The Chinese Path Series

The Internationalization of China's Economy

Chen Jiangsheng

Translated by Duan Feng, Zhang Yan, Liao Dongqiong

Proofread by Li Weibin

Paths International Ltd

中国财经出版传媒集团
经济科学出版社
Economic Science Press

Preface

The Chinese path refers to the path of socialism with distinctive Chinese characteristics. As Chinese President Xi Jinping points out, it is not an easy path. We are able to embark on this path thanks to the great endeavors of reform and opening up over the past 30 years and more, and the continuous quest made in the 60-plus years since the founding of the People's Republic of China (PRC). It is based on a thorough review of the evolution of the Chinese nation over more than 170 years since modern times and carrying forward the 5,000-year-long Chinese civilization. This path is deeply rooted in history and broadly based on China's present realities.

A right path leads to a bright future. The Chinese path is not only access to China's development and prosperity, but also a path of hope and promise to the rejuvenation of the Chinese nation. Only by forging the confidence in the path, theory, institution and culture can we advance along this path of socialism with Chinese characteristics. With this focus, *The Chinese Path Series* presents to readers an overview in practice, achievements and experiences as well as the past, present and future of the Chinese path.

The Chinese Path Series is divided into ten volumes with one hundred books on different topics. The main topics of the volumes are as follows: economic development, political advancement, cultural progress, social development, ecological conservation, national defense and armed forces building, diplomacy and international policies, the Party's leadership and building, localization of Marxism in China and views from other countries on the Chinese path. Each volume on a particular topic consists of several books which respectively throw light on exploration in practice, reform process, achievements, experiences and theoretical innovations of the Chinese path. Focusing on the practice in reform and opening up with the continuous exploration since the founding of the PRC, these books summarize on the development and inheritance of China's glorious civilization, which not only display a strong sense of the times, but also have profound historical appeal and future-oriented impact.

The series is conceived in its entirety and assigned to different authors. In terms of the writing, special attention has been paid to the combination of history and reality, as well as theory and practice at home and abroad. It gives a realistic and innovative interpretation of the practice, experience, process and theory of the Chinese path. Efforts are made on the distinctive and convincing expression in a global context. It helps to cast light on the "Chinese wisdom" and the "Chinese approach" that the Chinese path has contributed to the modernization of developing countries and solutions to human problems.

On the basis of the great achievements in China's development since the founding of the PRC, particularly since the reform and opening up, the Chinese nation, which had endured so much and for so long since the modern times, has achieved tremendous growth—it has stood up, become prosperous and grown in strength. The socialism with distinctive Chinese characteristics has shown great vitality and entered a new stage. This path has been expanded and is now at a new historical starting point. At this vital stage of development, the Economic Science Press of China Finance & Economy Media Group has designed and organized the compilation of *The Chinese Path Series*, which is of great significance in theory and practice.

The program of *The Chinese Path Series* was launched in 2015, and the first publications came out in 2017. The Series was listed in a couple of national key publication programs, the "90 kinds of selected publications in celebration of the 19th CPC National Congress", and National Publication Foundation.

Editorial Board of *The Chinese Path Series*

Contents

Chapter 1
Connotations, Characteristics and Course of China's Economic Internationalization

Since modern times, significant changes have taken place in China's external environment and social nature. They are not only the results of the long-term humiliation and oppression by western powers but also the achievements of the Chinese nation's continuous struggle and exploration. In fact, such resistance, exploration, and development mainly follow two lines: One is the development and stagnation of capitalism from the Opium War in 1840 to the founding of the People's Republic of China (PRC) in 1949. The other is the exploration and development of socialism since the 20th century, especially after the founding of the PRC. The conflict and collision between the two interweave the ups and downs of Chinese society since modern times and also outline the overall picture of China's economic development— from a rigid and forcedly open small-scale peasant economy and natural economy to a dynamic and actively open socialist market economy.

This development is mainly manifested in the modernization and internationalization of China's economy: the former is a catch-up to the times while the latter is a catch-up to the outside world. Although China re-opened its doors after the Opium War abolishing the policy of seclusion from the outside world introduced by the Ming and Qing Dynasty, such opening was forced, dependent and unequal, which had never brought China the development it deserved. Therefore, strictly speaking, the real, autonomous and all-around internationalization of China's economy starts from 1978 when China's reform and opening up policy successfully inspired people's enthusiasm, promoted continuous economic growth and finally blazed a trail of socialism with Chinese characteristics.

This chapter firstly defines the relevant concepts of China's economic internationalization and then analyzes its characteristics as well as divides stages. It should be noted that the internationalization of China's economy since modern times is not only rooted in China's native land but also profoundly influenced by the world. It is the main vein of China's economic and social development as well as an essential part of China's revolution and construction. Thus, whether to define the concept of China's economic internationalization or to discuss its characteristics and course, we have to put them within the context of the continuously developing world economy and combine them with the course of China's revolution, construction and reform.

1.1 Connotations of economic internationalization and China's economic internationalization

The internationalization of China's economy has some characteristics in common with that of any other country, but at the same time, it contains its specific features, which is mainly because China's economic development has a unique international and domestic environment and follows a unique developmental track. Especially since the founding of the PRC, the internationalization of China's economy has shown to be independent, truth-seeking and people-centered. Therefore, it is necessary to explain the connotations of economic internationalization and China's economic internationalization respectively.

1.1.1 Connotations of economic internationalization

Economic internationalization is defined as a process in which the economic development of a country or region transcends national borders, and the mutual connection with an infiltration of other countries or regions continue to expand and deepen[1]. People usually associate this concept with economic globalization, and even in daily use, there is no strict distinction between them. However, this book is mainly a study of the Chinese economy. The main concern is how China's economy has been continuously integrated into the world economy. As a matter of fact, it is necessary to distinguish between the two concepts (see Table 1–1 and Figure 1–1).

[1] Lu Dan, "The Connotation and Relevant Concepts on Economic Internationalization", *Economic Research Guide*, 2009(5).

Table 1–1 The differences between economic internationalization and economic globalization

Item	Perspective of research	Scope of contents	Time of generation
Economic internationalization	It is from the perspective of a country or region, to analyze the process and degree of its economic integration with that of the world.	The core contents are the internationalization of resources allocation, mainly including trade internationalization, capital internationalization, and production internationalization.	It was born in the 18th century, and a relatively scientific theoretical system was formed in the middle of the 19th century.
Economic globalization	It is from the perspective of the world's overall economy to analyze global economic problems.	It is with more extensive contents including production globalization, trade globalization, capital globalization, consumption globalization, the globalization of technological development and application and the globalization of information dissemination.	It was born after the Second World War, and in the middle of 1990s, its theoretical system was driven to maturity.

Source: Zhao Dongrong, *Policy Research on Chinese Economic Internationalization*, Nanjing: Nanjing University Press, 2000, pp. 16–18. Lu Xinde, "The Connotation and Features of Economic Internationalization", *Journal of Shandong University of Finance*, 2000(2).

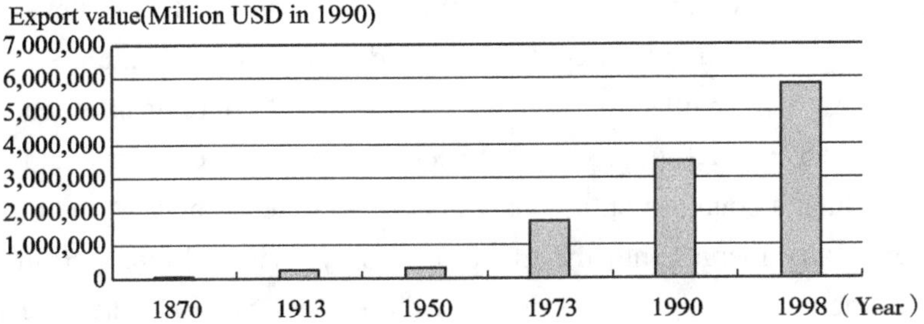

Figure 1–1 World constant export value

Source: Angus Maddison, translated by Wu Xiaoying et al., *The World Economy: A Millennial Perspective*, Beijing: Peking University Press, 2003, p. 359.

Economic internationalization falls into the historical category which is a dynamic process. The first industrial revolution saw the primary stage of economic internationalization. At the beginning of the 20th century, the capitalist economy entered its monopolistic stage, at a time when the international flow of capital and commodities expanded further; thus the economic internationalization entered a new era. Since the 1950s, the economic internationalization has undergone further developments, from commodity internationalization to capital internationalization and then to production internationalization. Since the 1980s and 1990s, the trend of economic internationalization has further surged in the world. Meanwhile, international economic ties and cooperation have made breakthroughs in both scope and depth. Knowledge and information networks, global trade liberalization, financial capital internationalization, production system multinationalization and operational mechanism assimilation have all been strengthened unprecedentedly. Thus, the process of economic internationalization has reached a higher level.

The contents of economic internationalization are highly comprehensive with resource allocation internationalization at its core, mainly including the internationalization of trade, capital, production and corresponding policies, systems, and technical standards. Internationalization of enterprise operation is the basis of economic internationalization. However, the development of economic internationalization is restricted by the international political and economic environment. Sound international political and economic relations inevitably push forward a country's economic internationalization process. On the contrary, such poor relations may impede this process. Besides, economic internationalization is also closely related to a country's economic development strategies as well as existing systems. Outward-oriented development strategies and free trade regimes are conducive to the development of economic internationalization. In contrast, inward-looking development strategies and protective trade systems will slow down its development. Economic internationalization is the result of an interactive process between the domestic economy and the global economy in which a country continuously opens its domestic market and the domestic economy gradually merges into the global economy. Within limits permitted by the domestic economy, the higher the degree of openness is, the faster the economic internationalization progress will be.

1.1.2 The connotations of China's economic internationalization

Corresponding to the concept of economic internationalization, China's economic internationalization refers to an economic developmental process in which China's economic development transcends national borders and is mutually linked, infiltrated with other economies with a continuously expanding and deepening trend.

Nevertheless, economic internationalization is based on the formed international markets, which means that all economies have relatively equal status in economic exchanges and follow specific market rules. This is not only the proper meaning of economic internationalization, but also the sine qua non for its sound development. However, these conditions were not met in modern China.The initial opening up of modern China was forced and oppressed, and China did not enjoy an equal position in economic exchanges as the outside world, which led to the fact that China's economy had never achieved a truly independent internationalization by 1949. After the founding of the PRC, it had been rejected by the western world for a long time. As a result, the Chinese economy before 1978 had to be in a semi-closed state with no reasonable conditions for economic interactions. In this sense, China had always been closed, or semi-closed by 1978, and the degree of internationalization of its economy was always quite low.

However, special attention should be paid to the fact that apart from the connotations of general economic internationalization, China's economic internationalization also contains two distinctive elements. One is its independent and equal economic interaction status. The other is an emphasis on the introduction of science and technology. Therefore, China's economic internationalization may also be regarded as a process in which China's economic development is continuously pursuing independence and its trade, investment and technological exchanges with other economies are continuously expanding and deepening.

1.2 The characteristics of China's economic internationalization

Economic internationalization depends not only on its own social and economic development but also on the overall level and situations of the world economy. Similarly, the process of China's economic internationalization also shows obvious particularities—in different stages, the characteristics of China's economic internationalization have alternated with the change of social nature and international situations. Generally speaking, China's economic internationalization has developed from passivity and imbalance to activity and soundness since the founding of the People's Republic of China in 1949.

1.2.1 The characteristics of China's economic internationalization between the opium war and the founding of new China

The road into internationalization of China's economy before the founding of the

PRC was bumpy and tortuous. In terms of the development of capitalism at this stage, it was also quite a dilemma as modern Chinese capitalist enterprises were still in a difficult position until 1933 when the Kuomintang was in the middle of its rule. Firstly, China's modern industrial production, excluding the output value of foreign industries in China, accounted for only 6% of national production. Secondly, modern mining production, including production by indigenous methods, accounted for only 12% of the total, with the majority under control of foreign capital.[1] Specifically speaking, the internationalization of the economy during this period mainly had the following characteristics.

1.2.1.1 Loss of autonomy

After the Opium War, due to the signing of a series of unequal treaties, China was gradually reduced from an independent sovereign country to a semi-colonial and semi-feudal country. China lost its status as an independent country in foreign relations. This was manifested in the economic field as a forced, involuntary and unbalanced opening to the outside world and it had been stamped with coercion and colonization in terms of the system, trade and personnel.

(1) *Seizure of the bargaining tariff and customs administrative power*

After the Opium War, foreign consuls in Shanghai headed by British consuls had been trying to seize China's customs administrative power. In 1850 and 1851, the British consul deliberately investigated two British merchant ships for tax evasion, trying to gain the trust of the Qing government and utilize the opportunity to seize the Chinese customs under cover of "legal trade" and "assisting the Chinese customs". In 1853, the Shanghai revolutionary group "Small Swords Society" responded to the Taiping Rebellion and occupied Shanghai including Shanghai customs. The British consul of Shanghai, Rutherford Alcock, took the opportunity to propose that foreigners participate in the management of customs, with agreement from the American and French consuls. Thus the consuls of the three countries and provincial governor of Shanghai Wu Jianzhang agreed: "It is well aware that customs work requires honest, bright and diligent employees who need to be familiar with foreign languages and cope with affairs according to relevant charts and rules, which are not easy to be met. Thus, foreign talents were needed because they can give us some help. It is the provincial governor's responsibility to appoint these foreign personnel. Meanwhile, the provincial

---

[1] Wang Jingyu, "The Development and Stagnation of Modern Chinese Capitalism", *Historical Research*, 1985(5).

governor should trust them and give them powers in order to improve the whole situation". According to their opinions, Wu Jianzhang established the Inspector-General of the Shanghai Maritime Customs Service on July 12, 1853, consisting of three foreigners from the UK, the US, and France respectively. In this way, the foreign invaders easily took customs power of this critical port.[1]

After the second Opium War, Article 10 of *the Sino-British (Sino-American, Sino-French) Trade Regulations* stipulated that "the Prime Minister shall invite the British (American and French) deputy to cater for tax affairs including strictly investigating tax evasion and other things." Due to the great power of Britain, the British Horatia Nelson Lay was appointed "Inspector-General of Chinese Maritime Customs Service" in 1859. He organized the Inspector-General of Guangzhou Maritime Customs Service on that year according to a set of methods adopted in Shanghai. From 1860 to 1863, Chaozhou, Ningbo, Fuzhou, Zhenjiang, Tianjin, Jiujiang, Xiamen, Hankou, Yantai (near the East China Sea) and other maritime customs services were established. Then, from 1863 to 1907, during Robert Hart's succession to Inspector-General of Chinese Maritime Customs Service, more than 30 more maritime customs services were set up.[2]

At this point, the administrative power of China's maritime customs services has completely fallen into the hands of the British invaders. This was equivalent to the fact that foreign invaders seized the key to China's "gate", being allowed to enter and leave China at will and plunder this country.

(2) *The gradual loss of control in the trade field*

The most significant change in foreign trade around 1842 was the change in nature. Before 1842, China's foreign trade was controlled by the Qing government and operated by its authorized Co-hong system.[3] Since 1842, the relationship between the domestic market and the global market has undergone major changes. It is the trading ports that connect the domestic market with the global market. In the trading ports, the comprador of foreign firms played a communicative role between the domestic market and the global market, and it was also these compradors who were among the first businessmen

---

[1] "Compilation Group of China's Modern Economic History", *China's Modern Economic History volume I*, Beijing: People's Publishing House, 1976, p. 74.

[2] "Compilation Group of China's Modern Economic History", *China's Modern Economic History volume I*, Beijing: People's Publishing House, 1976, p. 74.

[3] The Co-hong system, also called "Guangzhou trade system," is the foreign trade system of the Qing government based on a guild of Chinese merchants in Guangzhou.

playing actively in the modern market. Since then, China's foreign trade was not controlled by the Qing government but by the western businessmen.

There were less than 40 foreign firms in China before the Opium War. After the Opium War, the number had increased rapidly, to 440 by 1852.[1] After the 1870s, the distribution area of foreign firms at trading ports had expanded. Their assets also had increased, and foreign firms had expanded the scope from import and export trade to investment in shipping, finance, insurance, docks, warehouses, and industrial enterprises. These investments were for them to operate import and export trade services. The stock shipping companies established by the foreign firms had a monopoly position in China's foreign trade as well as domestic trade including transportation along the coastline and along the Yangtze River by virtue of the privileges of sailing obtained along these areas. Foreign firms relied on compradors to promote foreign goods and buy local goods. Backed by power, foreign firms utilized the activities of compradors to control China's import and export trade quickly.

Objectively speaking, compradors' activities had accelerated the development of commerce in China's urban and rural areas and the commercialization of some products, which helped to introduce western advanced craft, production technology and management experience, and to promote the modernization of China's economy as well as the convergence between the Chinese and the global market. However, compradors were only intermediate agents after the Qing government lost its independent trade rights. Thus, their existence was not for the development of China's own economy and could not bring about real development to China.

(3) *Trade of Chinese coolies*

From the 1940s to 1960s, imported foreign goods did not sell well. Thence, foreign firms engaged in selling Chinese workers while concentrating their capital on the opium trade. Such illegal activity was sheltered by foreign consuls in China. Some European countries were developing colonies in America, Southeast Asia and Australia where a massive demand for cheap labor was in place. Under cover of "contracted Chinese laborers", foreign traffickers cajoled Chinese workers to sign a lifetime indenture and sent them abroad. Before the Opium War, Portuguese, Spanish and Dutch businessmen smuggled Chinese laborers to other countries. After the Opium War, the businessmen from the United Kingdom, the United States, France and other countries joined such looting businesses of selling Chinese workers. They set up "pig houses", special "inns"

[1] Yao Xianglao, *Data of China's Modern Foreign Trade History*, Beijing: Zhonghua Book Company, 1957.

and "hoarding boats" alike at the trading ports to imprison coolies. Due to the condemnation of the slave trade worldwide as well as the decreasing supply of African slaves, western countries had to intensify their labor trafficking businesses in China. In the first half of the 19th century, there was an estimation of 320,000 Chinese workers going abroad with an average of 6,400 people per year. From 1850 to 1875, 1.28 million Chinese workers went abroad with an annual average of 51,000 people. During the voyages, Chinese workers suffered from inhuman torture with the mortality rate generally ranging from 40% to 50%, and sometimes up to 80%.

1.2.1.2 Relatively low level of internationalization

Although after the Opium War, China had no longer been closed to the outside world, no breakthroughs had been made in its economic internationalization due to the oppression of western powers and the slow economic and social development at home. Especially in the context of the accelerated development of the world economy since the second industrial revolution, modern China had enormously fallen backward in this respect. The most prominent characteristic of China's foreign trade in modern times was its semi-colonial nature. International trade was initially one of the driving forces for the development of capitalism, but the semi-colonial nature of modern China's foreign trade restricted its role in promoting the development of capitalism in the country.

On the whole, in the eighty years of history after 1870, although China's total import and export value showed a relatively obvious growth, this rate was not only lower than the average of the world but also even lower than rapidly developed countries such as the United States and Japan at that time.

Thus, it was suggested that China lagged behind not only in the overall economic development, but also in the path of economic internationalization (see Table 1–2).

Table 1–2 Real growth rates of commodity exports in China, the US, the UK, Japan and the World (1870–1950)

Unit: %

Country and region	1870–1913	1913–1950
Worldwide	3.4	0.9
China	2.6	1.1
The US	4.9	2.2
The UK	2.8	0
Japan	8.5	2.0

Source: Angus Maddison, translated by Wu Xiaoying et al., *The World Economy: A Millennial Perspective*, Beijing: Peking University Press, 2003, p. 359.

1.2.1.3 Unbalanced development of capitalism

During its forced openness to the outside world, China's economy also saw an unbalanced development of capitalism with the rapid expansion of foreign capital, the rapid development of domestic bureaucratic capital but the difficult development of national capitalism.

(1) *The rapid expansion of foreign capital*

Before the Sino-Japanese War in 1894–1895, foreign capitalism had already carried out capital export in China, though the amount was relatively small. At that time, the total investment of capitalist countries in China amounted to only about US$200–300 million[1], of which industrial investment accounted for only US$14 million. After the Sino-Japanese War in 1894–1895, the investment of imperialism had been increasing, choking China's financial and economic arteries.

As can be seen from Table 1–3, foreign investment in China reached US$1.5 billion in 1902 with an increase of 5–8 times compared with that before the Sino-Japanese War. After 1902, the amount had even increased dramatically. The figures indicated that enterprises directly invested in real estate, while loans and boxer indemnity were indirect investments. Besides, the proportion of direct investments was exceptionally high and increased year by year. If boxer indemnity exempted, the proportion of direct investment accounted for 65.1% in 1902, 66.3% in 1914 and 72.9% in 1930 of the total.

Of the total foreign investment, the UK, the US, France, Germany, Japan, and Russia accounted for the vast majority, with significant changes throughout. In 1902, Russia ranked first, with the UK second, Germany third, France fourth and the four countries together were responsible for more than 90% of the total investment. In 1914, the UK came first, with Russia second, Germany third, Japan fourth, and the four countries took up 77.2%; while in 1930, Japan came first, followed by the UK, France and the US with the total of the four countries accounted for 87.4% (see Table 1–4). The imbalance in political and economic development among imperialism had also been reflected in the investment in China. During the first World War, European imperialism lessened its aggression against China, giving the US and Japan the chance to enter. After the first World War, the strengths between imperialism had changed: Germany was a defeated country, so its power to invest abroad was not quite great. Meanwhile, France and the UK also suffered some losses in the war, especially France. After the

1 Wu Chengming, *Imperialism's Investment in China before 1949*, Beijing: People's Publishing House, 1955, p. 35.

October Revolution in Russia, the foreign policy of this country had fundamentally changed. Thus, the Soviet Union soon announced the cancellation of various rights and interests of Tsarist Russia in China. As for Japan and the US, they took the opportunity to make a windfall and stepped up their economic aggression against China.

Table 1-3 Total foreign investment in China in 1902, 1914 and 1930

Unit: US$ million

Year	Sum	Enterprise property	Real estate	Loan	Boxer indemnity
1902	1,509.309	478.277	50.100	284.400	696.532
1914	2,255.657	1,000.319	134.869	575.979	544.490
1930	3,487.559	1,977.063	440.392	897.150	172.954

Source: Wu Chengming, *Imperialism's Investment in China before 1949*, Beijing: People's Publishing House, 1955, p. 52.

Table 1-4 Investment in China by The UK, the US, France, Germany, Japan, and Russia in 1902, 1914 and 1930

Unit: US$ million

Year	The UK	The US	France	Germany	Japan	Russia	Other	Sum
1902	344.1	79.4	211.6	300.7	53.6	450.3	69.6	1,509.3
1914	644.6	99.1	282.5	385.7	290.9	400.2	92.7	2,255.7
1930	1047.0	285.7	304.8	174.6	1,411.6	—	263.5	3,487.6

Source: Wu Chengming, *Imperialism's Investment in China before 1949*, Beijing: People's Publishing House, 1955, p. 45.

(2) *The rapid development of China's bureaucratic capital*

By the middle of the 20th century, bureaucratic capital has dominated China's economy for nearly a century. The bureaucratic capital was formed along with the invasion of foreign capital. It was a transformed way for the traditional ruling class in Chinese society to adapt to the dominance of foreign capital. Under the banner of "defending China," bureaucratic groups had gradually capitalized and compradorized the controlled local power and built up the initial bureaucratic capital enterprises under the Self-strengthening Movement. This emerging force had also suppressed the Chinese people's demands for revolutions at home and resistance to foreign rulers. Although bureaucratic groups led by advocates for Self-strengthening Movement collapsed with the fall of the Qing Dynasty, China's bureaucratic capital was established ever since.

During the Beiyang Government period, both forms of bureaucratic capital, namely government-run private and privately-run government enterprises, had been further developed and thus the nature of bureaucratic capital had been fully manifested.

All warlords who had lost their monarch were more openly and obviously colluding with large foreign capital consortia, and the compradors' political nature was even more prominent. The rule of Beiyang Government did not last long, but it was an essential stage in regard to the evolution and expansion of bureaucratic capital.

Kuomintang's rule period was the third stage of bureaucratic capital evolution and also its heyday. At this stage, from 1927 to 1949 before the founding of the PRC was founded, China had reached a *pro forma* "unification," and bureaucratic capital also controlled China's economic arteries with the power of the central government. The Japanese invasion to China during this period (1931–1945) prompted the already pro-American / British monopoly capital consortia to take full refuge in these two countries, thus bringing the Chinese economy under the control of the American monopoly capital. Bureaucratic capital in this heyday stage fully embodied its rule nature and the obstacles to China's economic modernization. The development of China's bureaucratic capital is shown in Table 1–5.

Table 1–5 The Development of China's bureaucratic capital (1872–1913)

Period	Sum		Merchant-run			Government-run and Government-Merchant-joint-run		
	Number of plants established	Capital (Thousand yuan)	Number of plants established	Capital (Thousand yuan)	Capital proportion (%)	Number of plants established	Capital (Thousand yuan)	Capital proportion (%)
1872-1894	72	20,907	53	4,704	22	19	16,203	78
1895-1913	548	120,297	463	90,821	75	85	29,476	25

Source: The data between 1872 and 1894 in the table come from Yan Zhongping, *Selections of Data on Chinese Modern Economic History*, Beijing: China Social Sciences Press, 2012, p. 93; The data between 1895 and 1913 come from Wang Jingyu, *Data of Chinese Modern Industrial History, Volume II*, Beijing: Zhonghua Book Company, 1962, pp.870-919.

(3) *The difficult development of China's national capital*

The Chinese national capital originated from the Self-strengthening Movement with a short "boom" after the Sino-Japanese War in 1894–1895 but suffered from setbacks again after the 1930s. In a sense, although its development had never stopped, it always steered a narrow course between foreign capital and bureaucratic capital.

After the Sino-Japanese War in 1894–1895, China's national capitalism had a preliminary development but also showed great weaknesses at the same time with weak strength, small-scale, backward technology and bringing great limitations to its development. The reasons for such limitations were mainly the oppression of imperialism and the constraint of feudal forces. Besides, national capitalism was in relation with imperialism and feudalism, making it impossible to develop independently and thoroughly.

From the 1930s to 1940s, bureaucratic capitalism gradually monopolized the social economy, and Japan launched a war of aggression against China. After the First World War, the economic forces of European imperialist countries underwent a resurgence. Under the slogan of "returning to the market", they had significantly increased their export of goods and capital to China. Since 1919, the total value of China's import trade had surged. If the value in 1913 were 100, the value in 1919, 1920, 1921, 1922, 1923 and 1924 would be 113.6, 133.7, 158.9, 165.8, 162.0 and 178.6 respectively.[1] In order to expand the export of goods to China, imperialist countries had expanded many monopoly companies already established before the war and added more branches to further control the Chinese market. After 1921, the UK, the US and Japan launched fierce investment competitions in China. They strengthened their control of China's industrial capital and financial undertakings through the addition of factories, the establishment of banks and "Sino-foreign joint ventures", making China's finance and industry its accessories. Under the fierce impact of the imperialist economic forces, China's national capitalist industry and commerce gradually turned into depression.

1.2.2 The characteristics of China's economic internationalization since the founding of the People's Republic of China

Since the founding of the PRC, especially since the third plenary session of the 11th Communist Party of China (CPC) Central Committee, on the basis of former development experience and investigation on international situations, the CPC has opened up the path of socialism with Chinese characteristics, which has successfully led the development of our country and guided and promoted the process of China's economic internationalization. The historical process of our country's opening up to the outside world has formed its unique landscape of economic internationalization: On the one hand, China has continuously been integrated into the world economy while on the other hand, its economic strength has been continuously strengthened and its people's living standards have been continuously improved.

[1] Wang Ying, "The Development History of China National Capitalism", *Journal of Fujian Institute of Socialism*, 2005(1).

1.2.2.1 Adherence to the principle of independence[1]

The participation in economic globalization and the promotion of economic internationalization are only means while the development of China's comprehensive national strength and the improvement of people's living standards are the ultimate aims. The CPC has always adhered to the principle of independence and has successfully realized its rapid development in the process of economic internationalization.

After the founding of the PRC, Mao Zedong held on to the principle of independence mainly depending on self-reliance in economic construction supplemented by winning over foreign aid, which is comprehensive, complete and profound in theory. Then in terms of its guidance to practice, it was because the CPC adhered to this principle without hesitation that we have thwarted the blockade and strangulation by international capitalism, stopped the attempt by chauvinism of the Soviet Union to coerce and control, made a relatively rapid growth in the national economy, achieved great feats in initially changing the situations in China and greatly improved its international status during the 1950s and the middle of 1960s.

While adhering to Mao Zedong principle of independent economic construction, Deng Xiaoping made new explanations and gave full play to it according to the changed international and domestic situations, thus making it more comprehensive and completed. In April 1974, Deng Xiaoping, on behalf of the Chinese government, expounded thoroughly and systematically the principle of independence and self-reliance in economic development at the United Nations. He said: "what we mean by self-reliance is that we rely mainly on the strength and wisdom of our people, control our economic arteries, make full use of our resources, strive to increase food production and systematically and gradually develop our national economy. Independence and self-reliance are by no means divorced from the reality of specific countries. Instead, policymakers should determine their ways of self-reliance according to their specific conditions in different situations". Deng Xiaoping stressed that: As long as all countries, according to their own characteristics and conditions, adhere to the principle of independence and self-reliance, advance along this path and devote to their own economic construction, they will be determined to face a bright future. Of course, being independent and self-reliant is not to close China up, shut down China from the outside world, deny any foreign aid and refuse to learn from foreign countries. Deng Xiaoping

---

[1] This part of Deng Xiaoping's speech is quoted from Song Jihe, "Similarities and Differences of Thinking on Chinese Economy's Independent Development between Mao Zedong and Deng Xiaoping", *Journal of the Party School of Jinan Municipal Committee of CPC*, 1999(4).

advocated that all countries could carry out extensive economic and technological exchanges on the basis of equality, mutual benefit and mutual respect of national sovereignty, so as to learn from each other and speed up different countries' development of national economy, which is also conducive to consolidating their political independence. In short, independence suggests that all internal affairs of a country, including its economic development, should be decided and handled by its own government and people. The people of all countries have the right to choose and decide their own path of economic development according to their own conditions without interference from foreign forces.

Since the reform and opening up, Deng Xiaoping has repeatedly stressed the importance of proceeding from China's reality and taking its own independent road to construct economy. He pointed out: "China's modernization must start from China's reality. No matter revolution or construction, we must learn from foreign countries and draw their experiences. However, simply copying international experiences and models can never make success. It is the basic conclusion drawn from our long-term historical experiences that we should combine the basic principles of Marxism with our country's concrete practices and follow our own path of socialism with Chinese characteristics". China's affairs should be handled according to China's own situation. Independence and self-reliance have been our starting point from the past till now. This will continue to be true in the future. In response to the huge damage brought about by the ten years of domestic turmoil to our country's economic development, he made it clear that "to raise our country's scientific and technological level, we must, of course, rely on our own efforts, must develop our own creations, and must adhere to the policy of independence and self-reliance. However, independence is not keeping our doors closed, and self-reliance is not blindly excluding the help from foreign counties. Science and technology are the commonwealths created by humankind. Any nation or country needs to learn the strengths of other nationalities or countries and learn the advanced science and technology of them".

Since the 18th National Party Congress, the CPC Central Committee with general secretary Xi Jinping as its core has braved the wind and the waves and made great efforts in promoting economic internationalization, with special emphasis on handling the relationship between opening to the outside world and independence and on the necessity of adhering to the principle of independence and autonomy in the process of opening to the outside world. At the first glance, the two seem to be ambivalent, but in fact, the two are integrated into the whole development process of China with a common aim of realizing better achievements. To open to the outside world is to make good use of the domestic and international markets and resources to expand our country's economic development space and improve our country's economic operation efficiency. On the other hand, adhering to the principle of independence ensures that our country will strengthen its economic strength and enhance enterprises' international competitiveness in the whole opening-up process. At the beginning of the opening up, Deng Xiaoping emphasized: "on the one hand, we implement the policy of opening up; on the other hand, we still hold on to self-reliance advocated by Chairman Mao since the founding of the PRC".[1] After nearly 40 years of opening up, our country's opening level to the outside world continues to improve, and our ties with the world continue to deepen, but we still need to be conscious of the fact that "one has to be very strong if he wants to strike the iron." As a matter of fact, General Secretary Xi Jinping has continuously stressed the importance of the principle of independence on the process of opening up. "We must be assertive and follow our own independent path of development with its own characteristics".[2] Concerning the attitudes on opening up, we should steer its course between achieving win-win situations and bearing in mind the bottom line. Pursuing win-win cooperation complies with the theme of peace and development and is regarded as an indication of abandoning zero-sum thinking as well as an inevitable requirement for successfully pushing forward the opening up. Meanwhile, bearing clearly in mind the bottom line is vital for safeguarding our own legitimate rights and interests, because the purposes of opening up lie in developing our country's social productivity, enhancing our overall national strength and improving people's living standards. General Secretary Xi Jinping pointed out, "we must adhere to the path of peaceful development, but at the same time we can never give up our legitimate rights and interests or sacrifice the core interests of the country".[3]

1.2.2.2 Uphold the principle of seeking truth from facts

The principle of independence has established our determination and perseverance in the process of economic internationalization in the new era, while the principle of seeking truth from facts and a fair and pragmatic attitude is the important guarantee for policies' implementation and improvement.

---

1 *Selected Works of Deng Xiaoping*, Beijing: People's Publishing House, 2011, p. 406.

2 Du Shangze and Li Bingxin, "Speech Delivered by Xi Jinping at the Roundtable of South-South Cooperation", *People's Daily*, Sep.28, 2015.

3 Xi Jinping, *The Governance of China*, Beijing: Foreign Languages Press, 2014, p. 249.

(1) *The gradual formation of a full-dimensional mode of opening up*

Deng Xiaoping has established special economic zones and then further opened up coastal port cities and other coastal areas based on accumulated experience, thus stimulating the opening up of the inland to the outside world. Facts have proved that his design conforms to our country's realities. Uneven development of productive forces and various geological and cultural conditions for opening up in different cities have determined that we can only adopt a progressive strategy from point to surface and from exterior to interior. Special economic zones, coastal open up cities and areas served as the key points of opening up in the middle of early 1980s, and this was closely related to their superior conditions. From a historical viewpoint, they are located along the coast having a long tradition of economic contacts with overseas countries. Then, from a practical point of view, they are all relatively advanced and active regions in China's economic sector, initially having the basis for absorbing foreign technology, capital, and management experience. Moreover, in the era of the planned economy, they were already important bases for China's foreign trade, some of which were major ports for contact with the outside world. In stark contrast, influenced by various factors, the vast inland areas are inferior in their conditions for opening to the outside world.

The planning of the opening-up process cannot rely solely on good wishes and the exaggeration of the role of the subjective initiative but must take the existing facts as its starting point and utilize and create conditions. Deng Xiaoping's design is a vivid practice of Marxist methodology of seeking truth from facts. The strategy of gradually opening up from point to surface and from exterior to interior is also in line with the people's ideology. The reform and opening up must rely on the people to carry out it consciously. Without their support, it would be difficult to implement any good strategic concept. However, opening up is mainly to absorb good contents from western society, such an introduction will inevitably involve a question about the relationship between capitalism and socialism. Therefore, questions like "how we treat capitalism" and "how to analyze what has been introduced" require scientific answers from theory and practice. Ready-made answers could not be provided by a country that only stepped out from its closed state a moment ago. It is also clear enough that to push forward the opening policy on a large scale could not easily gain people's understanding and support. Therefore, the only correct option is to push forward the opening process experimentally and to explore a way to develop itself by drawing the beneficial results of capitalism through the pilot special economic zones. Even this kind of experiment has perplexed people. The debate about the nature of the special economic zones has been going on for a long time. However, it is also these debates and the success of experiments that have gradually raised people's awareness and made them treat what rationally comes from a capitalist society. The practice has educated the people, enhanced people's understanding and strengthened the awareness and urgency of reform and opening up, thus providing the ideological guarantee for promoting the opening-up process on a larger scale and in a deeper level.

(2) *From "bringing in" to "going global"*

Since entering into the 21st century, especially 18th CPC national congress, the CPC Central Committee has continued to adhere to the principle of seeking truth from facts and adjusted its opening up policy with times. One of the outstanding manifestations of the policy change is from "bringing in" to "going global". Since the opening up policy, our country has actively implemented the strategy of "bringing in", which is mainly to import foreign capital and advanced technologies. In this regard, our country has made great achievements. On the one hand, the net capital flow of foreign direct investment has constantly been rising from US$430 million in 1982[1] to US$126.27 billion in 2015[2]. On the other hand, the structure of foreign capital has been further optimized with the proportion of foreign capital in service industry reaching 55.4% from 2011 to 2014 and even reaching 61.1% in 2015[3].

Faced with progress and changes in the opening up process, Jiang Zemin proposed the integration of "bringing in" and "going global" as early as 1997. However, it was not until the 18th national congress that the CPC Central Committee more consciously and comprehensively proposed and implemented the "going global" strategy. In particular, the proposition and implementation of the Belt and Road Initiative have made a new look on our country's foreign investment cooperation.

It needs to be pointed out that the CPC Central Committee's emphasis on "going global" is not a simple denial of "bringing in". Instead, it means that we need to continue our emphasis on "bringing in" while we are pushing forward the "going global" strategy. Special attention needs to be paid on the optimization of the industrial structures of foreign investment.

---

[1] The data come from the World Bank Database, http://data.worldbank.org.cn/.

[2] The data come from the Commerce Data Center of the Ministry of Commerce, http://data.mofcom. gov.cn/channel/dwjhz/dwjhzs.html.

[3] The data come from the Commerce Data Center of the Ministry of Commerce, http://data.mofcom. gov.cn/channel/dwjhz/dwjhzs.html.

1.2.2.3 Always adopt a people-centered approach

In the whole process of economic internationalization in a new era, the CPC has always put people's interests first, with the faith that development is for the people, that it is reliant on the people, and that its fruits are shared by the people, which is a true implementation of the people-centered philosophy. Since the18th National Party Congress, the CPC Central Committee with General Secretary Xi Jinping at its core has been committed to implementing the philosophy of shared development in the process of economic internationalization. "Our people feel enthusiastic about life, look forward to better education, more stable work, more satisfied income, more reliable social security, a higher level of medical and health service, more comfortable living conditions and more beautiful environment, and hope that children can grow better, work better and live better. Their desire for a better life is our ultimate goal".

(1) *Rely on and work for the people in the process of economic internationalization*

Faced up with the complicated international situations and the heavy tasks for domestic reform and development, the CPC Central Committee has always looked everything from a long run and thought in big pictures with an insist on serving the people and relying on them in the opening up process.

First of all, the recognition of the fact that people are the creators of history is the source of our party's strength, which belongs to the mass view in the materialist conception of history. Our party is the Party of the Chinese people. No matter in what era, in what circumstances, and whether it is a revolution, construction or reform, people have always been the source of our party's strength. This is because our party comes from the people and returns to the people, fully representing the interests of the people and entirely relying on the people. At the beginning of his tenure as General Secretary of CPC, Xi Jinping pointed out that "people are the creators of history, the real heroes, and the source of our strength. We know very well that everyone's strength is limited, but as long as we unite as one, there will be no difficulties that cannot be overcome. Also, everyone's working hours are limited, but their dedication to serving the people wholeheartedly can be unlimited".[1] On December 5, 2013, General Secretary Xi Jinping stressed during the 11th Collective Study of the Political Bureau of the CPC Central Committee, "we must learn and keep in mind the fact that people are the creators of history and our reforms need to be dependent on them".[2]

[1] "Meeting of the Standing Committee of the 18th Political Bureau of the Central Committee with Chinese and Foreign Reporters", *People's* Daily, Nov.15, 2012.

[2] Xi Jinping, "Promoting the Whole Party's Learning and Understanding of Historical Materialism," Xinhua Website, http://news.xinhua-net.com/politics/2013-12/04/c_118421164.htm.

Secondly, he also emphasized that people are part of the central opening up and people-to-people exchanges should play a big part in it. Fundamentally speaking, the opening up of a country to the outside world begins with the exchanges of people, especially that of talents. Exchanges of people play a fundamental role in promoting the opening up of a country. If people are narrow-minded and reluctant to receive new things, it can never be a real opening up. Thus, opening up should focus on people and rely on people, with a push of them to be open-minded regarding vision, ideology, knowledge, and technology, and thus continuously raising the entire opening up to a higher level through learning and applying advanced knowledge and technology from the outside world.

Finally, people are an important driving force for opening up. People are the providers of the labor force and carriers of knowledge and technology. Only when they participate fully in the process and promote it actively, can the level of opening up be truly and effectively improved. In addition, people are direct practitioners. Thus, our party must optimize the top-level design of reform and opening up, steer it into the right direction and rely on people's strength to put it into reality.

(2) *Attach great importance to the development of productive forces and consolidation of economic foundation in the process of economic internationalization*

This is because the continuous development of productive forces plays a fundamental role in enhancing international competitiveness and raising the level of opening up. This is also because our goal of opening up is to make full use of the international and domestic markets and resources to develop our country's productive forces and consolidate our economic foundation.

The development of the domestic economy determines the competitiveness of domestic enterprises in the process of opening up, which in turn affects the level of opening up to the greater extent. The development of productive forces and the consolidation of the economic foundation have become essential foundations for opening up. During the 12th Five-year Plan, China's total trade volume accounted for a rising share of the world, and its trade structure was continuously optimized, which largely reflected the continuous development of China's productive forces. The 13th Five-year Plan is a decisive period for China's success to build a moderately prosperous society which also requires China to implement the great concept of opening and development to realize a higher level of opening to the outside world. Therefore, the 13th Five-year Plan clearly proposed that "we should speed up the optimization and upgrading of foreign trade and move from a big trading country to a powerful trading country", which requires the vigorous development of service trade and the promotion of exports of technology and capital-intensive products abroad and the adjustment of economic structure and the upgrading of industries at home.

The original intention of economic internationalization is to seek the improvement of national economic efficiency, people's living standards and comprehensive national strength. The CPC fully understands the overall situations at home and abroad, and thoroughly advances the implementation of the "going global" and "bringing in" strategies, further developing domestic productive forces, and consolidating China's economic foundation. Since the 18th National Party Congress, the most distinctive feature of China's opening up lies in the successful advancement of the "going global" strategy, especially with the continuous advancement of the Belt and Road Initiative which has successfully led the development China's foreign investment cooperation, making full use of domestic capital, technology and equipment, effectively easing the pressure of overcapacity at home and promoting the development of the national economy and productivity. At the same time, while vigorously promoting the "going global" strategy, China's "bringing in" strategy has also been implemented successfully with a continuous improvement in both quantity and quality. In 2015, the actual amount of foreign capital used in our country was US$126.27 billion, up 6.4% year on year, among which, the actual use of foreign capital in the service sector was US$77.18 billion, up 17.3% year on year, accounting for 61.1% of the country's total. The actual use of foreign capital in manufacturing was US$39.54 billion, basically the same as that of the previous year, accounting for 31.4% of the country's total, among which, the high-tech manufacturing sector continued to grow, with US$9.41 billion of actual used foreign investment, up 9.5% year on year, accounting for 23.8% of the total foreign investment actually used in manufacturing. However, steel, cement, electrolytic aluminum, shipbuilding, flat glass and other industries with serious overcapacity in the domestic market are basically not approved to set up new foreign-funded enterprises.[1] The steady inflow of foreign capital and the optimization of its structure have played an essential role in the transformation of our country's economic development mode, and in the promotion of industrial upgrading and innovation.

---

[1] "Illustrations on 2015's Inflow of Foreign Capital by Head of the Department of Foreign Investment Administration of the Ministry of Commerce", from the official website of the Ministry of Commerce.

1.3 The course of China's economic internationalization

The course of China's economic internationalization can be roughly divided into two big parts. One is the development and stagnation of capitalism from the Opium War to the eve of the founding of the PRC, and the other is the exploration and development of socialism since the founding of the PRC.

1.3.1 Classification criteria for China's economic internationalization stages

According to the above-discussed connotations of China's economic internationalization, apart from the general connotations of economic internationalization, China's economic internationalization also contains two unique elements, an independent and equal economic exchange position as well as an emphasis on an introduction of science and technology, special attention needs to be paid to these two elements when dividing stages. In summary, there are two critical aspects involved, namely nature and degree, which is the equal status in economic exchanges and the degree of economic internationalization.

1.3.1.1 Equal status in economic exchanges

The nature of economic internationalization refers to whether a country participates in international economic exchanges on an equal footing. Therefore, China's economic internationalization can be roughly divided into: (i) involuntary and unequal opening up before the founding of the PRC; (ii) voluntary and equal opening up after the founding of the PRC.

1.3.1.2 Degree of China's economic internationalization

The degree of economic internationalization mainly refers to the degree of a country's integration into the world economy usually in terms of the exchanges of trade, capital, and technology. Generally, trade dependence and capital dependence are used to explain the degree of trade internationalization capital internationalization.

Trade dependence: the total import and export volume / gross domestic product, reflecting economic sums' dependence on the international market. The larger the ratio is, the higher the degree of trade internationalization will be.

Capital dependence: total long-term capital flows / gross domestic product, reflecting total output's dependence on international capital. With the proportion of foreign capital in the total added, a bigger and more realistic picture of the reality can be unfolded. The larger the value is, the higher the degree of capital internationalization will be.

It needs to be pointed out that due to the particularity of China's economic internationalization, we will also take technological exchanges into account when dividing different stages.

1.3.2 Stages of China's economic internationalization

According to the criteria above, China's economic internationalization are divided into the following stages:

1.3.2.1 From the Opium War (1840) to the Eve of the Founding of the PRC (1949)

During this span, there were three climaxes of economic internationalization in China. Accordingly, they were three attempts to make China's economy take off. Specifically, they were firstly Self-strengthening Movement (1860s–1890s), secondly the ware of industrialization in early years of the Republic of China, and thirdly the reform carried out by the National Government of the Republic of China in the 1930s. According to Table 1–6, during the Self-strengthening Movement and 1930s, China's total export of goods increased significantly.

Table 1–6 Export values of commodities with constant prices

Unit: US$ million in 1990

Country	1870	1913	1929	1950
China	1,398	4,197	6,262	6,339

Source: Angus Maddison, translated by Wu Xiaoying et al., *The World Economy: A Millennial Perspective*, Beijing: Peking University Press, 2003, p. 358.

China's earliest economic internationalization and efforts at industrialization can be traced back to the 1950s. After being forced to open the doors, some officials presumed that the western powers were invincible because of their advanced ships and guns while China's lagging behind was due to the lack of cutting-edge weapons. Therefore, China must develop the weaponry industry in order to get improved. Due to the deterioration of the financial situation of the Qing government and the limitations of military enterprises, officials from the Self-strengthening Movement realized that only developing military industries could not help China to be powerful. Instead, they decided to develop civilian industries at first, adopting the strategy of being rich first and then powerful. As a result, they began to open "officially-built enterprises" and "private enterprises supervised by the government" since the middle of the 1870s.

Although the Self-strengthening Movement failed along with China's defeat in the Sino-Japanese War in 1894–1895, it produced China's first batch of modern industries and was the first attempt to industrialize since modern times. The principle of "holding traditional Chinese values while aided with modern Western management and technology" has influenced the historical process of China in the next century.

Then, the Revolution of 1911 overthrew the rule of the feudal Qing government and announced the establishment of a Republican regime. The newly established Republican government advocated freedom in industry and commerce, promulgated a series of decrees encouraging the development of industry and commerce, and carried out the preliminary construction of economic laws and regulations. This inspired the Chinese business community, which once attracted a high enthusiasm for investment. Moreover, during the first World War, the Western powers were too busy to look into the east, sharply reducing the volume of exported goods and at the same time, increasing the demand for various military materials. Thus, China's industrial development entered into a "golden age". However, followed with the invasion of the Western powers and their gain of rights to invest and set up factories in China, China's natural economy gradually disintegrated, and the economy in urban and rural areas was further semi-colonized. However, this process was long and bumpy. Chinese agricultural economy turned into commercial agriculture in an adaptation to the needs of the Western powers, but the feudal land relations were still preserved. The development of industries was adversely affected by social unrest and imperfect market. Although the bureaucratic capital was stronger than national capital, it lacked vitality. Thus, private industries were striving between foreign capital and bureaucrat capital. The basic economic situations in China had not changed, and the speed of economic internationalization was still very slow.

The third climax of China's economic internationalization occurred between 1927 and 1937. At this time, due to the elimination of warlords and the initial unification of the country, the National Government began to deal with issues in economic construction and made certain achievements, especially in the struggle for independence in tariffs. From 1928 to 1930, the government negotiated with a number of capitalist countries and signed tariff treaties in which all countries agreed to China's abolition of the bargaining tariffs, being independent in tariffs. From 1925 to 1933, the national government announced four times of changes in import tariffs. Thus, China's import tariffs were up to 34.3% in 1934 from lower than 3% between 1921 and 1922, 4.3% in 1928, 16.3% in 1931, 25.4% in 1933 and 34.3% in 1934. Independence in tariffs is an act of striving for equal rights by market players and raising import tariffs can serve as a protector for national industries to certain degrees.[1] Generally speaking, however, during this period, China did not achieve equal status in exchanges with the outside world, and there were no qualitative changes in China's economic internationalization development.

1.3.2.2 The development of the economic internationalization after the founding of the PRC

This can be roughly divided into two smaller sections: first, between the founding of the PRC and the inauguration of the reform and opening-up policy; second, since the reform and opening up.

(1) *China's economic internationalization between the founding of the PRC and the reform and opening-up policy*

After the founding of the PRC, with some developments in socialist construction and economic exchanges with the outside, China's economic internationalization has made some progress. However, due to the blockade by imperialists and the deterioration of Sino-Soviet relations during the 1950s and 1960s, coupled with some twists and turns in domestic economic construction, it is difficult for China to have extensive and authentic practices in opening its economy. Therefore, the level of economic internationalization at this stage was relatively low. The data in Table 1–7 show that although China's import and export trade volumes have almost increased by 20 times from 1950 to 1978, its total was quite small, only about US$20 billion.

Table 1–7 China's total import and export trade volumes (1950–1978)

Unit: US$ billion

Item	1950	1955	1960	1965	1970	1975	1978
Export trade volume	1.13	3.14	3.81	4.25	4.59	14.75	20.64

Source: National Bureau of Statistics of China, *Compilation of Statistics in Five Decades in China*, China Statistics Press, 1999.

(2) *China's economic internationalization since the reform and opening up*

Since the reform and opening up, China's economic internationalization has achieved brilliant results with world-first trade volume in goods and greater foreign investment drawn. This trend can be clearly reflected in Figure 1–2 and Figure 1–3.

[1] Gao Debu and Wang Jue, *An Economic History of the World*, Beijing: China Renmin University Press, 2001, p. 281.

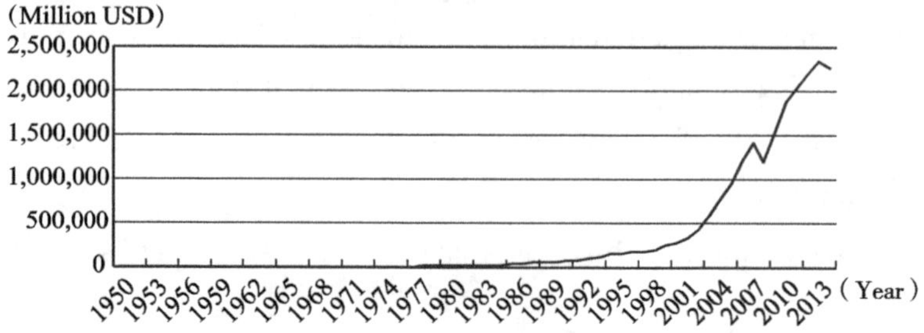

Figure 1–2 China's trade export volume in goods (1950–2013)

Source: http://unctadstat.unctad.org/wds/ReportFolders/reportFolders.aspx.

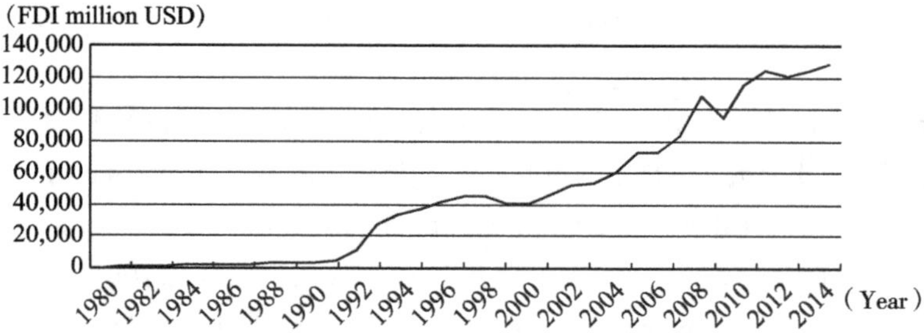

Figure 1–3 Foreign direct investment in China (1980–2014)

Source: http://unctadstat.unctad.org/wds/ReportFolders/reportFolders.aspx.

China's economic internationalization after the reform and opening up can be roughly divided into five minor stages. The first stage refers to the first decade after the reform and opening up, in which "a comprehensive reform was initiated, a socialist path with Chinese characteristics and basic lines were established, and brave reform steps were made". Remarkable results in "liberating the productive forces" has been made during this span with marked growth every few years, making the opening up into reality from points to lines and then to the surface.

The second stage lies in the 1990s. During this decade, China's economic internationalization stood the test of political and financial turmoil and forged ahead more firmly. Moreover, a series of systematic guiding theories, basic programs and reform aims of a socialist market economy were formed. Thus, this decade has witnessed new historical breakthroughs in reform and opening up. It has also achieved remarkable results in "liberating the productive forces". Concerning growth rate, the average annual economic growth between 1992 and 1996 was 12.1%. In the aspect of structural reforms, state management of the economy has changed from a mandate to an option. A new pattern of the basic economic system has taken into shape which keeps public ownership as the mainstay of the economy and allows diverse forms of ownership to develop side by side. After continuous reforms and developments at this stage, China has generally entered into a moderately prosperous society in all aspects, and its economic internationalization has accelerated.

The third stage sits at the beginning of the 21st century. At this stage, China, standing at a new historical starting point, has made sure the country's and the CPC's historical direction, held high the great banner of socialism with Chinese characteristics and begun an eight-year building of moderately prosperous society. In its first seven years, China's total economic output has maintained a double-digit growth, its economic internationalization has gone significantly further, and people's life has also been greatly improved. At the same time, fairness and justice have been paid special attention while the overall development was accelerating. China has entered into a new stage in which there were a more active dedication to a scientific, harmonious and peaceful development, an effort to perfect socialist market economy and coordination between economic, political, cultural and social schemes.

The fourth stage is in relation to China's dealings with the global financial crisis of 2008. China then has calmly responded to the crisis with corresponding measures, stabilized its economic growth and at the same time effectively restored the growth in trade and investment, making China the largest trading country in goods in 2013 and promoting the steady advancement of China's economic internationalization.

The fifth stage, a stage of acceleration in all aspects, begins with the 18th National Party Congress. Riding the historical trend of win-win cooperation, China has insisted on deepening reform and opening up in an all-around way and actively promoting the Belt and Road Initiative. Consequently, China has turned itself from a big trading country to a powerful trading country with developments of capital, technological and talent internationalization, in an attempt to build a community with a shared future for humankind.

Chapter 2 Internationalization of China's Economy before the Reform and Opening Up

We have divided the development of China's economic internationalization before 1978 into two stages: one is from the Opium War to the founding of the PRC, and the other is from the founding of the PRC to the reform and opening up. In terms of the structure of the chapter, first, the relevant economic thoughts will be sorted out; Second, the corresponding policies will be introduced; finally, the corresponding results of each stage will be summarized.

2.1 The internationalization of China's economy from the Opium War to the founding of the PRC

Between the Opium War and the founding of the PRC, China's economy and society had undergone a low point and at the same time, dynamic changes. At this stage, the internationalization of China's economy had a unique international environment and specific domestic conditions. Therefore, it also had its own characteristics and achievements. Generally speaking, the level of economic internationalization during this stage was relatively low.

2.1.1 The trend of thoughts in economic internationalization from the Opium War to the founding of the PRC

This stage was an era of dynamic changes in China's society, with various ideological trends constantly colliding with each other.

2.1.1.1 Perspectives from advocates for Self-strengthening Movement[1]

After the second Opium War, the economic aggression of foreign capitalism was further intensified, bringing more sufferings to the Chinese nation and the Chinese people. At the same time, it also objectively promoted the disintegration of China's natural economy and created conditions for the development of capitalism.

Under such circumstances, Zeng Guofan, a critical advocate for Self-strengthening Movement put forward the proposition of "learning to make weapons and ships from the Westerners which will benefit us forever." However, the scope of learning from the west was only limited to making weapons and ships, and this represented the early main thoughts of advocates for the Self-strengthening Movement.

Later on, another representative of the Movement, Li Hongzhang, had already noticed the great changes that had taken place in Chinese society at that time and he believed that the trade connections between China and foreign countries were "one of the biggest changes in more than 3,000 years". He proposed that in order to adapt to this kind of "change of situation", the government should make "reforms". What he called "making reforms", was to learn western science and technology, introduce foreign machinery and equipment, establish China's modern military industry. He believed that this was "the foundation of self-improvement while taking the skills of the foreign countries to become China's skills". Since the modern military industry started up, Li Hongzhang had turned his attention to weapons and ships and other equipments. This highly demanded iron and coal, and military industry consumed huge sums of funding. Therefore, he advocated using machines to mine iron ore, stressing that the move "had something to do with the plans to make the country rich and militarily strong". He also proposed that building railways "was actually a great plan for today's prosperity". In 1882, when Li Hongzhang was going to establish the Mechanical Textile Bureau, he also suggested that "all countries, old and new must be rich first and then be strong. If people are rich, the country will be inherently solid". What he meant was to seek rich from the development of civil industry, which had high profits and could not only provide raw materials for the military industry but also provide funds, so it is said that "the foundation of the country would also be solid". The Self-strengthening Movement encouraged to learn western science and technology, but none of them involved any changes in the social system, be it to promote "self-improvement" to establish modern military industry or to promote "prosperity" to develop the modern civilian industry.

---

1 Zhang Shoupeng, "Changes in Chinese Modern Economic Thinking", *Qinghai Social Sciences*, 1987(3).

Zhang Zhidong, a representative figure in the later period of Self-strengthening Movement, once summarized the thoughts of the movement as "learning both old and new", and "learning from both inside and outside", treating learning from the old as its essence and learning from the new as its practical use. Similarly, learning from inside could build our bones and souls while learning from outside could help us deal with the world. The so-called "building essence", "inside" and "bones and souls" in fact promoted that loyalty and filial piety be taken as the basis and Chinese classics and history learning as the foundation. "Scholars could be turned to the original pureness" and were able to consciously become feudal moralists. The difference between old feudal moralists and new feudal protectors lied in the fact that the new ones understood some western knowledge and advocated taking the western advanced science and technology to consolidate the feudal system. This is the fundamental characteristic of the Self-strengthening Movement's economic thought.

2.1.1.2 Perspectives from bourgeois reformists[1]

While representatives of the Self-strengthening Movement opposed the development of capitalism in China, the early bourgeois reformists represented by Wang Tao, Ma Jianzhong, Zheng Guanying, and Xue Fucheng advocated the development of capitalism in China. Wang Tao pointed out that capitalist countries were "relying on business in foreign countries" and "the prosperity of business meant the wealth for the whole country". He said that British businessmen "went as far as tens of thousands of miles away and made profits and enriched the country through different levies"; "Britain's society and people's livelihood depended entirely on commerce, and all the profits came from navigation". Ma Jianzhong also believed that foreign trade was a "source of wealth" for a country. the UK, France, Russia, the US and Germany "all got rich by foreign trade". Thus, in order to make China rich and powerful, we must vigorously develop foreign trade, increase exports and reduce imports. Silk and tea were the main export commodities in China. We should improve their quality and output, encourage silk and tea merchants to organize large companies, and reduce the tax rate on silk and tea so as to facilitate export. He also stressed the need to implement a tariff protection policy: "Foreign countries adopted the policy to levy more imports than exports." China should also adhere to this principle. Besides silk and tea, bulk export commodities such as cow leather, wool, brown sugar, cotton, and porcelain should also improve their competitiveness in the international market. Wang Tao and Ma

[1] Zhang Shoupeng, "Changes in Chinese Modern Economic Thinking", *Qinghai Social Sciences*, 1987(3).

Jianzhong's proposition of developing capitalist commodity economy was mercantilist.

Xue Fucheng and Zheng Guanying overturned the traditional Chinese saying of "scholar, farmer, industry, and business." Instead, they put the "business" in an important position of "holding the foundation of people's livelihood" and emphasized, "one of the best ways to amass money was to promote business". Thus, they raised the slogan of "building the country by doing business". Especially, Zheng Guanying had put forward the theory of "commercial warfare" with capitalist countries and expounded the strategies to protect businesses. He held that capitalist countries relied on the "militory war" and "commercial war" to invade other countries, which had their own characteristics and functions. "The militory war was short, and the disaster was obvious, while the commercial war lasted long, and the disaster was significant". Therefore, he proposed, "it was better to wage a commercial war rather than a military war".

Early bourgeois reformists believed that social wealth was mainly obtained in the circulation process, and the production process was subordinate to and served the circulation process. However, Zhang Rui, Number One Scholar in the late Qing Dynasty who personally engaged in industrial activities, had a new understanding of the status and role of industry. In 1895, he put forward that "people all said that foreign countries built their country by commerce, but this was too superficial because they did not understand that foreign countries got rich through the industry". Developing a capitalist industry was the only right way to "to raise people's standard of living and enrich the country". Kang Youwei, a bourgeois reformist, pointed out in 1898 that the world "had already entered the industrial age" while China was still an "agricultural country", so how could it compete with foreign countries? He also said, "a country that highly regarded agriculture was silly and conservative while a country that advocated industry would be fresher and wiser", promoting that China "should be designated as a country to value industry", "emphasizing the importance of materialism" and "encouraging the set-up of large factories to promote the industry". He stressed that only in this way could we "build a new country without fear of being oppressed". The so-called "an industrial country" meant the realization of capitalistindustrialization. He was the first Chinese to advocate China's industrialization. Liang Qichao also believed that China was a natural agricultural country in ancient times and that it was indeed reasonable and necessary to implement the policy of emphasizing agriculture. As for building a modern society, he also held that we must "build our country by industry" and vigorously develop new industries.

In order to revitalize China's economy, both the early bourgeois reformists and reformists had noticed the necessity of reforming China's feudal political system. For example, Wang Tao stressed that in order to achieve self-improvement, we need to realize autonomy first, that was, starting with the reform of the political system to achieve the country's prosperity. Zheng Guanying pointed out that in western capitalist countries, the fundamental solution to chaos and the foundation of prosperity are not all based on the strength of ships and weapons but on the unity of the upper and lower levels of the parliament and the rules and law. Before the Sino-Japanese war of 1894–1895, he advocated the establishment of a parliament, believing that the parliament administrated personnel to serve the public with the utmost justice. Meanwhile, efficiency was bound up with practicalities, so if China wanted to be a rich and powerful country, it must begin with the establishment of the House. This is the result of the bourgeois reformists' dissatisfaction and negation of the feudal autocratic system in an extremely cautious way. It is also the fundamental difference between them and Self-strengthening Movement advocates on the issue of learning from the west.

The bourgeois reformists are more radical than the early bourgeois reformists in their demands for the reform of the feudal political system, and their struggle against the feudal autocratic system of the Qing Dynasty is even fiercer. During the Reform Movement of 1898, Kang Youwei proposed to "adopt the developmental process of France, Russia and Japan," especially to follow the example of Japan's Meiji Restoration and implement the constitutional monarchy system. This shows the desire of the Chinese national bourgeoisie to change the feudal autocratic system and clears the way for the development of capitalism. After the failure of the Reform Movement of 1898, Liang Qichao fled to Japan, advocating protecting the emperor while making sharp criticism against the decadent Qing Dynasty. He pointed out that the country was not "the private property of the monarch", but was "the public asset of the nation". However, for thousands of years, feudal emperors had stolen this property from the public, and treated its citizens as his slaves. To change this situation, only a constitutional monarchy can be implemented. However, facts have proven that not overthrowing the feudal autocratic system and only changing China's politics with the constitutional monarchy system can never shatter the cause, so it was utterly impossible to create a good environment for the development of China's capitalist economy.

2.1.1.3 Perspectives from bourgeois revolutionaries

During the process of leading the bourgeois-democratic revolution of the old type, the Chinese bourgeois revolutionaries put forward the program of developing capitalism in China, which can also be regarded as the guiding ideology of the internationalization of China's economy. After Revolution of 1911, Sun Yat-sen elaborated on the grand plan to realize China's industrialization in his monograph *The International Development of China*. He proposed to open a northern port in Bohai Bay, and from this port, a northwest railway system was going to be built, reaching the northwest border, and then send people into Xinjiang and Mongolia, and open canals to connect the river courses in northern and central China with the northern port. Next, develop coal and iron ore in Shanxi province and set up iron and steel plants. Similarly, build an eastern port in Hangzhou Bay, to control and improve the Yangtze River system, to build an inland trade port, and to create a large cement factory. In Guangzhou Bay, build a southern port to become an international port to improve Guangzhou's water system. Build coastal commercial ports and fishing ports, shipyards, and a southwest railway system. Establish a railway system with a total length of 100,000 miles to connect with all parts of the country. Vigorously develop livelihood industry and printing industry. Mine coal, oil, copper, and other minerals and establish mining machinery factories and smelters, etc.[1]From the above, it can be seen that the plan proposed by Sun Yat-sen was a grand blueprint for the full realization of China's industrialization. Its proposition symbolized that China's thoughts of modern industrialization were initially established at the beginning of the 20th century. At the same time, it also indicated that the age-old agricultural thought had lost its dominance, and the modern industrialization thought has gradually taken the lead in the social and economic life.

As regards how to develop China's modern industry, Sun Yat-sen proposed that it should be conducted in two ways, one was personnel management, and the other was state management. He said, "if individuals are more suitable to take up the business, then let them do it. The state can reward them, and law can protect them instead. On the other hand, when individuals cannot do it well, let the state manage it instead". This shows that Sun Yat-sen not only wanted to mobilize the enthusiasm of the national bourgeoisie but also to advocate the use of state capitalism rather than private monopoly capitalism to develop China's modern industry. In order to achieve this goal, it is necessary to prevent the excessive expansion of private capital. In 1924, Sun Yat-sen explicitly put forward the principle of "regulation of capital" "any enterprises owned by its own nationals or foreigners, when they have the tendency to monopoly the whole

[1] Sun Yat-sen, *The International Development of China*, Beijing: Foreign Language Teaching and Research Press, 2011.

industry or the scale is far too large to be managed solely by any private sector such as banks, railways and air routes, shall be operated and managed by the state, so that the private capital system cannot manipulate the national economy and people's livelihood". This was not only to limit China's private capital so that it could not control the national economy and people's livelihood but also to prevent foreign monopoly capital from controlling China's economic lifeline. It reflected the desire of the middle and lower classes of the national bourgeoisie, who were simply unable to monopolize the national economy, but wanted to independently develop China's modern capitalist economy. In order to develop capitalism in China, the feudal autocratic rule must be completely overthrown to establish a bourgeois democratic republic. In the course of engagement in the democratic revolution of the old type, Sun Yat-sen made himself have a further understanding of the decadent rule of the Qing Dynasty through the struggle, and through the controversy with Kang Youwei, Liang Qichao and others who later turned into royalists. He established the idea of democratic revolution and founded the theory of "Three Principles of the People". After reorganizing the Kuomintang in 1924, Sun Yat-sen reinterpreted the Three principles of the People and developed the old Three Principles of the People into the new Three Principles of the People. The proposal and development of the Three Principles of the People symbolized the development of the Chinese national bourgeoisie's anti-imperialism and anti-feudalism ideology to a new height and also symbolized that they had stronger requirements and more specific ideas for the development of Chinese capitalism.[1]

2.1.1.4 Perspectives in the 1930s

In the 1930s, the discussion on foreign trade issues in ideological and theoretical circles became more mature, mainly focusing on the discussion on countermeasures to promote China's foreign trade. Typical viewpoints include:

Wu Yugan once deconstructed the causes of China's sluggish foreign trade and analyzed the ways to vitalize China's foreign trade. He advocated that abolishing the unequal treaties was the key and paid special attention to direct trade and foreign trade technology. These propositions reflected the needs of China's economic development under the new situation and the characteristics of the times.

Tang Youren put forward the theory of foreign trade balance, advocating that China should base itself on the reality of foreign trade deficit and should adopt flexible methods to offset the surplus, which was apparently a strategic thought of import and

---

[1] Zhang Shoupeng, "Changes in Chinese Modern Economic Thinking", *Qinghai Social Sciences*, 1987(3).

export trade.

Ma Yinchu proposed that reducing production costs was also a good way to strengthen export competition. He also proposed specific foreign trade policies to promote national economic construction. He also proposed to implement trade protection policies and control policies, saying "the only way out for China's economy was to control the economy". Ma Yinchu proposed to protect trade and control trade, but he did not deny the positive significance of free trade. His foreign trade policy thought not only adhered to the principle of free trade and of equal competition but also could flexibly formulate countermeasures according to changes in the international economic competition situation and the needs of domestic economic development.

Gu Xiangqun, a well-known figure in the financial sector, put forward the idea of promoting industrialization and promoting agriculture through the industry. He Bingxian, Director of the International Trade Bureau, put forward a proposal to expand exports. In particular, he put forward the idea of properly protecting tariff policies. He did not agree with over-protection of tariffs but believed that tariffs should "protect and promote the functions of industries and adjust the functions of foreign trade". In the aspect of how to vitalize foreign trade, the academic circles have put forward a series of countermeasures and policies.

Besides, Hu Shanheng discussed the exchange rate and conversion rate of foreign trade and advocated drawing up the exchange rate based on reality. Shen Zouting proposed the thinking about tax rate standard for balancing production cost. These thoughts were all typical of this period.[1]

2.1.2 Policies of economic internationalization between the Opium War and the founding of the PRC

Although this period had witnessed various economic trends of thought and generally all advocates agreed to learn from the west, due to the social turmoil and the change of government in China, there was no obvious continuity and consistency in the policies of this period. Therefore, three stages were mainly selected for discussion here.

2.1.2.1 The Self-strengthening Movement

The Self-strengthening Movement had carried out a series of reforms in diplomacy, military industry, civil industry and education. However, in the economic aspect, it

[1] Li Shujin, *Research on Thinking of Chinese Modern Foreign Trade*, Shanghai: Fudan University Press, 1996, p. 100.

mainly had the following practices:

First, establish the military industry. Zeng Guofan founded the earliest military factory Anqing Ordnance Institute in 1861. In 1862, Li Hongzhang founded the first Foreign Gun Bureau in Shanghai that technically relied on the British. In 1864, Li Hongzhang founded Suzhou Foreign Gun Bureau. Since then, Jiangnan Manufacturing Center, Jinling Manufacturing Bureau, Fuzhou Ship-Building Bureau, and Tianjin Machinery Bureau had been established one after another. By 1890, Zhang Zhidong had established Hubei Gun Factory. In total, 19 military factories had been built. These factories were China's first batch of modern industries. They were mainly military or military-related industries invested by the state which widely used advanced foreign technologies and equipment. However, the factory management adopted the feudal management mode under the condition that the market did not develop. Funds were allocated by the government, and products were generally distributed by the government to designated military units free of charge. Thus, the development of enterprises had nothing to do with their operations. Although these military industries did not operate in accordance with the mode of operation of the market at all, they were China's earliest industrial civilization and thus played a landmark role in China's economic history.

Second, develop the civil industry. Since the middle of the 1870s, the Self-strengthening Movement advocates had begun to adopt the state-run, state-and-private-joint-run and private-run-but-state-monitor strategies to build civilian industry under the slogan of "seeking wealth". These enterprises involved mining, smelting, transportation, textile and other industries, including the first shipping company, China Merchants Steamship Navigation Company, 1880-built railway system across north and south, 1878-operant Keelung coal mine (the first modern coal mine), 1893-completed Hanyang Iron Works (the first iron-making plant), Shanghai Mechanical Textile Bureau which was under construction since 1890 and the first modern cotton textile, Tianjin Telegraph Office which was the first telegraph office established in 1890, and later Kaiping Coal Mine, Mohe Gold Mine, and Hubei Official Textile Bureau and Spinning Bureau, etc.

2.1.2.2 Early Republic of China

After the victory of the Revolution of 1911, people were eager for the newly established bourgeois government to introduce China's economy into a new period, and China also witnessed various ideological trends and movements of saving the nation by industry. The Beiyang Government of China also complied with this social call to a certain extent, by enacting some laws and regulations that were conducive to the development of foreign trade and began to intentionally promote the development of foreign trade.

The first step was the promulgation of industrial decrees conducive to the development of foreign trade. Among them, documents that called for the development of mining industry, encouraged nationals to set up enterprises included the followings: *Operation Rules of Mining Ordinance*, *Registration Rules of Mining Ordinance*, *Mining Registration Regulations*, *State-owned Wasteland Reclamation Regulations*, *Mining Regulations*, etc. Laws and regulations issued by the Beiyang Government of China to encourage the development of agriculture and animal husbandry included: *Rules for Collecting Plant Diseases and Pests*, *Rules for Selecting Crops*, *Rules for the Dissemination and Study Bureau of Dinghai Fishery Technology*, *Rules and Regulations for the Administration of Dinghai Fishery Technology Disseminationand Study Bureau and Regulations on Incentives for Cotton Planting, Sugar Making and Sheep Herding*, etc. *Revision of the Articles of Association of the Central Agricultural Experimental Farm*, *Revision of the Articles of Association of the Breeding Livestock Experimental Farm*, *Revision of the Articles of Association of the Cotton Experimental Farm*, *Revision of the Articles of Association of the Forestry Experimental Farm*, *Articles of Association of the Sugar Experimental Farm*, *Articles of Association of the Tea Experimental Farm*, *Provisional Rules of the Peasant Association and Forest Law*, etc. Laws and regulations promulgated by the Beiyang Government of China to encourage the development of industry and commerce included: *Merchant General Rules*, *Company Registration Rules*, *Detailed Rules for the Implementation of Company Regulations*, *Company Regulations and Detailed Rules for the Implementation of Merchant General Rules*, etc.[1]

The second step was to promulgate the *Chamber of Commerce Law* and the *Trademark Law* to create a favorable environment for the development of foreign trade. *The Chamber of Commerce Law* stipulated in September 1914 that all local chambers of commerce should be replaced by the general chamber of commerce. In December 1915, the Beijing government announced the amendment of the Chamber of Commerce Law, adding a lot of contents and clauses, and perfecting various functions of the chamber of

[1] Luo Hongxi, *Research on China's Foreign Trade Diplomacy during the Republican Period* Doctoral Dissertation, Changsha: Hunan Normal University, 2014.

commerce. "The revised version had changed greatly in actual contents compared with the old one in 1914".[1] In 1918, the Beijing government also promulgated the Industrial and Commercial Association Rules and revised it in 1923, which stipulated that trade associations must maintain the economic interests of their peers, and "hold the principle of correcting the problems in this regard".[2] This regulation was, in fact, the first law in our country to regulate trade associations in an all-around way. Before May 1923, the management of trademarks was basically in a state of disunity because the management organizations were disorderly and complicated. In order to strengthen the competition with foreign investors, the Beiyang Government of China initially changed the chaotic situation in the late Qing Dynasty by promulgating the Trademark Law, establishing the trademark office, and publishing the trademark bulletin. It was a great progress in our country's trademark industry, which symbolized the preliminary construction of a relatively complete trademark management system in our country, and had also played some resistance to foreign infringement of our country's trademark rights.

2.1.2.3 In the 1930s

During this period, due to the initial unification of the country, the Nanjing National Government started to deal with the economic construction problem and made new progress in the foreign economy. The main policy measures adopted include:

First, strive for tariff autonomy. In the second half of 1928, the Nanjing National Government focused on "revising old treaties and issuing the new ones", in an effort to restore tariff autonomy, and to finalize the national tariff rules. In June 1928, the National Revolutionary Army occupied Beiping, and the Nanjing National Government nominally achieved national unity. The Ministry of Foreign Affairs at that time declared "The Declaration on Foreign Affairs" on one hand and announced the abolition of all unequal articles between China and foreign countries; on the other hand stating "constructing another structure" on its own on the basis of equality with the western European powers and separately establishing new treaties, followed by a series of diplomatic activities in an effort to gain access to tariff autonomy. The Nanjing National Government first signed *the Out-sorting Sino-US Relation Treaty*, in which the United States recognized China's tariff autonomy. Subsequently, the Nanjing National Government also negotiated with 11 countries, including Britain, to amend some signed

---

1 Shen Jiawu, et al., *Selected Economic Data during Zhang Qian's Tenure as Secretary of Agriculture and Commerce*, Nanjing: Nanjing University Press,1987, pp. 216 - 219.

2 Xie Zhenmin, *Legislative History of the Republic of China*, Beijing: China University of Political Science and Law Press, 1999, p. 599.

treaties, and successively signed new tariff treaties between November and December. Among these newly signed treaties, these countries recognized China's tariff autonomy. Instead, based on the equality principle, China would give these countries most-favored-nation treatment and national treatment. Only Japan, which had the largest trade share in China, run counter to the main trend and firmly refused to recognize China's tariff autonomy. However, after all, most countries had already admitted that China could independently formulate tax rules. In December 1928, the Nanjing National Government of the Republic of China announced that China would set a national tax rate from February 1, 1929. Since then, "the national government had enacted and promulgated new import and export tax rules one after another".[1]

Second, improve the financial system and reform the monetary system in a unified way. "The second stage of the development of modern China's banking system was the gradual improvement stage of the banking system, which took place between 1927 and 1949". The gradual improvement of the banking system in modern China was mainly signaled by the establishment of the central bank system, set-up of specialized banks and the formation of supervision system of banks.[2] In order to develop foreign trade, the Nanjing National Government started to establish a relatively modern banking system at the very beginning of its establishment. After the establishment of the Nanjing National Government in 1927, the "four-banks-and-two-bureaus" capital finance system was established including the Central Bank, the Bank of China, the Bank of Communications, Farmers Bank of China and Directorate-general of Postal Remittances and Central Trust of China. They had laid a foundation for the Nanjing National Government to control national finance and develop foreign trade. Besides, the currency system reform of the Nanjing National Government in 1935 replaced the silver dollar with paper money as the currency in circulation in the market, which was conducive to unifying China's currency system and stabilizing finance and foreign trade. It was a milestone in the history of China's foreign trade policy.

Third, organize industrial investment and strengthen the construction of infrastructure. The Nanjing National Government of the Republic of China recognized that "railway construction was important to boost production and increase exports by supplying large quantities of raw materials to other industrial countries". Meanwhile,

---

[1] Luo Hongxi, "Research on China's Foreign Trade Diplomacy during the Republican Period". Doctoral Dissertation, Changsha: Hunan Normal University, 2014.

[2] Guo Xianglin and Zhang Liying, *Research on Chinese Modern Market*, Shanghai University of Finance and Economics Press, 1999, p. 238.

"industrial countries, with their remaining manufactured goods, could assist our country in building railways, and at the same time assist our country in promoting production and export. In this way, our country could repay the debt of principal and interest to build railways". Therefore, the use of foreign capital to develop railway systems was "an act of mutual aid and mutual benefit between creditor and debtor countries". Under the general policy of utilizing foreign capital, the National Government started railway construction by borrowing foreign funds before the War of Resistance against Japanese Aggression. Starting from 1929, the National Government began to plan for the construction of railway, highway and harbor docks in accordance with Sun Yat-sen's *The International Development of China.* These projects were large-scale and time-consuming, so most of them had not been completed until the outbreak of the Anti-Japanese War. Meanwhile, in order to successively promote the development of foreign trade, on January 9, 1930, the Ministry of Industry and Commerce announced the Unifying Procedures of Metrology to guide all localities to abolish old equipment and reform new ones, providing a good circulation environment for promoting the development of foreign trade. On May 6, 1930, the Nanjing National Government promulgated the Trademark Law. Then, in January 1931, the Ministry of Industry promulgated The Detailed Rules for the Implementation of the Trademark Law to provide a good quality basis for promoting foreign trade[1].

2.1.3 Achievements of economic internationalization between the Opium War and the founding of the PRC

From the Opium War to the founding of the PRC, Chinese society was in profound changes and turmoil, with the economic development in this period lagging far behind the world average.Thus, the internationalization of the economy had not achieved good results either.

2.1.3.1 China's economic development level

From a vertical perspective, although China's GDP had generally developed during more than one hundred years from the Opium War to the founding of the PRC, the achievements were very poor, especially compared to the world average. As shown in Table 2–1, the proportion of China's GDP in the world dropped rapidly from a historical high of 32.9% in 1820 to only 5.2% in 1952. This substantial decline reflected the rapid downturn of China's economic strength and also the hardships and twists that China had

[1] Luo Hongxi, "Research on China's Foreign Trade Diplomacy during the Republican Period", Doctoral Dissertation, Changsha: Hunan Normal University, 2014.

experienced over the past over one hundred years. As shown in Table 2-2, since 1700, China's GDP per capita had basically stagnated and regressed for more than 250 years, falling from an equivalent to the world average to about 1/4 of the average level. Behind such statistics were the hardship of the Chinese people and the inevitable result of the overall economic recession in China. However, in terms of economic structure, China had made some obvious progress. According to Table 2-3, China's economy and society had undergone dramatic changes since modern times. The traditional natural economy was gradually disintegrating, and the modern market economy was beginning to sprout.

Table 2-1 Distribution of world GDP (1700-1952) Unit: %

Year	China	The US	Japan	Europe	India
1700	22.3	0.1	4.1	24.9	24.4
1820	32.9	1.8	3.0	26.6	16.0
1952	5.2	27.5	3.4	29.3	4.0

Source: Angus Maddison, translated by Wu Xiaoying et al., *Chinese Economic Performance in the Long Run*, Shanghai: Shanghai People's Publishing House, 2008, p. 36.

Table 2-2 Per capita GDP of China, the US, Japan and Europe (1700-1952) Unit:1990-level international dollar

Year	China	The US	Japan	Europe	World
1700	600	527	570	923	615
1820	600	1,257	669	1,090	667
1952	538	10,316	2,336	4,343	2,260

Source: Angus Maddison, translated by Wu Xiaoying et al., *Chinese Economic Performance in the Long Run*, Shanghai: Shanghai People's Publishing House, 2008, p. 36.

Table 2-3 Proportions of major industries' contributions to GDP in China (1890-1952) Unit: %

Major industries	1890	1913	1933	1952
Farming, fishing and forestry	68.5	67.0	64.0	55.7
Handicraft industry	7.7	7.7	7.4	7.4
Modern manufacturing	0.1	0.6	2.5	4.3
Mining industry	0.2	0.8	0.8	2.1
Modern transportation and commerce	0.4	0.8	1.5	2.8
Trade	8.2	9.0	9.4	9.3
Finance	0.3	0.5	0.7	10.4

Source: Angus Maddison, translated by Wu Xiaoying et al., *Chinese Economic Performance in the Long Run*, Shanghai: Shanghai People's Publishing House, 2008, p. 48.

2.1.3.2 Achievements of China's economic internationalization

Generally speaking, in the 80 years after 1870, although China's import and export value showed relatively obvious growth, the speed was not only lower than the world averagebut even lower than that of other countries such as the United States and Japan which developed rapidly at that time. This showed that China was not only lagging behind in the overall economic development but also lagging behind in the course of economic internationalization (see Table 2–4).

Table 2–4 Real growth rates of commodity exports in China, the US, the UK, Japan and the World (1870–1950)

Unit: %

Country	1870–1913	1913–1950
Worldwide	3.4	0.9
China	2.6	1.1
The US	4.9	2.2
The UK	2.8	0.0
Japan	8.5	2.0

Source: Angus Maddison, translated by Wu Xiaoying et al., *Chinese Economic Performance in the Long Run*, Shanghai: Shanghai People's Publishing House, 2008, p. 359.

Looking at the developments per capita, China had also achieved considerable growth in more than one hundred years in modern times. However, a horizontal comparison showed that China's growth was not only lagging behind Japan who successfully achieved an economic take-off but also not as good as developing countries such as India, thus causing the founding of the PRC to face an extremely severe economic construction foundation and domestic situation when it embarked on its economic construction (see Table 2–5).

Table 2–5 Per capita exports of China, India, and Japan (1850–1950)

Unit: USD, based on the current year's price and exchange rate

Year	China	India	Japan
1850	0.12	0.36	0.00
1870	0.28	1.01	0.44
1913	0.70	2.49	6.10
1929	1.36	3.39	15.32
1950	1.01	3.18	9.95

Source: Angus Maddison, translated by Wu Xiaoying et al., *Chinese Economic Performance in the Long Run*, Shanghai: Shanghai People's Publishing House, 2008, p. 48.

Of course, if we continue to examine the situation of foreign investment, we can easily find from Table 2–6 that in the first 30 years of the 20th century, there was also a relatively rapid accumulation of foreign capital at that time. However, the foreign capital at that time was to invade and plunder, which had little positive effect on China's economic development, which confirmed the importance of independence in international economic exchanges.

Table 2–6 Stock of foreign direct investment in China (1902–1936)

Unit: US$ million

Item	1902	1914	1931	1936
According to the same year's price	503.2	1,067.0	2,493.2	2,681.7
According to the price in 1931	922.5	1,784.0	2,493.2	2,681.7

Source: Angus Maddison, translated by Wu Xiaoying et al., *Chinese Economic Performance in the Long Run*, Shanghai: Shanghai People's Publishing House, 2008, p. 51.

2.2 The internationalization of China's economy between the founding of the PRC and the reform and opening up

The founding of the PRC changed China's semi-colony situation of being exploited and enslaved for a long time in modern times. China's foreign economic and trade relations have also undergone a historic turning point. China emerged from its unequal and exploited international trade status in a semi-colonial and semi-feudal society on the stage of international economic and trade in an equal and independent manner. New attempts have been made to internationalize the economy. However, due to changes in the world situation and the state of domestic economic development, the internationalization of economy in this period was still in a tortuous process.

2.2.1 Theories of opening up between the founding of the PRC and the reform and opening up

In the 1950s, our country's foreign trade theories, like the world's general opening-up theories, did not form a systematic system and were limited to some important viewpoints related to foreign trade. Among them, perspectives and solutions from the Party and State leaders were the most influential.

2.2.1.1 Foreign trade theories

During the economic construction in the early days after the founding of PRC, in order to restore and develop the national economy, and smash the imperialist conspiracy of blockade, embargo and containment against our country, the Communist Party of China (CPC) with Chairman Mao Zedong as its core has examined the current situation and was actively working with other socialist economies with the Soviet Union as the lead. At the end of 1949, Mao Zedong visited the Soviet Union and signed the Sino-Soviet Treaty of Friendship, the Agreement on China's Changchun Railway, Lvshunkou and Dalian, the Agreement on Loans to the People's Republic of China and the Soviet Union agreed to help China establish and transform 50 enterprises with a loan of US$100 million to China, which opened a new chapter in the practices of foreign economic exchanges in PRC. In the 1950s, a total of US$142.7 billion of loans were obtained from the Soviet Union, and 156 sets of equipment were mainly imported from the Soviet Union, promoting the development of modern industrial construction in the founding of the PRC. During this period, the Soviet Union also provided China with comprehensive technical assistance. For example, during the first Five-year Plan period, as many as 400 experts and consultants from the Soviet Union and other Eastern European countries worked in China. Besides, China also attached great importance to the development of economic exchanges and cooperation with Eastern European countries.

Zhou Enlai's thinking on foreign trade had an important impact on the development of foreign trade in the PRC. After the founding of the PRC, Zhou Enlai proposed that "we should think about ways to take active measures to develop foreign trade" and "facilitate the development of production and the prosperity of the economy". Based on China's basic national conditions, he clearly pointed out that in terms of China's backward economy and technology, its socialist modernization needed to "develop and expand economic, technological and cultural exchanges with other countries in the world"[1]. At that time, imperialist countries headed by the United States adopted a hostile attitude towards China by implementing an economic embargo policy in economics, the sovereignty non-recognizing policy in politics and the policy of intervention in the military. In response to this and with the consideration of China's harsh position in the international community, Zhou Enlai publicly announced that "we are willing to maintain peace with all countries that are willing to do so and to establish

---

[1] *Selected Works of Zhou Enlai*, Beijing: People's Publishing House, 1984, p.226.

or resume trade relations, in an effort to develop a peaceful economy. Any capitalist country who wishes to develop trade relations with us on the basis of equality and mutual benefit will not receive any discrimination from us".[1] Zhou Enlai's speech aroused widespread concern in the international community, and it was conducive to promote the development of foreign trade in our country, showing that Zhou Enlai was eager to develop the foreign trade and attached great importance to it.

In Zhou Enlai's view, after the founding of the PRC, although China achieved economic independence, it was still very backward in economy and culture. Meanwhile, China is also a large country with a huge population. It was precisely based on a correct and sober understanding of China's national conditions that Zhou Enlai had repeatedly expounded the necessity and urgency of China to implement foreign trade and promote socialist modernization. He stressed that, "China must admit its backwardness in economy and culture. For example, our industry is lagging behind England. Besides, Although our culture has a long history and is brilliant, it has been lagging behind since modern times, because the level of natural science and social science was very low either from the perspectives of quality or quantity". "Compared with developed countries, our mechanized level was far from modernization".[2] As estimated, China was at least 100 years behind western countries in economy. As China's economy and technology were backward, in order to carry out socialist construction, it was necessary to exchange information with foreign countries, carry out trade exchanges and technical cooperation, and could not adopt a closed-door policy of exclusion.

The principle of equality and reciprocity had always been Zhou Enlai's guiding ideology in handling relations, including trade relations, with other countries in the world. Zhou Enlai pointed out many times that the development of foreign trade and economic ties had never been unilateral but mutual and mutually beneficial. Zhou Enlai also extended foreign trade to economic cooperation with other countries, but the basis of such economic collaboration must also be equality and mutual benefits. Zhou Enlai pointed out that Asian and African countries needed to cooperate economically and culturally and such collaboration should be based on equality and mutual benefit without any privileged conditions. Zhou Enlai creatively put forward the strategic thought of developing economic cooperation with foreign countries based on his past

---

[1] Scientific Research Management Department of the Literature Research Office of the Central Committee of the Communist Party of China, *Research Collections of New China's 60 Years, Volume IV*, Beijing: Central Party Literature Publishing House, 2009.

[2] *Selected Works of Zhou Enlai on Diplomacy*, Beijing: Central Party Literature Publishing House, 1990, p. 83.

diplomatic experience and objective judgment of the international situation, which had guiding significance for our country to further expand foreign trade.

Zhou Enlai made an objective judgment about the world situation and standing on the world scientific and technological advancement, and he pointed out that China's modernization of economy and technology needed to carry out international co-operation. Under the conditions of socialized mass production, modern science and technology were even making significant progress within "only one day". Science is the decisive factor for China to build socialism. Thus, China should develop foreign economic exchanges and absorb the advanced achievements of other countries. He believed that "only when we get the most advanced science and technology can we have solid protection and great power, and can we lead our national economy to the forefront of the world economy".[1]

Liu Shaoqi, when he took over the work of guiding urban construction, treated foreign trade as a way for the founding of the PRC to participate in the world social reproduction and paid full attention to its strategic position in the development of the national economy, making pioneering contributions to the further development of foreign trade in the founding of the PRC. He believed that foreign trade had a great impact on the national economy and people's livelihood, and even the impact was decisive. Its mission was to develop production and turn the economy over. If it failed, it would be detrimental to the production and the turnover of the economy. We must effectively organize foreign trade, which is a crucial work and one of the people's greatest interests. In order to arrange foreign trade well, the State should regulate foreign trade and manage it. In the past, it was impossible to manage foreign trade because of imperialist aggression, but today it must be managed by the State. He profoundly expounded the urgency of our country's foreign trade work and the necessity of the management by the State under the international situation at that time.

To this end, Liu Shaoqi drafted the Decision of the CPC Central Committee on Foreign Trade and the Directive of the CPC Central Committee on Foreign Trade Policy. The two documents systematically expounded the principles and policies of the State in regulating and managing foreign trade, and clearly pointed out that the founding of the PRC would implement the basic foreign trade policy focusing on the newly democratic countries including the Soviet Union and Eastern Europe countries and take other capitalist countries into account. These two documents are historical documents in

[1] *Selected Works of Zhou Enlai*, Beijing: People's Publishing House, 1984, p. 226.

guiding the foreign trade work of the founding of the PRC and are the basic guidelines for formulating foreign trade policies and regulations later on.

Liu Shaoqi believed that the implementation of the State's foreign trade management policy must be guaranteed by corresponding organizations, rules and regulations. After the founding of the founding of the PRC, all levels of institutions from the central government to the local government should be fully established to improve the rules and regulations further. Besides, he also pointed out that it was necessary for the State to manage foreign trade, but "do not manage it too tightly to being strangled", and do not hinder legitimate import and export trade because of the state management.[1] He stressed that in order to do a good job in the foreign trade of the PRC, public-private relations, urban-rural relations, and internal-external relations must be handled well. We should adhere to the foreign trade guidelines of "unification and flexibility", correctly handle public-private relations, urban-rural relations, and internal-external relations, with the aim of making foreign trade work serve the development of the new democratic economy better. In the early days since the founding of the PRC, under the guidance of this policy, the Central Government formulated a series of foreign trade policies that took care of all aspects of relations, and better mobilized the enthusiasm of public and private sectors, urban and rural areas, and internal and external sectors to participate in the foreign trade of the PRC. The practice has proven that the foreign trade policy of "unification and flexibility" has played an important role in promoting the prosperity and development of of the PRC's economy.

2.2.1.2 Foreign capital theories

In the 1950s, the theoretical circle regarded the credit relationship between socialist countries as a form of economic cooperation. At that time, it was believed that the credit relations among socialist countries were different from those in the capitalist world, because international capitalist credit was a means of plunder, while socialist international credit was a sincere mutual-aid.

In the 1960s and 1970s, the "left-wing" trend of thought prevailed. Some people believed that foreign investment was "bringing in the wolf". Therefore, there were few theories of foreign investment at that stage. These theories were based on the spirit of self-reliance and the supplementation of foreign aid, and the obedience of economy to politics, so all analyses were not suitable for future developments.

---

[1] *China's Economic Development by Liu Shaoqi*, Beijing: Central Party Literature Publishing House, 1993, p. 81.

2.2.2 The economic internationalization policy between the founding of the PRC and the reform and opening up

2.2.2.1 Policy overview

At the beginning of the founding of PRC, the state management policy of foreign trade was implemented. Mao Zedong put forward at the Second Plenary Session of the Seventh Central Committee of the Communist Party of China held in March 1949 that, "it is impossible for the recovery and development of the national economy of the People's Republic of China without the state management policy of foreign trade". He also said that "after the Chinese revolution won on a country-broad scale and the issue of land ownership was solved, there are two basic contradictions. The first is inside, that is, the contradiction between the working class and the bourgeoisie. The second is outside, that is, the contradiction between China and the imperialist countries. Because of these, after the victory of the people's democratic revolution, the state power of the PRC led by the working class cannot be weakened but must be strengthened. Domestic regulation of capital and external control of foreign trade are the two basic policies in China's economic struggle".[1] According to the CPC Central Committee's decision on regulating foreign trade, the Common Program of the Chinese People's Political Consultative Conference (hereinafter referred to as "the Common Program") adopted in September 1949 stipulates that "... implement foreign trade state management policy, and also adopt a protective trade policy". Based on this, the state management policy of PRC on foreign trade was established. It was pointed out in the Common Program that, "the People's Republic of China can, on the basis of equality and mutual benefit, cooperate with foreign governments and nationals, resume and develop trade relations". This laid down the basic policies and principles for foreign economy and trade after the founding of the PRC.

Under the guidance of the Common Program on foreign trade policy, China has implemented the state-managed foreign trade policy in the early days after its founding. The contents include to adhere to the principle of equality and mutual benefit, to implement the construction policy of self-reliance, to develop foreign trade based on production, and to make overall consideration and appropriate arrangements for internal and external sales. The State has successively promulgated a series of policies to manage foreign trade and formulated relevant specific regulations and implementation measures. In accordance with the state management foreign trade policy, plan

---

[1] *Selected Works of Mao Zedong*, Beijing: People's Publishing House, 1991, p. 1433.

management was gradually strengthened, which meant that the national foreign trade activities would be placed under the centralized leadership and unified management of the State, and foreign economic activities would be carried out in a unified way in order to safeguard the independence of the country, promote the recovery and development of the national economy, and ensure the smooth progress of socialist transformation and construction.

In the process of foreign trade management by the State and given the special domestic and international environments in the early days after the founding of the PRC, Zhou Enlai proposed that China should adopt flexible and diversified foreign trade methods under the general principle of "independence and self-reliance, centralization and unity". According to Zhou Enlai's instructions, in July 1950, the Ministry of Trade held a national import and export conference to study China's foreign trade methods and channels and to divide the trading scope ran by the State and by the private enterprises. The meeting has decided that the state should monopoly the purchase and marketing of imported and exported goods and besides three other means of management should be implemented to unify and regulate the imported and exported of goods, i.e. "International Trade Research Association", "Professional Groups of Trade Councils and Associations" and "Joint Operation". This mode of foreign trade, in which the State and the private sector complement each other and both the State and the private enterprises run concurrently has strong flexibility. These flexible and diverse forms and methods of foreign trade have laid a good foundation for China to further expand its economic and trade ties with other countries in the future.

2.2.2.2 Three heights of foreign economic elements introduction

During this period, China's foreign economic elements introduction had three large-scale climaxes, which can be represented by the three figures of 156, 43 and 78. "156" refers to 156 projects established in China with the help of the Soviet Union in the first Five-year Plan period in the 1950s. "43" refers to the introduction of US$4.3 billion-worth sets of equipment from Western countries in the early 1970s, and this is the well-known "43 plan". "78" refers to the sign of an agreement to import US$7.8 billion-worth sets of technical equipment, and this move was once called "the Leap to the West". These three heights had different international and domestic backgrounds, and the imported targets, the means, and guiding ideology were also different. They covered the evolution history of China's import and opening to the outside world before the reform and opening up.

(1) *The basic process of the three heights of introduction*

Before the founding of the PRC, the Chinese Communist Party had already seen the importance of introducing foreign capital and technical equipment. In 1944, Mao Zedong talked with Xie Weisi in Yan' an, a member of the US military observation group. Mao said that China's industrialization in the future must be supported by free enterprises and foreign capital. China could provide "an investment place" and "an export market" of heavy industry products for the United States. Meanwhile, China could use industrial raw materials and agricultural products as the "compensation" for American investment and trade.[1] However, after the outbreak of China's Civil War, the United States began to support the Kuomintang, so the Chinese Communist Party quickly turned its attention to the Soviet Union. In December 1946, representatives of the Soviet Union's Ministry of Foreign Trade held the first tradetalk with the Northeast Administrative Commission, and they agreed that the North-East exchanged grain and coal for military goods, civilian goods and raw materials from the Soviet Union. At that time, some railway power stations were repaired mainly for wartime needs, not to a level of introduction and construction. On February 16, 1949, The central committee of the CPC instructed the Northern China Bureau and the Northeast Bureau to develop import and export trade with the Soviet Union as much as possible and Western countries were lower priorities. This has confirmed the basic principles of China's foreign trade.[2]

The formation process of the "156 projects"[3]: Between December 1949 and February 1950, Mao Zedong visited the Soviet Union and held the highest talks with the Soviet side. Economic assistance was taken as the most important issue, and the Soviet Union had signed an agreement to allow loans to China, and the Soviet government expressed its willingness to help China design and construct projects and provide complete sets of equipment and materials in batches. After Zhou Enlai, Chen Yun, Li

---

[1] Dong Zhikai et al., *Mao Zedong's Economic Thinking during Yan'an Period*, Xi'an: Shaanxi People's Education Press, 1993, pp. 114-115.

[2] The State Archives Administration of the People's Republic of China, *Selections of Party Literature of the CPC Central Committee, Volume XVIII*, Beijing: Central Party School Press, 1992, pp. 136-137.

[3] The basic materials for the "156 projects" have not been systematically sorted out in the past, including which items, how many items included, and there were different opinions. In 1983, after a long-term investigation of a large number of archives of the National Development and Reform Commission, the Central Archives and the State Economic Commission by the Basic Construction and Integration Bureau, the formation, changes, scale and progress of the "156" projects were sorted out for the first time. It was counted that there were 150 projects and the findings were written in "Construction Condition of 156 Projects during the First Five-Year Plan (150 implemented)".

Fuchun and others went to the Soviet Union, both sides had successively agreed on the first batch of 50 key projects that the Soviet Union would help China resume and build up by the end of 1952, mainly including coal, electricity and other energy industries, steel, nonferrous metals, chemical, and other raw materials industries and national defense industries. In 1953, focusing on the national defense industry, the Soviet Union signed the second batch of Sino-Soviet agreements on the supply of complete sets of equipment construction projects, totaling 91projects. In 1954, the Soviet Union signed the third batch of Sino-Soviet agreements introducing 15 energy industry and raw material industry projects from the Soviet Union to China, and they had decided to expand the scope of original supply of the 14 equipment packages. So far, the total number of aid projects signed with the Soviet Union had reached 156, and this was announced in1955, in the First Five-year Plan, known as "156 projects". Later, due to the renaming of some projects, the double counting of some projects, and the unbuilt projects, the factually implemented projects was 150.[1]

Heavy industry accounted for 97% of the complete sets of equipment projects imported from the Soviet Union, mainly including basic industry and national defense industry projects. Looking at the composition of investment, energy industry accounted for 34.3%, metallurgical industry for 22%, mechanical industry for 15.7%, chemical industry for 7.9% and national defense industry for about 12%. In the actual completion of the First Five-year Plan, the energy industry accounted for 28.6%, the metallurgical industry for 22%, the mechanical industry for 18.5%, the chemical industry for 7.8% and the national defense industry for 14%. Furthermore, 694 construction units above the quota have also been deployed. Of the 150 projects of the program, the total investment was estimated to be RMB18.78 billion (the original total investment had been estimated to be RMB20.27 billion). However, excluding the suspension of Sanmenxia Water Conservancy Project and reduced investment in military projects by RMB14.9 billion, the factual completion of the projects was worth RMB19.63 billion at around 104.5%. The completion and operation of these projects have given birth to China's first batch of large-scale modern enterprises, greatly enhanced the capability of China's heavy industry and military industry, and filled a number of gaps in production technology. Thus, the foundation for China's industrialization has been initially established. During the First Five-year Plan period, among the newly added production

[1] The Basic Construction and Integration Bureau of the National Development and Reform Commission. "Construction Condition of 156 Projects during the First Five-Year Plan (150 actually implemented)", Jun. 8, 1983.

capability, 79.1% of iron-making, 72.9% of steel-making, 81.1% of steel-rolling, 100% of aluminum smelting and automobile manufacturing and 65.9% of power generating machines were all provided by the "156 projects".[1] High-grade alloy steel, silicon steel sheets, composite stainless steel plates, seamless steel pipes, jet planes, tanks, large-caliber guns, warning radars, automobiles, medium tractors, and ten thousand tons of seagoing ships, large-capacity complete sets of thermal power, hydraulic power generation equipment, large-capacity blast furnace equipment, combined coal mining machine and new machine tools, etc. that could not be produced in the past were now being produced in China.[2]

With the aid of the Soviet Union, China's introduction of economic elements during this period has witnessed an unprecedented scale. In the 1950s, China had got investment in technology and equipment from the Soviet Union which was worth 7.69 billion rubles (around RMB7.3 billion). Among them, 3.2% was completed between 1950 and 1952, 57.1% in 1953–1957 and 39.6% in 1958–1959. During the same period, the total investment in technology and equipment imported from Eastern European countries was 3.08 billion rubles (equivalent to RMB2.93 billion).[3] The above total was RMB10.23 billion, equivalent to US$4.04 billion based on the average exchange rate in the 1950s or to US$3.909 billion based on the 1959's exchange rate.

The formation process of the "43 plan": In the 1960s, China's foreign trade was shrinking. Mao Zedong once considered expanding the introduction of economic elements from the West. He told the delegation of French parliamentarians, "we oppose capitalism, and you may oppose communism. However, cooperation is still possible". "I hope you will reverse any embargo on strategic goods." "I said, one day we will break through this gap".[4] He even put forward, at a certain time, that, "the Japanese can also come to China to set up factories, mine iron ores and we can learn technologies from them"[5]. However, due to the continued blockade by the West, only a batch of

---

1 The Basic Construction and Integration Bureau of the National Development and Reform Commission. "Construction Condition of 156 Projects during the First Five-Year Plan (150 actually implemented)", Jun. 8, 1983.

2 Peng Min, *Basic Construction of Contemporary China, Volume I*, Beijing: China Social Sciences Press, 1989, pp. 54-56.

3 Peng Min, *Basic Construction of Contemporary China, Volume I*, Beijing: China Social Sciences Press, 1989.

4 *Selected Works of Mao Zedong on Diplomacy*, Beijing: Central Party Literature Publishing House & World Affairs Press, 1993, p. 520.

5 "Mao Zedong's Speech on Jan.7, 1964, when Listening to the Report of the Labor Exchange Conference", *Compilation of Major Events of the National Economic and Social Development Plan of the People's Republic of China*, Beijing: Hongqi Press, 1987, p. 212.

automobiles and petrochemical manufacturing equipment were imported from France and the UK, and the introduction from foreign countries almost completely stopped at the early stage of the "Cultural Revolution." In the early 1970s, Western countries had an economic crisis and were eager to find overseas markets. Also, Sino-US relations eased, and China returned to the United Nations, removing from being blockaded. China has created favorable conditions for itself to expand its import from foreign countries. On January 22, 1972, Li Xiannian, Ji Dengkui and Hua Guofeng jointly submitted to Zhou Enlai the Report of the National Development and Reform Commission on the import of complete sets of chemical fiber and chemical fertilizer technical equipment, suggesting introducing 4 sets of new chemical fiber technology equipment, 2 sets of chemical fertilizer equipment and some key equipments and materials urgently needed by China, which would cost about US$400 million. On February 5, this report was again introduced to Chairman Mao by Zhou Enlai and won Chairman Mao's approval.[1] On August 6, the National Development and Reform Commission formally submitted a report on the import of 17-meter rolling mills. On August 21, Mao Zedong and Zhou Enlai approved it. On November 7, the National Development and Reform Commission submitted another report recommending the import of 23 sets of chemical equipment worth US$600 million. While Zhou Enlai approved it, he demanded to adopt a large-scale integration introduction plan.

On January 5, 1973, the National Development and Reform Commission submitted the "Report on Increasing the Import of Equipment and Expanding Economic Exchanges" to summarize the previous stage and plan future foreign import projects. It was suggested that US$4.3 billion of complete equipment be imported in the next 3 to 5 years. This was commonly referred to as the "43 plan" and was the second large-scale introduction plan after the "156 projects" and also a major step to break the closed-door situation during the "Cultural Revolution." Later, another batch of projects has been added on the basis of this plan, with a planned total import value of US$5.14 billion. With the equipment and through domestic matching and renovation, a total investment of about RMB20 billion has been made, and 27 large-scale industrial projects have been built, all of which would be put into operation by 1982 and would achieve good economic benefits. For example, after the Wuhan Iron and Steel Group put into operation the 1.7-meter rolling mill in 1984, the profit tax reached RMB685 million,

---

[1] "Report of the National Planning Revolution Committee on the import of complete sets of chemical fiber and chemical fertilizer technical equipment". Chen Donglin, "The Second Height of China's Introduction from Foreign Countries in the Early 1970s", *Research on the History of the Communist Party of China*, 1996(3).

1.66 times higher than that of 1979 before the operation. Meanwhile, the imported advanced technology has also been promoted and transplanted in the same industry in other places of China to promote the advancement of the technology in domestic steel-rolling and steel-making. Driven by the "43 plan", other important import projects also included: import colored kinescope production technology projects from the United States and purchase old and new ships with foreign exchange loans to form ocean-navigating fleets and buy British trident planes, etc.

The "43 plan" has promoted a breakthrough in China's foreign trade. The total foreign trade volume in 1973 was 2.4 times larger than that in 1970, and the volume in 1974 was even 3.2 times larger than that in 1970. The introduction of complete sets of equipment and advanced technology has promoted the development of China's basic industries, especially the metallurgical, chemical fertilizer and petrochemical industries, and provided the necessary material conditions for the economic growth in the 1980s.

The "78 plan": In 1976, the people of the whole country fervently hoped to speed up the pace of construction. In November 1977, on the basis of *the Outline of the 10-Year Plan (1976–1985)* re-formulated in 1975, the National Population and Family Planning Commission re-stressed that by the year 2000, several major battles would be fought in three distinct stages and 120 large-scale projects would be built. Furthermore, by the end of the 20th century, China's output of major industrial products needed to be close to, equivalent to and even exceed that of the most developed capitalist countries. The same held true for China's various economic and technological indicators. The main way to realize this large-scale construction plan was to expand the introduction of foreign capital and equipment. Since the beginning of 1978, China has sent a number of central delegations led by Gu Mu, Lin Hujia and Li Yimang to Europe, Japan, and other countries as well as Hong Kong and Macao regions in China. After returning home, in June 1978, these people made a report on a meeting of the Political Bureau of the Central Committee presided over by Hua Guofeng. Gu Mu pointed out that there had already been a big gap in development levels between China and foreign countries, so we should make use of the favorable opportunity of excess foreign capital to expand the introduction from foreign countries. Ye Jianying, Li Xiannian and other Central leaders who attended the meeting expressed their warm support. Hua Guofeng immediately requested that Gu Mu sort out several measures in this regard and present them to the State Council Meeting on Theoretical Matters for discussion.[1] From July 6 to

---

[1] Cao Pu, "Gu Mu and Reform and Opening up during 1978–1988", *Hundred Year Tide*, 2001(11).

September 9, the State Council convened a meeting on theoretical matters, and more than 60 Heads of Ministries and Commissions attended and made presentations, among which, the introduction of economic elements from foreign countries was an important agenda. Hua Guofeng and Li Xiannian made several speeches and cut in for a long time. On July 11, Li Renjun, Deputy Director of the National Development and Reform Commission, introduced the arrangements for the introduction and proposed a scale of RMB50 billion.

The realities of China's introduction of economic elements from foreign countries in 1978 were as follows: On March 11, the State Council approved the reports of the National Population and Family Planning Commission, the Construction Committee and other departments, deciding to import complete sets of equipment from Japan and build a large steel plant in Baoshan Shanghai with a projected annual output of 6.5 million tons of iron and 6.7 million tons of steel, with a total investment of RMB21.4 billion, including US$4.8 billion foreign exchange and RMB7 billion domestic investment. On March 20, the National Population and Family Planning Commission and the Construction Committee issued the 1978 Plan for the Introduction of New technologies and Complete sets of Equipment, approving relevant departments to use US$8.56 billion foreign exchange. That year's turnover was US$5.92 billion, and that year's used foreign exchange was US$1.17 billion.[1] The plan actually reached an agreed amount of US$7.8 billion, so it was called "7.8 billion plan". On December 5, the Ministry of Chemical Industry reported to the National Development and Reform Commission and the State Council that nine import projects of complete chemical equipment were signed with foreign countries within the same year. Daqing Petrochemical Plant, Shandong Petrochemical Plant, and Beijing Dongfanghong Chemical Plant each had one set of 300,000 tons of ethylene production units; Nanjing Petrochemical Complex had two sets of 300,000 tons of ethylene units; Jilin Chemical Industry Company had one set of key equipment for 110,000 tons of ethylene; Zhejiang Chemical Fertilizer Plant, Xinjiang Chemical Fertilizer Plant and Ningxia Chemical Fertilizer Plant each had one set of 300,000 tons of ammonia production plant; and Shanxi Chemical Fertilizer Plant had 300,000 tons ammonia operation equipment. These nine projects needed domestic engineering investment of more than RMB16 billion. In addition, 100 sets of integrated coal mining units, Dexing Copper Base,

---

1 Bai Hejin, *Economic Summary of the People's Republic of China (1978–2001)*, Beijing: China Planning Press, 2002, p. 2.

Guizhou Aluminum Factory, Shanghai Chemical Fiber Phase-II Project, Yizheng Chemical Fiber Factory, Pingdingshan Cord Factory, Shandong Synthetic Leather Factory, Lanzhou Synthetic Leather Factory, Yunnan Wuna Factory, Huolinhe Coal Mine, Kailuan Coal Mine, and Color television projects were signed and included in the whole introduction plan in 1978. The above 22 key projects required US$13 billion of foreign exchange, equivalent to RMB39 billion. The total would be more than RMB60 billion, plus more than RMB20 billion domestic engineering investment.[1] Throughout 1978, all projects signed were worth US$5.8 billion, equivalent to 89.2% of the total amount of US$6.5 billion that China had imported from 1950 to 1977.

(2) *The domestic and international situations of the three heights of foreign import*

Significant changes in the domestic and international background were the main reason for the obvious differences in the guiding ideology, objects, means and scale for the three introductions.

The domestic and international background for "156 projects" was the expanding socialist camp so the Chinese Communist Party which would soon become the ruling party would naturally seek support from it. In February 1949, Mikoyan, a member of the Political Bureau of the Communist party of Soviet Union, held talks with leaders of the CPC Central Committee in Xibaipo, Hebei province. Liu Shaoqi said, "without the help of the Soviet Union and other people's democratic countries, it is inconceivable to establish the industrial base for the founding of the PRC." Mao Zedong said, "in order to shorten the transitional period, we need economic assistance. We believe that the assistance can only be obtained from the Soviet Union and other new democratic countries. We need a three-year (1949–1951) loan totaling US$300 million, with an annual principal and interest of US$100 million. We hope that the loan will include some equipment, oil, other goods and money needed to maintain the strength of the *renminbi*".[2] The outbreak of the Korean War has also forced China to implement a "one-sided" foreign policy more firmly and finally formed a policy of relying on Soviet aid and taking self-reliance into account while mainly learning from the Soviet Union. The Soviet Union's path towards national industrialization and planned economy system in the 1920s and 30s were the dreaming goals of China. The First Five-year Plan approved at the second session of the first National People's Congress in 1955 clearly

---

[1] Fang Weizhong ed., *Major Economic Events of the People's Republic of China (1949-1980)*, Beijing: China Social Sciences Press, 1984, pp. 609 - 610.

[2] A. M. Ledovskikh, "Secret Talks Between Mikoyan and Mao Zedong (January-February, 1949)", Part II, *Literature of Chinese Communist Party*, 1996(3).

pointed out that, the basic task of the plan was to "concentrate major efforts on industrial construction centered on 156 construction units designed by the Soviet Union to help our country and consisting of 694 construction units above the quota"; "the 156 units were complete sets of equipment designed and supplied with the help of the Soviet Union, which was a great advantage to ensure the completion of the plan".[1]

While striving for the Soviet Union's aid, the Chinese leaders also paid attention to the importance of self-reliance. Mao Zedong emphasized as early as on the Xibaipo Meeting that "this did not mean that we should not only rely on others, but we also needed self-reliance. If the Soviet Union could not provide anything, then we would not complain".[2] In January 1950, he again gave instructions to the officials at home when he was in the Soviet Union, "it is better to borrow less rather than to borrow more in the following few years".[3] After the outbreak of the Korean War, China had to increase its loan from the Soviet Union because of the rising demand. Even so, during the whole the First Five-year Plan period, loans from abroad were only RMB3.635 billion, accounting for only 2.7% of the State's fiscal revenue.[4]

Through the introduction of the "156 projects", China has made great achievements in economic construction. First of all, the introduction of the complete sets of Soviet projects has helped China establish a large number of backbone enterprises and facilities. The implementation of the same planned economic system as that of the Soviet Union has brought this kind of introduction and construction into line with each other with high efficiency and short cycle. For example, FAW Group in Changchun only took three years to prepare for and start in operation. Besides, while introducing complete sets of equipment, new design and artifact technologies have been introduced at the same time. For example, more than 2/3 of the 4,000 new products in the machinery industry were developed by copying Soviet design drawings.[5] Finally, from 1949 to 1960, the Soviet Union has altogether sent more than 18,000 experts to

---

[1] Party Documents Research Office of the CPC Central Committee, *Selected Important Documents since the Founding of the People's Republic of China Volume V*, Beijing: Central Party Literature Publishing House, 1993, pp. 410-426.

[2] A. M. Ledovskikh, "Secret Talks Between Mikoyan and Mao Zedong (January-February, 1949)", Part II, *Literature of Chinese Communist Party*, 1996(3).

[3] *Mao Zedong's Manuscripts since the Founding of the People's Republic of China Volume I*, Beijing: Central Party Literature Publishing House, p. 213.

[4] *China's Contemporary Finance Volume I*, Beijing: China Social Sciences Press, 1988, p. 120.

[5] Wang Zhangbao, "50 Years' Technology Introduction in Chinese Mechanical Industry", *Journal of Dialectics of Nature*, 2000(1).

China. Among them, the number of experts who came to China during the "156 projects" period (1954–1958) accounted for more than 60%.[1] A large number of professional and technical personnel have been trained for China and have become the backbone of China's economic construction for decades.

Under the historical conditions at that time, the introduction also produced some adverse effects. Firstly, too much emphasis has been placed on the introduction of construction and production. At one time there was a tendency to blindly learn from the Soviet Union and the country's manufacturing level and innovation capability were neglected, so the country's strength for sustainable development was also neglected. Some of the imported designs and projects, such as the Sanmenxia Water Conservancy Project, have failed because they did not take China's national conditions into account. Secondly, among all introduced projects, the labor division of imported industries was too detailed, for example, the establishment of many large but single-product military enterprises following the example of the Soviet Union. From the perspective of the introducing method, such large-scale introductions relying on the support of the Soviet Union was abnormal, so it was bound to be unstable with the change of political situations, and it did not enable us to obtain some normal international trade experience and integration pattern. Therefore, when the Soviet Union suddenly terminated its aid in 1960, some projects were caught off guard and many imported construction projects fell into suspense. China then had to re-explore its own foreign trade path.

The domestic and international situations faced with when the "43 plan" was underway included the following: Sino-US relations have softened, and China joined the United Nations. Although China corrected some "left" mistakes, the similar "Cultural Revolution" path continued and had not been fundamentally changed. Therefore, the most urgent task was to open a gap and resume and expand economic exchanges with foreign countries. This kind of strategic decision could not be made without Mao Zedong. In 1972, Mao Zedong heard a waiter in the South complaining that he could not buy the chemical fiber cloth supplied by the limited quota, so Chairman Mao said why not expand the production. Zhou Enlai immediately seized on this seemingly non-important expression of Mao Zedong and asked the National Development and Reform Commission to prepare for the introduction of chemical fiber production equipment. In February, Mao Zedong said in his talks with Nixon, "you want to make exchanges with us including personnel exchanges and want to do some small

[1] Shen Zhihua, *Soviet Experts in China (1948–1960)*, Beijing: China Radio International Press, 2003, p. 408.

business. However, we would never agree. For more than a decade, we said if you did not solve major problems with us, we would not agree on anything small, including me. Later, I found out that you were still right, so I invited you to play table tennis".[1] Chairman Mao made use of this conversation to criticize the mistake of being closed to the outside world and showed his determination to prepare for the development of foreign trade. Zhou Enlai, Li Xiannian, Yu Qiuli, Chen Yun and Deng Xiaoping actively carried out this decision and formed the guiding ideology of undertaking the domestic economic construction, satisfying living needs of the people and further breaking the western economic barriers through introduction and exchanges.

Through this introduction, a new pattern of foreign trade has generally been formed, as Chen Yun pointed out that, "in the past, 75% of our foreign trade was from the Soviet Union and Eastern European countries and only 25% was from capitalist countries. Now, we have changed them to 75% from the capitalist countries and 25% from the Soviet Union and Eastern Europe". "Is this trend settled? I think so".[2] According to the principle of placing the majority of the introduced equipment in the coastal cities while putting only a small amount of equipment in inland cities proposed in the "43 plan", "the coastal cities have a good foundation for industry, which can enable imported equipment to be put into operation as soon as possible and copied as soon as possible," and "the faster the coastal industry can develop, the more beneficial it is to the promotion of mainland construction in the long run".[3] Thus, the strategic layout of the one-sided emphasis on the third-line construction and war readiness formed in the late 1960s was adjusted. More preciously, it was Zhou Enlai who recognized how to use foreign capital. In June 1973, he met with an American banker Rockefeller and said, "it is a cost-effective channel to promote the development of trade between us through the banks of the two countries. On this point, we even could not compete with Taiwan region's Yan Jiagan. He suggested introducing foreign capital from the United States and Japan, importing raw materials to process products and exporting these processed products. Furthermore, Taiwan region has set a tax-free port in Kaohsiung, like Hong Kong. In this way, Taiwan region's trade volume has increased

---

1 "table tennis" refers to the "Table Tennis Diplomacy" initiated by inviting the US table tennis team to visit China. *Selected Works of Mao Zedong on Diplomacy*, Beijing: Central Party Literature Publishing House & World Affairs Press, 1993, p. 595.

2 *Selected Works of Chen Yun,Volume III*, Beijing: People's Publishing House, 1995, p. 217.

3 "Report of the National Planning Revolution Commission on Instructions for Increasing Equipment Import and Expanding Economic Exchanges", Chen Donglin, "The Second Height of China's Introduction from Foreign Countries in the Early 1970s", *Research on the History of the Communist Party of China*, 1996(3).

substantially".[1] In October when Zhou Enlai resumed talks with Australian Prime Minister Whitlam, he re-emphasized that, Chiang Kai-shek had Kaohsiung in Taiwan region as a free port which levied no tax. Thus, raw materials were imported to build factories, and Taiwan region's cheap labor was greatly utilized, producing commodities sold back to these foreign countries. This would attract a lot of foreign capital to invest in Taiwan region.[2]

The "43 plan" was carried out in the struggle with the "ultra-left wings". In terms of the way of introduction, at that time, the emphasis was solely placed on the introduction of complete sets of equipment, ignoring the introduction of individual technologies and equipment. Meanwhile, few technical personnel were sent abroad for leaning, and few foreign experts were invited to China to communicate with us.

The domestic and international environment that China has faced during the implementation of the "78 plan" has changed dramatically compared with the former two heights, bringing China's ideology a new leap. The international environment at that time was very favorable. The United States had just withdrawn from the Vietnam War and was unable to interfere with other regional affairs. The Soviet Union was paying attention to Afghanistan and had no time and energy to watch for other countries. More importantly, the Cold War was at a low point. In terms of economy, Western countries have just emerged from the economic depression and had more free funds, so they urgently needed to expand overseas markets. Wherever the Chinese delegation visited in 1978, Western officials and businessmen showed their strong intention to develop economic cooperation with China. During Gu Mu's talks with French President Giscard d'Estaing at that time, the French Ambassador to China told Gu Mu that France was willing to invest 10 of the 120 major projects that China was planning. In the Federal Republic of Germany, the governor of Baden-Württemberg said that he could lend US$5 billion to China and the agreement could be signed immediately. North Rhine-Westphalia State said even US$10 billion would not be a problem. Besides, Japan, South Korea and other countries and regions have achieved their economic take-off through the introduction, which has become a model for other Asiatic countries. Since the early 1970s, while continuing to develop processing and export industries, Taiwan of China has begun to promote the import-substitution strategy for the second time.

---

[1] *Selected Works of Zhou Enlai on Economy*, Beijing: Central Party Literature Publishing house, 1993, pp. 644-645.

[2] *The Chronicle Biography of Zhou Enlai 1949 – 1976, Volume II*, Beijing: Central Party Literature Publishing house, 1997, pp. 630 - 631.

Till 1978, the proportion of heavy industry production exceeded that of light industry for the first time, and Taiwan of China began to have a relatively complete industrial system.

All these have stimulated the Chinese leaders to take a positive attitude towards import and introduction and formed the guiding ideology of accelerating the expansion of the introduction from foreign countries. In February 1978 when the Political Bureau of the Central Committee discussed the "10-year Plan", Deng Xiaoping pointed out that, "after introducing advanced technology, we need to copy and improve it and this is nothing small. The key is iron and steel. If the production volume of iron and steel cannot go up, it will not be possible to develop large-scale industries. We must seize the time and speed up negotiations if we want to make introductions as early as possible. As for common markets, it is also necessary to quickly send people to carry out technical investigations." Ye Jianying said that, as for the import problem, the Central Government should seize the opportunity more tightly and quickly. Otherwise, another three or eight years would soon pass away. The meeting initially confirmed the scale of US$18 billion imported from other countries. Hua Guofeng requested that US$18 billion imports could be handled together. After hearing the report on the foreign visit of Lin Hujia and Gu Mu in June, Hua Guofeng said, "regarding the use of foreign funds to build several large coal mines, iron, and steel plants and chemical fiber plants, as long as the Central Government has decided on the project, you could just embark on the work so firstly made 2 million tons of chemical fiber implemented by the Planning, Economic and Construction Commission.[1] At present, France has offered more than US$2 billion for us to use. In fact, it could also be more because even US$5 billion was okay. The Federal Republic of Germany has offered US$20 billion, and Japan was even more active. We should open our eyes, and the negotiation time should not be too long. We should finalize the project as early as possible and make a long list at first. Then we will do it one by one."[2] On June 22, Deng Xiaoping talked with Yu Qiuli, Gu Mu, and Kang Shien and proposed that we should make a bigger deal with foreign countries, winning US$50 billion at first. The capitalist crisis should be properly utilized because the opportunity should not be missed. Rather, we need to be bolder and take more steps. After listening to Lin Hujia's report, he added, "Don't just talk. Once you have got it

[1] *The Chronicle Biography of Deng Xiaoping 1975 – 1997, Volume I*, Beijing: Central Party Literature Publishing House, 2004, p.267.

[2] The National Development and Reform Commission of the People's Republic of China, "Issues in Economic Guidance after the Crushing the 'Gang of Four'", Nov. 15, 1980.

right, start right away. Thus, we can work out hundreds of projects firstly, including coal mines, nonferrous metals, oil, power plants and electron, military industry, transportation, and provender mill, and these projects can start next year".[1] In summer on the State Council Meeting on Theoretical Matters, Hua Guofeng put forward new requirements and said, "the 10-year Plan needs to be revised, and China has the conditions to speed up the pace of its modernization and must open its eyes on the issue of introduction. Let's be a little bit bolder, do more things, and move faster".

During the implementation of the "78 plan", there was a tendency to rush for success. During the whole year of 1978, about half of the US$7.8 billion agreement was signed in a short period of 10 days from December 20 of that year.[2] The introduction of such a large number of projects at the same time was a great burden on a country's financial Power and a great impact on the entire national economy. As early as June, Deng Xiaoping had already warned that "we should be careful and cautious about the whole introduction projects", and "we should divide them into two groups, one with more urgent ones, the other with other projects, so we should finish them one by one according to priorities, and there is no hurry to finish them within just one or two years".[3] In December 1978 when Central Working Conference was held, Chen Yun pointed out that, "the introduction of industrial projects should be carried out step by step rather than all at the same time. Although the latter plan looks very fast, it cannot achieve any similar effective results to the former plan".[4] This was the first time that the problem of imbalance has been brought before the whole Party. In March 1979, Chen Yun and Li Xiannian jointly wrote to the Central Government, suggesting that it was better to take two or three years to adjust the economy first so as to correct the imbalance problem. The central government agreed on this proposition after an investigation. Deng Xiaoping pointed out that, "the predominant task now is to make adjustments. First of all, we must have the determination to do the job well. In the past, we emphasize the production of grains and later steel, but now we have to make our own

---

[1] Li Zhenghua, *Preparation and Operation of China's Reform and Opening up*, Beijing: Contemporary China Publishing House, 2002, p. 267.

[2] Peng Min, *Basic Construction of Contemporary China, Volume I*, Beijing: China Social Sciences Press, 1989, p.241.

[3] *Collected Works by Deng Xiaoping on Military Affairs, VolumeIII*, Beijing: Military Science Publishing House & Central Party Literature Publishing House, 2004, p.136.

[4] China Literature Research Office of the Central Committee of the Communist Party, *The Chronicle Biography of Chen Yun, Volume II*, Beijing: Central Party Literature Publishing House, 2000, p. 229.

conclusions".[1] In June 1979, the State formally adopted the policy of "adjustment, reform, reorganization and improvement" and decided to take three years to complete the adjustment of the national economy, strictly control the scale of the introduction, and focus on the introduction of individual items with little investment, quick efficiency and high exchange rate.[2] Among 22 key import projects, several have fallen into suspense including Yizheng Chemical Fiber Factory. As for the Baoshan Iron and Steel Factory which has borrowed RMB20 billion after Chen Yun's many on-site investigations, he reported to the central government and decided to continue introducing a full set of technical equipment for its construction.

Despite all kinds of problems, the "78 plan" has greatly broken through the previous introduction framework and has important pioneering significance. During the "156 projects" period, China mainly relied on borrowing money from the Soviet Union at an annual interest rate of 1%, lower than that of the Soviet Union's loans to Eastern European countries (2%) at that time and that given to the industry by domestic banks in China (3.24%).[3] As an additional condition to the loan, the Soviet Union requested China to use tungsten, antimony, lead, tin, rubber and other materials as repayment starting from 1955. This was, to a certain extent, mutual barter support between socialist countries and did not have the universal significance of international trade. During the "43 plan" period, China highly promoted the non-external-debt and non-internal-debt as an achievement, paying foreign exchange dependent entirely on tapping the potential of generating large sums of foreign exchange and adopting the methods of extension, installment payment, and compensation trade. Because the government was unwilling to fall into debts, the expansion of the import scale was limited. Starting from the "78 plan", the government firstly emphasized self-reliance but later was entirely dependent on large-scale borrowing. At first, the government simply introduced technology and equipment from abroad but then China began to attract foreign investment and establish joint ventures at home. In the beginning, the government only borrowed debts, but later

---

[1] China Literature Research Office of the Central Committee of the Communist Party, *The Chronicle Biography of Chen Yun, Volume II*, Beijing: Central Party Literature Publishing House, 2000, p. 242.

[2] "Li Xiannian's Speech at the Central Working Conference on Apr. 5, 1979", *Selected Important Documents since the Third Plenary Session of the Central CommitteeVolume I*, Beijing: People's Publishing House, 1982, pp.126-127.

[3] "Chinese Academy of Social Sciences & the State Archives Administration of the People's Republic of China", *Selected Files Data of the People's Republic of China's Economy during 1953–1957(of basic construction investment and building industry)*, Beijing: China City Economy and Society Press, 1989, p.99.

China started to issue foreign debts abroad and even had the idea of establishing special zones.

Borrowing from abroad was criticized during the "Cultural Revolution". Until April 1978, Foreign Trade Minister Li Qiang also pointed out, we could do the following: First, compensation trade; Second, the processing with materials supplied by customers and with given samples; Third, the use of brand registration of foreign trademark; Fourth, cooperative production; Fifth, consignment sale; Sixth, installment payment and deferred payment. However, borrowing money from foreign countries and setting up joint ventures with foreign countries are not allowed. In June, when listening to Gu Mu and others' reports, Deng Xiaoping decisively put forward that, "the installment payment should be suspended, but instead we can receive compensation trade and bank loans".[1] Since then, the gate began to open. In November at the Central Working Conference of the CPC Central Committee, the policy of making full use of the current favorable situations to absorb foreign capital and technology was determined. On December 15, Li Qiang announced in Hong Kong that "China has recently decided to cancel the stipulation of refusing the government-to-government loans and foreign investment in China. Basically, the two practices mentioned above are normal in the international trade arena".[2]

The method of issuing foreign debts overseas to support the introduction began with Yizheng Chemical Fiber Project, which was one of the 22 key projects. After the project was stopped, Rong Yiren, President of the China International Trust and Investment Corporation, continued to explore new methods with the support of Deng Xiaoping because of the real needs in China. Finally, China successfully issued 10 billion yen bonds in Japan in 1981 and imported major equipment and technology from Germany and Japan respectively. The project started in January 1982, the first production unit was put into operation in 1984 and the second phase of the project was completed in 1990, forming a production capacity of 500,000 tons of polyester. This fund-raising was called "the Yizheng Mode", which set a precedent for major national projects to be supported by issuing bonds abroad rather than government financial allocation.

The idea of setting up special economic zones has also sprouted in the climax of the introduction. After Hua Guofeng visited North Korea and returned home, Ren Zhongyi,

---

1 Li Zhenghua, "An Important Meeting for Preparing Reform and Opening Up", *Reference Data of State History*, Vol. 214.

2 Li Zhenghua, *Preparation and Operation of China's Reform and Opening up*, Beijing: Contemporary China Publishing House, 2002, pp. 272-274.

Secretary of Liaoning Provincial Party Committee, proposed to him that Dalian, which had more contacts with Japan, should be built as a window for the northern economy. Hua Guofeng soon approved the report and sent people to Liaoning for investigation, which was put on hold because the conditions were not proper. In April 1979, after listening to a report by Xi Zhongxun, Secretary of the Guangdong Provincial Party Committee, the Political Bureau of the Central Committee approved setting special zones in Guangdong and Fujian. Not long after, Deng Xiaoping listened to Gu Mu and others' report and proposed that "we can draw a line in a place and call it a special zone. In the past, Shaanxi, Gansu, and Ningxia were the special administrative region. The central government has no money, so we want you to do it yourself!"[1] Different from the previous two heights, these introduction methods in "plan 78" had strong vitality and continued to be adopted from the 1980s and 1990s to the 21st century, becoming a bridge for China to integrate into the world economy.

2.2.3 Achievements of economic internationalization between the founding of the PRC and the reform and opening up

In the stage of socialist exploration, although China's economic construction has undergone some mistakes, the whole conditions of economic construction have improved. One outstanding achievement was the continuity of economic development and the continuous improvement of people's standard of living and safety. As shown in Table 2–7 and Table 2–8, China not only reversed the trend of economic recession but also had a good growth rate. Taking into consideration the domestic and international situation during this period, it is even more valuable to achieve such results.

Similarly, the state-managed trade system made important achievements in the early days after the founding of the PRC. In 1951, China's total foreign trade volume reached US$1.955 billion, exceeding the highest level reached before the founding of the PRC in 1928 (US$1.533 billion). From 1952 to 1957, China's total import and export growth rate index was 161.8%, import growth rate index was 133.3%, and export growth rate index was 201.1%. From 1950 to 1956, China's annual export growth rate reached 17%. Furthermore, between 1950 and 1956, China's export volume had increased from US$550 million to US$1.65 billion, while the import volume rose from US$580 million to US$1.56 billion. The structure of export commodities has also

[1] Party Literature Research Center of the CPC Central Committee, *The Chronicle Biography of Deng Xiaoping 1975–1997*, Beijing: Central Party Literature Publishing House, 2004, p.117.

undergone obvious changes, from single agricultural and sideline products and raw materials to diversified products. However, like a highly centralized planned economic system, the trade system managed by the State has its own inevitable defects. The state-managed foreign trade policy had greatly restricted the scope and scale of China's trade. According to statistics, until 1979, the total import and export volume of our country was only US$29.34 billion among which the export volume was only US$13.66 billion, only accounting for the world's total export volume's 0.8%, ranking only 32nd among countries and regions worldwide. State-managed foreign trade system managed too tightly, lacked flexibility and could not motivate small businesses' activity.[1]

Table 2–7 Per capita GDP growth rate of China, Japan and the United States (1913–1978)

Unit: %

Country	1913–1952	1952–1978
China	-0.1	2.3
Japan	1.3	6.7
The US	1.7	2.2

Source: Angus Maddison, *translated by Wu Xiaoying et al., Chinese Economic Performance in the Long Run*, Shanghai: Shanghai People's Publishing House, 2008, p. 59.

Table 2–8 China's position in the world economic structure (1913–1978)

Unit: %

Item	1913	1952	1978
Proportions in world GDP	8.8	4.6	4.9
Proportions of GDP per capita in the world average	41.7	23.8	22.1
Proportions in world export volume	1.6	1.0	0.8

Source: Angus Maddison, *translated by Wu Xiaoying et al., Chinese Economic Performance in the Long Run*, Shanghai: Shanghai People's Publishing House, 2008, p. 57.

Overall, during this stage, China started to carry out economic construction and exploration independently. Either in terms of the total economic volume or the GDP per capita, China has made fast improvements. Meanwhile, China's economic internationalization has also begun to produce greater results.

[1] Su Ling, "Strategic Decisions and Basic Experience of Foreign Trade during the Early Foundation of New China", *Research Collections of New China's 60 Years, Volume IV*, Beijing: Central Party Literature Publishing House, 2009.

Chapter 3
The Development of China's Economic Internationalization

The reform and opening up is an important policy in Chinese history as well as a landmark of the internationalization of China's economy, which leads to the most critical and effective progress of China's economic internationalization. Since the 1970s, the establishment of diplomatic relations with the United States and Japan, along with the starting of economic globalization, has provided a relatively stable and favorable external environment for China's development. At the same time,the ten-year "Cultural Revolution" in China has just come to an end, calling for an urgent rebuilding of its suffered economy. Against such international and domestic context, the Communist Party of China centered on economic construction and opened to the outside world, following the main themes of times. Since then, China's economic internationalization has entered a high-speed development channel while China's development has become inseparable from the world economy.

3.1 Internationalization of China's economy at the beginning of reform and opening up

What is the most significant historical event after the founding of the PRC? There is no doubt that it is the reform and opening up. In other words, it is the Third Plenary Session of the 11th Central Committee of the Communist Party of China in 1978 in which the policy of reform and opening up was made. However, how can a meeting of just five days become such a great historical turning point? Moreover, why didn't the reform and opening up start immediately after the downfall of the "Gang of Four" in 1976, but wait for another two years, after the Third Plenary Session of the 11th Central Committee?

To find out the answers, two different "voices" in China from 1976 to 1978 should be figured out. Reform is always taken for granted to achieve economic development nowadays, so is opening up to outside. However, under the conditions and the ideology of that time, what has been taken for granted today encountered plenty of difficulties.

3.1.1 Forerunner of opening up: going abroad and examining ourselves in the "mirror"

Limited by the international situation and domestic conditions, China had not achieved open development indeed within a long time since the founding of the People's Republic of China. Although great progress had been made in economic construction, China still lagged behind the advanced countries around the world. What's worse, the ten-year of "Cultural Revolution" led to a more severe situation for China's economic development. In 1955, China's gross national product accounted for 4.7% of the global total but dropped to 1% in 1978. The average annual consumption of grain per capita in China was only 190.5kg in 1978, lower than 197.5kg in 1952. The national average salary of workers was RMB575 in 1976, less than RMB583 in 1966. For more than a decade, salaries had not increased while the actual living standard declined. What's more, the national capital profit rate of industrial enterprises in 1976 was only half of that in 1965, and the loss-making enterprises accounted for one-third of the total. The import and export volume in 1976 was only US$13.4 billion while the foreign exchange reserves were only US$0.58 billion. Under the circumstances at that time, opening up to outside became the key to break the economic predicaments.

Speaking from an objective perspective, although the central government carried out "two whatevers" within a certain time after the downfall of the "Gang of Four", the overall development in China did not regress but advanced in those two years, especially in the aspect of opening up. In fact, China had been already considering opening up to the outside world in the two years before the Third Plenary Session of the 11th Central Committee. In a talk with Hu Yaobang and Tan Qilong in July 1978, Hua Guofeng said: "The Central Committee has put forward a 10-year plan and a 23-year blueprint, but the problem that remains now is that the thoughts of senior cadres still lag behind. What should we do? Go abroad more and investigate more..." Obviously, the meaning of the words is to go abroad to have a look. Actually, the main leaders of the CPC Central Committee, including Deng Xiaoping and Hua Guofeng, had made their minds to open up to the outside world, learn from advanced international experience, import advanced technology as well as equipment and develop economic cooperation with foreign counterparts in May 1978 at the latest. What they were considering and exploring is how to open up to the outside world instead of whether to open or not.[1]

Due to the interruption of the "Cultural Revolution," most people at home had no idea about the development outside China at that time.

After the "Cultural Revolution", people were eager to know the changes in the outside world. Therefore, the National Development and Reform Commission proposed to "seriously organize the inspection work abroad" for the first time in a submitted report on the introduction to the Political Bureau of the Central Committeeon July 26th, 1977. Hua Guofeng also pointed out that, "To carry out the four modernizations, we must adhere to the principles of independence and self-reliance and learn from advanced foreign experience. If you want to learn from other countries, you have to go global to investigate... find out something useful and helpful abroad and figure out the weaknesses of capitalism, from which we can learn lessons." As a consequence, the State Council arranged numerous delegations of ministries and commissions to visit abroad since the second half of 1977.[2] China's economic internationalization slowly moved on again after blocked by the "Cultural Revolution" for many years.

(1) *A craze for studying abroad*

In 1978, when the domestic public was all concerned about the criterion of truth, the government set off a huge upsurge of the overseas investigation. According to the statistics from the Hong Kong and Macao Affairs Office of the State Council at that time, 529 batches of 3,213 people went abroad and visited Hong Kong from January to the end of November in 1978.

Among these delegations, the group headed by Gu Mu to the five Western European countries was the highest according to the administrative levels. It was also the first economic delegation headed by a national leader from China to western countries after the founding of the PRC.

Before their departure, Deng Xiaoping specifically talked to Gu Mu and asked for extensive contacts, detailed investigation and in-depth study during their visit to have

---

[1] Document Research Office of the Central Committee of the Communist Party of China, *Recalling Deng Xiaoping(Part I)*, Beijing: Central Party Literature Publishing House, 1998, p. 156.

[2] Cao Pu, *Some Important Issues in the Study of the History of Reform and Opening up*, Fuzhou: Fujian People's Publishing House, 2014, pp.15-16.

a better understanding about the development of modern industry in western countries and learn from the advanced and good managerial experience of capitalist countries. From May to June in 1978, Gu Mu with the Chinese economic delegation paid their visit to five western European countries, including France, Switzerland, Belgium, Denmark and the Federal Republic of Germany. According to members of the delegation, they had not thought that the global modernization had developed to such a degree that science and technology, as well as the living standard of people in western Europe, had far exceeded that of China. In Germany, an open-pit coal mine with an annual output of 50 million tons of lignite required only 2,000 workers, while 160,000 workers were needed in China, 80 times of that in Germany. In Bern, a Swiss company with only 12 employees, the installed capacity of a low-flow faucet hydroelectric power station was 25,000 kilowatts. In contrast, the installed capacity of Jiangkou Hydro-power Station in Jiangxi Province of China was 26,000 kilowatts with 298 employees, more 20% workers than Bern. Saul Mel Steel Mill in Marseille, France could produce an annual output of 3.5 million tons steel with 7,000 workers while 2.3 million tons steelrequired 67,000 workers in Wuhan Iron and Steel Corp in China, 14.5 times of that in France.[1]

During Gu Mu's visit to Europe, he not only saw the huge gap between China and other European countries in economy, science, technology, and other aspects but also felt local government officials' and business people's strong desire to establish economic and trade relations with China. At the meeting with then French President Valéry Giscard d'Estaing, French ambassador to China said to Gu Mu: "I heard that you are going to launch 120 major projects. We France would like to make our contribution. Would you like to grant us ten projects?" In Germany, some governors' showed their willingness that they could provide even billions of dollars in loans for China. It could be seen from these statements that they were eager to find a way out for their surplus capital and it was possible to speed up China's economic construction by using foreign capital.[2]

After returning home, the delegation gave a report to then Vice Premier Wang Zhen and Kang Shien and members of Political Bureau of the Central Committee, including Hua Guofeng, Ye Jianying, Li Xiannian, Wu Lanfu, Ji Dengkui, Su Zhenhua,

---

[1] Cao Pu, *Some Important Issues in the Study of the History of Reform and Opening up*, Fuzhou: Fujian People's Publishing House, 2014, p. 17.

[2] Li Lanqing, *Breaking Out—Days of Early Opening Up*, Beijing: Central Party Literature Publishing House, 2008, p. 53.

Wu De, Chen Xilian, Nie Rongzhen, Chen Muhua in late June.Gu Mu recalled that the report lasted a long time from 3: 30 p.m. to 11: 00 p.m, in which he highlighted the following three points. Firstly, after the Second World War, the European capitalist countries had indeed achieved unprecedented economic development, especially the rapid development of science and technology, the wide application of electronic technology and much-improved labor productivity. Compared with these countries, China lagged far behind, and the situation was quite severe. What was worthy of learning lay in many ways, such as the economic operation mechanism of these countries, the governmental regulation of the economy and the handling of social conflicts.Secondly, most of these countries were friendly to China. They attached great importance to developing economic and trade exchanges with China because of over capitalization and the needs of the market for technology and commodities. Many things could be done as long as we tried. Thirdly, numerous internationally accepted approaches to developing international economic exchanges could be adopted to accelerate the modernization of China, including sellers' credit, buyers' credit, compensation trade, Sino-foreign cooperative production, foreign direct investment absorption and so on. According to Gu Mu, central leaders paid great attention to his report at that time. He wrote in his memoir, "All the leaders present at the meeting delivered speeches to emphasize that the acceleration of socialist construction was mainly based on domestic conditions and principles of independence and self-reliance. At the same time, the introduction to advanced international technology could not be ignored. In doing so, we should expand exports, increase receipt of proceeds, speed up the growth of non-trade foreign exchange earnings and develop international economic cooperation...From a strategical perspective, Marshal Ye Jianying stressed, 'We have not fought with Western Europe for decades. They want China to become a force for world stability. We need their advanced technology. They have too much capital and need markets for technology. The focus of introducing technology should be in Western Europe.' Marshal Nie Rongzhen firmly said, 'In the past, our propaganda to the western countries was unbalanced and hypocritical to some degree, which bounded us in turn. Gu Mu's investigation was quite comprehensive as everything deserved our attention was involved. What and from which country to introduce should be decided! Don't talk on paper!' At this meeting, many leaders of the Central Committee have suggested that we should be vigilant to an unbalanced emphasis on centralization and unification, which means that everything should be in our own hands and managed by ourselves. Li Xiannian said that the Ministry of Foreign Trade emphasized a foreign trade control system, which was said to have been proposed by Chairman Mao. However, it was told to the domestic bourgeoisie at the Second Plenary Session of the Seventh Central Committee according to the situation at that time. But for now, the time had come for the two initiatives to be brought into play under the central unification plan. There was no doubt that attention must be paid to unification when it came to the outside world, but it could not be limited in the Ministry of Foreign Trade. At the end of the report meeting, the central leadership asked me, as well as my colleagues,to study further and summarize several items for discussion in the State Council".[1] Deng Xiaoping had a talk with Gu Mu soon after the report meeting. After listening to Gu's report, he made a speech, of which the central meaning could be concluded as follows. Firstly, an introduction is necessary. Secondly, we should make up our mind to borrow some money from abroad for construction. Lastly, it is a race against time, so we should take actions as soon as possible. It can be said that this visit provides an essential basis for the policy of opening up to the outside.[2]

Besides, there were many other delegations. The Chinese delegation of agricultural mechanization visited Italy, France, the UK and Denmark from April 27 to June 27. A Chinese agrarian delegation composed of leaders in charge of agriculture in Fujian, Anhui, Hunan, Jiangsu and Sichuan provinces and researchers in rice and agricultural machinery visited Japan from May 9 to June 9. The Chinese capital construction delegation were invited to visit Japan from May 13 to June 13. A delegation of 26 representatives from Chinese agricultural departments in Heilongjiang, Hubei, Shaanxi, Shanxi, Shandong, Tianjin and the Ministry of Agriculture and Forestry was invited to visit the US from July 25 to September 8. The Chinese forestry delegation visited Austria and Romania successively from August 3 to 26. A Chinese agricultural delegation of 23 representatives led by Beijing, Liaoning, Jilin, Henan and Hebei, the National Federation of Supply and Marketing Cooperatives and the Ministry of Agriculture and Forestry visited Romania, Federal Germany, and France from August 10 to September 23. From August 10 to September 9, the delegation of Chinese agriculture, composed of 12 representatives from the Ministry of Agriculture and Forestry, the National Farm and Land Reclamation Administration and leaders and technicians from Heilongjiang, Xinjiang and Ningxia Land Reclamation Departments was invited to Canada. From September 7 to October

---

[1] Gu Mu ed., *Reminiscences of Gu Mu*, Beijing: Central Party Literature Publishing House, 2014, p. 327.

[2] Zhang Shujun and GaoXinmin, *The People's Republic of China in 1978*, Shijiazhuang: Hebei People's Publishing House, 2001, p. 186.

8, the Chinese finance and economics delegation visited Yugoslavia and Romania. At the same time, the Chinese agriculture delegation visited Japan. A delegation from the State Economic Commission was invited to visit Japan to study the management of Japanese industrial enterprises from October 31 to December 5. A delegation from the State Planning Commission was invited to visit Yugoslavia, focusing on the planning work of Yugoslavia From November 15 to 29.[1] After each delegation returned from abroad, they wrote reports about their impressions and suggestions combining what they have seen and heard. Therefore, the leadership of the CPC Central Committee and the State Council could have a more accurate understanding of the world situation.

(2) *Frequently visits by leaders*

The importance attached to opening up can also be seen from the frequent visits by senior leaders. Within the year of 1978, 12 leaders above the ranks of vice premier or vice-chairman visited 51 countries successively in 20 times. The leaders of the Party and the state went abroad in person to feel the pulse of world development. Deng Yingchao visited Cambodia in January, and Li Xiannian visited the Philippines and Bangladesh in March; Chen Muhua visited Somalia, Gabon, and Cameroon in April while Hua Guofeng visited Romania and Yugoslavia in September. And Wang Zhen visited the UK in November...

Among those leaders, Deng Xiaoping made the largest number of visits. In 1978, he made four trips to eight countries. Among these trips, he was deeply impressed by his visits to Japan and Singapore. On October 22, 1978, Deng Xiaoping visited Japan at the invitation of the Japanese government. Japan, as a close neighbor of China and the only developed country in Asia at that time, had always attracted the attention of China. Especially after World War Ⅱ, Japan was rebuilt from the ruins just within 20 years and became a world economic power, of which the experience naturally attracted China. Deng Xiaoping visited some large modern factories during his visits. By comparison, he had a personal feeling about the huge gap between China and Japan in economy and technology.

While visiting the Nissan car factory Deng Xiaoping watched and learned about the production of automated equipment. In his speech, he pointed out: "China is undergoing modernization and we are grateful to the industrially developed countries, especially the Japanese industry for their assistance". On October 26, when taking the

[1] Zhang Shujun and GaoXinmin, *The People's Republic of China in 1978*, Shijiazhuang: Hebei People's Publishing House, 2001, pp. 187-190.

Shinkansen “Hikari-81” super express train, travelling from Tokyo to Kyoto at a speed of 210 kilometers per hour, he was asked by a Japanese reporter to talk about his opinions, he said: “It is really fast and it seems to urge people to run. This is the very vehicle that is suitable for.[1]

At a press conference attended by more than 400 Japanese journalists and foreign correspondents in Japan, Deng Xiaoping answered questions about Sino-Japanese relations and pointed out: “There is much room for economic cooperation between China and Japan. We can learn from Japan in various aspects and also introduce Japan's science and technology and even funds. We have signed a long-term trade agreement about US$20 billion.However, one is not enough. It should be doubled and even trebled”.[2] Deng Xiaoping also talked about his feelings about his visit to Japan with the head of the Chinese organization in Singapore, saying that: “During our visit to Japan, we talked about our poverty everywhere ... We have too many conventions, and it is not easy to change them all at once. Thirty houses have been built in the Qianmen area of Beijing, which look good outside but not inside. Therefore, delegations were sent outside to learn from other countries. We should use our wits and learn to think, avoiding regarding ourselves as the best. What's more, we should compare ourselves with the international standards, not the domestic.”[3]When Deng Xiaoping visited Singapore in November of the same year, he was deeply impressed by Singapore's successful experience in attracting foreign investment to develop its economy. After visiting the Yulang Town Industrial Park in Singapore on November 13 and listening to its introduction in detail, he immediately said that he would bring Singapore's experience into China.He also said in his speech later: “I went to Singapore to learn how they use the foreign capital. Foreigners' setting up factories in Singapore benefits Singapore a lot. Firstly, 35% of the profits of foreign-funded enterprises should be paid to the country as taxes, which increases the country's income. Secondly, workers benefit from the labor income.Lastly, its service industry is driven by those factories, which promotes the revenue doubtlessly.We have to make such a determination that after we weigh the pros and cons, even some losses can be acceptable to eventually build up production capacity in China and drive some of our

---

[1] Party Literature Research Center of the CPC Central Committee, *The Chronicle Biography of Deng Xiaoping 1975–1997(Part I)*, Beijing: Central Party Literature Publishing House, 2004, pp.409, 413.

[2] “Vice Premier Deng's Meeting with the Press in Tokyo”, *People's Daily*, Oct. 26, 1978.

[3] Party Literature Research Center of the CPC Central Committee, *The Chronicle Biography of Deng Xiaoping 1975–1997(Part I)*, Beijing: Central Party Literature Publishing House, 2004, p. 429.

enterprises. In my opinion, it is a pity not to make full use of foreign capital when it comes to financial issues."[1]

For Deng Xiaoping, he clearly recognized the widening gap between China and the developed countries and also saw opportunities for China's development through these visits.On June 23, 1978, Deng Xiaoping met with the outgoing Romanian ambassador to China, Nicolae Gavrilescu and talked about the large-scale visit: "For China, making foreign things serve China is an important part of self-reliance". "We have sent many delegations to Europe and Japan and found that there are many things we could make use of. Many countries are willing to provide us with funds and technology without harsh terms which is good for us politically and economically. Why not try? With favorable international and domestic conditions, so long as we make up our minds to do it, we can definitely speed up the construction". On September 12, during the meeting with Kim II-Sung in North Korea, Deng Xiaoping further talked about the huge shock brought by these visits and said: "We must take advanced international technology as our starting point for modernization.Recently, some of our comrades went out to visit, and the more they looked, the more they felt that we were lagging behind.What is modernization? Things were the same in the 1950s but different in 1960s and more different in 1970s". On October 10, during a meeting with the press delegation of the Federal Republic of Germany headed by Georg Negwer, Deng Xiaoping pointed out again: "China has contributed to the world in history.However, it has been stagnant for a long time, and its development is slow. Now it is time for us to learn from the rest of the world. In the past, we learned advanced science and technology from foreign countries which was called 'worshiping foreign countries and fawning on foreign countries' in a certain period. We have come to understand how stupid this argument is.Therefore, we have sent many people abroad to familiarize themselves with the outside world. A country can never develop itself with closed doors … To achieve modernization, we must learn to learn and get international help. We should introduce international advanced technology and equipment as the starting point for our development".[2] Deng Xiaoping explicitly used the word "opening" for the first time in answering the guest's questions and solemnly stressed: "You asked us whether our opening policy is contrary to traditions.Our practice is that those good traditions must be preserved on the premise of new policies

---

1 *Selected Works of Deng Xiaoping, Volume II*, People's Publishing House, 1994, p. 199.

2 Party Literature Research Center of the CPC Central Committee, *The Chronicle Biography of Deng Xiaoping 1975–1997(Part I)*, Beijing: Central Party Literature Publishing House, 2004, pp. 329, 372-373, 398-399.

determined according to new circumstances...We introduce advanced technology to develop productive forces and improve people's living standards, which is beneficial to our socialist country and the socialist system".[1]

By witnessing the development of the outside world and comparing ourselves with this "mirror"of international development, the cadres within the Party have been greatly shocked besides Deng Xiaoping.It also strengthened the determination of opening up and prompted positive changes in China's foreign economic policy.At the end of the discussion on the criterion of truth, the balance of power within the Party was biased toward the practical criterion. To be honest, it was also closely related to the personal visiting experience of the party cadres.Finally, the Third Plenary Session of the 11th CPC Central Committee held from December 18 to 22, 1978 became a turning point.

3.1.2 Windows of opening up: founding and development of special economic zones (SEZ)

Opening up to the outside world is a topic that China's economic internationalization cannot go around. At the beginning of reform and opening up, the economic internationalization of China mainly laid in the special economic zones. It can be said that the founding of the special economic zones marks the start of China's economic internationalization process after the "Cultural Revolution".

The establishment and development of special economic zones are not smooth sailings. The process of establishing special economic zones can be roughly divided into three stages: initial creation, twists, and turns as well as development.From the perspective of materialist dialectics, it is a spiral process of creation, debate, questioning and developing, a process of development of negation and negation and a process of continuous creation and verification in practice with all kinds of prejudice and interference eliminated. All in all, it is an essential stage of China's economic internationalization.

(1) *The Establishment of the SEZ*

Although the basic policy of opening to the outside world has been determined at the Third Plenary Session of the 11th Central Committee, how to open to the outside world is still under thinking and exploration.

At that time, Guangdong took the first step.At the Central Working Conference

[1] *Selected Works of Deng Xiaoping, Volume II*, People's Publishing House, 1994, p. 133.

held before the Third Plenary Session of the 11th Central Committee, Xi Zhongxun said in his speech that he hoped the Central Committee would give Guangdong more support and room for local authorities to deal with problems flexibly, and allow Guangdong to absorb funds from Hong Kong and Macao and to carry out "the three-processing and one compensation", which had won the approval and support of the participants. Therefore, Xi Zhongxun's confidence and determination to open up to the outside world were strengthened.[1] After Xi Zhongxun returned to Guangdong, the Guangdong Provincial Party Committee held the fourth session of the Second Standing Committee expansion meeting from January 8 to 25, 1979, which centered on the discussion of how to implement the spirit of the Third Plenary Session of the Eleventh Central Committee and then realize the shift of work priorities. On January 8, Wang Quanguo said at the meeting: "Guangdong is adjacent to Hong Kong and Macao. Under the good international context, there is much to be done in this regard. We should try to be more flexible and dauntless. With 55 million people, can't Guangdong catch up with Taiwan? We should organize some researches and studies to make plans, including reforming the superstructure, and then report to the central government to ask some special provisions for Guangdong and authorize it more power before the national system is settled. It is conceivable that if the industry is given a free hand in processing and assembly, certain joint ventures and compensation trade while the agriculture in the use of foreign capital, technology and the international market to establish and develop a number of agricultural, livestock and aquatic products bases, and if larger projects are introduced and corresponding transportation construction can keep up with the development, the economy of Guangdong will definitely develop rapidly, and people's income will increase significantly, which will make greater contributions to the country".[2] On January 25, Xi Zhongxun made a concluding speech at the meeting, in which he clearly pointed out: "Guangdong is adjacent to Hong Kong and Macao, which is favorable for the four modernizations. We can use the foreign capital, introduce advanced technology and equipment and engage in compensation trade, processing and assembly, and cooperative operations, on which the central leading comrades have made clear instructions that we must be decisive, bold and feel free to speed up its development of industrial and agricultural

---

[1] Xi Zhongxun Administrating Guangdong editorial Committee, *Xi Zhongxun Administrating Guangdong Province*, Beijing: Central Party History Publishing House, 2007, p.233.

[2] Luo Musheng, *Draft of the development History of Chinese Special Economic Zones*, Guangdong: Guangdong People's Publishing House, 1999, p. 7.

production".At that time, a letter from Hong Kong manufacturers who asked for returning to Guangzhou to open a factory was sent to Deng Xiaoping. Soon Deng Xiaoping made a statement: "Guangdong can feel free to do it in this regard".[1]

After the enlarged meeting of the Standing Committee of the Provincial Party Committee, Xi Zhongxun, Yang Shangkun and other provincial party committee leaders had gone to various places with the working groups to convey the spirit of the Third Plenary Session of the Eleventh Central Committee and conduct investigations and studies on the spot since February 3, 1979. On March 3, Xi Zhongxun hosted a meeting of the Standing Committee of the Provincial Party Committee in Guangzhou. According to the results of surveys, they discussed whether to delineate a pilot area in Guangdong to attract foreign investment and introduce advanced foreign technology. Wu Nansheng, secretary of the provincial party committee, said: "If the provincial party committee agrees, I am willing to go to Shantou to have a try". At that time, the Standing Committee members reached an agreement on the proposal of setting up pilot areas. Xi Zhongxun immediately said: "If we do it, the whole province will do it. We make a draft on it first, and I will take it to Beijing when the Central Working Conference is held in April".[2]

The CPC Central Committee Work Conference was held in Beijing to discuss economic adjustments from April 5 to 28, 1979. Xi Zhongxun and Wang Quanguo attended the meeting on behalf of Guangdong. On April 8, Xi Zhongxun said at the South Central Group meeting: "Guangdong is close to Hong Kong and Macao. We should make full use of this advantage and actively conduct foreign economic and technological exchanges. In this regard, I hope that the central authorities will delegate us some power and let Guangdong take a step earlier. It seems that the proper relationship between the central and local governments is involved in the areas of planning, finance, foreign trade, foreign exchange, materials, foreign economic and technological exchanges and so on. An old saying goes that 'small as the sparrow is, it possesses all its internal organs'. As a province, Guangdong is as large as one or several countries abroad. However, the provincial governments have little power while the central government controls too much, which is not conducive to the development of the national economy. Our request is to delegate powers to lower levels and be more

---

[1] "Speech by Comrade Wang Quanguo at Central Working Conference with Central South Group", *Documents of the Third Enlarged Meeting of the Fourth Standing Provincial Party Committee in Guangdong*, Apr.10, 1974.

[2] Xi Zhongxun Administrating Guangdong Province editorial committee, *Xi Zhongxun Administrating Guangdong Province*, Beijing: Central Party History Publishing House, 2007, pp. 235-236.

flexible under the centralized and unified leadership of the country. In doing so, it will benefit both the local areas and our country consistently".[1]

This proposal has brought up controversies. Liu Tianfu, deputy director of the Guangdong Revolutionary Committee at that time, said in his memory: "I remember that once Xi Zhongxun and I reported to the central leading comrades in Beijing. When we proposed that the central government should give Guangdong greater autonomy and allow us to try a special export zone referring to the successful experience of foreign countries and 'Four Asian Tigers' to speed up Guangdong's economic development, a deputy prime minister threw 'cold water' on it. He said that if Guangdong did this, it was necessary to pull up 7,000 kilometers of barbed wire on the border to separate Guangdong from neighboring provinces. We listened to him and were greatly surprised. Obviously, he was worried that once the country was opened, capitalism would flood in like a flood of beasts. Therefore, the idea of using barbed wire to isolate Guangdong from the provinces of Fujian, Jiangxi, Hunan, and Guangxi was put forward". Fortunately, Deng Xiaoping and other leaders attach great importance to this proposal.[2]

On April 17, Xi Zhongxun attended the meeting of the conveners of the Central Working Conference held by the Political Bureau of the CPC Central Committee and reported to the leaders including Hua Guofeng and Deng Xiaoping. He said: "We have discussed among the provincial party committee. We come to the meeting and hope that the central government will give priority to Guangdong to take a step earlier this time". "If Guangdong is an 'independent country', it would surpass Hong Kong now". When Deng Xiaoping listened to the report, he interjected: "Americans asked me, would you become capitalism in this way?[3] I said that the money we earned would not be in the pockets of Comrades like Hua Guofeng or us. We adhere to the ownership by the whole people, and thus socialism will not change into capitalism. If Guangdong does this, per capita income will reach RMB1,000 to 2,000, then they will not ask the central government for money. There are 80 million people in Guangdong and Fujian, which is equal to one country. There is no harm in their getting rich first".[4]

---

1 "Speech by Comrade Xi Zhongxun at Central Working Conference with Central South Group", *Documents of the Third Enlarged Meeting of the Fourth Standing Provincial Party Committee in Guangdong*, Apr.8, 1974.

2 Liu Tianfu, *Reminiscences of Liu Tianfu*, Beijing: Central Party History Publishing House, 1995, p. 434.

3 Zhang Hanqing, "Xi Zhongxun in the Reform and Opening Up of Guangdong Province", *Reform Career of Xi Zhongxun*, Beijing: Central Party History Publishing House, 2002, p. 549.

4 Party Literature Research Center of the CPC Central Committee, *The Chronicle Biography of Deng Xiaoping 1975–1997(Part I)*, Beijing: Central Party Literature Publishing House, 2004, p. 506.

Hua Guofeng also responded to Xi Zhongxun's request at the meeting and said: "It should be clear to delegate power to lower levels". And he also said: "Gu Mu should go to Guangdong to study how to work out the problem raised by Xiaoping. Zhuhai and Baoan those two counties should focus on the processing industry, while Shenzhen the sand. Now China Resources Company is contracted and bounded. We should give it a free hand. Zhongxun said that if Guangdong were a country, it would have been developed before...To carry out institutional reforms, Guangdong can employ a new system and act as an experiment for major reforms."[1]

During the meeting, Xi Zhongxun also mentioned that Guangdong intended to observe and follow the form of foreign processing zones to study and experiment. According to the international practice, places were to be set up in Shenzhen, Zhuhai, and the important hometown of overseas Chinese, Shantou, as they were adjacent to Hong Kong and Macao. This place would practice separately as an investment place for overseas Chinese, Hong Kong and Macao compatriots and foreign businessmen and organize production according to the needs of the international market. We initially named it as "Trade cooperation zone".[2] Deng Xiaoping totally agreed and immediately showed his affirmation and support. When Gu Mu raised the question of the naming of places with special regional policies in Shenzhen, Zhuhai, Shantou, and other areas, facing varied opinions on it from different people, Deng Xiaoping said: "It is still called the Special Economic Zones, similar to the name of Shaanxi-Gansu-Ningxia Special Administration Region(SAR). There is no money in the central government, but favorable policies can be given to you so that you can do it yourself and find a way out".[3] Therefore, the "trade cooperation zone" proposed by Guangdong was officially renamed "Export Special Zone" in the document of the Central Working Conference. According to Deng Xiaoping's proposal, the Central Working Conference formally discussed the proposals of Guangdong Province and Fujian Province and formed the *Regulations on Vigorously Developing Foreign Trade to Increase Foreign Exchange Income*. In the section of "Trial Export Special Zone", it is proposed to draw out special zones in some areas along the coast. Shenzhen and Zhuhai can try first.

According to the instructions of the central government, Gu Mu and more than 10

---

[1] Cultural and Historical Records Committee of CPPCC National Committee of Guangdong Province, *Origins of Special Economic Zones*, Guangdong: Guangdong People's Publishing House, 2002, p. 192.

[2] Wu Nansheng, "The Foundation of Special Economic Zones", *Guangdong Party Committee History*, 1998(6).

[3] Party Literature Research Center of the CPC Central Committee, *The Chronicle Biography of Deng Xiaoping 1975–1997(Part I)*, Beijing: Central Party Literature Publishing House, 2004, p. 510.

responsible leaders from the State Council Import and Export Office, the State Planning Commission, the State Construction Committee, the Ministry of Foreign Trade, the Ministry of Finance, and the Ministry of Materials visited Guangdong and Fujian from May 11 to June 5, 1979. According to the recommendations of the Gu Mu and the current situation, the two provinces drafted reports on how to make use of advantages to expand the opening up and submitted them to the central government.

After careful study and discussion on the reports of the two provinces, the Central Committee of the CPC and the State Council issued the 50th document *the Central Committee of the CPC and the State Council approve and forward two reports by CPC Guangdong Provincial Committee and the Fujian Provincial Committee on the implementation of special policies and flexible measures in the foreign economy* on July 19, 1979. The approval statements pointed out: "Guangdong and Fujian, close to Hong Kong and Macao, where there are many overseas Chinese, enjoy abundant resources and many other favorable factors for accelerating their economic development. The central government has decided to implement special policies and flexible measures for the foreign economic activities in the two provinces, giving the local authorities more initiative to full play their advantages and seize the current favorable international opportunities. Thus they can take the leading step and develop the economy as soon as possible". "The economic management system recommended in the two reports is to implement all-round responsibility system under the unified leadership of the central government. The Central Committee and the State Council agreed to try in principle.""Exporting special zones can be firstly tried in Shenzhen and Zhuhai. After accumulating experience, it can be promoted in Shantou and Xiamen".[1]

After the release of the policy, the construction of the special exporting zones has also entered the implementation stage. During the company of the Danish Queen's visit to Guangzhou on September 22, 1979, Gu Mu had a meeting with Xi Zhongxun and Yang Shangkun. Gu Mu pointed out that the central government wanted Guangdong to take the first step and it was necessary to make a big move in Guangdong. Guangdong needed to speed up and seize the time to walk ahead of the country. In addition to its economy, Guangdong had the task of accumulating experience and blazing a trail. Gu Mu also hoped that Liu Tianfu and others would

[1] The State Committee Office for Economic System Reform, *Compilation of Economic System Reform Documents (1978–1983)*, Beijing: China Financial & Economic Publishing House, 1984, p. 471.

"have a little bit of the spirit of Sun Wukong, and not be bound by the rules and regulations".[1] From September 25 to October 3, Xi Zhongxun and Yang Shangkun went to Beijing to attend the Fourth Plenary Session of the 11th Central Committee of the Communist Party of China and the meeting of secretaries of the Party Committee of the provinces, municipalities and autonomous regions held by the Central Committee, and reported to Deng Xiaoping on the work of Guangdong. Deng Xiaoping instructed that: "Do whatever you can do. It is fine to name the two places divided from Shenzhen and Zhuhai as special zones. In the future, when Taiwan and Hong Kong come back, they will also be called that. In 1937, Shaanxi-Gansu-Ningxia was our special zone. It is fine as long as the places belong to our country".[2] It can be seen that the central leadership at that time was quite tolerant of the special zones. I hope that the special zones will soon explore a road for China's opening up to the outside world.

(2) *The Development Period of the SEZ*

However, the construction of the special zones encountered troubles and resistance soon.

First of all, it is the name. As we know, that things are called by their right names is very important. The name of special zones is inappropriately reflected in two aspects. One is improper positioning, and the other is unclear regulations.

From the perspective of positioning, Deng Xiaoping named it as "Special Zone" while the central document also called it "Export Special Zone." Therefore, the earliest construction of the Special Zone was to make extensive use of foreign capital, introduce advanced technology and set up factories to increase export earnings and develop international trading.

However, with the deepening of the opening up, the understanding of the "Special Zone" in Guangdong and Fujian has gradually changed into that a "Special Zone" should be both a base for production and export, and a frontier, window or trial area of China's reform and opening up, through which China can be able to observe changes in world economic trends, science and technology, and market supply and demand, learn and introduce advanced technology and management experience from other countries, and try new ways to accelerate China's economic reform and development. Considering the functions that the "Special Zone" should play, it is

[1] Liu Tianfu, *Reminiscences of Liu Tianfu*, Beijing: Central Party History Publishing House, 1995, p. 444.

[2] Zhong Jian ed., *Report of Chinese Economic Special Zones Development (2010)*, Beijing: China Social Sciences Academic Press, 2010, p. 480.

obvious that the name "Export Special Zone" is somewhat narrow and cannot fully reflect them. The Guangdong Provincial Committee of the CPC convened a symposium on the work of the special zones involving leaders in Shenzhen, Zhuhai, Shantou and relevant departments of the provincial government to discuss the principles, policies, and practices for the establishment of the Special Zone on October 31, 1979. At that meeting, everyone agreed that the "Export Special Zone" should be changed into "Special Economic Zone", which had richer connotations and was considered being the most relevant to the original intention of the special zone.[1]

On November 17, Gu Mu, on behalf of the Central Committee of the CPC and the State Council, hosted the meeting of Guangdong and Fujian provinces in Jingxi Hotel. In the report, Wu Nansheng proposed that the name of the "Export Special Zone" should be changed into "Special Economic Zone", which has a more accurate meaning.

From March 24 to 30, 1980, Gu Mu was entrusted by the Central Committee of the CPC and the State Council to host the meeting of Guangdong and Fujian provinces in Guangzhou. The meeting was mainly to check the implementation of Document No. 50 in 1979 and further study some important policies in the special zone. The hard work of the two provinces was recognized and the proposal of Guangdong Province to rename the "Export Special Zone" as "Special Economic Zone" was adopted in the meeting. On March 30th, the "Guangdong and Fujian Provinces Working Conference Minutes" was formed after extensive discussions. And then, the Central Committee of the CPC and the State Council approved and forwarded the Minutes, and officially renamed the "Special Zone" as "Special Economic Zone" on May 16.

From the perspective of statutes, there isn't any precedent for "special economic zones" in China, which makes the establishment of the SEZ lack legal basis. What's more, the management of the SEZ is particularly difficult, and Shenzhen has even experienced large-scale smuggling because of the unclear legal provisions during the early time. The State Council commissioned Guangdong to draft the "Regulations on Special Economic Zones in Guangdong Province" since August 1979. On December 27, 1979, the Second Session of the Fifth Session of the People's Congress of Guangdong Province reviewed and approved the "Regulations on Special Economic Zones in Guangdong Province(Draft)". On April 22, 1980, the Third Session of the

[1] Cao Pu, *Some Important Issues in the Study of the History of Reform and Opening up*, Fuzhou: Fujian People's Publishing House, 2014, p. 148.

Standing Committee of the Fifth Session of the People's Congress of Guangdong Province passed the revised "Regulations on the Special Economic Zone of Guangdong Province". Afterward, "Regulations on Special Economic Zones in Guangdong Province" were finally submitted to the Standing Committee of the Fifth National People's Congress at the fifteenth meeting in August 1980 after repeated demonstration and revision by the State Import and Export Management Committee with the insistence of Guangdong Province to make the regulations more authoritative. On August 21, Jiang Zemin, who was deputy director of the State Import and Export Administration Committee and entrusted by the State Council, made a statement at the meeting on the establishment of special economic zones in Guangdong and Fujian provinces and the "Regulations on Special Economic Zones in Guangdong Province". On August 26, the 15th meeting of the Standing Committee of the Fifth National People's Congress approved the "Regulations on Special Economic Zones in Guangdong Province" and announced its implementation on the same day. The approval of the "Regulations on the Special Economic Zones of Guangdong Province" marks the legal basis for the trial of special economic zones and is a programmatic document in the history of the construction of the SEZ. This "Regulations" consists of 6 chapters and 26 articles, which reflect the degree of economic opening up of China's special economic zones and special measures for economic development. To sum up, they are mainly as follows: The first is to encourage foreign investment on the premise of safeguarding China's sovereignty and interests and protect the legitimate rights and interests of investors while adhering to the principle of equality and mutual benefits;the second is to give special preferential treatment to investors, and the last is to implement a set of management systems adapted to the nature and requirements of the special zones.[1]

The second is mainly about whether the SEZ belongs to capitalism or socialism. The criticism from the "ultra-left" ideology is the biggest resistance to the construction of special economic zones.

Although the Party's top leaders have decided to shift the focus to economic construction after the Third Plenary Session of the 11th CPC Central Committee, the influence from the "Cultural Revolution" for many years is not to dissipate easily, which can be seen from the central working conference in April 1979. At that time,

---

[1] Cao Pu, *Some Important Issues in the Study of the History of Reform and Opening up*, Fuzhou: Fujian People's Publishing House, 2014, p. 150.

some senior central cadres were skeptical about Guangdong's opening up to the outside world, because they were afraid of something bad of capitalism sneaking in through the special zones.Even after the central government officially issued a policy allowing Guangdong and Fujian to set up special economic zones, opposition still exists, with some accusing such as "the special zones are 'enclaves' of international bourgeoisie", "the special zones are the same with Hong Kong and capitalist" and "the special zones have changed into concessions". As the special economic zones mainly implement the market regulation, there is no doubt that those who have long believed that socialism must employ the system of a planned economy are impacted conceptually. Therefore,they are raising the question of whether the special economic zones belong to capitalism or socialism.

Under such context, Gu Mu presided over the State Council's work conference in Beijing for Guangdong and Fujian provinces and special zones, which was attended not only by leaders of the two provinces but also by many economists.Participants from the two provinces reported that some departments of the State Council had always been full of worries about policy implementation since the central government proposed to implement special policies and flexible measures in Guangdong and Fujian provinces.The worries were fears of slipping into the capitalist road, upsetting the overall situation of the national economy, making mistakes and out of control of the management with greater import and export rights to special economic zones.Therefore, a note "Guangdong and Fujian are no exception" had been added to many documents for fear that the two provinces would go beyond the "track." The leading comrades of the two provinces believed that in fact, the central authorities had not yet given them something truly special, flexible and advanced. However, some people were so afraid to do that.[1] It can be seen that there was a big misunderstanding of the special economic zones, and the development of the special economic zones was blocked by some ideas at that time.

Therefore, Ren Zhongyi and Xiang Nan, the first secretary of the Fujian Provincial Committee, proposed at the meeting that we could set a few principles for the two provinces. First, do not take the capitalist road; Second, adhere to the four basic principles; Third, resolutely complete the tasks stipulated by the central government; Fourth, do not be a special party member; Fifth, implement a unified

---

[1] Li Lanqing, *Breaking Out—Days of Early Opening Up*, Beijing: Central Party Literature Publishing House, 2008, p. 124.

foreign policy. With these principles, the central government should let us go without too much control.There was only one request from the two provinces: "Deregulation and decentralization". The meeting was a success, unifying the understanding of the special economic zones. "Minutes of Working Meetings of Guangdong and Fujian Provinces and Special Economic Zones," the result of the meeting, was submitted to the Central Committee, which was approved and forwarded by the Central Committee of the CPC and the State Council in the document in 1981 on July 19, 1981.[1] The Minute answered and solved three questions. First, it further clarified the main contents of implementing special policies and flexible measures in the two provinces. Second, it further clarified the vague understanding on the issue of piloting special economic zones. Third, it further formulated ten policies and measures to promote the development of special economic zones.By this document, more specific special policies and flexible measures for special economic zones were gradually formed.

The meeting had far-reaching effects, as Liu Tianfu mentioned in his memory: "The meeting was a great success...The responsible comrades of the central departments have 'emancipated' or 'semi-emancipated' their minds. Moreover, the two provinces are in the right and self-confident and strongly supported by the theoretical circle...The meeting better coordinated and resolved the relationship between the relevant departments of the central government and the two provinces, further loosening the ties and delegating power to help the two provinces to be really special, flexible and go first".[2]Gu Mu later said in his memoir: "In the more than 20 years since then, although there have been many adjustments to the specific regulations, and some aspects have developed while some aspects have ceased to be implemented, all work has been carried out according to this framework on the whole.It has played an important role in the establishment and development of the special zones".[3]

However, immediately after the "deregulation and decentralization" comes the need to face the unhealthy tendencies and lawlessness from the economic field. Liu Tianfu recalled: "Although we were wary of smuggling and took some corresponding measures after the opening up of the country in 1979, due to the inadequate

---

[1] Li Lanqing, *Breaking Out—Days of Early Opening Up*, Beijing: Central Party Literature Publishing House, 2008, p. 125.

[2] Liu Tianfu, *Reminiscences of Liu Tianfu*, Beijing: Central Party History Publishing House, 1995, p. 466.

[3] Gu Mu ed., *Reminiscences of Gu Mu*, Beijing: Central Party Literature Publishing House, 2014, p. 331.

preparation for the fight against capitalist corrosion and criminal activities in the economic field under the new situation, and the lack of experience and unsound coastal prevention, including the unqualified anti-smuggling team, equipment nor other measures to combat smuggling, criminals at home and abroad got their chances. Overseas smuggling groups and criminals in some parts of Guangdong conspired with each other to carry out smuggling and speculation".[1] There were serious smuggling and bootlegging along the coast in Guangdong, Fujian and Zhejiang provinces, resulting in the phenomena that "fishermen do not fish, workers do not work, and farmers do not farm, students do not go to school" and "they rush to sell smuggled goods in the streets and along the roads".[2] As a result, smuggling and bootlegging activities in some coastal areas continued and intensified despite repeated prohibitions. From the second half of 1980 to the first half of 1981, such practice developed into a very rampant level and even became an unprecedented trend.According to statistics, more than 9,000 smuggling and speculation cases were seized in Guangdong province in 1979, four times more than in 1978. Moreover, the situation had become more severe since 1979 with more than 4,000 smuggling cases captured in the first quarter.[3]

On July 13, 1980, Guangdong provincial party committee and provincial government issued "Instructions on Resolutely Combating Smuggling and Speculation". In 1981, the three southeast provinces, Guangdong, Fujian, and Zhejiang, organized two joint anti-smuggling operations. However, the lack of anti-smuggling experience had limited the effectiveness of anti-smuggling operations. Instead of being effectively curbed, smuggling activities were on the rise, attracting more attention from the central government.

On January 11, 1982, according to Deng Xiaoping's and Chen Yun's suggestions, the Central Committee decided to crack down on smuggling activities and issued the "Urgent Notice of the Central Committee of the Communist Party of China on Resolving the Problem of Cadre Smuggling and Selling Private Goods" in which a vigorous crackdown was demanded.

To study how to implement the Urgent Notice better and effectively combat smuggling, the Central Secretariat held a meeting of Guangdong and Fujian provinces in Beijing from February 11 to 13, 1982. Participants recalled that the atmosphere was

---

1 Liu Tianfu ed., *Reminiscences of Liu Tianfu*, Beijing: Central Party History Publishing House, 1995, p. 473.

2 Liang Lingguang ed., *Reminiscences of Liang Lingguang*, Beijing: Central Party History Publishing House, 1996, p. 538.

3 Liu Tianfu ed., *Reminiscences of Liu Tianfu*, Beijing:Central Party History Publishing House, 1995, p. 474.

intensive at that time. Many leaders talked about the relationship between the anti-smuggling struggle and implementing special policies, flexible measures and piloting special economic zones in the two provinces at the meeting. Moreover, a material called "Origin of the Old Chinese Concession" was issued, actually alluding to the suspicion that the special zone offered land to foreign investors for compensation at that time.

Judging from the situation at that time, most leading cadres agreed that the central government would severely crack down on illegal and criminal acts in the economic field, and also believed that it would be conducive to a better opening to the outside world.However, some people who were deeply influenced by the "ultra-left" trend of thought and used to rigid monopoly system attributed the causes of smuggling and bootlegging to opening up to the outside world, labeling Guangdong, Fujian and special economic zones as "another rampant attack of capitalism against us" and "the source of parallel imports", even claiming that "Guangdong will collapse within three months". They proposed to take back all the rights that have already been delegated and stipulate a variety of restrictive measures, and even required that the central government cancel "special policies and flexible measures" and close down the special economic zones. At that time, the pressure on the two provinces and special zones were palpable.At a meeting in 1998, Gu Mu said: "There was a 'bleak autumn wind' in the first half of 1982".[1]

It can be said that the development of the special economic zones has been facing many difficulties since 1982 with repeatedly increased handover tasks and restrictions from "rules and regulations" but the smaller scope for special and flexible policies and measures.Even the comrades who were in charge of the work of the special zones also had concerns. "Some of them did receive such a warning: Aren't you afraid of the ship of the special zone capsizing when you board"?[2]

(3) *Rapid Development of the SEZ*

The construction of the special zone is mired in a quagmire. If opening up is blocked, the process of China's economic internationalization will inevitably have a huge retreat.

At this moment, Deng Xiaoping personally took the lead. He and other leaders comrades of the Central Committee have been paying close attention to the construction

---

[1] Li Lanqing, *Breaking Out—Days of Early Opening Up*, Beijing: Central Party Literature Publishing House,2008, pp. 136, 137, 139.

[2] Gu Mu ed., *Reminiscences of Gu Mu*, Beijing: Central Party Literature Publishing House, 2014, p. 337.

of special economic zones. We can look at some conversations of leading comrades of the Central Committee since the establishment of the special economic zones:

At the central working conference in December 1980, Deng Xiaoping said: "the decision to set up several special economic zones in Guangdong and Fujian provinces must continue...On the premise of independence and self-reliance, we should continue to implement a series of defined economic policies of opening to the outside world, draw lessons from the past and then improve ourselves". During the meeting, he earnestly said to the leaders of Guangdong province: "The special economic zones must adhere to its original guiding policy, and the pace can be slowed down.""Slowing down is due to temporary difficulties in the national economy. What is the most fundamental is that the original policy cannot be changed and the special economic zones must be continued firmly".[1]

At the beginning of 1982, when smuggling activities were rampant in Fujian, Guangdong, Deng Xiaoping made it clear that the observation and implementation of the policy of opening up should not be affected by the fight against smuggling and corrosion, emphasizing the correct implementation of the policy of opening up and invigorating the economy at home and further running the special zone.[2]In the talk with Hu Qiaomu and Deng Liqun on April 3, 1982, he also pointed out: "We will carry out the fight against serious criminal activities in the economic field to the end.We must work with our two hands together, not just one. One is to adhere to the policy of opening up and invigorating the economy at home, which has been proved by practice and cannot be wavered at all. What needs improvement in practice must be seriously done. The other is to fight against criminal activities in the economic field for a long time and persistently with clear minds and wariness.Without this hand, we will deviate from the socialist direction and modernization will not be well done."[3]

On October 30, 1982, Chen Yun instructed in the "Preliminary Summary of Pilot Special Economic Zones" submitted to the CPC Central Committee and the State Council by the Guangdong Provincial Party Committee and provincial government:

---

[1] Li Lanqing, *Breaking Out—Days of Early Opening Up*, Beijing: Central Party Literature Publishing House, 2008, p. 141.

[2] Li Lanqing, *Breaking Out—Days of Early Opening Up*, Beijing: Central Party Literature Publishing House, 2008, p. 142.

[3] Party Literature Research Center of the CPC Central Committee, *The Chronicle Biography of Deng Xiaoping 1975–1997(Part I)*, Beijing: Central Party Literature Publishing House, 2004, p. 810.

"The preliminary summary of the pilot special economic zones in Guangdong on October 22 is good." "To develop the SEZ better,lessons must be constantly drawn from previous experience. Hu Yaobang, general secretary of the CPC Central Committee, gave affirmation and support to the work of the Special Economic Zones when he visited Shenzhen in February 1983, and wrote a slogan for Shenzhen:"Special things are done in special ways while new things in new ways with unchanged positions." In March, Wang Zhen visited Guangzhou. When he heard that some people believed that the establishment of the special zone was to develop capitalism, he retorted: "These people are even behind those who held westernization, and not as good as Zheng Guanying at that time. They said that smuggling has increased and we have been eroded by bourgeois ideology. Will there be no smuggling without opening up? Of course, there is.The key is how you manage it. Must be open, closed-door can only lead to backwardness".[1]

The support of Deng Xiaoping and the leading comrades of the Central Committee is like a cardiotonic, greatly inspiring the workers of the SEZ in the most challenging times. As Chairman Mao once said, "There is no right to speak without investigation".Deng Xiaoping decided to take a look at the development of the SEZ personally in the face of various "left" questions and accusations in society.

What is more interesting is that high-level officials from the central government came to visit the special economic zones intensively and unanimously praised the work in the zones after returning home from 1983 to the beginning of 1984, which also prompted Deng Xiaoping to make his decision to visit the zones in person.Deng Xiaoping visited Guangzhou, Shenzhen, Zhuhai, Xiamen, and Shanghai successively from January 22 to February 16, 1984.

On January 24, 1984, Deng Xiaoping arrived at Guangzhou Railway Station on a special train and said to Liu Tianfu and Liang Lingguang: "The establishment of special economic zones was initiated by me and decided by the central government. Whether it succeeds or not, I want to take a look". On January 28, in a meeting with Henry Fok and Ma Wanqi, he said: "I initiated the establishment of the zones. It seems that it is right". On January 29, he wrote an inscription for Zhuhai that "Zhuhai Special Economic Zone is good". On February 1, he wrote an inscription "Shenzhen's development and experience have proved that our policy of establishing the Special

---

[1] Li Lanqing, *Breaking Out—Days of Early Opening Up*, Beijing: Central Party Literature Publishing House, 2008, pp. 140-141.

Economic Zone is correct" for Shenzhen. On February 9, he wrote another inscription for Xiamen that "Run the Special Economic Zone faster and better". On February 14, during the visit to Shanghai, he pointed out: "At present, the opening policy is not a matter of how to close it but is not open enough".[1]

On February 24, on the 7th day after returning to Beijing, Deng Xiaoping called Hu Yaobang, Zhao Ziyang, Wan Li, Yang Shangkun, Yao Yilin, Hu Qili and Song Ping to have a talk. Deng Xiaoping said: "Recently, I went to Guangdong and Fujian to see three special economic zones, and also to Shanghai to see Baoshan iron and steel plant. I have some perceptual knowledge.We should set up special economic zones and implement the policy of opening to the outside world with a clear guiding ideology, that is, not to close but to open more...SEZ in Xiamen is too small to activate the economy of Fujian Province as a whole...In addition to existing special economic zones, we might consider opening more port cities, such as Dalian and Qingdao.We would not call them special economic zones, but policies similar to those in the zones could be pursued there.We also need to develop Hainan Island".[2] At the end of the talk, Deng Xiaoping also designated Yao Yilin and Song Ping to report the contents of the talk to Chen Yun. Chen Yun later made it clear that he was in favor of Deng Xiaoping's idea of opening wider to the outside world.

According to Deng Xiaoping's proposal, the Secretariat of the CPC Central Committee and the State Council held a forum on coastal cities in Beijing from March 26 to April 6, 1984. The "Minutes of the forum on Coastal Cities" according to the contents of the forum was approved and forwarded with the document in 1984 issued by General Office of the CPC Central Committee on May 4, deciding to further open 14 coastal port cities from Dalian to Beihai and agreeing to implement a series of special policies and measures in expanding local authority and giving preferential treatment to foreign investors.

Since 1985, the Central Committee of the CPC and the State Council have successively listed the Yangtze River Delta, Pearl River Delta, Xiamen-Zhangzhou-Quanzhou Triangle Area in Southern Fujian, Shandong Peninsula, Liaodong Peninsula, Bohai Bay Area in Hebei and Beibu Gulf Area in Guangxi in the coastal economic

---

[1] Party Literature Research Center of the CPC Central Committee, *The Chronicle Biography of Deng Xiaoping 1975–1997(Part II)*, Beijing: Central Party Literature Publishing House, 2004, pp. 954, 956, 957, 958, 960.

[2] Party Literature Research Center of the CPC Central Committee, *The Chronicle Biography of Deng Xiaoping 1975–1997(Part II)*, Beijing: Central Party Literature Publishing House, 2004, pp. 963-964.

development zone, thus forming a large coastal frontier for China's external development in the eastern coastal area.[1]

On April 13, 1988, the first session of the Seventh National People's Congress adopted the decision on the establishment of Hainan Province and the resolution on the establishment of Hainan Special Economic Zone. China's largest special economic zone was officially born.

So far, the overall layout of China's coastal areas as all-around bases for the opening to the outside world has formed, and the stalled process of China's economic internationalization has accelerated again.

It can be said that speeches of Deng Xiaoping during his visits to Shenzhen and other places and seminars in some coastal cities in 1984 marked that China's opening to the outside world entered a new stage of accelerated development in the 1980s. The year 1984 also became a new milestone in further opening up and went down in history. Before that year, we still had the mentality of "testing water" and "worrying" about setting up special economic zones. Some even regarded it as a "scourge" alien to socialism. After that, from the top leadership of the central government to local departments, we have unified their thinking and strengthened their confidence in opening to the outside world and doing a good job in the special economic zones.

On June 12, 1987, Deng Xiaoping said in a meeting with Stefan Colossez, a member of the Central Presidium of the Communists League of Yugoslavia: "Now I can boldly say that our decision to establish special economic zones is not only correct but also successful.All doubts can be dispelled".[2] This is Deng Xiaoping's historical evaluation, and conclusion of China's special zone policy on the basis of "Practice is the only criterion for testing the truth".

Now looking back at the difficulties of the special economic zones at the beginning of the reform and opening up, Li Hao, who was the party secretary and mayor of Shenzhen from 1985 to 1993, said: "There was much discussion about the special economic zones from 1979 to 1984. Should we set up the special economic zone? Was it capitalist or socialist? Was it successful or unsuccessful? There were many voices of opposition...Without Deng Xiaoping's decision, no special zone would be established. Without his affirmation in 1984, our special zone would have been

[1] Huang Zhongping, et al., *Records of 30 years' Reform and Opening Up*, Beijing: People's Publishing House, 2009, p. 58.

[2] Party Literature Research Center of the CPC Central Committee, *The Chronicle Biography of Deng Xiaoping 1975–1997(Part II)*, Beijing: Central Party Literature Publishing House, 2004, p. 1194.

closed down and there would have no future practice and experience".[1] Gu Mu said: "Deng Xiaoping's talk in Beijing after his visits to the south... is of significance and plays important roles. The guiding ideology of 'opening rather than close' has been deeply rooted in the hearts of people and ended the discussion about the right and wrong to set up special economic zones and ushered in the 'spring' of opening to the outside world".[2]

As the window for China's opening to the outside world, the special economic zone has fully proved its correctness and necessity in practice. Even today, it is still an important way to internationalize China's economy. Just as Deng Xiaoping believed, it was only after the "Cultural Revolution"that China shifted its focus to economic work. It was also due to the tortuous process of the establishment and development of special economic zones in the 1980s that China's determination to persist in opening to the outside world and building special economic zones was strengthened.The practice of special economic zones has also provided valuable experience and lessons for the overall opening up of China's economy and accelerated the process of internationalization of China's economy.

3.1.3 Achievements of China's economic internationalization at the beginning of reform and opening up

Reform and opening up in China mainly consist of internal reform and external opening up, which is aimed to realize the transition of economic system through reform and introduce foreign capital and technology through opening up, so that reform and opening up can promote each other as well as China's economic development.In the process of economic transition and opening to the outside world, China's economy has also gradually integrated into the global one and realized its internationalization.

However, we now think that the 1980s are the initial stage of China's reform and opening up and the beginning of China's economic internationalization. Therefore, the results of China's economic internationalization at this stage must have some specific characteristics, because China's economic transformation is slow, gradually shifting from a planned economy to a planned economy and supplemented by market

[1] City History Office of Shenzhen Municipality, *Interview with Li Hao on Shenzhen Special Economic Zone*, Shenzhen: Haitian Publishing House, 2010, p. 214.

[2] Gu Mu, "Deng Xiaoping Led Us to Open to the Outside World", *Memories of Deng Xiaoping (Part I)*, Beijing: Central Party Literature Publishing House, 1998, p. 161.

regulation, rather than "shock therapy" in Russia. Therefore, although various economic data have increased rapidly, they are easily influenced by policies and thus the increase is still relatively gentle on the whole in this period.

So what benefits did the internationalization of China's economy bring to China during this period? In 1987, Deng Xiaoping said, "Our decision to establish a special economic zone is not only correct but also successful". What is the basis?We can review what achievements China has made in its economic internationalization at the beginning of reform and opening up:

(1) *The National Economy Is Developing Rapidly*

As can be seen from Figure 3–1, China's GDP grew slowly before 1978, reaching RMB145.7 billion in 1960, while it reached RMB362.41 billion in 1978 at the beginning of reform and opening up, about 2.5 times within 18 years.By 1988, the total GDP was RMB1,492.23 billion, a fourfold increase over ten years compared with that in 1978. Even the per capita GDP was only RMB119 in 1952 and then RMB379 in 1979, increasing less than four times. However, the per capita GDP reached RMB1,355 in 1988, nearly up four times than that within ten years.This change is quite surprising.

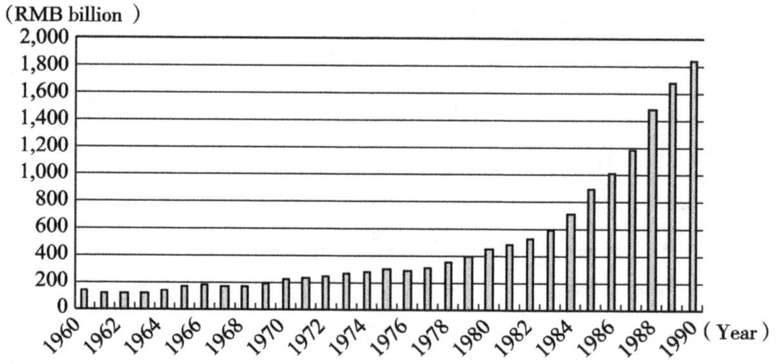

Figure 3–1 Gross national GDP from 1960 to 1990

Source: *Compilation of Statistical Data for the Fifty Years of New China*, Beijing: China Statistics Press, 1999.

For the GDP growth, it can be seen from Figure 3–2 that although China's GDP growth in the 20 years before the reform and opening up experienced a 19% annual growth in one year, it fluctuated greatly and even experienced negative growth for several times.The high growth rate in a particular year is mainly influenced by the trend of pursuing instant success at that time, which is done at the expense of overdraft resources. Moreover, the GDP growth rates areal ways below 10% from the 1970s to the time before the reform and opening up, which shows that China's economic development was not good in both "quality" and "quantity". However, the GDP growth rate has remained above 10% for a long time after the reform and opening up in 1978, especially Deng Xiaoping's talk in 1984 officially establishing the construction of special economic zones. The development of special economic zones is more remarkable. The first four special economic zones, such as Shenzhen, had a total industrial output value of only RMB5.5 billion in 1985, but RMB49.5 billion in 1990, up more than eight times within five years with an average annual growth rate of 50%, which definitely benefits from the opening up and economic internationalization.

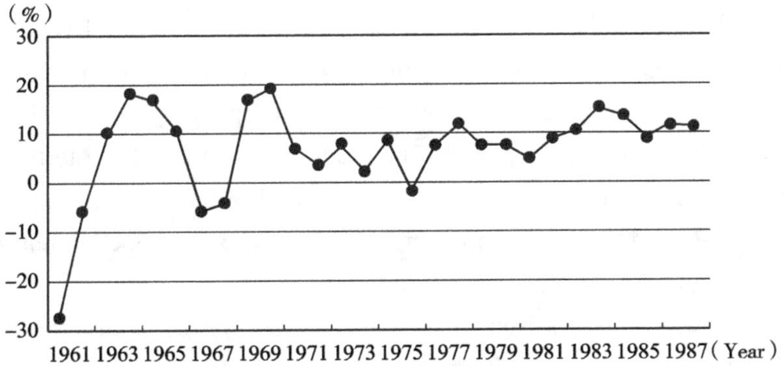

Figure 3–2 China's GDP growth rate from 1961 to 1987

Source: World Bank Database, http://data.worldbank.org.cn/.

As for the development of the whole national economy, China's heavy industry increased by 97 times, light industry 21 times and agriculture 2.7 times from 1949 to 1979. Apparently, the heavy industry is too heavy while the light industry is too light. In 1988, light industry increased by 4.3 times and heavy industry increased 3.5 times compared with 1979. The proportion of light industry in total industrial output value also increased from 43.7% in 1979 to 49.3% in 1988, which shows that the government has realized the problem of the heavy industry's high proportion. With the reform and opening up, especially in the crackdown on smuggling and bootlegging along the coast, common people's urgent demand for industrial consumer goods was realized by the government and then adjusts its industrial structure.

As for the employment population in various industries, the proportion of the total employed population in the primary industry employment decreased from 69.8% in 1979 to 59.3% in 1988, while the employment population in the secondary industry increased from 17.6% to 22.3%. Among the cities, the number of employed people in the secondary industry has increased tremendously especially in Guangdong, Fujian, Jiangsu and other coastal open cities.The number of employed people in the secondary industry in Guangdong and Jiangsu was 3.811 million and 4.8673 million respectively while 16.0711 million and 12.51 million respectively in 1988.What is more interesting is the tertiary industry, which employed 18.81 million people in 1952, 51.76 million in 1979, an increase of more than 30 million employers within 30 years.Moreover, the number reached 99.33 million in 1988 with an increase of more than 40 million in just 10 years, which includes that Guangdong increased from 2.648 million employers in 1979 to 6.438 million in 1988, Fujian from 1.058 million to 2.556 million, Jiangsu from 2.96 million to 5.973 million, Zhejiang from 3.06 million to 4.169 million and Shandong from 2.53 million to 5.11 million.It can be said that the open coastal provinces have absorbed a large number of employed people in the tertiary industry and greatly promoted its development. The total output value of the tertiary industry has increased from RMB8.658 billion in 1979 to RMB45.101 billion in 1988, a five-fold increase in 10 years.From experience, the more developed countries tend to have the higher the proportion of tertiary industry in GDP.[1]

It is not difficult to see from these data that special economic zones, as open bases, did play an important role in the economic internationalization at the beginning of the reform and opening up as a large amount of growth came from special economic zones.

(2) *Preliminary development of foreign trade*

China, which accounted for one-fifth of the world's population in 1978, accounted for only 0.75% of the world's exports, while the United States accounted for 10.8%, Japan for 7.5% and Federal Germany for 10.9%.The world economy was first formed as a result of international trade. China, which accounted for such a low proportion of international trade, was undoubtedly outside the world economic system at that time.[2]

---

[1] General Statistics Department of the National Bureau of Statistics, *Compendium of Statistical Data for the Fifty Years of New China*, Beijing: China Statistics Press, 1999.

[2] Xiao Guoliang and Sui Fuming eds., *Economic History of the People's Republic of China 1949–2010*, Beijing: Peking University Press, 2011, p. 178.

After opening to the outside world in 1978, the situation began to be improved. As mentioned before, China was not closed in the late period of the "Cultural Revolution", China mainly hoped to establish an independent and self-reliant economic system through import substitution at that time. After the reform and opening up, due to a large-scale overseas visit in 1978, China was attracted by the development models of Japan and the "Four Tigers" in Asia and decided to adopt an export-oriented policy. However, in order to steadily push forward the reform, we implemented the policy of combining import substitution with export-oriented at the beginning of the reform and opening up. China first reformed its foreign trade system to develop its foreign trade in this process vigorously.

First of all, foreign trade management authority has been gradually decentralized since 1979. The central government delegates power to local authorities and departments, and the local authorities and departments delegate power lower levels. In 1982, the Ministry of Foreign Trade and the State Import and Export Administration Commission, the Foreign Investment Administration Commission and the Ministry of Foreign Economic Relations were merged into the Ministry of Foreign Economic Relations and Trade, which was mainly charge of foreign trade.The government has relaxed its administrative control over the right to foreign trade and no longer worked out and issued foreign trade acquisition and allocation plans since 1985. Instead, regions and foreign trade departments could directly contact suppliers to decide their supply of goods according to export planning tasks and market supply and demand. Many productive enterprises and industries also obtained the right to manage foreign trade themselves, gradually overcoming the long-standing problems of separation of industry and trade and disconnection between production and sales.

Secondly, exports were awarded while imports were limited. The average legal tariff rate in China reached 56% in 1982 and only dropped to 43.2% in 1992. After opening to the outside world in the early 1980s, quotas, licenses, and other ways were still widely used to restrict imports. By the end of the 1980s, the number of licensed commodities reached 53 categories, accounting for 46% of all imported commodities.[1] What mentioned above were mainly related to China's lack of foreign exchange reserves at that time. The original intention in establishing special zones was to generate foreign exchange through export.

---

[1] Wu Jinglian, *Tutorial on Economic Reform in Contemporary China*, Shanghai: Shanghai Far East Publishers, 2015, p. 321.

Thirdly, the exchange rate system has been reformed accordingly. In August 1979, the State Council promulgated "Regulations on Several Issues Concerning Vigorously Developing Foreign Trade to Increase Foreign Exchange Income" and decided to set another new kind of exchange rates from 1981 besides the official exchange rates for non-trade income and expenses, which was named the internal settlement price of foreign exchange for trade (hereinafter referred to as the internal settlement price) and aimed at the settlement of import and export trade and the accounting of foreign trade unit economic efficiency, setting a precedent for the dual exchange rate of renminbi.The internal settlement exchange rate was determined according to the cost of exchange for exports at that time and had been fixed at the level of US$1 to RMB2.80 for the next four years. However, the public quotation for non-trade settlement had maintained at around US$1 to RMB1.5 In 1980, China resumed its legal status with the International Monetary Fund. According to the relevant regulations of the International Monetary Fund, member states can implement multiple exchange rates, but the transition time to a single exchange rate must be shortened as soon as possible.

Finally, the development of foreign trade called for the strengthening of customs management. In February 1980, the General Administration of Customs and the General Administration of Import and Export Commodity Inspection were separated from the Ministry of Foreign Trade. At the same time, it is stipulated that all provinces, municipalities and autonomous regions exercise supervision and leadership over local customs. *The Customs Law of the People's Republic of China* of 1984 stipulates that "the State Council shall set up the General Administration of Customs to uniformly administer the national customs" and establish a vertical customs management system. In short, the foreign trade authority began to be delegated to lower levels, and a unified foreign trade management authority was formed at this stage, so did the unified customs administration and management system. Moreover, the exchange rate system changed from double exchange rates to a single exchange rate. All of these changes are conducive to the development of foreign trade and opening to the outside world.[1]

The effect is obvious. China's total import and export trade was RMB35.5 billion in 1978, but it had reached RMB382.1 billion in 1988 with a tenfold increase, in which

[1] Xiao Guoliang and Sui Fuming eds., *Economic History of the People's Republic of China 1949–2010*, Beijing: Peking University Press, 2011, pp. 199–200.

special economic zones played an important role. The export volume of 12 coastal provinces (including autonomous regions and municipalities directly under the central government) in 1990 was nearly US$40 billion, accounting for about two-thirds of the total export volume of the country, which is enough to show the promotion of special economic zone policies to the development of foreign trade.What is funny is that China's foreign trade was in deficit for four consecutive years from 1984 to 1989 under China's policy of "awarding exports and restricting imports" which is not only affected the policies at that time but also reflects the huge market in China. Once the market is opened up, enormous demand could be generated.

At the same time, the structure of China's export products also changed. The introduction of foreign capital and the realization of processing trade promoted not only economic development but also the transformation and upgrading of the foreign trade structure. In 1978, primary product exports accounted for 54.8% of total exports while industrial finished products accounted for 45.2%. However, the proportion of industrial finished products exports, reaching 63.6%, had greatly exceeded that of primary products in 1986.

At that time, the growth rate of China's foreign trade was far higher than the average growth rate of world trade. The basic reasons for the rapid growth are not only the expansion of China's economic scale and the resulting increase in international competitiveness but also the rapid development of processing trade. China has implemented the policy of "three to one compensation" since the late 1970s. Moreover, then the open strategy of "large-volume import and export" was implemented in the mid and late 1980s. Adapting to the international situation of industrial transfer, this strategy provides the chance to give full play to China's comparative advantage in the international division of labor, land and other factors at a lower price.So great achievements have been made.[1]

Although the foreign trade volume was still small from today's point of view, this was undoubtedly a good start and indicated that China had gradually integrated into the world economic system from relative close, which was important in the process of economic internationalization.

(3) *Introducing foreign capital*

In January 1985, Deng Xiaoping stressed during a meeting with a delegation

[1] Wu Jinglian, *Tutorial on Economic Reform in Contemporary China*, Shanghai: Shanghai Far East Publishers, 2015, pp. 322-323.

from Hong Kong Nuclear Investment Co. ltd. that "China's policy of opening to the outside world and attracting foreign investmentis a long-term and lasting policy".[1] The most significant and influential achievement was the effective use of foreign capital since China's opening to the outside world. In that period, the main purpose of China's foreign capital utilization was to alleviate the shortage of domestic capital and foreign exchange, speed up the system transition and promote economic development.

China has been taking a series of preferential measures to attract foreign capital since the reform and opening up. As shown in Table 3-1, China's introduction of foreign capital is increasing year by year.The proportion of GDP is also getting higher and higher, and the number of enterprises established by using foreign capital is also on the rise.

Table 3-1 Direct foreign investment

Year	Number of enterprises	Actual use of foreign capital (US$ billion)	Proportion to GDP (%)
1979-1982	920	1.769	—
1983	638	0.920	0.3
1984	2,166	1.420	0.5
1985	3,073	1.856	0.6
1986	1,498	2.244	0.8
1987	2,233	2.314	0.7
1988	5,945	3.194	0.8
1989	5,779	3.392	0.8
1990	7,273	3.487	0.9

Source: Ministry of Commerce of the People's Republic of China.

In July 1979, the Second Plenary Session of the Fifth National People's Congress passed and promulgated the *Law of the People's Republic of China on Sino-foreign Joint Ventures*, allowing the introduction of foreign capital. In May 1983, the State Council held the first national conference on the utilization of foreign capital to further relax the policy on it. During that period, the establishment of special economic zones has also promoted the gradual development of foreign investment in China. In October 1986, the State Council promulgated the "Regulations on Encouraging Foreign Investment" to promote the improvement of the environment for foreign investment

[1] GuWenfu and Ding Wen, "Opening up Will Not Lead to Capitalism with Socialism Taking the Priority", *People's Daily*, Jan.20, 1985.

and to give preferential treatment to foreign investment in taxation and other fields.In December 1987, relevant departments formulated relative regulations to guide the direction of foreign investment in order to create a good environment for foreign investment and improve the structure of foreign investment. A series of policies and measures had enabled foreign direct investment in China to continue to develop steadily in the early days of reform and opening up.

The special economic zones have undoubtedly done exceptionally well in introducing foreign capital. The core task of China's special economic zones is to introduce foreign capital and advanced technology, hoping that the regions open to the outside world can make effective use of international resources and become the forerunner of China's opening to the outside world. According to statistics, 14 coastal open cities introduced more than US$10 billion of foreign direct investment, accounting for about 70% of the total foreign investment, and put into operation more than 2,000 foreign-invested ventures from 1986 to 1990. During this period, Hong Kong was the largest source of capital. According to the data, the number of enterprises invested by Hong Kong reached 1,721, accounting for 77.07% of the total foreign capital enterprises and Hong Kong, Macao, Taiwan invested enterprises in the country, while the amount of capital imported from Hong Kong reached US$1.587 billion, accounting for 68.64% of the total in 1987.[1] We can imagine how outstanding the results of opening up Guangdong and establishing Shenzhen and Zhuhai Special Economic Zones with the help of Hong Kong and Macao were in those days.

Seeing from the investment direction, foreign investment in China is mainly concentrated in labor-intensive industries, especially in manufacturing. Most of China's foreign trade during this period was also formed by foreign investment and processing trade, which created an advantage for China to undertake international industrial transfer after the 1990s.

In the early days of reform and opening up, although the cost of land and labor was low and the government issued preferential policies, low-level small investments were attracted mainly as an area for opening up in China was small. However, the spillover effect of foreign investment has gradually emerged with the deepening opening up, greatly promoting the subsequent economic development of China.

On the whole, the reform and opening up have a far-reaching impact on the internationalization of China's economy. After opening to the outside world in 1978,

---

[1] Data from Ministry of Commerce: http://www.mofcom.gov.cn/article/ae/ai/200812/20081205962396.html.

China's economy has made great progress in terms of both quantity and quality, to which the development of special economic zones have contributed a lot.

Looking back now, although the achievements of China's economic internationalization at the beginning of the reform and opening up in the 1980s may not be comparable to those achieved after the 1990s and the 21st century, the role of this period in exploring the mode of opening to the outside world cannot be ignored. More importantly, as a prerequisite for joining the world economy is the implementation of the market economy system, the market adjustment measures adopted in the special zone at this time have enabled China to accumulate experience and lessons in developing a market economy and laid a good foundation for China to build a socialist market economy and promote deeper economic internationalization. The opening up of this period enabled China to integrate into the world economy, which can be regarded as the starting point of China's economic internationalization.

3.2 The internationalization of China's economy in the 1990s

In the ten years from 1978 to 1988, China's reform and opening up achieved remarkable results and initial success. China's economic development had made great progress, and people's lives had been significantly improved. However, some new problems have been exposed along with unsettled problems since the 1990s. New debates have arisen about whether China should realize internationalization and how to do it with economic internationalization.

3.2.1 Two disputes: the twists and turns in the economic internationalization in the 1990s

When it comes to the opening up of new China, reform is always inevitable. Economic internationalization means economic exchanges with other countries in the world, especially the western developed countries. Therefore, once China's economic internationalization goes further than before, the emancipation of people's mind happens because of different ideologies from the western countries.

As mentioned earlier, China's reform and opening up has always been controversial both within the Party and among the people. At the beginning of the establishment of special economic zones, some people worried about whether the opening up would bring in capitalism. Only at the insistence of Deng Xiaoping and other party leaders did domestic opposition "disappear". China's reform and opening up did not stop in the 1980s but continued despite bumps.

If the road to China's economic internationalization was bumpy in the 1980s, the 1990s was full of thorns. Since 1990, change has occurred, which is shown in the following two aspects.

Firstly, China's position in the world economy has not been fundamentally changed, although it has made great achievements in the decade of reform. If we look at the figures alone, it is even worse. China's GNP per capita dropped from the last 24th to 21st from the bottom in the world from 1980 to 1989. Compared with the average GNP per capita of low-income countries, China dropped from 12% higher to only 6% higher.The gap with developed countries was still widening.In 1980, the GNP per capita in China was 2.55% of that in the United States, and it dropped to 1.67% in 1989.[1]Meanwhile, many deep-seated contradictions and problems accumulated in the process of domestic reform, which had become a serious obstacle to further deepening the reform, such as overheating of investment, the imbalance between industry and agriculture, serious inflation, the fact that the total social demand far exceeded the total social supply and others. The setback in the price reform of 1988 further intensified the contradiction in the domestic economic structure.

Secondly, the development of eastern European countries was generally in trouble and even suffered an economic collapse in the 1980s. Besides, countries and regions with developed capitalist and emerging market economies, especially the "Four Asian Tigers" have achieved more significant economic development at that time, which also caused enormous pressure on China, making an urgent need for a higher economic growth rate.

With the dual changes in the domestic and international environment, the question of whether to open up has been raised again. Many people have different views on the establishment of special economic zones, the development of the non-public economy and what socialism is. Does socialism have a market economy? Are reform and opening up threatening national security or promoting national development? Finally, the focuses are on whether the market economy is "capitalist" or "socialist," and the ownership should be "public" or "private". Although Deng

[1] Xiao Guoliang and Sui Fuming eds., *Economic History of the People's Republic of China 1949–2010*, Beijing: Peking University Press, 2011, p. 243.

Xiaoping said "not to argue", all kinds of arguments over these issues continued unabated for several years. Actually, China entered the 1990s in the debate.

(1) *Dispute over the Capitalism or Socialism of the Reform*

After the Third Plenary Session of the 11th CPC Central Committee, especially after formally proposing "developing the socialist commodity economy" at the Third Plenary Session of the 12th CPC Central Committee, China's economic system reform focused on the reform of planning system to develop the commodity economy. During that period, "commodity economy" was used instead of "market economy", because "market economy" was "capitalism" while "planned economy" was "socialism" in many people's minds in China. They held that socialist countries must adopt a planned economic system. If China adopted a market economy, it meant that socialism was given up.However, the commodity economy and the market economy are similar to each other. Even the communique of the Third Plenary Session of the 12th Central Committee said: "To reform the planning system, we must first break through the traditional concept of opposing the planned economy and the commodity economy".[1] It can be seen that the commodity economy and the market economy are identical in that context. Even so, there was still no mention of "market economy", which showed that people's rigid understanding of "market economy". In fact, the reform of China's economic system is essential to replace the resource allocation method based on administrative orders with the one based on the market mechanism. Therefore, the term "market economy" is more explicit, and the use of "commodity economy" is only a temporary solution.

With the development of reform, the understanding of the relationship between "plan and market" is constantly breaking through. On February 6,1987, Deng Xiaoping pointed out in his talk with Yang Shangkun, Wanli, and others about the preparations for the Thirteenth National Congress and the report draft of it: "Why does it refer to capitalism when we talk about the market? Only the plan is socialist? They are both means of developing the productive forces.So long as they serve that purpose, we should make use of them. If they serve socialism, they are socialist while if they serve capitalism, they are capitalist. It is not correct to say that planning is only socialist because there is a planning department in Japan and there is also planning in the United States. At one time, we copied the Soviet model of economic development and had a planned economy. Later, we adjusted the economic system into a plan-based

[1] "The CPC Central Committee's Decisions on Economic System Reform", *the Compilation of Documents from the Third Plenary Session of the Previous Central Committee Since the Reform and Opening up*, Beijing: People's Publishing House, 2013, p 29.

one complemented with marketing, but we should not talk about it anymore now".[1] Therefore, the report of the 13th National Congress did not mention planned economy in the economic system reform, and went further on the discussion of the relationship between "planning and marketing" pointing out: "The development of socialist commodity economy cannot be separated from the development and perfection of the market. The use of market regulation is by no means equal to the establishment of capitalism...In general, the new economic operation mechanism should be the one that the government regulates the market while the market guides enterprises". It was also after the 13th National Congress that domestic academic circles began to use the term "socialist market economy" directly. In February 1988, Ma Hong, director of the Development Research Center of the State Council, asked at a central meeting: What is the difference between "a socialist commodity economy" and "a socialist market economy"? The main leaders of the State Council replied: "Speaking from the reality, there is no difference. The using of commodity economy is to make it more acceptable for more people.The commodity economy mentioned at the Thirteenth National Congress is the market economy.Two statements, but the same meaning".[2] From this, we can see that the understanding of "market economy" was much improved at that time.

However, due to changes in the international and domestic situation, the "market economy" began to be criticized in 1989, and the idea of "planned economy" rose again with the "left trend of thought".

At that time, some people thought privatization was privatization.[3] Some people said: "Privatization and marketization belong to capitalism, ...China's reform must not take the road of privatization and marketization but the socialist one".[4]Some people also said: "...Making the market the main allocator of resources, and neglecting or even weakening and negating the important role of the planned economy will inevitably lead to the collapse of the socialist public sector of the economy".[5] Others said: "Planned economy is a basic feature of the socialist economy, which is fundamentally opposed to a market economy". "Socialist society cannot adopt a

---

[1] Party Literature Research Center of the CPC Central Committee, *The Chronicle Biography of Deng Xiaoping 1975–1997(Part II)*, Beijing: Central Party Literature Publishing House, 2004, p. 1168.

[2] Cao Pu, *Some Important Issues in the Study of the History of Reform and Opening up*, Fuzhou: Fujian People's Publishing House, 2014, p. 278.

[3] Wu Shuchun, "Reform and Opening Up Must Maintain Socialist Orientation", *People's Daily*, Nov.17, 1989.

[4] Jiang Xuemo, "China's Reform Cannot Take the Path of Private Market", *People's Daily*, May 29, 1991.

[5] "China Cannot Fully Implement Market Economy", *Guangming Daily*, Oct.28, 1989.

market economy but only planned economy, which is determined by the nature of the socialist economy". "In the process of economic reform, the erroneous idea of rejecting socialist planned economy completely and replacing it with market economy appeared due to the rampant trend of bourgeois liberalization. In fact, it is to deny the basic economic system in our country fundamentally". "Planned economy and market economy are fundamentally opposed to each other, but it is by no means to say that planned economy and market regulation are also incompatible, because the market, market regulation, and market economy are concepts with different connotations, which cannot be confused".[1]

Although these articles safeguarded socialism to a certain extent under the political environment at that time, they were mixed with some "ultra-left" ideas and totally denied the "market economy" direction of reform. What these critical articles have in common is to combine the plan and the market with the basic system of society. They believed that "adhering to the socialist system is to keep the planned economy", and re-raised the propositions that "planned economy is equal to socialism", "market economy is capitalism" and "engaging in market economy" is "engaging in bourgeois liberalization", the essence of which was to ask whether the reform is "socialist" or "capitalist". In such an atmosphere of public opinion, there were naturally fewer people mentioning "reform and opening up".

China's GDP grew at a double-digit rate on average from 1984 to 1988. Affected by the public opinion mentioned before, the GDP growth rate was only 4.1% in 1989 and further decreased to 3.8% in 1990, revealing a severe decline in economic growth.The growth rate of foreign trade was also affected with the annual growth rate of imports and exports dropping from 12% in 1987 and 24% in 1988 to 9% in 1989 and 3% in 1990. What's worse, the growth rate of imports dropped to –10% in 1990. The vague attitude and controversy in China towards the market economy not only slowed down China's economic growth but also seriously interfered with its economic internationalization process. Restoring the status of contracting party to GATT was an essential step in the internationalization of China's economy. However, some western forces blocked China on the grounds that China did not develop a market economy at that time, showing that China's attitude towards the market economy had affected the view of the international community on us and played a decisive role in the direction

---

[1] Hu Naiwu and Yuan Zhenyu, "Create an Operation Mechanism Coordinating Planned Economy and Market", *People's Daily*, Nov.27, 1989.

of China's economic internationalization.

At the critical moment, Deng Xiaoping once again stepped forward. On June 9, 1989, he said in an interview with cadres from the martial-law troops in the capital that the planned economy and market regulation would still be combined in the future.[1](The original version goes that "we will continue to adhere to the combination of planned economy and market economy, and it cannot be changed".)[2]

When talking with Jiang Zemin, Yang Shangkun and Li Peng on December 24, 1990, he pointed out: "We must understand theoretically that the distinction between capitalism and socialism does not lie in the question of whether it is a plan or a market.Socialism has regulation by market forces while capitalism has control through planning. Don't think that adopting a market economy is to take the capitalist road. It is not that way. Both a planned economy and a market economy are necessary. If we do not engage in the market, we will even know nothing about the world, and we will inevitably lag behind".[3] He specifically told Li Peng not to mention the priority to the planned economy.[4]

From January 28 to February 18, 1991, Deng Xiaoping visited Shanghai and delivered a series of speeches. When talking about the development of Shanghai, he repeatedly mentioned that Shanghai should be open and reformed with emancipated minds. On February 6, in a conversation with Zhu Rongji, he further pointed out: "It is difficult to develop the economy without opening up...Don't think that the planned economy is socialism while the market economy is capitalism.It is not the case. Both of them are means to develop the country and the market can also serve socialism".[5]

The speech from the top undoubtedly inspired people. In the early of 1991, Jiefang Daily in Shanghai published several articles with the signature Huangfu Ping successively. The thoughts in the articles continued the spirit of Deng Xiaoping's speeches in Shanghai. Moreover, they explicitly supported reform and opening up and supported that socialism could also adopt a market economy, which attracted public attention. The articles pointedly said: "In the new situation of deepening reform and

---

1 *Selected Works of Deng Xiaoping, Volume Ⅲ*, People's Publishing House, 1993, p. 306.

2 Wu Jinglian, "The Key Points of Three Speeches at a Symposium (October-December 1991)", *Planned Economy or Market Economy*, China Economic Publishig House, 1993, p. 113.

3 Party Literature Research Center of the CPC Central Committee, *The Chronicle Biography of Deng Xiaoping 1975–1997(Part Ⅱ)*, Beijing: Central Party Literature Publishing House, 2004, p. 1323.

4 Chen Jinhua, *State Memory*, Beijing:Central Party History Publishing House, 2005.p. 213.

5 *Selected Works of Deng Xiaoping, Volume Ⅲ*, People's Publishing House, 1993, p. 367.

opening up, we should prevent ourselves from falling into a 'new ideological deadlock'. The development of the social commodity economy and the socialist market cannot be simply equated with capitalism".[1] "Shanghai will take a big step in opening upin the 1990s...If we are still constrained by the criticism of 'whether it is capitalist or socialist to develop a market economy', we will surely miss the opportunity".[2]

On July 1, 1991, Jiang Zemin said in his speech at the celebration of the 70th anniversary of the founding of the CPC: "Planning and marketing, as means of regulating the economy, are objectively needed for the development of the commodity economy based on socialized mass production, so the use of these means within a certain range is not a sign to distinguish the socialist economy from the capitalist economy".[3]

From these series of events, it can be seen that the central government shows a firm attitude in pushing forward the market-oriented reform and is constantly developing and deepening it, while firmly taking the system reform as the principal means to push forward the opening up. After a year, Deng Xiaoping visited Wuchang, Shenzhen, Zhuhai, Shanghai and other places at the age of 88 from January 18 to February 21, 1992, and delivered the great talks during his inspection, giving clear opinions on some important theories, routes, principles, and policies concerned at home and abroad. Especially the contents involving the market and plan, opening to the outside world had stimulated the internationalization of China's economy since then and finally ended the debate that whether it is capitalist or socialist to develop a market economy. In his talks, he pointed out: "More plans or more markets are not the essential difference between socialism and capitalism.A planned economy is not equivalent to socialism, because there is planning in capitalist countries while a market economy is not capitalist, because there are markets under socialism too.Plans and markets are both economic measures".[4] "If socialism wants to win the advantages compared with capitalism, it must boldly absorb and learn from all achievements of human society as well as all the advanced management methods reflecting the laws of modern socialized production from all countries in the world, including capitalist

---

[1] Huangfu Ping, "Reform and Opening up Needing New Ideas", *Jiefang Daily*, Mar.2, 1991.

[2] Huangfu Ping, "Strengthening the Awareness of Reform and Opening Up", *Jiefang Daily*, Mar.2, 1991.

[3] Jiang Zemin, "Speech at the 70th Anniversary of Communist Party of China", *People's Daily*, Jul.2, 1991.

[4] *Selected Works of Deng Xiaoping, Volume Ⅲ*, People's Publishing House, 1993, p. 373.

developed countries".[1]

He urged: "We should be bolder and dare to experiment in reform and opening up. Do not behave like a woman with small feet who can only take small steps. If you see the chance, seize it and try. There will be no good or new road to take and no new career without the spirits of breaking through and taking risks. Who dares to say that he can take no risks and be sure of everything he does?"[2] He also gave instructions to the fact that China's economic development should depend on opening up: "Seize the opportunity to develop and the core is to develop the economy...Where conditions permit, we should try our best to speed up. As long as we talk about efficiency, quality, and export-oriented economy, there is nothing to worry about".[3]

After Deng Xiaoping's south tour talks were conveyed, they caused strong responses and huge shocks at home and abroad. The contents of the talks were rich and profound, which answered the most concerned and debated questions in China at that time and were major theoretical breakthroughs in China's reform and opening up and the adaption of Marxism to the Chinese context. Gong Yuzhi, former vice president of the Party School of the Central Committee of the CPC and executive vice director of the Party History Research Office of the Central Committee, once said: "The south tour talks have been identified as the final chapter of the third volume of Selected Works of Deng Xiaoping. It is a masterpiece representing Deng Xiaoping's theory of building socialism with Chinese characteristics".

Deng Xiaoping's south tour talks also laid the ideological foundation for the 14th CPC National Congress and made theoretical preparations for it. The 14th Party Congress officially announced in October 1992: "The goal of China's economic system reform is to establish a socialist market economic system". China's economic reform and development started again from a new starting point, so did the process of internationalization of China's economy shelved in the debate.

(2) *The dispute between public and private ownership*

The last dispute was settled in 1992. After that, China's economic reform and internationalization have developed to a certain extent. With the deepening of reform, we have gradually touched the "deep water area" in 1997. The issue at that time was related to the core of the economic system: ownership.

---

1 *Selected Works of Deng Xiaoping, Volume Ⅲ*, People's Publishing House, 1993, p. 373.

2 *Selected Works of Deng Xiaoping, Volume Ⅲ*, People's Publishing House, 1993, p. 372.

3 *Selected Works of Deng Xiaoping, Volume Ⅲ*, People's Publishing House, 1993, p. 375.

The non-public economy has made great progress at that time.Although the total amount of the state-owned economy has increased, its share in the economy was continuously declining. By the mid-1990s, it accounted for about 50% of the industry, while the private economy had developed rapidly with industrial output value reaching RMB1,522.8 billion in 2002 from RMB9.7 billion in 1989, up 158 times within 14 years.[1]

Deng Xiaoping made a special statement on the ownership in the three kinds of foreign-invested ventures and special zones in his south tour talks: "In Shenzhen, public ownership plays the main part, while foreign investment accounts for only a quarter.For foreign investment, we can also benefit from taxation, labor services, and other aspects. Set up more foreign-invested ventures and don't be afraid. So long as we keep a clear mind, there is no cause for alarm. We have advantages as we have large and medium-sized state-owned enterprises and township enterprises and more importantly, we take charge of them.Some people think that more foreign capital will lead to more capitalism and more foreign-invested enterprises mean being more capitalist and developing capitalism.These people lack basic knowledge. For these foreign-invested enterprises, although foreign investors earn some money according to the current laws and policies, the government collects taxes and workers earn their wages from them. What's more, we can also learn technology and management and get information from them and open up the market through them. Therefore, the foreign-invested enterprises are restricted by the whole political and economic conditions in our country and are a beneficial supplement to the socialist economy, which is conducive to socialism indeed".[2]Since then, the amount of foreign capital introduced and the degree of opening to the outside world in coastal areas have been increasing, and the private economy has been active, accommodating a large number of employers. About 20 million unemployed people in the reform of state-owned enterprises have flocked to private enterprises.

In the face of the ever-decreasing state-owned economy and the ever-increasing private economy since the establishment of the socialist market economy system, some people ask the questions: Will the public ownership be reformed if the reform continues? If there is no public ownership, is it still the socialism? So the dispute over the capitalism or socialism of the reform in 1992 came back but changed into the

---

1 Wang Huanpei, *Research on Current Chinese Private Economy*, Hunan Science & Technology Press, 2006, pp. 114-116.

2 *Selected Works of Deng Xiaoping, Volume III*, People's Publishing House, 1993, p. 373.

dispute between "public" and "private" ownership.

This debate is essentially a continuation of various debates in our country since China's reform and opening up. This debate originated from macro-control in 1995 through which China's economy achieved a soft landing, but some problems gradually emerged, the state-owned enterprises being the first to bear the brunt. Under such conditions, what should we do? In the second half of 1995, the central government put forward a reform idea for state-owned enterprises "to manage large enterprises well while relaxing control over small ones". "Managing large enterprises" means concentrating on a number of large state-owned enterprises that are vital to the country, and "Relaxing control over small ones" means allowing merging, leasing, contracting or selling the small state-owned enterprises. As a matter of fact, "relaxing control over small enterprises" is to liberalize their ownership. As the reform of state-owned enterprises has touched the level of ownership, it causes conflicts and disputes.

Since 1995, some people have been voicing the fear that the change of ownership structure will lead to the deterioration of socialism and nurture the soil for the bourgeoisie. A well-known article *Some Factors Affecting National Security* was widely circulated at that time, believing that the change in the proportion of state-owned economy and the private economy at that time in China was in danger of bourgeois liberalization. There are also similar articles, such as *Preliminary Discussion on the Internal and External Situation and Major Threats of China's National Security in the Next 120 Years*, *Some Theoretical and Policy Issues on Adhering to the Dominant Position of Public Ownership* and *Trends and Characteristics of Capitalist Liberalization Since 1992*, all of which are anonymous. They all believe that reform cannot involve the ownership and oppose reform and opening up in the name of "Marxism." What's more, they believe that socialism in China is dangerous if there are any components of the private economy.

With constant debates, everyone focuses his eyes on the central government. Experience tells us that opinions at the highest level often play a decisive role in China.

On May 29, 1997, Jiang Zemin delivered an important speech at the graduation ceremony of the provincial and ministerial cadre training class of the CPC Central Party School, which can be regarded the most important speech before the 15th national congress and preparations for the 15th national congress.

There are two main points in the speech: one is to hold high Deng Xiaoping's banner, and the other is to adhere to the theory of the primary stage of socialism. There is nothing new in these two points, which are discussed at the 12th and the 13th national congress. However, we can find that the significance of this speech is more than it reveals the determination of the top leaders of the central government to continue reform and opening up.

In his speech, Jiang Zemin pointed out: "Practice has proved that we are not breaking away from socialism but building it on the ground so that socialism is truly thriving in China".[1] "Strive to find a form of public ownership that can greatly promote the development of productive forces, and all modes of operation and organizational forms that reflect the laws of socialized production can be used boldly".[2] These statements are the first public answer to the dispute over the capitalism or socialism of reform from the top leaders of the central government, from which we can see the attitude of the top leaders to the debate. In Deng Xiaoping's words, we should be "alert to the right, but mainly to prevent 'left'" to convey confidence to the whole nation that China's reform complies with socialism, and China's economic internationalization will not stagnate.

On September 12, 1997, the 15th National Congress of the Communist Party of China was held, and Jiang Zemin delivered a speech. There were greater breakthroughs in the issue of ownership at this conference, mainly summarized as the following four points: Firstly, the ownership structure of our country was clearly defined. "Public ownership as the main body and the common development of various ownership economies is a basic economic system in the primary stage of socialism in China".[3] Secondly, we redefined the meaning of public ownership economy. "The public ownership economy includes not only the state-owned economy and the collective economy but also the state-owned and collective components of the mixed ownership economy".[4] Thirdly, it illustrates the leading role of the state-owned economy." The dominant position of public ownership is mainly embodied in the following two aspects. One is that public assets are dominant in total social assets and

---

[1] Wang Xinqing, "Jiang Zemin Emphasized at the Graduation Ceremony of a Senior Course for Ministerial Officials and Provincial Heads at the CPC Central Committee's Party School: Hold High the Banner of Deng Xiaoping Theory of Socialism with Chinese Characteristics and Grasp the Opportunity to Promote Our Career in the 21st Century", *People's Daily*, May 30, 1997.

[2] Wang Xinqing, "Jiang Zemin Emphasized at the Graduation Ceremony of a Senior Course for Ministerial Officials and Provincial Heads at the CPC Central Committee's Party School: Hold High the Banner of Deng Xiaoping Theory of Socialism with Chinese Characteristics and Grasp the Opportunity to Promote Our Career in the 21st Century", *People's Daily*, May 30, 1997.

[3] *Selected Works of Jiang Zemin (Volume II)*, Beijing: People's Publishing House, 2006, p.19.

[4] *Selected Works of Jiang Zemin (Volume II)*, Beijing: People's Publishing House, 2006, p.19.

the other is that the state-owned economy controls the lifelines of the national economy and plays a leading role in economic development...The leading role of the state-owned economy mainly shows in the power of control...As long as we stick to public ownership as the main body and the government controls the lifelines of the national economy, the control power and competitiveness of the state-owned economy will be enhanced. Moreover, on this premise, a little reduction of the proportion of the state-owned economy will not affect the socialist nature of our country".[1] Fourthly, it points out the diversification of public ownership. "All the management methods and organizational forms that reflect the laws of socialized production can be used boldly.Efforts should be made to find a form of public ownership that can greatly promote the development of productive forces".[2]

Li Peng said at a discussion meeting of the 15th National Congress that the 15th National Congress was another liberation of our minds. Indeed, the 15th National Congress broke new ground in the ownership theory and ultimately ended the debate over the ownership clarifying people's confusion and doubts.It further developed the theory of socialism with Chinese characteristics on the basis of safeguarding China's socialist system, providing powerful theoretical support and ideological weapon for continuing to promote economic internationalization and deepening economic system reform.

Theory guides practice and ideological emancipation often go ahead of revolutionary construction. The two debates in China in the 1990s were another liberation of the Chinese Communist Party's mind after the Third Plenary Session of the 11th Central Committee, providing the impetus for China's reform and opening up.On this basis, China began to establish a socialist market economic system and cleared the obstacles to the internationalization of China's economy from the economic system by adhering to the socialist system, thus significantly promoting the internationalization of China's economy.

3.2.2 Institutional reform promotes opening to the outside world: reforms in the process of economic internationalization in the 1990s

The debates and disturbance in the Chinese ideological circle in the 1990s not only determined the direction of China's road in theory but also were embodied deeply

---

[1] *Selected Works of Jiang Zemin (Volume II)*, Beijing: People's Publishing House, 2006, pp. 19–20.

[2] *Selected Works of Jiang Zemin (Volume II)*, Beijing: People's Publishing House, 2006, p.20.

in practice. Deng Xiaoping's south tour talks, the 14th, and 15th National Congresses all have become policies that have been put into practice to promote China's economic system reform and its economic internationalization. There is no doubt that China's opening up to the outside world has been inseparable from reformas well as the advance of ideological emancipation since 1978. The road of China's economic internationalization has been accompanied by constant reform of the economic system. The greatness of the Communist Party of China is that it can maintain calm and continue its reform to upgrade itself to a higher level while making outstanding achievements. That is to say, reform is an everlasting task and should be carried out along the development of the country. In the 1990s, China continued to push forward the reform of the economic system on the basis of the great achievements made in the 1980s, making the internationalization of China's economy more in-depth.

During this period, the establishment of a socialist market economic system was the core task, and all other reforms were carried out closely around it. Indeed, it is essential to establishing the socialist market economy system in the internationalization of China's economy.

Learning from the historical experiences and lessons, closing the country to the outside world means backwardness and suppression from others. Opening up is the only way for China to develop itself. However, the contradiction between the world economic rules and the domestic economic system is becoming more and more prominent with the development of China's opening up and the improvement of economic internationalization.Especially after the disintegration of the Soviet Union in the 1990s, the world economy has increasingly formed a pattern headed by the United States.The internationalization of China's economy is actually a process of continuous integration into this world economic pattern, which requires us to accept the trade rules formulated by western developed countries to a certain extent. We do not need to do that unless we can stand on our own feet, but when we are not strong enough, to stand on our own feet is obviously unrealistic, and the only way out is to bide our time and seek chances for development. The foundation of the world economic rules is the market economy. One of the important reasons why China's "re-entry" the GATT is full of difficulties is that China's market economy status is not recognized by other countries. If China wants to further open up to the outside world and promotes its economic internationalization and international market influence, whether to establish a market economy system is an inseparable topic. In the early 1990s, the debate over the nature of the reform is a debate that whether China should implement a market economy system or not to a large extent.

Deng Xiaoping's south tour talks in 1992 ended the debate with the statement that China must persist in reform and opening up to the outside world to develop itself. However, what kind of model should be chosen for the economic system reform has become a new topic, because Deng Xiaoping explained the relationship between the plan and the market in his talks without mentioning that what kind of model our economic system should be.At that time, there were three representative views on what kind of target model to set for China's economic system reform at the 14th Party Congress to be held in the second half of that year: the first is to establish a socialist commodity economic system combining planning with the market. The second is a planned socialist market economic system while the third is a socialist market economic system.[1]

The central government has also been thinking deeply about this question and holds many seminars to discuss it. On April 30, 1992, Jiang Zemin chaired a meeting of the Standing Committee of the Political Bureau of the Central Committee to discuss the first draft of the report submitted by the drafting group of the 14th National Congress.He said at the meeting: "The 14th National Congress should go further in the relationship of planning and marketing, which is a major issue related to the overall situation of reform, opening up and modernization".[2] In an important speech delivered at the provincial and ministerial level cadre training class of the Central Party School on June 9, he talked about how to deeply understand and fully implement Deng Xiaoping's south tour talks from nine aspects. When it comes to planning and marketing, he made it clear: "In my personal view,I would like to use the term 'socialist market economic system'. A planned commodity economy is a planned market economy. The socialist economy is planned from the very beginning, which has always been clear in people's mind. The question of whether or not to cancel the plan will not arise because of the lack of the word 'planned'... Therefore, I think the use of the 'socialist market economy system' can be accepted by most cadres and the masses. Although it is my personal view, I have talked about it with some comrades in the Central Committee, and most of them agreed".[3]

On June 12, three days after this speech, Jiang Zemin reported to Deng Xiaoping

---

[1] Cao Pu, *Some Important Issues in the Study of the History of Reform and Opening up*, Fuzhou: Fujian People's Publishing House, 2014, p. 289.

[2] *Selected Works of Jiang Zemin (Volume II)*, Beijing: People's Publishing House, 2006, p. 210.

[3] *Selected Works of Jiang Zemin (Volume II)*, Beijing: People's Publishing House, 2006, pp. 201–202.

the proposal of the use of "socialist market economic system" and was approved by Deng Xiaoping.Deng Xiaoping said: "In fact, we are doing this. Shenzhen is adopting a socialist market economy. There will be no competition and comparison, and even no development of science and technology without a market economy." He also said: "The speech in the Party School can be preceded by internal documents first.If it is well reflected, it can be further promoted. The 14th National Congress will have a theme in this way".[1] After careful discussion by the party committees of the 30 provinces, municipalities and autonomous regions in the country, it was widely accepted.

On this basis, the 14th Party Congress officially announced in October 1992: "The goal of China's economic system reform is to establish a socialist market economic system" and pointed out: "The socialist market economic system we want to establish is to enable the market to play a fundamental role in the allocation of resources under the macro-control of the socialist country, so that economic activities will follow the requirements of the law of value and can adapt to changes in the relationship between supply and demand.""The establishment and improvement of the socialist market economy system is a long process and a complex task about social system." "We believe that the market economy under the socialist conditions should and can be run better than the market economy under the capitalist one".[2] The 14th Party Congress marks the final establishment of the goal to the reform the socialist market economy system.

According to the goals and tasks set by the 14th National Congress to establish a socialist market economy system, the CPC Central Committee and the State Council successively made a series of major arrangements to formulate the overall plan of the socialist market economy system and promote reform and opening up and the internationalization of China's economy.

Since 1993, China has striven to make breakthroughs in the change of the operating mechanism of state-owned enterprises, development of various markets, reforms of price, labor wage system, social security, urban housing system, fiscal and taxation systems and financial systems, as well as the improvement and strengthening

[1] Party Literature Research Center of the CPC Central Committee, *The Chronicle Biography of Deng Xiaoping 1975–1997(Part II)*, Beijing: Central Party Literature Publishing House, 2004, pp. 1347–1348.

[2] Jiang Zemin, "Accelerating Reform and Opening Up and Modernization Construction and Seize a Larger Success in Socialism with Chinese Characteristics—Report at the 14th National Congress of the Communist Party of China", *People's Daily*, Oct.21, 1992.

of macroeconomic management to finally establish a socialist market system.

In March 1993, the First Session of the Eighth National People's Congress amended Article 15 of the Constitution to read: "The country implements a socialist market economy." It was the first time that the socialist market economy had been written into the fundamental law of our country.

The Third Plenary Session of the 14th CPC Central Committee formally considered and adopted the Decision on Several Issues Concerning the Establishment of a Socialist Market Economy System (hereinafter referred to as the Decision), further concretizing the objectives and basic principles of the economic system reform proposed by the 14th CPC Central Committee from November 11 to 14, 1993. The Decision constructed the basic framework of the socialist market economy system and became the guiding principles and blueprint for establishing the socialist market economy system in China in the 1990s, which had a significant and far-reaching impact on its reform and opening up and socialist modernization as the Chinese government and people had more confidence in reform and opening up, and another trend of economic internationalization had been set off.

According to the deployment of the 14th National Congress and the 3rd Plenary Session of the 14th CPC Central Committee, China's economic system reform entered a new stage of overall advancement and key breakthroughs, especially in the areas of taxation, finance, foreign exchange, foreign trade, investment, price and state-owned enterprise reform since 1994. From the perspective of economic internationalization, all of them could be seenin the reform of state-owned enterprise and foreign economic system.

(1) *State-owned enterprise reforms*

The reform of state-owned enterprises has always been a focus of China's economic system reform.Before Deng Xiaoping's south tour talks, the reform of state-owned enterprises can be divided into four stages: the first stage (1978–1980) takes the expansion of the pilot project of enterprise autonomy as a breakthrough, the main contents of which are power expansion, tax reduction, and profit concession, giving enterprises a certain amount of independent property and management rights. The second stage (1981–1982) is mainly to test the economic responsibility system. In 1980, enterprises in some regions began to try out various forms of responsibility system for profits and losses, and measures such as scoring wages, piece-rate wages and floating wages, combining production responsibility system with economic benefits, and gradually forming an economic responsibility system combining responsibility and rights. The third stage (1983–1986) focuses on the replacement of profit submission with tax payment. In June 1983, the first step of tax reform was carried out in pilot areas around the country in the form of a combination of profit submission with tax payment. In September 1984, it was transitioned to a complete replacement of profit submission with tax payment, thus promoting the growth of national fiscal revenue. The fourth stage (1987–1991) is to improve the operating mechanism of enterprises and implement the contract system with the main focuses on "a fixed requirement of handing over combined with keeping exceeding profits while making up for deficit themselves", thus mobilizing the enthusiasm of enterprises and workers and promoting the development of enterprise production by breaking the big pot.[1] After the 14th National Congress, the reform of state-owned enterprises is aimed at establishing a modern enterprise system.

From the reform of state-owned enterprises, we can see that China's economic reform, from the development of commodity economy to the establishment of a socialist market economy, has gradually realized the transition from a planned economy to a market economy. As the main body of the market economy, enterprises are naturally the focus of the reform, especially after we formally proposed the establishment of a socialist market economy system.

Enterprises in the western market economy do not include state-owned enterprises, because the foundation of the modern market economy lies in the property right system, but state-owned enterprises are not clear on this point. A property right is an economic category that meets the requirements of the development of a modern market economy. Modern property right system is essential to the modern market economy. The market economy is aimed at seeking profits as much as possible under the effect of the market mechanism. All activities of the market economy are based on and around property rights.In order to establish a socialist market economy system in China, we must first improve the modern property right system. The reason why the reform of state-owned enterprises is so essential to the construction of the socialist market economy system in China is that it involves the core of the modern market economy: the property right system.

Although consensus has been reached on the understanding that socialism can also develop a market economy after the talks in the south, how to reform became a

---

[1] Xi Jieren ed., *Encyclopedic Dictionary on Scientific Outlook of Development*, Shanghai: Shanghai Lexicographic Publishing House, 2007, p. 76.

difficulty, especially in dealing with the relationship between state-owned enterprises and private enterprises, as well as the reform of state-owned enterprises themselves. The reform of state-owned enterprises is crucial. On the one hand, state-owned enterprises, a product of the traditional planned economy, have property rights owned by the state and the collective with unclear rights, responsibilities, and ownership. Therefore they are in an inferior position in market competition with low earning efficiency and unrestrained spending called “state-owned enterprise disease,” which is not conducive to the development of the market economy. The state-owned enterprises have even become an important excuse that western developed countries have not recognized China’s market economy status for a long time. On the other hand, public ownership is the foundation of our system as a socialist country, and we cannot take the road of complete privatization, which has been proved wrong in Russia. Therefore, China cannot abandon state-owned enterprises. However, if the proportion of the state-owned economy is too large, it is not conducive to the development of a market economy. Thus it can be concluded that dealing well with the property rights of the state-owned economy and promoting the reform of state-owned enterprises have already affected the success of the socialist market economy and whether China’s economy can be in line with international standards.

Therefore, it is not surprising that after the 14th National Congress in 1992, the reform of state-owned enterprises has shifted from the distribution relationship to the stage focusing on the reform of property rights, and the construction of modern enterprise system based on the reform of property rights system has become the basic content of the reform of state-owned enterprises. In November 1993, the Third Plenary Session of the 14th Central Committee of the Communist Party of China adopted the Decision on Several Issues Concerning the Establishment of a Socialist Market Economy System, which stated that deepening the reform of state-owned enterprises must “focus on the innovation of the enterprise system” and required the establishment of a modern enterprise system “with clear property rights and responsibilities, separation from government and scientific management”. This indicates that the state-owned enterprise reform has shifted from decentralization to enterprise system innovation with property right reform as its core.

On December 29, 1993, the Fifth Session of the Eighth National People’s Congress passed the “Company Law of the People’s Republic of China” (hereinafter referred to as “Company Law”) and proposed that companies invested by different property rights should have equal legal status.The promulgation of the Company Law not only provides legal basis and guarantee for the shareholding reform of state-owned enterprises but also plays an important role in regulating the market operation of all enterprises with different ownership. On March 2, 1994, the State Economic and Trade Commission issued "Some Opinions on Transforming the Operating Mechanism of State-owned Enterprises to Establish a Modern Enterprise System" (hereinafter referred to as "Opinions") and proposed the implementation of the "Transformation of System" Plan, in which the following goals are involved. Firstly, the 14 business autonomous rights granted by the Regulation on the Mechanism of Conversion of Industrial Enterprises Owned by the Whole People will be implemented by about 10,000 large and medium-sized state-owned enterprises within two years to lay a solid foundation for enterprises to transfer their organizational structure and enter the market. Secondly, the state will supervise the state-owned assets of 1,000 key enterprises related to the national economy and people's livelihood in batches by appointing a supervisory board. Thirdly, 100 large and medium-sized state-owned enterprises of different types will be selected for the pilot projects of establishing a modern enterprise system under the leadership and deployment agreed by the State Council. Fourthly, the comprehensive reform pilot of "optimizing the capital structure and enhancing the strength of enterprises" will be tested in 10 cities (later expanded to 18).The "Opinions" put forward that "Transformation of System" is an organic whole, which is the direction and task of the enterprise reform as a whole and implementation plan of key breakthroughs in the enterprise reform. In November 1994, the State Council held a national working conference for pilot areas on the establishment of a modern enterprise system. Since 1995, the State Economic and Trade Commission has focused its efforts on the four pilot projects approved by the State Council: The first is the establishment of a modern enterprise system in 100 state-owned enterprises.The second is to actively carry out the pilot work of "optimizing capital structure" in 18 cities, which was later increased to 58 cities and even 111 cities in 1997. The third is to do a good job in the pilot work of 56 enterprise groups and 3 state holding companies, and vigorously promote the reform of small state-owned enterprises through joint-stock system, leasing, bankruptcy and sale according to the policy of "manage large enterprises well while relaxing control over small ones" put forward by the Fifth Plenary Session of the 14th CPC Central Committee in 1995.In addition to the above pilot units managed by the central government, various regions have also identified some pilot enterprises, reaching 2,343 totally, covering 31 provinces, autonomous regions, and municipalities.By the end of 1996, the pilot project had achieved initial results. Among the 100 enterprises, the remaining 98 have been fundamentally restructured except for the one disintegrated and the other merged.After a corporate restructuring, the total assets of these enterprises reached RMB360.08 billion, an increase by RMB99.45 billion and 27.6% over the amount before the reform. Owner's equity was RMB123.18 billion, an increase of RMB38.3 billion and 31.1%. The asset-liability ratio of enterprises dropped from 67.59% to 62.28%.Significant progress has also been made in the selection of 2,343 pilot enterprises around the country.By the end of 1996, the asset-liability ratio of all pilot enterprises was 65.8%, down 2.4% than that of the previous year. The asset appreciation rate was 26.5%. The number of pilot enterprises redirected into social service agencies reached 2,265 with 611 thousand surplus employees.The pilot practice shows that the establishment of a modern enterprise system by state-owned enterprises can be successful.[1] However, since there is no emphasis on reorganizing the original state-owned enterprises into real ones through equity diversification, the vast majority of the enterprises participating in the pilot project have only completed the transformation of corporatization in form and become "wholly state-owned companies", not meeting the due standards of corporate enterprises.

The 15th National Congress in 1997 further proposed that we should focus on improving the whole state-owned economy, managing large enterprises well while relaxing control over small ones to carry out a strategic restructuring of state-owned enterprises and finally incorporate the reform of state-owned enterprises into the reform of the whole social and economic ownership structure.The 15th National Congress and the First Plenary Session of the 15th Central Committee issued a "mobilization order" to the whole party and the people of the whole country for the reform and relief of state-owned enterprises that most state-owned large and medium-sized loss-making enterprises will be freed from difficulties through reform, restructuring, transformation and strengthening managementin about three years, striving to establish a modern enterprise system by the end of the 20th century for most large and medium-sized state-owned backbone enterprises.Then it will take a long time to complete the strategic adjustment of the state-owned economy and the strategic reorganization of the state-owned enterprises, form a more reasonable layout and structure, and establish a complete modern enterprise system.This is the "two

[1] Dong Fureng ed., *Economic History of the People's Republic of China, Volume II*, Beijing: Economic Science Press, 1999, pp. 396-397.

goals in three years" for state-owned enterprises to reform and extricate themselves from difficulties. On March 19, 1998, Zhu Rongji proposed at a press conference held at the first session of the Ninth National People's Congress that the task of the current government was "one guarantee, three in position and five reforms" in which the reform of state-owned enterprises was included.

With a series of measures, the reform of state-owned enterprises has been fruitful, and their competitiveness in the market has been significantly enhanced. China has also realized the accelerated transformation from the old planned economy to the socialist market economy, promoting the further expansion of the role of the market mechanism throughout the 1990s and significantly enhancing its economic vitality, leading to the accelerated development of China's economic internationalization and laying a foundation for Chinese enterprises to step on the international stage in the future.

(2) *The accelerated development of opening to the outside world*

After Deng Xiaoping's south tour talks in the 1990s, we adhered to the basic national policy of opening up to the outside world in the face of the globalization of economy and technology. A new round of climax in China's opening up to the outside world came with a new situation of opening up to the outside world as we learned from the experience of opening up to the outside world in the 1980s and greatly expanded the areas and scopes of opening up to the outside world.

Firstly, the regions and fields of opening to the outside world have been further expanded.

After entering the 1990s, the government put forward the "Strategy for Four Areas" for opening up to the outside world, focusing on accelerating the development and opening up of the four kinds of areas, and further expanding the open zones:

Coastal areas. The development of the Pearl River Delta, the Yangtze River Delta, Bohai Bay, and Beibu Gulf is the focus. Among the four, the Yangtze River Delta and Beibu Gulf have not developed as well as the other two regions in the past; thus more actions are expected in the future.

Border areas. The focus of northern border areas in Xinjiang, Inner Mongolia and Heilongjiang is to develop and strengthen economic and trade exchanges with the countries of Commonwealth of Independent States. The southwest focuses on developing the border areas of Yunnan and Guangxi to exploit the trade routes to South and Southeast Asia. On March 9, 1992, the State Council decided to open Heihe City and Suifenhe city in Heilongjiang, Manzhouli City in Inner Mongolia and

Hunchun City in Jilin. On June 9, the three border cities of Yining, Bole, and Tacheng in Xinjiang, Pingxiang City and Dongxing Town in Guangxi, Wanding City, Ruili City and Hekou County in Yunnan were further opened. The Erenhot city in Inner Mongolia was further opened on July 30 of the same year. For these border cities, the government adopted the special policies similar to that of open coastal cities.

Areas along the river.Taking Pudong Development Zone as the leading role and the construction of the Three Gorges Project as an opportunity, promoting the comprehensive development and opening up of the Yangtze River valley below Chongqing is focused to link east and west and radiate north and south.As early as April 17, 1980, the State Council approved the opening of eight foreign trade ports along the Yangtze River, namely Zhangjiagang, Nantong, Nanjing, Wuhu, Jiujiang, Wuhan, Chenglingji and Chongqing. The last five inland ports are only open to national ships.In 1991, these ports were expanded to be open to foreign vessels. In July of next year, Wuhu, Jiujiang, Yueyang, Chongqing and Wuhan were listed as open inland cities, implementing the same open policy as coastal open cities.

Areas along the road.As part of the Eurasia Continental Bridge, the economic development along the railway from Lianyungang to Alashankou in Xinjiang in China, especially along the northwest, is still relatively backward, the development of which is of great significance to changing the economic backwardness of China as a whole.In June 1992, the State Council first opened the three provincial inland capitals of Urumqi, Kunming, and Nanning, and in July opened another 15 provincial capitals such as Taiyuan and Hefei. So far, China had opened all provincial capitals except Lhasa in Tibet.

The implementation of this strategy enabled China to realize an all-around geographical opening from coastal areas to inland areas in the mid-1990s, forming a new pattern of opening to the outside world.

At the same time, the industrial fields open to the outside world has also been expanding, mainly by encouraging foreign investment in infrastructure and basic industries while allowing foreign investors to gradually enter the service industry, such as setting up joint-venture retails and wholesale commercial enterprises. The establishment of Sino-foreign joint banks and insurance companies were expanded from special zones to major cities. What's more, Sino-foreign joint or cooperative commodity inspection authorities were set up, and the accounting market is opened up. Further progress has also been made in the form of utilizing foreign capital, mainly by adding wholly foreign-owned enterprises and implementing some new forms of utilizing foreign capital, such as BOT.

Second, the development of special economic zones has been further deepened.

It seems doubtful whether the SEZ will still exist when opening up to the outside world in an all-round way with expanding the opening area.Deng Xiaoping's south tour talks directly mentioned the advantages of special economic zones and recognized its important role, laying the foundation for the further deepening of the special economic zone in the 1990s.

On June 20, 1994, Jiang Zemin solemnly made "three unchanging" commitments to the development of special economic zones when he visited Shenzhen. "The central government's determination to develop special economic zones will remain unchanged;The central government's basic policies towards special economic zones remains unchanged. The status and role of special economic zones in the national reform, opening up and modernization will remain unchanged." He proposed, "The development of special economic zones should run through the whole process of socialist modernization. It is wrong to think that the status and role of special economic zones can be weakened or even gradually eliminated under the new situation of all-around opening up in the country".[1] He also requested Special Economic Zones to create new advantages and attain a higher goal. According to this requirement, the special economic zones maintained a sustained and rapid development of the national economy from 1995 to 2000. The GDP of Shenzhen Special Economic Zone increased from RMB61.5 billion in 1994 to RMB143.6 billion in 1999, an annual increase of 18.5%. The GDP per capita rose from RMB19.5 thousand to RMB35.9 thousand. The per capita disposable income of residents increased from RMB10.9 thousand to RMB20.2 thousand. The total import and export volume of foreign trade increased from US$34.98 billion to US$50.43 billion, of which the total export volume increased from US$18.3 billion to US$28.2 billion. Fiscal revenue in the local budget risen from RMB7.44 billion to RMB18.48 billion.With the enhancement of economic strength, Shenzhen's contribution to the country is increasing with a cumulative central fiscal revenue of RMB102 billion over the past five years.[2]

At the same time, the development of Shanghai Pudong Special Economic Zone has made a significant contribution to the opening up of coastal and riverside areas on the basis of previous experience.As an important coastal city, Shanghai was not among

---

[1] *Selected Works of Jiang Zemin (Volume I)*, Beijing: People's Publishing House, 2006, p. 374.

[2] Ren Weidong, He Jinsong and Li Nanling, "Sailing and Navigating the Sea", *Guangming Daily*, Aug.28, 2000.

the first special economic zones, which made a pity for the central leaders. Deng Xiaoping also admitted this pity. During his visit to Shanghai in February 1991, he said on Pudong development: "The four special economic zones were determined in that year mainly because of geographical conditions...However, we did not take the intellectual advantages of Shanghai into account. If Shanghai had listed in special economic zones at that time, it would be totally different now. Although Shanghai is one of the fourteen coastal open cities, it is too ordinary".[1] In 1992, the State Council set up Pudong New Area in Shanghai, announced the establishment of a national development zone, and granted a series of new preferential policies to Pudong New Area after the 14th National Congress. Firstly, the approval authority for investment projects in Shanghai was expanded. The second is to authorize Shanghai the right to raise matching funds in five aspects. According to the goals and actual needs of Pudong's development and opening up, Shanghai has also formulated a master plan and a number of policies and measures so that the development and opening up of Pudong could be regulated and brought into a legal and standardized track. The reform and opening up of Pudong New Area have created breakthroughs under the leadership of the CPC Central Committee. GDP in Pudong increased from RMB6 billion in 1990 to RMB108.2 billion in 2001, with an average annual GDP growth rate of 19.6%. Its foreign trade exports rose from US$1.2 billion in 1993 to US$13.6 billion in 2002. Regarding actual utilization of foreign capital, there were only 37 foreign investment projects in Pudong before the central government announced the open of Pudong. By February 1995, 2,836 investment projects from 48 countries and regions had been approved, with a total investment of US$10.88 billion and a contractual investment of US$6.28 billion. By the 10th anniversary of its development and opening up, more than 6,000 foreign investment projects had been attracted with a total investment of nearly US$30 billion. Pudong became China's most attractive international financial and trade zone soon, providing a solid and powerful impetus for Shanghai's fast growth throughout the 1990s and making a new engine of economic growth in Shanghai and even the whole country.

Third, the capacity of foreign capital utilization has been further improved.

The active use of foreign capital is an important policy put forward by Deng Xiaoping to accelerate China's socialist modernization. The 14th National Congress

---

[1] Party Literature Research Center of the CPC Central Committee, *The Chronicle Biography of Deng Xiaoping 1975–1997(Part I)*, Beijing: Central Party Literature Publishing House, 2004, p. 1327.

put forward: "The fields of utilizing foreign capital should be expanded. A more flexible approach should be adopted to continue the improvement of the investment environment and provide more favorable conditions and adequate legal protection for foreign investment. Following the industrial policy, foreign investment should be actively attracted to invest mainly in infrastructure, basic industries and technological transformation of enterprises, capital-intensive and technology-intensive industries, and in finance, commerce, tourism, real estate and other fields as appropriate".[1] After 1992, since the labor-intensive coastal industries were saturated, foreign investment was attracted to capital-intensive, technology-intensive and cost-effective projects. The sources of foreign investment have also changed with more and larger enterprise groups and multinational companies from developed countries in Europe and the United States joining investment in China. At the end of 1995, 200 of the world's top 500 companies invested in China, targeting China's huge market where they can produce and sell products, which led to an increasingly competitive domestic market. Under such context, the requirement came that we should not only continue to use foreign capital and improve the level of foreign capital utilization but also take into account the protection of national industries when it came to the foreign capital. To adapt to the new changes,policies of utilizing foreign capital underwent great changes with insisting on exchanging technology with the market. The policies of utilizing foreign capital also shifted from preferential treatment to integration with the international community and improvement of the investment environment.

While actively utilizing foreign capital and the work of "bringing in" were fruitful, the government put forward the strategy "going global", encouraging Chinese enterprises to go abroad to make better use of both domestic and foreign markets and resources. On December 24, 1997, when meeting with representatives of the National Foreign Capital Work Conference, Jiang Zemin said, "We should not only actively attract foreign enterprises to invest and set up factories in China, but also guide and organize powerful domestic enterprises to going global to invest and set up factories abroad, making use of local markets and resources… 'bringing in' and 'going global' are two closely related and mutually reinforcing aspects of our basic national policy of opening to the outside world".[2] Since the 1990s, Chinese enterprises actively carried out transnational operations, achieving remarkable results of the "going global"

---

1 *Selected Works of Jiang Zemin (Volume I)*, Beijing: People's Publishing House, 2006, p. 230.

2 *Selected Works of Jiang Zemin (Volume II)*, Beijing: People's Publishing House, 2006, p. 92.

strategy. The combination of "bringing in" and "going global" strategies played an important role in promoting the development of China's export-oriented economy.

Fourth, the system of opening to the outside world will be further integrated.

With the rising position in international trade of China, the government demanded to resume its legal seat in GATT in 1982 to further strengthen its international trade exchanges and promote economic internationalization. By the 1990s, negotiations entered an essential stage. To meet the requirements of GATT, China actively pushed forward the reform of its opening-up system.

With regard to the reform of the foreign trade system, the State Council issued the "Decision on Further Deepening the Reform of the Foreign Trade System"on January 11, 1994, confirming that the objectives of the reform of China's foreign trade system were to unify policies, liberalize management, compete on an equal footing, assume sole responsibility for its profits and losses, integrate industry and trade, implement the agency system and establish an operating mechanism adapted to the prevailing rules of the international economy. Therefore, the following reforms in the foreign trade system were carried out. Firstly, the guiding plan for the total import and export volume, export collection and import use of foreign exchange were adopted while the mandatory plan for foreign trade was canceled. Secondly, the measures for the administration of export quotas were further improved to control the commodities to be managed and relax the commodities needing no control. Thirdly, measures for the administration of export licenses were further enhanced.Fourthly, adjustment of the tariff rate structure continued to reduce the overall tariff level. Fifthly, import and export management rights were granted to qualified production enterprises, commercial enterprises, material enterprises, and scientific research institutes to change the state of lagging behind in the transformation of the management mechanism of foreign trade enterprises. The sixth was encouragement and acceleration of the development of overseas investment enterprises. Lastly, sound foreign trade laws were established in combination with international practices and international quality certification standards were actively promoted to speed up the integration of foreign trade systems with the international community. On May 16, 1994, the Foreign Trade Law was promulgated and implemented. These measures enabled China to improve its openness. At the same time, foreign trade enterprises were encouraged to take a big step towards a new foreign trade system that conforms to China's national conditions and international practices.

As for the foreign exchange management system, the renminbi exchange rates has been merged into a single managed floating exchange rate system based on the supply and demand of the foreign exchange market since January 1, 1994. The exchange rate of renminbi had new features in the new foreign exchange management system. Firstly, the renminbi exchange rate is no longer directly designated and announced by the official administrative authorities, but determined and adjusted by the designated foreign exchange banks themselves. Secondly, the exchange rate set by designated banks is based on market supply and demand. Thirdly, the exchange rate formed on the basis of market supply and demand is unified. In this system, the following reforms have been adopted: First of all, foreign exchange retention and surrender have been abolished, and the bank settlement system has been implemented.The second is to implement a bank remittance system, thus realizing free convertibility of renminbi under the current account. The third is to establish a unified and standardized inter-bank foreign exchange trading market to replace the original decentralized foreign exchange swap centers set up by administrative divisions. The fourth is to prohibit foreign currency pricing, settlement, and circulation in China. The last is to carry out macro-control over foreign exchange and international payments in economic and legal ways instead of the mandatory plan of foreign exchange receipts and payments. At the same time, to realize smooth and fast renminbi current account reform, the People's Bank of China announced a series of foreign exchange system reform measures in 1996, including the following contents.The People's Bank of China promulgated the "Regulations of the People's Republic of China on Foreign Exchange Control" on January 29, announcing the removal of exchange restrictions on non-trade and non-business transactions under certain current accounts from April 1. On May 13, the Administration of Foreign Exchange issued "Measures for Domestic Residents to Exchange Foreign Exchange for Private Purposes" to eliminate the exchange restrictions on the private foreign exchange. On June 26, the People's Bank of China issued "Regulations on Foreign Exchange Settlement, Sale and Payment" to incorporate foreign-invested enterprises into the bank's foreign exchange settlement and remittance system, and announced that the remaining few exchange restrictions and relevant laws and regulations would be abolished. On December 1, the Chinese government announced the realization of the free exchange of renminbi under the current account ahead of schedule. China had allowed some export enterprises and foreign-funded enterprises to retain 15% of their foreign exchange earnings since October 15, 1997.

The transformation of the foreign trade system from centralized and unified management to the expansion of local autonomy and enterprise autonomy, and of the exchange rate system from a fixed exchange rate system with overvalued renminbi exchange rate to a two-tier exchange rate system and then a single floating exchange rate system, is in line with the deepening of the country's opening to the outside world and the changes of its opening-up strategy. The management approach has also gradually changed from the traditional planning method to the marketing, which has dramatically improved the economic environment outside China and played an important role in attracting foreign investment and developing an export-oriented economy, thus pushing China's foreign economic system into line with international standards and accelerating China's economic internationalization.

From the regional expansion of opening up to the reform of the external system, China successfully promoted the great development of its opening up in the 1990s. With the establishment of the socialist economic system, the improvement of the opening up led to a more close connection between China's economy and the larger. The opening up also played a more and more important role in driving the development of China's economy as well as the sound development of China's economic internationalization.

In short, China took a series of reform measures in the 1990s with the goal of establishing a socialist market economic system. Both the reform of state-owned enterprises and the adjustment of its opening-up strategy were aimed at marketization, laying a foundation for the improvement of Chinese enterprises' international competitiveness and the connection of China's market and trade rules with international standards, thus promoting the internationalization of China's economy.

3.2.3 Towards the new century: achievements of economic internationalization in the 1990s

The international environment and situation were favorable for China in the early days of reform and opening up when China's economy was not significantly affected by the outside world because the level of opening to the outside world and the degree of economic internationalization were not high at that time. However, with the deepening of China's opening to the outside world and the acceleration of economic globalization, China began to face some problems brought about by opening up when we went deep into the world economic system and benefited from opening up.The global environment in the 1990s was unstable, and the external conditions for China's development were not favorable. The changes in the world's political and economic pattern caused by the collapse of the Soviet Union in 1991 and the impact of the Asian financial crisis on East Asian emerging economies in 1997 taught China a lesson in the internationalization of its economy. Luckily, leaders of the Party and government followed the main themes of "peace and development" with their great perception. Seizing the opportunity of globalization and calming domestic disputes, they persisted in reform and opening up to develop the country, thus ushering in a new round of economic growth in China in the 1990s. The opening to the outside world and economic internationalization of China made great progress during that period. The internationalization of the economy was not only the reason for the progress but also a result of it. That is to say, on the one hand, it was because of the constant reform of the economic system and the promotion of economic internationalization that China's economy achieved incredible results in the 1990s. On the other hand, rapid economic development became one of the driving forces for us to continuously promote economic internationalization.

On the whole, the Communist Party of China handed over a satisfactory answer to history in the last decade of the 20th century. Today, the following achievements made at that time are still praise worthy when we look back on them.

(1) *The economy is growing rapidly*

The speed of China's economic development is worthy of affirmation throughout the 1990s. Only in 1990 and 1991, when the international situation was unstable and domestic disputes led to the obstruction of reform and opening up, certain declines happened in economic growth. China's economic growth rate reached 14.2% in 1992 by continuing the reform and opening up and implementing the reform of the socialist market economic system with disputes inside China being eliminated, which showed the profound impact of economic internationalization on China's economy. From 1992 to 2000, China's GDP grew at an average annual rate of 10.4%, faster than that of 3% in the world economy in the same period, becoming one of the fastest growing countries in the world.Per capita GDP increased from RMB2,334 in 1992 to quadrupled RMB8,717 in 2001, realizing the historic leaps from living in poverty to having access to basic material needs, and then to moderate prosperity.

From Figure 3–3, we can also see that although GDP has maintained a high growth rate, there are fluctuations. In 1992, after Deng Xiaoping's south tour talks, a round of rapid growth was set off, with double-digit growth of 13.9% and 13% respectively in 1993 and 1994. This economic prosperity was mainly brought about by investment in industrial equipment and real estate, which grew by about 44% in 1992 and 62% in 1993.The sharp increase in the use of resources also led to a rapid increase in prices, with the retail price index rising 21.7% in 1994 and the consumer price rising 24.1%. Such high-speed growth led to high inflation. Therefore, the government immediately tightened monetary policy and restricted banks' large-scale loans. At the end of 1996, China's economy completed a "soft landing" with GDP growth dropping to 10%, commodity retail price index to 6.1% and consumer price index to 8.3%.In November 1997, China entered the deflation stage as inflation broke the baseline. Retail prices of commodities fell by about 2.6% in 1998 and 3% in 1999. At the same time, the Asian financial crisis from 1997 to 1998 led to unfavorable exports and insufficient consumption, which also contributed to economic fluctuations. Affected by these factors, China's GDP growth continued to decline, with 7.8% and 7.6% in 1998 and 1999 respectively. However, under the correct guidance of the Party and the government, the pressure was insisted on achieving economic recovery. Also, GDP growth reached 8.4% in 2000 and began to recover.

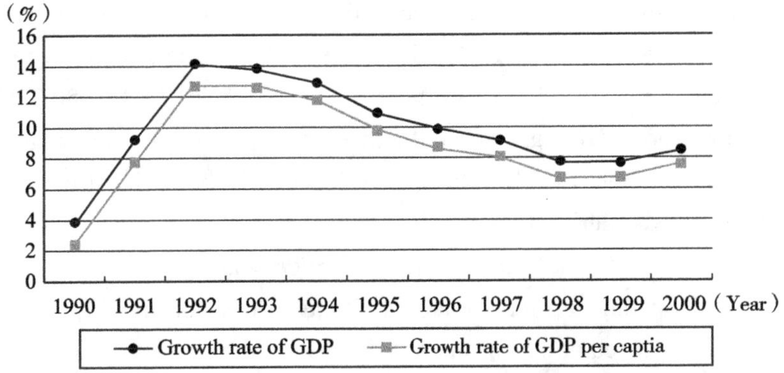

Figure 3–3 Changes in China's GDP and per capita GDP

Source: National Bureau of Statistics.

Let's look back on China's economic growth since the reform and opening up in 1978. As shown in Figure 3–4, we can see that China's economy has not been out of the cycle of "thrive when relaxed but stagnate when controlled". GDP growth is mainly driven by investment, and thus once the investment is curbed, it will decline rapidly. Since the second half of the 1990s, it gradually tended to be stable, which also shows that China's economy is moving towards a benign growth track.

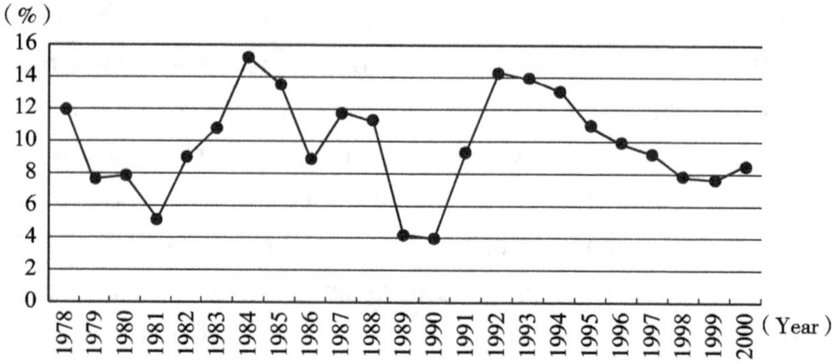

Figure 3–4 China's GDP growth rate

Source: World Bank Database, http: / /data. worldbank. org. cn /.

(2) *Economic restructuring has achieved remarkable results*

In the 1990s, with the continuous advancement of economic internationalization, important steps were taken in China's strategic adjustment of economic structure. The industrial structure had been continuously improved, realizing a more coordinated structure of the three industries and improved quality and efficiency of economic growth. The proportion of the added value of the three industries in GDP was adjusted from 21.8: 43.4: 34.8 in 1992 to 14.4: 45.1: 40.5 in 2001. The structure of employees in the three industries was adjusted from 58.5: 21.7: 19.8 in 1992 to 50:22.3: 22.7 in 2001. The proportion of GDP growth in the three industries is also constantly changing, from 1.2: 9.2: 3.8 in 1992 to 0.4: 3.9: 4 in 2001.[1]China's industrial structure had been continuously improved during this decade.

(3) *The growth and structural changes in foreign trade*

Reform and opening up have enabled China to develop quickly from a closed economy to a semi-closed and semi-open economy. With the formation of an all-round opening up pattern in the 1990s, China has become the most open market and economy among all emerging economies.At the same time of promoting the rapid development of economic internationalization, important achievements were made in its opening up to the outside world.

Speaking of the foreign trade, both rapid progress and breakthroughs were achieved on the original basis.

The first was the increase in trade volume.As could be seen from Table 3–2, the total import and export volume increased nearly threefold from US$84.94 billion in

---

[1] Xiao Guoliang and Sui Fuming eds., *Economic History of the People's Republic of China 1949–2010*, Beijing: Peking University Press, 2011,pp. 249-274.

1992 to US$249.20 billion in 2000.Total trade volume accounted for less than 1% of the world's in 1978 but up to nearly 5% in 2001. Moreover, its position in global trade rose from the 32nd at the beginning of opening up to the 6th in 2001. Furthermore, except for 1993, China's foreign trade had shown a trade surplus since 1992, which changed the situation of China's insufficient foreign exchange earning capacity and long-term deficit in foreign trade revenue and expenditure.

Table 3-2 The proportion and ranking of China's exports in the world

Year	World import and export volume (US$ billion)	China's total exports (US$ billion)	Share in the world (%)	China's rank in the world
1978	1,300.1	9.75	0.75	32
1989	3,036.1	52.54	1.73	14
1991	3,530.0	71.84	2.04	13
1992	3,700.0	84.94	2.30	11
1997	5,455.0	182.79	3.35	10
1998	5,405.0	183.76	3.40	9
2000	6,358.0	249.20	3.92	7
2001	6,162.4	288.10	4.68	6

Source: China Customs Statistics and WTO Website.

The second was the change in the mode of import and export trade. Processing trade accounts for the major proportion of China's foreign trade, which consisted of processing with imported materials and processing with supplied materials from customers. During the early days of reform and opening up, the development of processing trade had already begun to take shape.As shown in Table 3-3,China's total foreign processing trade was US$1.666 billion in 1980, accounting for 4.4% of the total foreign trade in that year. In 1988, the total processing trade rose to US$28.851 billion, of which the processing trade accounted for 28.1%. During this period, the proportion of processing with supplied materials was still higher than that of imported processing, although it was declining. The processing trade had further developed on the whole in the 1990s. In 1990, the proportion of processing with imported materials in the total volume of import and export was still only 38.3%, but more than half after 1996. Although it declined in the 21st century, it still accounted for a large proportion. It could be concluded that processing trade was the primary way of China's foreign trade in the 1990s. At the same time, for the change in quantity, the structure of processing trade transformed into a larger proportion of processing with imported materials. The positions of processing with supplied materials and processing with imported materials were reversed since 1989. Processing with imported materials became the main part of processing trade throughout the 1990s, and by the end of the 20th century, its proportion had reached 70% in processing trade.

Table 3-3 Changes in China's processing trade (1980–2001)

Year	Import and export volume (US$ billion)	Processing trade (US$ billion)	Processing with supplied materials		Processing with imported materials		Proportion processing trade to the import and export (%)
			Sum (US$ billion)	Proportion to the processing trade (%)	Sum (US$ billion)	Proportion to the processing trade (%)	
1980	37.800	1.666	1.330	79.8	0.336	20.2	4.4
1988	102.780	28.851	16.158	56.0	12.693	44.0	28.1
1989	111.680	36.161	16.912	46.8	19.249	53.2	32.4
1990	115.440	44.191	19.178	43.4	25.013	56.6	38.3
1991	135.630	57.487	23.859	41.5	33.628	58.5	42.4
1992	165.530	71.156	27.943	39.3	43.213	60.7	43.0
1993	195.700	80.617	28.929	35.9	51.688	64.1	41.2
1994	236.620	104.546	33.274	31.8	71.272	68.2	44.2
1995	280.860	132.080	26.895	27.9	95.185	72.1	47.0
1996	289.910	146.500	42.000	28.7	104.500	71.3	50.5
1997	325.010	169.810	50.200	29.6	119.500	70.4	52.2
1998	323.930	173.040	50.600	29.2	122.440	70.8	53.4
1999	360.630	184.460	59.330	32.2	125.130	67.8	51.1
2000	474.320	230.300	69.090	30.0	161.210	70.0	48.6

Source: Jin Zhesong and Li Jun,*China's foreign trade growth and economic development-review and prospect of the 30th anniversary of reform and opening up*, China Renmin University Press, 2008, p. 27.

Finally, the types of commodities exported changed. Since the reform and opening up, most of the foreign investment attracted by China concentrated in manufacturing with different distributions in different periods.In the 1980s, having seized the historic opportunity of the transfer of international labor-intensive industry represented by light textile products to developing countries, China focused on the processing trade of light textile products and cultivating a large number of export-oriented industries such as textiles, clothing, footwear, toys, bags, plastic products and so on. The total import and export volume reached US$711.5 billion from 1980 to

1989, which was 48 times as the total import and export volume from the founding of New China to the reform and opening up. For export, China ranked the 14th in 1989 among countries from the 26th in 1980. In the 1980s, the light textile industry added 61% exports and also attracted a large amount of foreign investment, especially from Japan. Until 1997, Japan's major investment projects in China shifted from the textile industry to electrical appliances, machinery, and other fields.

Similar to what happened in the 1980s, China seized the opportunity of international industrial restructuring in the 1990s, greatly promoting the development and export expansion of the mechanical and electrical industry. As shown in Table 3–4, about 50% of the increased import and export volume in the 1990s was realized by mechanical and electrical products. Such change in the structure of import and export also proves that the internal structure of China's manufacturing industry in the 1990s has been adjusted and continuously improved, which strengthens the competitiveness of China's exports in the world.

Table 3–4 Increased exports of China in the 1990s Unit: US$ billion

Item	National exports	Export of mechanical and electrical products
Year 1990	62.09	11.09
Year 1999	194.93	76.96
Increased from 1990 to 1999	132.84	65.87
The proportion of new exports of mechanical and electrical products (%)	—	49.6

Source: Ministry of Commerce of China: Statistical compilation of import and export of mechanical and electrical products from 1980 to 2002.

(4) *The introduction of foreign capital was further developed*

Since the reform and opening up, the economic development had largely depended on the introduction of foreign capital.After Deng Xiaoping's talks in the south, China had a more active and open attitude towards foreign investment, and foreign investment utilization had been continuously improved.In November 1993, the Third Plenary Session of the 14th Central Committee adopted the "Decision on Several Issues Concerning the Establishment of a Socialist Market Economy System", proposing to improve the investment environment and management for larger scales of investment and scopes of capital introduction, further open up the domestic market for foreign-invested enterprises with national treatments as much as possible, and improve the management of foreign-invested enterprises based on laws for giving full play to the advantages of China's labor resources and the size of the domestic market to attract foreign capital and technology and promote economic and trade development.

From Figure 3–5, we can see that although China's utilization of foreign capital has been increasing since the reform and opening up, the actual rapid growth took place in the 1990s, especially after 1992. During this period, China's foreign capital utilization was at a stage with rapid growth, ranking first among developing countries according to the absorption of foreign capital. More than 400 of the world's top 500 enterprises invested in China. By the end of 2001, more than 390,000 foreign-invested enterprises had been allowed to set up in China, while 6,310 enterprises of various kinds had been set up overseas.

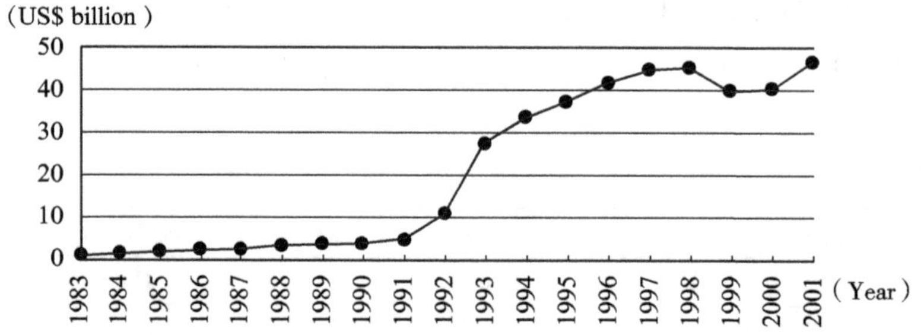

Figure 3–5 Actual utilization of foreign direct investment in China

Source: National Bureau of Statistics.

The introduction of a large amount of foreign capital greatly contributed to China's economic and social development during this period with lots of benefits.

On the one hand, the improvement of foreign capital utilization strengthened the overall strength of foreign trade.In the 1980s, we mainly adopted cooperative management and compensation trade in the using of foreign capital because of our insufficient experience in using foreign capital and unfamiliarity of foreign investors with China's investment environment. During the five years from 1979 to 1983, the amount of contracted foreign direct investment was US$687.39 million, of which 47% were from Sino-foreign cooperative enterprises, 12% were compensation trade, and only 5.9% were wholly foreign-owned enterprises. After entering the 1990s, wholly foreign-owned enterprises began to develop rapidly. Of the foreign-invested enterprises set up in 1997, 9046 were Sino-foreign joint ventures while 9604 were wholly foreign-owned enterprises. Wholly foreign-owned enterprises surpassed joint ventures for the first time, making the foreign direct investment the main way to utilize foreign capital. A large number of multinational companies flooded into China, making China quickly be a part the global division of labor system with the advantages of a large market and labor resources, thus promoting the rapid growth of foreign trade and enhancing its competitiveness in the international market.At the same time, as foreign-invested enterprises brought about technology diffusion effect and technology spillover, the overall industrial technology in China had been improved, and its export mode and structure had been further optimized when the investment priority of large multinational companies gradually shifted to high-tech fields.In addition, the advanced operative modes of multinational corporations also set good examples for competition as they strengthened the competition mechanism and stimulated the awareness of competition among domestic enterprises, greatly shortening the process of domestic enterprises participating in the international market competition and further enhancing China's overall foreign trade strength.

On the other hand, it greatly promoted the growth of China's foreign trade. With the establishment and improvement of the socialist market mechanism, state-owned enterprises no longer dominated foreign trade of China as more and more individuals and private enterprises were participating in international trade. Foreign-funded enterprises, collective enterprises, and private enterprises became the main forces of import and export trade, especially foreign direct investment enterprises, which gradually developed into the leading force of China's foreign trade. The import and export volume of foreign direct investment enterprises increased from US$43.75 billion in 1992 to US$25.91 billion in 2001 with a respective increase of the proportion to the total import and export volume in China from 26.4% to 50.8%. What's more, the contribution of foreign direct investment enterprises in export to China's exports reached 64%.[1]As shown in Table 3–5, foreign-invested enterprises accounted for just over a quarter of China's processing trade in 1990, but they accounted for 72% in 2000. As mentioned before, processing trade was the major part of China's foreign trade, which suggested that foreign-invested enterprises played a huge role in China's foreign trade.

[1] Research Institute of Ministry of Commerce, *China's 30 years of Foreign Trade*, Beijing: China Commerce and Trade Press, 2008, p. 146.

Table 3–5 The import and export volume and proportion of processing trade of foreign–invested enterprises in the 1990s

Year	Processing trade import and export (US$ billion)	Proportion of processing trade volume of foreign-invested in the whole country (%)
1990	12.70	28.7
1995	79.12	59.9
2000	165.77	72.0

Source: Ministry of Commerce Research Institute, *China's Foreign Trade for 30 Years*, China Business Press, 2008, p.160.

(5) *Successfully resisted the asian financial Crisis*

When it comes to China's economic internationalization in the 1990s, we have to mention the Asian financial crisis in 1997, which was a severe challenge to China's economic internationalization at that time. The successful settlement provided valuable experience for financial reform and risk prevention in the process of economic internationalization.

The Asian financial crisis is also called the Asian financial storm. At the beginning of 1997, international speculators led by George Soros with his "hedge fund" speculated wildly in Asian stock and foreign exchange markets through various channels. In order to avoid the impact of international hot money, some Asian emerging economies led by Thailand, took the initiative to lower their currencies against the US dollar, resulting in a series of chain reactions. On July 2, the Thai Ministry of Finance and the Central Bank announced the floating exchange rate system for the Thai baht, abandoning the exchange rate system linking Thai baht with the US dollar, which had been used for 14 years since 1984. The Thai baht dropped by 20% on that day, thus triggering a financial storm lasted for two years in which the entire East and Southeast Asia except China's mainland were involved. Affected by the crisis, currencies like the Philippine peso, Indonesian shield, Malaysian ringgit and so on depreciated significantly in succession. The Korean won devalued in October while the Japanese yen in November. In 1998, the Asian financial crisis continued to spread and worsen, affecting Russia, Latin America and other countries and regions like dominoes, causing great fluctuations in the global foreign exchange market and stock market and resulting in continued turbulence in the international financial market and a severe impact on the world economy.

Due to China's prudent fiscal policy and a series of measures taken to prevent financial risks in previous years, the capital account had not been opened, and the flow of international funds was strictly controlled, so the direct impact of the crisis on China was limited.

Before the outbreak of the financial crisis, China maintained the stability of the finance with a series of macro-control measures such as deepening financial reform, stabilizing the renminbi exchange rate, strengthening the supervision of financial institutions and securities markets, and prudently opening up the financial market. The national financial work conference held in January 1997 further proposed to effectively rectify the financial order to prevent and defuse financial risks by banning illegally established financial institutions and preventing non-financial enterprises from engaging in financial business. In March, Zhu Rongji proposed at the First Session of the Ninth National People's Congress that 1997 should be the "Year of Preventing Financial Risks". Then relevant departments issued a series of documents to strengthen the supervision of the stock and securities markets, all of which were helpful for China to cope with the impact of the Asian financial crisis.[1]

However, the economic depression in other countries indirectly affected China because of the acceleration of China's economic internationalization and the increasingly close ties with these countries, especially Southeast Asian countries who were important trading partners of China. Therefore, the financial crisis still had an inevitable impact on China.

On the one hand, competitiveness in export was weakened and the export slowed down. Imports from Southeast Asian countries with devalued currencies accounted for a high proportion of China's foreign trade exports. To some extent,the devaluation of their currencies stimulated exports and reduced imports. Besides, the slowdown in economic growth reduced their import demand for China.The data showed that in the first quarter of 1998, China's total import and export volume increased by 8.3% with a drop in the growth rate of 3.4%, of which exports increased by 12.8% with a drop of 12.9%. It could be seen that China's total import and export volume dropped rapidly due to the crisis. On the other hand, the inflow of foreign capital into China decreased. Southeast Asian countries were the main regions for China to absorb foreign investment, accounting for more than 80% of China's total foreign investment. The financial crisis greatly weakened the economic strength of Southeast Asian countries

---

[1] Cao Pu, *Contemporary Chinese Reform and Opening Up, Part II*, Beijing: People's Publishing House, 2016, p. 504.

and reduced their corresponding foreign investment. At the same time, the devaluation of Southeast Asian countries' currencies was conducive to their absorption of long-term international investment. They also successively adopted new policies for absorbing foreign investment, resulting in an increasing competition for China. China utilized US$64.4 billion of foreign capital in 1997 with an increase of 17.5% over 1996, which included US$45.3 billion of foreign direct investment, up by 8.5% but down by 2.5% in the growth rate than that of 1996. In that year, the utilization of contracted foreign capital was US$61.7 billion, down by 24.2% from 1996, which directly affected the growth of China's actual utilization of foreign capital in 1998.[1] The corresponding data are shown in the previous tables or figures.

Affected by the crisis, the development of the economy in China slowed down with deflation appearing and enormous pressure on the depreciation of the renminbi. After calmly analyzed the situation, the CPC Central Committee took a series of targeted measures to effectively deal with the financial crisis.

In July 1998, considering the sharp drop in the growth of foreign trade exports and the lack of domestic demand for economic development, the Central Committee of the CPC decided to implement an active fiscal policy and a prudent monetary policy by issuing long-term construction bonds to commercial banks from the central government, and then increasing investment to infrastructure construction. At the same time, the government also took some measures like export tax rebates and combating smuggling to boost exports as they devoted to improving people's lives by increasing the income of middle and low-income earners. From 1998 to 2000, RMB365 billion of long-term construction bonds were issued in public for three consecutive years and successfully drove nearly RMB750 billion of bank loans, which increased investment in fixed assets, greatly accelerated the pace of infrastructure construction, driving the development of a number of related industries and the increase of employment, and effectively boosted domestic demand. By 2000, the national economy had seen a vital turnaround, and economic development began to recover steadily.

Facing the high pressure of renminbi devaluation, the Chinese government made a solemn promise to the world that renminbi would not depreciate after weighing the pros and cons and considering carefully.In an interview with *Japan's Economic News* at the end of November 1997, Zhu Rongji said that

[1] Feng Wenli, *From the Asian Financial Crisis to International Financial Crisis*, Beijing: Metallurgical Industry Press, 2009, p. 7.

China would never devalue the renminbi to promote the export of its products.This was the first time the Chinese government had publicly announced that the renminbi exchange rate would not depreciate. In December 1997, at the informal meeting of the China-ASEAN summit in Kuala Lumpur, Jiang Zemin solemnly announced once again that China would maintain the stability of the renminbi exchange rate.In February 1998, at the Second Plenary Session of the 15th CPC Central Committee, Jiang Zemin pointed out that maintaining the stability of the renminbi exchange rate was not only related to the confidence of the people and the stability of our economy and society, but also a strong support for Hong Kong's financial stability as well as Asia and the world economy.In March 1998, at a press conference held at the first session of the Ninth National People's Congress, Zhu Rongji listed "No Depreciating of renminbi" as an important part of the "One Assurance" task of China. Not making things worse and taking advantage of the danger of others, the government insisted on not devaluing the renminbi and offered more than US$4 billion in financial aid to Thailand and other countries, voluntarily making self-sacrifice to share tremendous difficulties and risks, which made significant contributions to easing the pressure on Asian countries, stabilizing the Asian financial order, and promoting the recovery and development of Southeast Asian economies. In return, the government won the praise of being a major responsible power.[1]

The CPC Central Committee began to attach importance to the prevention of international financial risks because of the impact from the Asian financial crisis. In November 1997, the CPC Central Committee and the State Council convened a national financial work conference to make comprehensive arrangements to prevent and defuse financial risks. In November 1998, they decided to reform the People's Bank of China by abolishing provincial branches and setting up nine branches across provinces to strengthen the management of it. Those measures laid a foundation for the internationalization of China's financial management and risk monitoring.

Looking at the last ten years of the 20th century, we cherish more as the development achievements nowadays have not come easily. At the most challenging time of international socialism, we did not deviate from our original intention and went astray. We did not lose ourselves and took a detour although we achieved rapid economic development.We are so glad that our party and government have chosen a correct path to seek truth from facts by adhering to the center of economic

[1] *Cao Pu, Contemporary Chinese Reform and Opening Up (Part II)*, People's Publishing House, 2016, p. 506.

construction, reform and opening up and the four basic principles. Finally, we take the road of economic internationalization by seizing opportunities, closely linking China's national conditions with world trends and following the historical trend of globalization. As we have carried out a number of effective reforms and achieved initial success in economic internationalization, giving a satisfactory answer to the people all over the country, China could greet the new millennium with a new face and enter the new century.

3.3 The internationalization of China's economy at the beginning of the 21st century

If the internationalization of China's economy was at the initial stage in the 1980s, and at the development stage in the 1990s, then in the first eight years of the 21st century it was at the rapid development stage.

Since the new century, we have continued to stride forward with the momentum brought about by the high-speed development in the 1990s. Although increasingly prominent issues in domestic development such as resource and environmental constraints and unfair income distribution during this period, China's economic internationalization has made rapid progress. After joining the WTO in particular, China's economy as a whole has benefited from globalization.

On November 15, 1999, China and the United States signed a bilateral agreement on China's accession to the WTO in Beijing, finally removing the biggest obstacle to China's accession to the WTO before the new millennium. On December 11, 2001, China officially became a member of the WTO, ending its 15-year long journey to WTO. At that time, only a few people could realize the meaning of "joining the WTO" and how much it would contribute to China's economic development and internationalization in the new century.

Today, to review the internationalization of China's economy from 2000 to 2008, we must look back at the history of China's accession to the WTO.

3.3.1 A 15-year long journey of entering the WTO: a critical turning point of China's economic internationalization

The World Trade Organization (WTO for short) is an international organization dedicated to monitoring and liberalizing the world trade, whose predecessor was the

General Agreement on Tariffs and Trade (GATT), established in 1947 to prevent the recurrence of trade wars between countries that happened before the Second World War, to eliminate differential treatment in international trade and to promote freedom of international trade.

According to the original idea, GATT was an interim agreement that would soon be replaced by the International Trade Organization (ITO), a specialized agency of the United Nations (UN). However, due to the differences in foreign economic policies of various countries and the legal difficulties encountered by most governments in ratifying such a wide-ranging and tightly organized international treaty, the *Charter of the International Trade Organization* was not passed by most national parliaments,including the US parliaments. Thus, the validity of GATT was extended again and again, and it was revised several times to adapt to the changing circumstances. Although GATT had played a vital role in international trade for a long time, its loose organization, a limitation outside organizations and institutions, was turning unsuitable to the increasingly complex world trade. Therefore, in the 1990s, it was imperative to establish a world trade organization. The European Community (EC) first proposed a "Multilateral Trade Organization" initiative in 1990 and was supported by the United States, Canada, and other countries. Later in 1993, the United States proposed to change the "Multilateral Trade Organization" to "World Trade Organization." In April of the following year, the participants in the Uruguay Round adopted *the Marrakesh Agreement for the Establishment of the World Trade Organization* in Morocco. On January 1, 1995, the World Trade Organization was formally established. Up to then, GATT had been "temporarily applied" for nearly half a century.

China is a founding member of GATT. However, after the founding of the People's Republic of China on October 1, 1949, the KMT authorities that had retreated to the Taiwan region announced its withdrawal from GATT in 1950, fearing that the new China led by the Communist Party of China would benefit from the GATT. Although its withdrawal was in accordance with established legal procedures at that time, the KMT authorities, in fact, had no right to represent China since October 1, 1949. Thus, the withdrawal is illegal and invalid.Therefore, decades later, China's re-entry into GATT is "resumption", that is, the resumption of its status as a founding member of GATT.

In 1965, the application of Taiwan, China, to send observers to attend the

Conference of Parties (COP) was accepted by GATT. However, after the lawful seat of the People's Republic of China in the United Nations was restored on the UN General Assembly(UNGA) on October 25, 1971, the 7th GATT COP, referring to the UN Resolution No. 2758 revoked the observer ship of Taiwan, China on November 16, 1971.

According to international practice, it should be natural for the People's Republic of China to resume the legal status of GATT at this time. However, China decided not to participate with two reasons: First, GATT was considered to be a rich-country club, which had less than half the membership of the United Nations at that time, most of which were developed countries.Second, GATT was engaged in a market economy, which meant capitalism to China at that time.

However, the situation had changed. After the reform and opening up in 1978 in particular, China's economy undergone tremendous changes, with increasingly more foreign economic and trade activities day by day, whose role in the national economy was getting continuously important. Besides, as many developing countries had participated in GATT, the Chinese government began to attach importance to it. At the same time, with the reform of the domestic economic system and the development of the market economy (then called commodity economy), China's foreign trade had initially become eligible to join the multilateral trading system. All the changes made China's economy more dependent on the degree of economic internationalization. Resuming GATT seat was an inevitable choice objectively, made mainly for the following reasons: First, it was conducive to China's foreign trade, which totaled about US$20.6 billion in 1978, and reached US$73.85 billion in 1986, of which the trade volume with GATT contracting states accounted for about 85%. The "resumption" helped China to benefit from the multilateral trading system with unconditional MFN treatment in a fair and stable foreign trade environment; Second, it would deepen China's economic system reform. In accordance with GATT requirements and rules after its "resumption," China had to reform its foreign trade system in terms of transparency and unification of foreign trade policies and regulations to compete internationally. Third, it was conducive to curbing other countries' trade protectionism. In 1984, China formally joined the *Multifibre Agreement*, with the garment export steadily developed and some textile trade disputes preferably settled. Knowing the different treatments between being a contracting state to the GATT and not, China was determined to "resume". Fourth, it was conducive to China's participation in international economic affairs and the formulation of trade rules. Only by resuming its status as a contracting party to GATT to acquire an active "voice" in international trade exchanges can China truly integrate into the gradually open family of global multilateral trading systems, participating in world economic affairs as a master rather than a bystander. Only by doing so can China's economy truly realize internationalization.

In January 1983, the State Council decided to apply for the restoration of China's status as a contracting party to GATT. After a period of preparation, China formally claimed the "resumption" on July 10, 1986, which marks the beginning of China's eight-year "resumption to the GATT" negotiations and seven-year "accession to the WTO" negotiations.

(1) *Journey of "resumption" and "entry into WTO"*

China's negotiations on "resumption" and "accession" can be roughly divided into three stages.

From July 10, 1986, to 1992 is the first stage when the "resumption" negotiations began. China's formal application submitted to GATT Director General Arthur Dunkel for "resumption" on July 11, 1986, marks the beginning of the nine-year-long "resumption" negotiations. Before 1989, due to China's domestic reform and opening up and good political relations with countries like the US, countries in Europe, and Japan at that time, the "resumption" negotiations were once very smooth. However, with the economic sanctions imposed on China by western countries led by the US, in which the temporary suspension of China's "resumption" was a major element, the results of previous negotiations were in danger for a time.

China's foreign trade system was reviewed in this stage. The contracting parties judged whether China's foreign trade system met the basic requirements of GATT, of which implementing a market system was a prerequisite for GATT to accept China. Shi Guangsheng, former minister of the State Foreign Trade and Economic Cooperation, wrote in his memory: "Under such circumstance at that time, although China's economic system reform was always developing towards marketization, the market economy was forbidden in China until 1991. We could not describe China's economic system clearly, nor could the contracting parties understand. It was not until the beginning of 1992 that the core issues of the first stage of negotiations were solved when Deng Xiaoping suggested that a market economy, not equal to capitalism, could run within the socialist system. After that, in October, on the 14th Party Congress, a resolution was passed to establish a socialist market economy system".[1]

The second stage, from 1992 to January 1995, is the breakthrough stage of the "resumption of GATT" negotiations and the start-up stage of the "accession to WTO" negotiations. After Deng Xiaoping's South Talks and the 14th Party Congress held in 1992, China's reform and opening up entered a new stage, with the long-puzzling problem in China's "resumption" negotiations solved that what kind of economic system was China implementing. The "resumption" negotiations, which had stalled at one time, were restarted and entered the substantive phase. From March 1993 to July 1994, the GATT China Working Group held five consecutive meetings to substantively negotiate on the protocol to restore China's status as a contracting party. In November 1993, Jiang Zemin went to Seattle, the United States, to attend the first informal meeting of leaders of Asia-Pacific Economic Cooperation(APEC). During his meeting with then US President Clinton,Jiang Zemin expounded three principles for China to deal with the "resumption" issues:First, as an international organization, GATT would be incomplete without China;Second, China would participate as a developing country, undoubtedly; Third, China would participate with the balance of power and obligation. In order to show its sincerity to "rejoin the GATT", since the second half of 1994, the Chinese government has introduced a series of major reform measures in foreign trade, foreign exchange, and taxation, greatly reducing tariffs on nearly 3,000 types of imported goods.Subsequently, China took the initiative to propose a package to GATT, including tariff concessions, measures to reduce non-trade tariffs and opening up trade in services, and launched the "sprint" negotiations of over 50 days with major contracting parties, aiming to "rejoin the GATT" at the end of that year.[2] However, since the only thing that could pressure on China then in the US trade policy towards China was the resumption negotiations, the United States no longer emphasized tariff concessions and reductions in non-tariff measures but stressed that China could not be accepted as a developing country.Besides, as the major western developed countries realized that China's "resumption" might impact themselves, the contracting parties overcharged China.This unreasonable demand, ignoring China's economic development stage and requiring China to assume the obligations of developed countries in GATT, violated China's basic principle of "resumption." On November 28,

[1] Ouyang Song and GaoYongzhong ed., *Oral History of Reform and Opening Up*, Beijing: China Renmin University Press, 2013, p.502.

[2] Cao Pu, *Contemporary Chinese Reform and Opening Up, Part II*, Beijing: People's Publishing House, 2016, p.523.

1994, the "re-entry" talks broke down, failing to reach an agreement, and China failed to "break a blockade" as expected.

The third stage is the negotiation stage of "joining the WTO", from January 1995 to December 11, 2001. As the talks on "resumption" failed in 1994, and the WTO was formally established on January 1, 1995, China's "resumption" began to shift.On June 3, 1995, China became an observer of the WTO. On July 11, 1995, China formally applied to join the WTO.Since then, China's negotiations changed from "rejoining the GATT" into "accession to WTO". Compared with the resumption of GATT as a contracting state, accession to the WTO was further complicated. Moreover,the membership of the WTO was enriched, greatly increasing its management scope. All these enhanced the complexity and difficulty of China's entry into the WTO. In November 1996, Jiang Zemin met with the re-elected US President Clinton at the APEC summit held in the Philippines, and both sides decided to speed up the negotiation of China's accession to the WTO. From the end of 1996 to the beginning of 1997, Canada, Japan, the EU, and the US had successively held bilateral consultations with China's negotiating delegation in Beijing on China's accession to the WTO. Among them, the China-US and China-EU negotiations were the most difficult. However, with the agreement between China and the US finally reached in November 1999, the biggest obstacle to China's "entry into the WTO" was removed. After the bilateral negotiations were concluded, the WTO held its 18th China Working Group Meeting on September 17, 2001, on which it adopted all the legal documents for China's accession, marking the end of all negotiations on China's accession to the WTO, which had lasted for 15 years. On November 10, 2001, at 18: 35 local time, the decision for China to join the WTO was reviewed and adopted consensually on the 4th Ministerial Conference of the WTO held in Doha, Qatar. On November 11, 2001, the representatives of the Chinese government signed the protocol and submitted China's instruments of ratification on China's accession to the WTO to the WTO Secretariat. Thirty days later, on December 11, 2001, China officially became a member of the WTO.

(2) *The China-US and China-EU negotiations*

In particular, according to the requirements of WTO, China must first complete bilateral negotiations with trade interested parties if wanted to join the WTO. For this reason, China conducted bilateral negotiations with 37 WTO members. The first agreement was reached with Hungary in May 1997 and the last with Mexico on September 13, 2001. However, during the process, the most difficult negotiations, as mentioned earlier, were those with the US and the EU, with 25 rounds of China-US negotiations and 15 rounds of China-EU negotiations, that featured wide scope, rich content, and long-lasting hardship. Shi Guangsheng said in his recollection: "The United States was negotiating as a 'leader', representing all the WTO members. China was charged the highest price in the toughest negotiation with the US, which was full of political interference and dramatic. While the 'leadership' of the US was recognized by many members, waiting to enjoy the negotiation outcomes between the US and China ... With the same charge as that of the US, however, the EU insisted on not eating 'leftovers' from the United States, making the negotiations the same tough and dramatic".[1]

As the most powerful developed country in the world, the United States inevitably became China's main opponent in negotiating at the very beginning. At first, in the 1980s, when China-US relations were in a "honeymoon period" and America's main rival in the world then, the Soviet Union, was not yet disintegrated, together with China's reform and opening up since 1978 which made western countries, led by the US look forward to China's reform prospects, countries in GATT wanted to adopt China despite that China had failed to meet GATT's requirements in many respects. The China-US "resumption" negotiations thus went smoothly then, and China was expected to "re-entry" at one time. However, with the influence of domestic political turmoil in China in 1989, western developed countries led by the US violently interfered in China's internal affairs and imposed economic sanctions on China, one of whose major contents was preventing China from "re-entry". China's working group was forced to suspend its work for one year and ten months. Finally, the "re-entry" talks resumed in the second half of 1991 with the efforts made by then Premier Li Peng, who had written to the heads of governments of all GATT contracting parties and by the Chinese government in international diplomacy. However, because the US overcharged China in the subsequent talks, no progress was made in the "resumption" negotiations to the end.

With the start of China's accession negotiations, the 10th round of bilateral talks between China and the US was held on February 12, 1996, on which China responded point by point to the 28 requirements listed in the *Informal Documentation on China's Accession to the WTO* (the so-called *Traffic Map*) submitted by the US on November

---

[1] Ouyang Song and Gao Yongzhong ed., *Oral History of Reform and Opening Up*, Beijing: China Renmin University Press, 2013, p.505.

28, 1995. From September 16 to 17, 1996, China and the US held the 11th round of consultations, when the US made strategic adjustments to China's accession to the WTO. From October 7 to 9, 1996, from the end of 1996 to the beginning of 1997, and from April 24 to 30, 1997, China and the US held the 12th, 13th and 14th rounds of consultations.[1]

Then US President Clinton visited China in June 1998, hoping to make significant diplomatic achievements during his term of office before stepping down, and wanted to make the agreement reached by China and the US on China's accession to the WTO an important outcome of his visit. For this reason, US Trade Representative Charlene Barshefsky came to China for talks twice with substantial progress made. The two sides could reach an agreement with further efforts, just waiting for Clinton's arrival in China. However, during Clinton's visit to China, there was a great deal of bickering in the United States. Many people in the US Congress blamed Clinton for his visiting China and the agreement signed as a gift to the Chinese. Influenced by US domestic politics, Clinton did not contribute to promoting negotiations after his visit. Besides, the conditions proposed by Barshefsky became increasingly stringent. As a result, the two sides still failed to reach an agreement.

On March 15, 1999, then Premier Zhu Rongji said at the Chinese and foreign press conference: "China has been negotiating for 'rejoining GATT' and 'accession into WTO' for 13 years, during which black hair has turned grey. So now it is time to conclude such negotiations. Now there are conditions and possibilities. First, WTO members have already known that without China, WTO would not be representative, neglecting the potentially largest market. Second, with the deepening of China's reform and opening up and the accumulation of experience, the regulatory capacity and affordability of foreign trade have been improved for the problems that may be brought about by China's accession to the WTO. Therefore, China is ready to make the biggest concession for joining the WTO".[2]

In April 1999, then Premier Zhu Rongji visited the United States and held talks with Clinton on China's accession to the WTO, with great concessions made and favorable conditions given by China. Meanwhile, the negotiations between trade representatives of China and the US were also in anxious advance around the clock in Washington. On April 10, the two sides reached the *China-US Agreement on*

---

[1] Zhou Hanmin ed., *China's Entry into WTO*, Shanghai: Wenhui Press, 2011, p.41.

[2] "Premier Zhu Rongji's Meeting with the Press at the Second Session of the 9th National Party Congress", *People's Daily*, Mar.16, 1999.

Agricultural Cooperation, an essential component of China's WTO accession package, and then issued the *China-US Joint Statement*. At this time, the two sides were close to reaching an agreement. However, as the US side misjudged its domestic political situation, thinking that its Congress could not approve, together with its hope to force China to make more concessions, the opportunity to sign was missed. However, there was an overwhelming response in the US business community during Premier Zhu Rongji's visit to various parts of the United States, publicizing China's reform and opening up and China's rapid economic development, especially after the United States unilaterally announced the so-called "*China-US Negotiation List*" (which was actually the charge list from the US to China)to eliminate its domestic opposition. Thinking this a perfect result of the negotiations, the US business community strongly supported it, and US domestic public opinion began to turn with Clinton severely criticized. At that time, the US attitude changed again. Hoping to reach an agreement with China, US negotiating delegation arrived in Beijing the next day after Chinese delegation's return and started negotiations on China's accession to the WTO with Chinese negotiating team led by Long Yongtu, China's chief negotiator. Focusing on market access, legal and procedural issues, this negotiation finally failed because the US side still insisted on high charges.

On May 8, 1999, the appalling bombing of Chinese embassy in Yugoslavia by NATO led by the US caused great indignation among our people and the people of the world, bringing China-US relations to the bottom, and the Central Committee decided to suspend China-US bilateral negotiations.More than a month later, the United States tried actively to restore its relations with China with a series of friendly actions. Clinton called then President Jiang Zemin many times, saying that the bombing was a mistake, apologizing to China and proposing to restart bilateral negotiations. Jiang Zemin said that in the current situation of China-US relations, it was inappropriate for China and the United States to talk about the WTO bilateral agreement until the bombing incident was properly resolved. This situation continued for several months.[1] Until September 11, when Jiang Zemin and Clinton met at the APEC summit in Auckland, New Zealand when the bombing incident had primarily been handled, and China-US relations had eased, the central government decided to resume negotiations on the condition that China must be granted unconditional most-favored-nation (MFN)

[1] Ouyang Song and GaoYongzhong ed., *Oral History of Reform and Opening Up*, Beijing: China Renmin University Press, 2013, p.512.

treatment, which was consented by then President Clinton. Both sides expressed that further efforts would be devoted to reaching an early agreement on China's accession to the WTO. At this point, the China-US "WTO accession" negotiations resumed, which had been suspended for four months.

On September 27, 1999, China and the United States resumed consultations, but the negotiation was not encouraging. On October 16, Clinton called Jiang Zemin to express his willingness to show the bottom line of US negotiations, in an effort to reach an agreement between the two countries before the WTO Ministerial Meeting to be held in Seattle on November 30. Clinton was very sorry that he had not signed on Zhu Rongji's visit to the US in April. For Clinton, he hoped that China's accession to the WTO would, of course, be in the interests of the United States at the first place.China's entry into the WTO would bring at least the following advantages for the United States: it was conducive to opening up Chinese market so as to expand its exports to China; to the standardization of China's economic activities so as to facilitate US companies to run business in China; and to promoting China's reform, which was in line with the US strategic vision... However, more still he expected for more personal political capital. He thought that his management of the domestic economy was impeccable and what he lacked was diplomatic achievements, with not solving the problem of China's accession to the WTO as a "diplomatic regret" that he had always sought to make up. A senior official in White House said: "If we can still get it(the agreement not reached in Zhu Rongji's visit), we may catch it and run away". Given these considerations, the United States began to act positively since late October, with Clinton called Jiang Zemin again on November 6 to agree on China's "joining the WTO".

For China, the will to reach a bilateral agreement between China and the United States was equally strong, which was, after all, the biggest obstacle to China's entry into the WTO. So, not long after the call between leaders of the two countries, on November 10, 1999, US trade negotiator Barshefsky and presidential assistant Sparling sent by Clinton arrived in Beijing to start a new round of bilateral talks. The 6-day negotiation attracted the world's attention.

On November 11, 1999, around 14: 52 p.m. to 15: 45 p.m., the talks broke down, and the US delegation was ready to return home. On November 12, Zhu Rongji met with Barshefsky, who agreed to remain in Beijing for negotiations on fundamental telecommunication issues. On November 13, the talks were deadlocked again, and the US delegation again proposed to return. On November 14, Zhu Rongji and Wu Yi met with Barshefsky again to exchange views on relevant issues. Barshefsky, believing it was necessary to continue talking, decided to stay. Then the negotiations were quickened. On November 15, on the 6th day of the talks, at 15:32 pm, China and the United States signed the *Bilateral Agreement on China's Accession to the WTO.* China-US negotiations on China's "joining the WTO" were finally crowned with success.[1]

When the news came out that China and the United States reached an agreement on the 15th, catching the world's attention, the New York Stock Exchange(NYSE) had closed. However, on the 16th and 17th, the share price of 6 companies rose by at least 60%, which were among the 9 Chinese companies listed on the NYSE and Nasdaq Stock Exchange.Leaders from all over the world also made speeches welcoming the bilateral agreement between China and the United States. Singapore Prime Minister Goh Chok Tong believed that this was positive for the establishment of a global free trade system.Japanese Prime Minister Keizo Obuchi welcomed the conclusion of this agreement. Australian Trade Minister Mark Weil said the agreement between China and the United States paved the way for China's accession to the WTO. Italian Foreign Trade Minister Fasino said that China-US *Bilateral Agreement on China's Accession to the WTO* was a strategic and decisive step in the history of the WTO. The UK, France, Germany, Canada, and other countries also expressed their congratulations and support. A spokesman for the European Commission also immediately expressed a positive attitude, hoping to quickly conclude negotiations with China on its accession to the WTO.

The negotiation between China and the United States, which lasted for 13 years, can be described to have been through many twists and turns. After the success of China-US negotiations, the statements made by the governments of various countries proved that the Sino-US bilateral negotiations were the biggest obstacle to China's entry into the WTO, with most countries looking at the US "wink." After this obstacle was removed, public opinion generally believed that China might join the WTO in 1999. However, that was not the case. The China-EU negotiations were unexpectedly tough. 80% of the conditions for China's entry into the WTO put forward by EU were the same as those by the US, which meant that EU would still haggle with China over the remaining 20%. The EU, thinking the economic aggregate of its 15 countries was larger than that of the United States and was a force to be reckoned with, did not want

[1] Zhou Hanmin ed., *China's Entry into WTO*, Shanghai: Wenhui Press, 2011, pp. 42-43.

to eat the "leftovers" of Americans, which caused great difficulties to the Chinese negotiating team.

In January and February 2000, China and the EU held two rounds of talks in Brussels and Beijing, respectively. As the gap between the two sides still existed in some key areas, no agreement was reached. Since March 28, 2000, another round of talks was held by the EU and China in Beijing, attracting the attention of China's top leaders. However, in the following four days, kinds of news was only showing that the two sides had not made a significant breakthrough. On the morning of March 31, the latest round of talks between China and the EU on China's accession to the WTO ended, with both sides had made some progress but failed to reach a final agreement. China's journey to "join the WTO" experienced another twist.

After months' stalemate, on May 15, 2000, China and the EU held another "WTO accession" negotiation in Beijing. EU delegation included EU Trade Commissioner Lamy, Director General of Trade Department Bessel, et. al. The Chinese delegation included Minister of Foreign Trade and Economic Cooperation Shi Guangsheng, Vice Minister of Foreign Trade and Economic Cooperation Long Yongtu, et. al. Before the talks began, both sides expressed their hope that this would be the last round of talks and their confidence in the successful conclusion of the talks. This negotiation lasted for five days. After repeated pondering, Shi Guangsheng's negotiating team believed that though the major issues must not be compromised any more, several insurance companies and banks attracting EU's special attention could be granted. By doing so, China finally solved the problem, only being slightly affected but showing its respect to the EU.[1] At 18:18, on May 19, 2000, Shi Guangsheng and Lamy signed agreements on behalf of the two sides in the MOFTEC (Ministry of Foreign Trade and Economic Cooperation) Building. Thus, bilateral agreements between China and EU was reached.

After the negotiations with the United States and the European Union was ended, the "WTO accession" negotiations continued for another year or so, blocked on agricultural issues in multilateral negotiations, with the amount of domestic support for agriculture as the focus of the debate. According to WTO regulations, the maximum amount of support for agriculture in developing countries should not exceed 10% of their agricultural GDP, while for developed countries it should not exceed 5%. Some developed countries required China to comply with the standards of developed

[1] Ouyang Song and GaoYongzhong ed., *Oral History of Reform and Opening Up*, Beijing: China Renmin University Press, 2013, p.509.

countries in agriculture, which was neither in line with China's actual national conditions nor its principle of "joining the WTO". Because of this, the "WTO accession" negotiations were suspended for half a year, and the APEC meeting held in Shanghai in June 2001 became an opportunity on which Shi Guangsheng and US representatives reached an agreement that China's maximum support for agriculture should not exceed 8.5% of the gross agricultural production, which was very close to the level of developing countries. Once the United States had shown its attitude, other countries, including the EU, also agreed; thus the matter was resolved.

(3) *Debate on the pros and cons of China's entry into WTO*

December 11, 2001, would surely go down in the history of China's economic internationalization, on which China officially became a member of the WTO, satisfactorily ending its 15-year journey into the WTO, leading the internationalization of China's economy to a new stage in the new century. However, the success of China's entry into the WTO did not mean that the road to China's economic internationalization was as flat as a board. On the contrary, China's entry into the WTO was a double-edged sword. Like a giant ship, China was entering a deep sea of international competition, with its enterprises entering a fierce "era of competition".

For our state and national industry, was "joining the WTO" a feast of shared globalization or a scourge? In the past 15 years, similar debates continued about the negotiations. To sum up, there were no more than three views. One view held that China's entry into the WTO was equal to an immediate and full opening of the market, and equal to full implementation of the market economy, thinking that a large number of foreign products and services would march into China and strongly impact China's economy. This view, believing that "joining the WTO" was entering a game full of traps, can be called "trap theory" or "blindly pessimistic theory". According to another view, the day when China joined the WTO should be the time for China to have completed the practicing of the market economy and to enjoy the benefits of global multilateral trade and investment, believing that export, employment, GDP and so on would increase dramatically soon. Thinking entering WTO as entering a game full of flowers, this view can be named "flower theory" or " blindly optimistic theory." The third view was that China's accession to the WTO as a developing country had both advantages and disadvantages for its economy. While in general, the advantages were believed to outweigh the disadvantages. We can call this view "dialectical theory.[1] Regardless of the stances, the starting point of these arguments was, for China,whether the benefits of "joining WTO" would outweigh the harms or not.

Each viewpoint had its reason at the time, and the debate on the pros and cons accompanied China's accession to the WTO all the way. Fifteen years' tough negotiations were long enough for the Chinese to calmly analyze the significance of China's accession to the WTO. Ours never giving up to join the WTO was an obvious answer to that question. No country that was in long-term isolation and lacked competitive pressure could be able to gain momentum for progress. The reason why we wanted to join the WTO, despite all the difficulties and obstacles, was that China's reform and opening up were consistent with "joining the WTO", aiming to realize the great rejuvenation of the Chinese nation. At the beginning of the new century, China's reform and opening up became a consensus, with establishing China's position in the international division of labor system and global industrial restructuring as soon as possible being an inherent and inexorable demand for further development. The only way for China to locate this position was to fully participate in the international economic system, deeply integrating into the world economy. Admittedly, China's entry into the WTO had a lot of uncertainties for the immature Chinese market, but we could not miss the good opportunity of integrating into the world economy by emphasizing our particularity. We should be brave in fighting on the world stage and learn to "dance with wolves".

"Joining the WTO" was indeed a "double-edged sword"with both opportunities and challenges. No one at that time could give a definite answer to the question that whether it would be beneficial or harmful to China. However, it is certain that China has achieved unprecedented development during the 20 years from 1978 to 2000, through continuous opening up to promote economic internationalization. The practice made in the last 20 years of the 20th century has proved that economic internationalization is correct, necessary and feasible. China's entry into the WTO would be a milestone in the history of China's economic internationalization, marking the great progress of China's opening to the outside world, which would surely promote China's deeper integration into the world economic system. In this sense, it is not difficult to understand why joining the WTO is so vital.

---

[1] Zhang Ying and Zhang Aiping ed., *Modem Market Economy Foundation*, Harbin: Northeast Forestry University Press, 2006, p.235.

Green hills cannot stop the river flowing, to the vast ocean it keeps advancing. Globalization is a historical trend, and China's accession to the WTO was, and still is, the trend of the future that cannot be stopped. We could either follow the trend to seize the opportunity and develop, or act against the tide, which may result in our being thrown aside. Today, it seems that China has chosen the right way.

3.3.2 Measures on China's economic internationalization at the beginning of the 21st century

The triumphant entry into the WTO at the turn of the millennium was a great event for China to celebrate. At the turn of the 21st century, China's economic internationalization was at a new starting point. Although there were many concerns that China's "joining the WTO" was like "a sheep entering a tiger's mouth" for China, it had to dance with the "wolves" and must do it perfectly to catch up with the developed countries and truly realize the great rejuvenation of the Chinese nation. China's "accession to the WTO" was an opportunity rather than a challenge. Only by taking this opportunity to speed up reform can China win the opportunity to truly develop at the beginning of the new century.

In accordance with the requirements of WTO, China adopted a series of policies and principles in reforms, particularly in foreign trade, exchange rate, finance, and service industry. While fulfilling its obligations as a member of WTO, China has dramatically promoted the internationalization of its economy.

3.3.2.1 The Increased Liberalization of Trade in Goods

In the field of trade in goods, mainly involving the primary and secondary industries, tariff and non-tariff measures are important indicators of a country's degree of opening up. China had drastically lowered tariffs before joining the WTO, with the general tariff level fell from 42.5% in 1992 to 15% in 2000, which still failed to meet the WTO requirement for tariffs. According to the *Protocol on China's Accession to the WTO*, China should reduce tariffs during the transitional period after its entry to open up its market. People usually call 2001–2004 the "Pre-transition period," and 2004–2006 the "Post-transition period." While after 2008, the general transition period of China's accession to the WTO was ended. Under the framework of WTO, the major industries in China's trade in goods have significantly changed.

(1) *The trade in agricultural products was one of the issues hotly debated during China's accession to the WTO, and was also a matter to which close attention was paid by all sectors of China's domestic community after the accession*

Regarding trade liberalization of agricultural products, in a nutshell, China mainly made the following commitments: the first one was made to reduce tariffs to 14.5% by 2004, mostly on processed products such as animal products, fruits, and vegetables. The second was made by China to expand market access, promising to impose ceiling binding on tariffs on all agricultural products after its accession to the WTO, with the arithmetic average tariff declined from 19.9% in 2001 to 15.8% in 2004 and 15.1% in 2008. China canceled the planned management of foreign trade in some sensitive commodities with the tariff quota system, gradually expanding the quota proportion to non-state-owned enterprises, and stipulated that single-stage tariff as a protective measure would only be allowed for certain agricultural products after a certain period of time. The third is to cut domestic support, not providing export subsidies for agricultural products.At the same time, the price subsidy for agricultural products should not exceed 8.5% of gross agricultural production.[1]

On its entry into WTO, China began to fulfill its commitments. As for agricultural products tariffs, typical tariffs such as beef tariff dropped from 31.8% to 12%, apple tariff dropped from 22% to 10%, and potato tariff dropped from 24% to 15%. China's agricultural tariff reduction was far higher than the average reduction of 36% for developed members and 24% for developing members. China's average tariff of agricultural products before joining was 23.2%, which dropped to 18.5% in 2002, 16.8% in 2003, 15.6% in 2004, 15.3% in 2005 and 15.2% in 2007. By 2008, the average tariff level of China's agricultural products was far lower than the average world tariff level of 62%, making China one of the countries with the lowest agricultural tariff level worldwide.

With regard to expanding market access, the import license and import quotas for two types of agricultural products, sugar and tobacco, were immediately abolished and a single tariff system was introduced upon China's accession to the WTO. On September 27, 2003, the Ministry of Commerce of China issued the *Interim Measures for the Administration of Import Tariff Quota of Agricultural Products* and the *Interim Measures for the Administration of Import Tariff Quota of Chemical Fertilizer*, which was subsequently revised and improved in the implementation. An open and

---

[1] Chen Xiaohong ed., *Basic Knowledge of WTO*, Haikou: Hainan Publishing House, 2002, p.195.

transparent tariff quota management system was established for the import of bulk commodities such as grain, cotton, oil, sugar, wool, and fertilizer. The State Publication and Reform Commission, the Ministry of Commerce and other competent state departments kept announcing on time the annual tariff quota quantity and the applying qualification and procedures each year, fully reflecting the principle of fairness, justice, and transparency. The import allowance for these bulk commodities under the tariff rate quota system had been gradually expanded from 2002 to 2005, which was fully in line with China's accession commitment, among which, wheat increased from 8.468 million tons in 2002 to 9.636 million tons in 2005, corn increased from 5.85 million tons to 7.2 million tons, rice increased from 3.99 million tons to 5.32 million tons, soybean oil increased from 2.518 million tons to 3.587 million tons, sugar increased from 1.764 million tons to 1.945 million tons, wool increased from 0.2645 million tons to 0.287 million tons, wool tops increased from 72.5 thousand tons to 80 thousand tons, and cotton increased from 0.8185 million tons to 0.894 million tons. While as of the fertilizer, urea risen from 1.3 million tons to 2.8 million tons, compound fertilizer increased from 2.835 million tons to 3.29 million tons, and phosphate fertilizer has been increased from 5.67 million tons to 6.56 million tons.[1] The actual import volume was self-regulated according to the supply and demand of China's domestic market. The enlargement of tariff quotas not only met the needs of the domestic market, but also provided other WTO members with great opportunities for market access.

The tariff quota expansion for products,except fertilizer and vegetable oil, came to an end in 2004, when China's commitment to expand the tariff quota for these products had been fully achieved. In 2008, the proportion of agricultural products in state-owned trade was declining, except that of wheat which maintained 90% in state-owned trade. In 2005, China abolished the import designated operating system for wool and wool tops. On January 1, 2006, China terminated tariff quota management for vegetable oil with a single tariff of 9%. In 2006, tariff quota expansion for fertilizer reached the end, with compound fertilizer reached 3.45 million tons in 2008, increasing at an annual rate of 5%, and tariff quotas of other products remained at the highest promised level reached in 2004. In 2006, China introduced three kinds of commodities under import license management, importing US$91.83 billion of commodities under tariff quotas, import licenses and state-run trade

[1] Chen Xiaohong ed., *Basic Knowledge of WTO*, Haikou: Hainan Publishing House, 2002.

management throughout the year, which only accounted for 11.6% of total imports.[1]It can be said that non-tariff barriers in China's agricultural products market were gradually reduced.

In reducing the domestic support for agriculture, China has continued the long adopted industrial inclination policy of "emphasizing industry and constricting agriculture" after its accession. During this period, China's domestic agricultural support policy was adjusted mainly in three aspects with more attention paid first to the growth of farmers' income; second to the protection of farmers' rights and interests, including giving national treatment to farmers and funding for education and health services in rural areas; and third to ecological construction and environmental protection.[2]

(2) *There were many kinds of manufactured goods of complex varieties in China*

It was impossible for China to only open its advantageous industries but close the inferior ones to enter the WTO. Therefore, how to seize the opportunity of "joining the WTO" to expand our export of advantageous manufactured goods and enhance the international competitiveness of inferior manufactured goods was the focus of policies during this period. The representative developments of textile and automobile industries are taken as examples.

Textiles are the products of the most competitive advantages in China's foreign trade. Since 1996, China has become the world's largest supplier of textile exports, covering nearly one-sixth of the global textile market. After its entry into the WTO, on the one hand, China's textile export environment was much improved with significantly reduced trade barriers. At the same time, we could make full use of WTO membership to safeguard the interests of China's textile industry under trade protectionism of Europe and the United States. On the other hand, with the reduction of tariffs and the cancellation of import licenses, the prices of textile raw materials and finished products were in line with international standards.The average import tax rate of China's textiles and clothing dropped to 11.64% from 2002 to 2005, significantly reducing the cost of textiles. Moreover, the proportion of imported raw materials in export products increased significantly, improving international competitiveness. It can be said that China has enjoyed various benefits brought about by the liberalization of the textile trade. However, China's textile industry also encountered new challenges.

---

[1] Wang Zixian ed., *30 Years' Foreign Economy and Trade Of China Since Reform and Opening Up*, Beijing: Economy & Management Publishing House, 2008. p.165.

[2]:Lu Qied, *A Summary of WTO (2nd Edition)*, Shanghai: Fudan University Press, 2008, p.213.

On January 1, 2005, the textile trade quota system was canceled as scheduled, realizing the integration of textile trade. While as other countries were worried about the damage brought about to their industries by the influx of Chinese textiles, they begun to impose restrictive measures on Chinese textiles, such as anti-dumping, safeguard measures, special safeguard measures, in particular, technical barriers to trade and labor standards. According to the provisions of *China's Accession Protocol* and other documents, from the effective date of the *WTO Agreement* to December 31, 2008,if a WTO member believed that an increase in imports of textiles originating in China had caused confusion in its market, it could request to negotiate with China and impose quotas or quantitative restrictions on China's related products for less than a year. After China's accession to the WTO, reports on China's "special safeguards" application in the textile sector were endless. Just in the first half of 2005, 16 investigations on special safeguard measures were launched by the US and some European countries, all aiming at Chinese textiles. China's textile exports continued to undergo trade frictions during this period.

As a matter of fact, in order to curb the rapid export of textiles, China has substantially increased the tariffs on 148 kinds of textiles since January 1, 2005, and on other 74 kinds of textiles again on May 20. However, western countries did not appreciate China's goodwill, but instead, they imposed restrictions on the seven kinds of textiles sold to the US and two kinds of textiles sold to the EU in the same year. In response, on June 1, 2005, China canceled its export duties on 81 kinds of textiles and pointed out that the important condition—"market disruption"—specifically put forward by the US and EU did not actually exist, shocking both the US and EU. In order to ensure a smooth transition of free trade in the textile industry, China and EU reached a new agreement on textile import and export, which required that since January 1, 2008, export quotas would be abolished while imports would be subject to a "dual license supervision system" for joint surveillance for one year.

The automobile was just the opposite of textiles. Instead of a competitive industry of China, it has always been an infant industry protected by high tariffs, a market that other countries expected China to open. Joining the WTO was a severe challenge to China's domestic automobile industry. In accordance with China's "accession" commitment, import quotas and licensing restrictions would be removed in 2005, after which the auto import tariff would be the only protection means; the annual tariff cuts on imported cars would be 10%, resulting in the import tariff on completely built up (CBU) vehicles be reduced to 25% and the tariff on the imported auto parts to 10%

before 2006; foreign investment access conditions would also be loosened to provide other countries with the car market access.

The *Automobile Industry Development Policy* issued in 2004 can be said to have strictly complied with WTO regulations, greatly promoting the prosperity and standardization of China's imported automobile market. According to the regulations, by 2006, the duty on CBU reduced to 25% from 69.2% before joining. At the same time, in terms of the new automobile industry policy, starting from 2005, all import port free trade zones were not allowed to carry out the bonded warehousing services and display (sales) business of imported automobiles. That is to say, great changes were seen in the management of imported cars. Some implicit tax policies were introduced into the new industrial policies to make up for the damage caused by the cancellation of the localization rate to domestically produced vehicles. After the "land clearance" policy was put into practice, some functions of the bonded area were canceled, which meant that all the bonded areas at the import ports should not store cars with a purpose of entering the domestic market. This change had a far-reaching impact on the domestic imported automobile market. "Land clearance" restricted foreign cars from entering the Chinese market by increasing the financial pressure on car imports, which is an example of *Auto Industry Development Policy* fully utilizing WTO principles to protect the domestic car market.

Of course, the impact of tariff reduction on the price of imported cars was very limited in practice, because even if the tariff reached the bottom line as scheduled, the price of imported vehicles did not have an advantage over that of domestic cars. The "land clearance" policy also restrained the entry of imported vehicles to a certain extent. However, due to the quality gap between domestic and imported cars, the quality of cars also became an important factor, like the price, affecting the Chinese car market. Two focuses of the new policy were: on the one hand, adhering to the principle of combining the introduction of technology with an independent opening; on the other hand, controlling the import of vehicle parts and encouraging technology research and development in enterprises. China's automobile industry and market were greatly promoted, advancing with more stable steps and better performance in the WTO environment.

In the years after its entry into the WTO, China actively took measures to promote the freedom of trade in goods significantly. As for tariffs, after the accession, China actively fulfilled its commitment by drastically reducing tariffs six times in 2008. China's average tariff level gradually decreased from 15.3% before joining the

WTO to 12.7% in 2002,11% in 2003, 10.4% in 2004, 9.9% in 2005 and 9.8% in 2007. It can be said that three years after China joined the WTO, most of China's commitments on tariffs were fulfilled, and the transition period enjoyed by China was basically ended in 2005. Since then, tariffs on only a small number of products still needed to be cut as promised. Compared with other major WTO members, China's bound tariff rate reached 100%, with the actual tariffs consistent with the binding tariffs.

In terms of non-tariff measures, China's products subject to import quota and license management were reduced from thousands of tax numbers in the early 1990s to 424 tax numbers (based on 8-digit tax numbers) before its joining the WTO. For these 424 products, China had completely abolished quota and license management by 2005, according to the schedule stipulated in the legal documents of WTO accession. With the exception of a very few products, such as precursor chemicals, which must be subject to import license control under relevant international conventions, China's import non-tariff measures were all eliminated, fulfilling the commitments to join the WTO.

3.3.2.2 The gradually opening up of the market in service trade[1]

The process of opening up the service industry in China is a process of constantly reforming domestic regulations, lowering and reducing barriers to trade and investment of this sector to promote the free flow of service elements, mainly by giving foreign service providers national treatment, reducing market access restrictions on them, relaxing domestic regulations and enhancing the transparency of service trade policies. After China's entry into WTO, it gradually opened up domestic service trade according to the promised schedule, and even fulfilled its commitments in banking, insurance, tourism, and other fields in advance, thus forming a pattern of all-round opening up of the service industry.

By the end of 2007, China had opened 100 of the 160 service trade sectors classified by the WTO, accounting for 62.5%, which was close to the average level of developed members. As for the number of businesses in existence, in 2006, 7141 foreign-invested enterprises were newly established in China's service industry according to WTO industry classification standards, accounting for 17.2% of the total

---

[1] Wang Zixian ed., *30 Years' Foreign Economy and Trade Of China Since Reform and Opening Up*, Beijing: Economy and Management Publishing House,2008, pp.166-168; Fan Ying, "An Analysis of China's Openness since the Entry into WTO", *Intertrade*, 2012(10); Pei Changhong ed., *Research on Reform and Opening Up and Circulation Reform for 30 years of China*, Beijing: Economy and Management Publishing House, 2008, pp.160-166.

number of newly established foreign-invested enterprises in the country. The actual use of foreign capital in this sector amounted to US$21.14 billion, accounting for 30.4% of the total amount of foreign capital used in the country. Foreign investment's entering into China's service industry effectively promoted China's service industry and even the whole economy.

(1) *Financial services*

In the banking sector, for foreign banks, China fully opened its foreign exchange business in 2001 when it joined the WTO and removed all geographical restrictions at the end of 2006 on renminbi business, opening the renminbi business for Chinese residents at the same time. The scope and field of renminbi business of foreign banks were the same as those of Chinese banks. In 2008, foreign banks operated more than 100 kinds of businesses in the 12 basic business areas stipulated in the regulations, with further simplified standards and procedures for market access than three years ago. Besides, China also encouraged qualified overseas investors to participate in the restructuring and transformation of China's financial institutions and increased the proportion of Chinese commercial banks with a single foreign institution as a shareholder from 15% to 20%. If the total proportion of foreign investment was less than 25%, the nature and business scope of the invested institution would not change.

By the end of 2004, foreign banks had set up 211 business organizations in China, including 167 branches of foreign banks with 19 sub-branches, 14 foreign corporate bodies with 11 branches and affiliated institutions, and 220 representative offices of foreign banks, accounting for 1.84% of the total assets of banking financial institutions. At the same time, foreign banks also entered Chinese banks as strategic investors, whose investment rising from US$0.26 billion in 2003 to US$32.8 billion in 2009, increased by 126 times in 6 years.[1]

In the field of insurance, since the WTO accession, the business scope and established area of foreign insurance companies have gradually expanded. On December 11, 2004, the WTO "transition period" of China's insurance industry ended. The restrictions on the region and business scope of foreign-funded insurance companies were finally lifted. Thus, foreign-funded insurance companies could set up offices in any city in China. Foreign life insurance companies in China were also allowed to provide all non-life insurance services to both Chinese and foreign citizens except for legal services and to set up sole proprietorship subsidiaries in China. Since

---

[1] *China Banking Regulatory Commission 2009 Report*. http://www.cbrc.gov.cn/chinese/home/doc View/20100615A314C942DEE7DD34FF395FFCEB671E00.html.

the beginning of 2004, foreign insurance companies set up new branches in China almost monthly.

In the field of securities, China was much more cautious about the internationalization, approving three special overseas members of Shanghai Securities Exchange(SSE) and 3 of Shenzhen Stock Exchange(SZSE) respectively. Overseas securities institutions held 46 B-share seats on SSE and 21 on SZSE, with three approved foreign-shared securities companies and 20 fund management companies with foreign capital equity.Besides, the *Interim Measures for the Administration of Domestic Securities Investment by Qualified Foreign Institutional Investors(QFII)* came into effect in December 2002. It was a new transitional measure for China to introduce foreign capital and open up the securities market to a limited extent in the case of non-full convertibility of the renminbi. By the end of October 2004, 27 overseas institutions had been eligible for QFII, with a permitted investment amount of US$3 billion. Another 11 institutions (including four foreign banks) were authorized to carry out QFII custody business.

(2) *Retail and services sector*

In 2004, China lifted restrictions on the region, equity, and quantity of foreign-invested commercial enterprises. Subsequently, foreign retail giants accelerated their expansion in China, with 80% of the world's top 50 retailers entered China, Carrefour, Wal-Mart, B&Q, and Huatang included. Wal-Mart and Carrefour both opened more than 55 large-scale approved stores. However, the opening up of the retail industry did not lead to the collapse of local retailers across a broad front. Although the entry of foreign retailers did put enormous pressure on local retailers, and in many cities in China, there was even the phenomenon of "opening of foreign-funded hypermarkets accompanied bankruptcy of several state-owned commercial enterprises," local retailers sought their market positions amid pressure, achieving development and growth of their own. In 2006, domestic foreign retailers realized sales of more than RMB200 billion, accounting for only 3% of the total retail sales of social consumer goods in 2005 (excluding local approval items). The model of multinational retail giants——chain operation, management experience, and a sophisticated centralized purchasing system was quickly copied to local enterprises, thus prompting some regional local retail enterprises that already of considerable strength. Local retail enterprises continuously strengthened their competitiveness through equity financing and merger and acquisition. For example, after China's entry into the WTO, dozens of retail enterprises were successfully listed, like Wumart, Shanghai Hualian, and Jingkelong. These chain giants, such as Beijing's Wumart Group with over 500 stores, have developed comprehensive formats, including hypermarkets, general merchandise stores(GMS), convenience stores and shopping malls, competing with multinational retailers face-to-face in the regional market.

(3) *Tourism services*

In terms of the specific contents of China's WTO accession negotiations, the opening of tourism was mainly in the fields of hotels and travel agencies. In order to meet the requirements of WTO accession, the National Tourism Administration concentrated on the clean-up of regulations and rules in 2001, confirming that 23 items should be retained, 27 modified, and 19 abolished. Since 2002, ten sectoral regulations were developed according to actual needs, of which two were revised ones, and one was supplemented. In 2003, the *Book of China's Tourism Regulations* was published, fulfilling the obligation to facilitate WTO members' access to tourism regulations. In 2001, the National Tourism Administration cooperated with relevant departments topromote revising the *Regulations on Travel Agency Management* concerning foreign access promptly. In 2003, the National Tourism Administration, together with the Ministry of Commerce, formulated *Interim Provision on the Establishment of Foreign Holding and Wholly Foreign-owned Travel Agencies*, fulfilling the promise in advance to allow the establishment of foreign holding and wholly-owned travel agencies, which was revised in February 2005, and in December of the same year, the supplementary provisions of it were also promulgated, providing legal protection for further fulfilling the commitments of WTO accession. At the same time, China also fulfilled the relevant commitments in the fields of hotels (including apartment buildings) and restaurants on schedule, setting no restrictions on the establishment of sole proprietorship enterprises.

On December 1, 2003, Beijing Rihang Travel Agency (China) Co., Ltd., the first wholly foreign-owned travel agency approved by the National Tourism Administration, officially opened in Beijing. According to the promise made by China at the time of joining WTO, wholly-foreign-funded travel agencies were allowed to be set up before November 10, 2007. The opening of Beijing Rihang Travel Agency (China) Co., Ltd., marked that this promise was fulfilled over three years earlier. In February 2005, in terms of regional restrictions on the establishment of foreign-funded travel agencies according to the commitment, the National Tourism Administration and the Ministry of Commerce announced the lifting of the geographical restrictions in the *Establishment of Foreign-controlled and Wholly Foreign-owned Travel Agencies*

Tentative Provisions (Revised). By the end of 2007, 49 international hotel brands had entered the Chinese market. The number of travel agencies set up by foreign investors in China was 25, of which 11 were wholly owned, five were of foreign ownership, and 9 were joint ventures. Judging from the scale and strength of tourism enterprises, China already had five tourism groups with fixed assets of more than RMB10 billion in 2007, preliminarily enjoying international competitiveness. The gap between domestic and international tourism enterprises was narrowing. Also, for Chinese tourists, though traveling abroad was not a content of China's "WTO accession" commitments, it was more convenient to travel abroad after China's entering WTO, with an increasing number of overseas tourist destinations. In 2001, there were only 18 outbound tourism destinations for Chinese citizens (including Hong Kong and Macao SAR), and 67 travel agencies organizing outbound tourism. While in 2007, there were 132 countries and regions as outbound tourism destinations for Chinese citizens. Regarding inbound tourism, China has become one of the most attractive and safest tourist destinations in the world. In 2005, 46.8 million overnight visitors entered the country, ranking 4th in the world.

(4) *Transport services*

China has fulfilled its commitment to join the WTO on transportation services. As far as market admittance was concerned, by 2006, China's road transport industry had attracted 388 foreign investment projects, with the actual use of foreign capital of US$1.12 billion. In 2006, highway and railway transportation industry held 70 projects with foreign capital, including 44 wholly-owned projects and 4 M&A projects. By 2006, China's shipping industry had attracted 227 foreign-invested projects, with the actual cumulative use of foreign capital of US$2.21 billion. In 2006, the shipping industry added 49 foreign-funded projects, including 21 wholly-owned enterprises and 2 M&As, and as of 2006, China's civil aviation industry had attracted 48 foreign investment projects, with the actual cumulative use of foreign capital of US$0.41 billion. In 2006, the civil aviation industry added 12 foreign investment projects, including one wholly-owned project and 2 M&A projects. Overall, the degree of openness of transport services was lower than that of other service sectors, which was not owing to the low level of China's open commitment. From the perspective of commitment level, there was no quantitative or geographical restriction on transportation services. Though the market access level was slightly higher than that of other service sectors, the trade of commercial forms in the transportation industry was far weaker than that of other service industries. The main reason was that the transportation service was especially regulated by domestic regulations.Under the condition that China's relevant transportation regulations were not perfect, the cost of providing services through commercial presence by foreign businessmen was unpredictable, with unnecessarily increasing risks. To this end, China launched a series of policies and regulations such as *Provisions of the People's Republic of China on the Conditions for Maritime Administrative Licensing*, which was promulgated and implemented to make clear the conditions for permitting foreign ships to enter non-open waters, as well as the conditions of examination and approval for vessels entering and exiting ports, and the conditions for issuing ships' nationality certificates, so as to further standardize and improve the system of maritime government procedures. In April 2006, the Ministry of Communications, the National Development and Reform Commission, and the State Administration of Industry and Commerce jointly released the *Announcement on Publishing the Survey Conclusion on the Terminal Handling Charge(THC) of International Liner Transportation*, not completely prohibiting the collection of THC, but understanding the issue of detaining bills of lading and goods for shipping companies to force the owner of cargo to pay the THC as a civil dispute which was free from administration.

(5) *Communication service industry*

Since December 11, 2005, China has allowed foreign express companies to set up wholly-owned enterprises. Besides, with the reality of international mail express business conducted by them in China taken into account, foreign-funded enterprises were allowed to continue operating international mail express business after handling postal entrustment procedures. From the perspective of relevant laws and policies, as early as September 20, 2000 the State Council had passed the *Regulations on Telecommunications of the People's Republic of China* to comprehensively and meticulously regulate the telecommunications market, resources, constructions, and security to provide legislative guarantees for further regulating and standardizing the development of telecommunications market. In May 2006, the State Council promulgated the *Regulations on the Protection of the Rights of Communication through Information Network* to stipulate the rights of obligee to disseminate information, including those of authors, performers, producers of audio and video recordings, etc., protecting and promoting the creation and dissemination of information works. In 2005, the State Council passed the *Programme for the Reform of the Postal Service* to clarify that the core of postal reform was to separate government and enterprises and to reorganize the State Post Bureau and China Post

Group Corporation, clarifying their mutual responsibilities and reaffirming the State Post Bureau as the national postal regulatory body to practice unified supervision over the postal market, including universal service and courier service, and China Post Group Corporation as a postal service provider to participate in fair competition in the postal market. By the end of 2006, 31 foreign-invested express delivery companies had registered in China, and 167 international freight agent service enterprises and 372 branches operating international mail express business had received the "postal entrustment certificates." In terms of telecommunications services, in 2002, the State Council promulgated the *Regulations on the Management of Telecommunications Enterprises with Foreign Investment*, gradually liberalizing the restrictions on foreign investment in the Chinese telecommunications market, and removing geographical and other restrictions. As of 2006, 14 foreign-owned telecom companies had been formally approved the operation license of the telecom business to be mainly engaged in businesses like information service, internet data center, internet access service, call center and so on. Among the value-added telecommunication services, there are currently more than 20,000 enterprises that have obtained business licenses in China, with which foreign-funded companies have entered China Telecom's value-added operation market through mergers and acquisitions, joint ventures and equity participation.

(6) *Construction and related service industries*

After joining the WTO, China issued the *Regulations and Supplements on the Administration of Foreign-Invested Construction Enterprises*, *Implementation Measures for Qualification Management* and so on concerning construction enterprises; in terms of construction designing enterprises, China issued the *Regulations and Supplements on the Administration of Foreign-Invested Construction Designing Enterprises*, *Detailed Rules for Implementation on the Administration of Foreign-invested Construction and Engineering Design Enterprises*, *Tentative Provisions on Administration of Foreign Enterprises Engaging in Construction Work Design Activities in the Peoples Republic of China*, etc.; in terms of consultancy corporates, China issued *Regulations on the Administration of Foreign-invested Construction Engineering Service Enterprises*, *Management Procedures of Engineering Cost Consulting Enterprises*, *Measures for the Qualification Accreditation of the Bidding Agencies of Engineering Construction Projects*, etc.; and in terms of the project general contract and project management, China issued *Guidance on Cultivating and Developing Project General Contract and Project Management Enterprises*, *Trial Measures on Projects Management for*

Construction Engineerings, *Code of Construction Project Management* and so on. With the implementation of unified standards for market access for domestic and foreign enterprises, foreign enterprises could apply in accordance with the relevant provisions of qualification management. After approval, foreign-invested designing, construction, and engineering service enterprises could enjoy national treatment. Besides, after foreign-invested enterprises' obtaining the qualification certificates for construction enterprises or engineering design enterprises, the scope of contracted projects would enjoy equal treatment as domestic enterprises for wholly foreign-owned, foreign-invested, cooperative design enterprises and China-foreign joint ventures and cooperative construction enterprises. Through the promulgation of a series of related laws and regulations, China's commitment to openness in the construction industry and related services sectors promised during the WTO accession was realized. By the end of 2006, China's construction industry had 3,456 projects utilizing foreign investment, with the actual use of US$9.39 billion foreign capital. In 2006, 2,410 foreign-invested enterprises were newly established in real estate, making an increase of 14.1% over 2005; 358 foreign-invested construction enterprises were newly approved in the country, including 261 wholly foreign-owned projects and 8 M&A projects, whose actual use of foreign investment was US$8.83 billion, with a year-on-year growth of 52.7%, accounting for 33.7% and 38.9% of the total foreign direct investment in the national service trade, respectively, making this industry with the most foreign investment utilized in the service trade field.

It is through this series of reform policies and measures that China fulfilled the open commitments to service trade and further promoted the sustainable development of China's economy, making China's service trade continue to grow. According to WTO's statistics, in 2007, the total import and export volume of China's service trade exceeded US$256 billion, making China the world's 5th largest service trade country. Among them, the import of services trade was US$129 billion, and the export value was US$127 billion, resulting in a service trade deficit of US$20 billion.

3.3.2.3 Deepen the reform of the foreign trade system[1]

Since the determination to apply for "re-entry", China has carried out drastic reforms to promote the marketization in the field of foreign trade to make it comply

[1] Pei Changhong ed., *Research on Reform and Opening Up and Circulation Reform for 30 years of China*, Beijing: Economy and Management Publishing House, 2008, p.81; Wang Zixian ed., *30 Years' Foreign Economy and Trade of China Since Reform and Opening Up*, Beijing: Economy & Management Publishing House, 2008, p.170.

with WTO rules. It can be said that China has fundamentally solved the problem of compatibility with the WTO multilateral trading system. However, as China was still in economic transformation, many details had to be further improved. From 2001 to 2006, China was in a transitional period to join the WTO, during which significant adjustments were made to the foreign trade system which was not in accordance with or fit for the WTO multilateral rules.

(1) *Improve the legal system related to trade*

In order to meet the needs of joining the WTO, China has begun to clean up and revise a number of foreign trade laws and regulations since 1999. By the end of December 2002, nearly 30 departments of the State Council had cleaned and revised laws and regulations concerning foreign economic relations, with 1,400 regulations cleared, of which 559 were abolished, and 197 were revised. Thirty-one provinces, autonomous regions, municipalities and 49 larger cities in the country had modified, repealed or stopped implementing 190,000 local regulations, rules of local governments and relevant documents and other policies and measures, with more than 2,300 pieces of laws, administrative regulations and departmental rules formulated, revised and repealed at the central level alone. Among them, *Law on China-foreign Equity Joint Ventures*, *Law on China-foreign Cooperative Joint Ventures*, *Foreign Investment Enterprise Law* and their detailed rules for implementation were revised, and the requirements on foreign exchange balance, local procurement, export performance and filing of enterprise production plans for foreign-invested enterprises were eliminated. In terms of import and export trade management, related regulations such as *Regulations of the PRC on the Import and Export Control of Goods*, *Regulations on the Import and Export Control of Technologies*, *Anti-Dumping Rules*, *Countervailing Regulation of The People's Republic of China* and *the PRC Regulation on Safeguards Measures* were successively implemented. In the area of intellectual property rights protection, China revised the *Patent Law*, *Trademark Law*, *Copyright Law* and *Regulations on Computer Software Protection*, formulated and implemented the *Regulations on the Protection of Layout Design of Integrated Circuits*, basically meeting the requirements of the WTO agreement on *Trade Related to Intellectual Property Rights (TRIPS)*.

While cleaning up and formulating regulations and policies, China also paid more attention to maintaining the transparency of its foreign trade policy. According to the transparency requirements related to China's WTO accession, regulations, policies, and measures related to trade and investment formulated by the central and local governments should be published in designated journals. More and more public opinions began to be solicited in the process of formulating laws, regulations, and policies, giving the public and all stakeholders the opportunity to fully express their views.

The Ministry of Commerce also set up the WTO Notification Advisory Board in accordance with its commitment, and published the *Consultation Measures on WTO Notification Advisory Board of Chinese Government(Provisional)*, and *Registration Form of Consultation Measures on China's Government's WTO Notification Advisory Board* to provide information on China's trade policy, fulfilling its obligation to notify China's trade policies and measures in accordance with the requirements of various specific WTO agreements. Relevant departments also established two national inquiry points—concerning the WTO *Implementation of the Health Measures Agreement* and the WTO *Technical Trade Barriers Agreement*—which was informed to the WTO. On January 1, 2006, the Chinese government portal was officially opened, marking the beginning of a new stage in the openness of Chinese government affairs and government innovation. Fifty-five departments and direct units of the State Council set up open government leading groups and their offices, 36 departments and units set up an open system of government affairs, showing that advanced legal concepts such as transparency and censorship were going to spread from the trade field to other legislative practices in China.

(2) *The right to operate foreign trade changed from under examination and approval system to under the registration system*

The complete liberalization of foreign trading rights was a crucial step for China to fulfill its commitment to joining the WTO. According to the commitments in article 5.1 of *Protocol on the Accession of the People's Republic of China* and paragraph 84 (a) of *Report of the Working Party on the Accession of China*, the examination and approval of foreign trade rights should be canceled within 3 years after China's accession, and the right to operate foreign trade in goods and technology should be liberalized. The *Foreign Trade Law* was revised and passed by the 8th Session of the Standing Committee of the 10th National People's Congress on April 6, 2004, removing restrictions on private production and circulation enterprises entering the field of foreign trade, implementing the same standards and procedures as for public enterprises. The import and export business qualifications were divided into two categories: foreign trade circulation and self-operated import and export, with the former subject to the approval by the Ministry of Commerce, and the latter delegated to the provincial foreign trade department for registration. The 50-year examination and approval system for foreign trade rights was abolished, utterly liberalizing the right to operate foreign trade, stipulating the system of registration and filing for foreign trade operators, with which foreign trade operators were only required to register for the record. On June 25, 2004, the Ministry of Commerce issued *Ministry Order No.14 of 2004* and the *Filling and Registration Measures for Foreign Trade Operators*, which came into force on July 1 after extensive consultation. At this point, China fulfilled its promise six months in advance to liberalize its foreign trade rights made when China joined the WTO. By the end of 2004, 33,742 foreign trade operators across the country had registered by the law. Among them, domestic enterprises increased by 26.92% from 25,027 a year earlier to 31,764(including 575 state-owned enterprises, 388 collective-owned enterprise, 15,032 private enterprises, 15,065 limited liability companies and 704 of other types), together with 421 Hong kong-Macao- Taiwan invested enterprises, 1,154 foreign-invested enterprises and 403 self-employed enterprises. The abolition of the examination and approval system gave enterprises and individuals to the highest degree the autonomy in foreign trade operations, which was conducive to changing government functions, reducing the cost of enterprises and individuals engaged in foreign trade and improving the efficiency of foreign trade operations, thus stimulating the enthusiasm of market players.

(3) *Establish trade friction coping mechanism*[1]

As has been noted, after China's entry into the WTO, foreign trade friction did not decrease but on the contrary, increased. Since 2001, cases of anti-dumping and safeguard measures against Chinese products continued to occur, leading China's export products to suffer from increasing discriminatory restrictions. As about 1/3 of the world's anti-dumping cases were aimed at Chinese products, it can be said that China entered a high-incidence season of trade frictions. In the face of this situation, our government, in accordance with the relevant WTO rules, on the one hand, made full use of the WTO dispute settlement mechanism and platform to intensify negotiations and handle trade disputes with relevant members. Remarkable results were achieved with the establishment of the "four-body interaction" working mechanism, China's guiding enterprises to respond to lawsuits, strengthening legal defense and other measures. In the 23 special safeguard investigations since 2003, 21

[1] Pei Changhong ed., *Research on Reform and Opening Up and Circulation Reform for 30 years of China*, Beijing: Economy & Management Publishing House, 2008, p.83.

cases were successfully resolved, having properly handled trade disputes with members and guaranteed export safety. On the other hand, in order to prevent the impact of excessive imports on domestic industries, China also accelerated the establishment of an overall import warning system, expanding the monitoring scope of the industrial security database to 8,000 enterprises in 15 key industries such as petrochemical, machinery and light industry, established and improved its own technical standards, strengthened the links between the government, industry associations and enterprises, and improved the import supervision and rapid response capability. Since 2003, China initiated anti-dumping investigations on 26 kinds of imported products and took measures in 62 cases, involving industries like chemical, paper, textile, light industry, and agricultural products with nearly US$3 billion. Reasonable use of WTO rules has effectively maintained the safety of China's domestic industries.

3.3.2.4 Further reform on the foreign exchange administration system[1]

China's entry into WTO challenged its foreign exchange administration system. On the one hand, in line with the need to improve the socialist market economy restructuring and to fulfill its WTO commitments, China's opening up to the outside world was continuously expanding, enlarging the main body, scale and enriching forms of economic intercourse with the outside world. As the domestic and foreign economies become increasingly interconnected, foreign exchange management becomes more difficult with increasing costs, posing a challenge to the foreign exchange management model mainly based on quantity control and administrative examination and approval. On the other hand, as China's situation of foreign exchange shortage was radically improved, the management thinking practiced in the past that encouraging inflow and restricting outflow now needed adjusting. To this end, in the new era, China's foreign exchange management departments mainly took the following measures:

(1) *Foreign exchange control over current accounts*

After joining the WTO, the foreign exchange management gradually shifted from focusing on foreign exchange income to the balance of foreign exchange outflow and inflow, further easing the renminbi exchange restrictions.

---

[1] Jin Zhesong and Li Jun, *Foreign Trade Growth and Economic Development of China—Retrospect, and Prospect of the 30 Years' Reform and Opening Up*, Beijing: China Renmin University Press, 2008, pp.150-156; Pei Changhong ed., *Research on Reform and Opening Up and Circulation Reform for 30 years of China*, Beijing: Economy & Management Publishing House,2008, pp.289, 292, 293, 296.

China's gradual shift from mandatory foreign exchange settlement to voluntary foreign exchange settlement was manifested by the continuous expansion of the limited quota of foreign exchange account. In October 2002, the State Administration of Foreign Exchange (SAFE) relaxed the standard for Chinese enterprises to open foreign exchange current account, unifying the conditions for opening foreign exchange accounts for Chinese and foreign enterprises, and merged the settlement accounts and special accounts of current accounts into foreign exchange current accounts under a uniformly applied quota management, namely, the quota of accounts should be approved at 20% of enterprises' foreign exchange earnings for current accounts last year and the quota of new enterprises should not exceed an equivalent of US$100,000. In September 2003, the Foreign Exchange Bureau relaxed the quota of foreign exchange current accounts of internationally contracted construction projects, international shipping, and international bidding, raising the quota limit check standard from 20% to 100% of the current account foreign exchange income of enterprises in the previous year. In May 2004, the Foreign Exchange Bureau increased the proportion of held foreign exchange in the current account to 30% or 50% of the foreign exchange income of the previous year. In February 2005, the Foreign Exchange Bureau further relaxed the limit on the quota of foreign exchange current accounts, extending the time limit for domestic institutions with above quota settlement from 10 working days to 90 days, allowing domestic institutions to retain their foreign exchange funds within 90 days after the balance of their foreign exchange current accounts exceeding the approved quota, expanding the scope of enterprises with foreign exchange current account quota checked at 100% of their actual foreign exchange earnings. For import and export enterprises and production enterprises that needed to retain their foreign exchange earnings of current accounts in full due to actual business needs, the current account limit could be approved at 100% of their actual foreign exchange earnings. In August 2005, the Foreign Exchange Bureau increased the reserved spot exchange proportion of foreign exchange current account again, prescribing that the reserved spot exchange proportion of a foreign institution could rise from 30% to 50% if its foreign exchange expenditure was below 80% of its foreign exchange income of the current account in the previous year, and rise from 50% to 80% if beyond 80%; and that for a newly opened account which had no foreign exchange income of a current account in the previous year, it could retain foreign exchange equivalent to no more than US$200,000. In April 2006, China canceled the pre-approval for opening foreign exchange current accounts and adjusted the approval method of account quota, which was checked by 50% or 80% of income but is now checked by the sum of 80% of the income and 50% of the expenditure of current account foreign exchange in the previous year. For domestic institutions that did not have foreign exchange revenue and expenditure in the previous year and needed to open foreign exchange current accounts, the initially limited quota was raised from the equivalent of US$200,000 to US$500,000, and enterprises with import payment needs were allowed to purchase foreign exchange in advance. In August 2007, the Foreign Exchange Bureau officially canceled the quota management of foreign exchange current accounts, leaving domestic institutions able to keep their foreign exchange income of current account on their own, marking the official replacement of the compulsory foreign exchange settlement system that had been implemented in China since 1994 by the voluntary foreign exchange settlement system.

Simplify the administration of verification for foreign exchange payment and receipt of exports. Since 2001, China has carried out a series of reforms to promote trade facilitation in the verification of export collection. In August 2001, the export collection subsystem of enforcement system (ES) at the electronic port was officially operated nationwide, and the electronic accounts of paper for verification of export earnings and export declaration were established in the common data center at the electronic port in China. In December 2001, the link of presenting documents to the State Administration of Foreign Exchange before collecting foreign exchange was canceled, allowing enterprises to conduct cancellation after verification on a monthly and centralized basis, and a verification system of differences was adopted. In March 2003, the export reporting system was launched, realizing the mass downloading of logistics information by the e-port law enforcement system and the stabilization of capital information flow by the balance-of-payments (BOP) declare system, and customs and foreign exchange management authorities were interconnected, strengthening the management of real-time data sharing. Therefore, the role of verification sheets in the management of export collection was weakened. Thus the trade facilitation measures of batch write-off and total write-off could be quickly popularized and applied. In October 2003, the State Administration of Foreign Exchange promulgated and implemented a new *Administrative Measures for Verification of Export Customs Declaration*, reformed the original write-off measures according to the new features in export in recent years, and formulated corresponding implementation rules. With regard to the verification of import exchange payments, in

December 2004, the State Administration of Foreign Exchange promulgated the *Administrative Measures on Cancellation and Verification of Differences of Foreign Exchange Paid for Imports*, conducting verification management of differences on cancellation and applying business of foreign exchange paid for imports to further promote trade facilitation.

With the continuous expansion of trade management rights, in order to facilitate individuals to carry out foreign trade, in August 2004, the State Administration of Foreign Exchange issued the *Notice on Foreign Exchange Management Related to Individual Foreign Trade Operations*, which regulated foreign exchange receipt and payment behavior for individuals engaged in trade in goods, handling technology import and export, and conducting service trade. As the scale of individual foreign exchange receipts and payments continued to expand, the State Administration of Foreign Exchange improved individual foreign exchange management according to the overall opening process of the country and the international balance of payments situation, raising the individual foreign exchange purchase limit five times and simplifying the purchase and payment vouchers. According to the new situation of personal foreign exchange receipts and payments, in order to fully facilitate foreign exchange receipts and payments activities in personal trade and clarify individual capital project transactions, the Foreign Exchange Administration Department issued *Measures for the Administration of Individual Foreign Exchange* at the end of 2006, followed by *Detailed Rules for the Implementation of Personal Foreign Exchange Management Measures* to implement classification management under the main supervision on individual foreign exchange management, that is, to distinguish domestic and overseas individuals by the transaction subject and current and capital projects by the nature of the transaction. According to the convertibility principle of the current account, there was no restriction on foreign exchange receipts and payments of the current personal account, with the bank conducting authenticity verification and the Foreign Exchange Administration Department responsible for supervision, inspection and data analysis afterward. While according to the process of convertibility of capital items, the foreign exchange receipts and payments under the individual capital projects should be managed as necessary, and the Foreign Exchange Administration Department should implement the filing system or approval system according to the administrative license for cross-border foreign exchange transactions in individual capital projects.

(2) *Foreign exchange control over capital accounts*

During this period, measures were taken to simplify the foreign exchange management procedures for capital projects and selectively liberalize the trading limits for some capital projects, with the formally established foreign exchange management reform framework in which renminbi current account was fully convertible, and capital account was selectively convertible.

Carefully open up domestic securities investment. Foreign investors were only allowed to invest in B-shares issued in China and H-shares, N-shares, and other foreign currency stocks and foreign currency bonds issued abroad, not being allowed to invest in domestic renminbi-denominated stocks and bonds. Foreign investors were allowed to set up China-foreign joint venture securities companies but were only allowed to underwrite A shares, underwrite and trade B shares, H shares, government, and corporate bonds, and to initiate a fund. In October 2001, the Ministry of Foreign Trade and Economic Cooperation, the Ministry of Finance and the People's Bank of China jointly issued the *Interim Provisions for Financial AMCs with Foreign Investment to Engage in the Reorganization and Disposition of Assets*, allowing foreign capital of financial asset management corporations to participate in asset restructuring and disposal. In June 2002, the CSRC issued the *Rules for the Establishment of Foreign-shared Securities Companies* to allow foreign-funded securities investment, including domestic securities companies that were changed by overseas shareholders assigning or subscribing for their shares, or securities companies jointly funded by overseas shareholders and domestic shareholders. In November 2002, the CSRC and the People's Bank of China jointly issued *Provisional Administrative Measures on Domestic Securities Investment by Qualified Foreign Institutional Investors*, proposing that Chinese foreign fund management agencies, insurance companies, securities companies, and other asset management agencies that were approved by the CSRC to invest in China's securities market and had obtained the approval of the State Administration of Foreign Exchange may entrust domestic commercial banks as asset custodians and domestic securities companies to handle securities trading activities in China. Qualified foreign institutional investors could hold 10%–20% of the tradable shares of domestic listed companies. Closed funds could remit the principal after three years, and other funds can remit the principal after one year. Subsequently, the State Administration of Foreign Exchange issued the *Interim Provisions on Foreign Exchange Management of Securities Investment in China by Qualified Foreign Institutional Investors*, giving a detailed description of the foreign exchange business related there to and allowing qualified investors to transfer their investments to each other.

Adjust foreign exchange management policies for foreign direct investment. Investment in financial, insurance, securities, and other service industries was allowed, and foreign investors were encouraged to participate in the reorganization and restructuring of state-owned enterprises and state-owned commercial banks by means of mergers and acquisitions. In November 2002, the State Council issued the *Decision on Canceling the First Batch of Administrative Approval Projects*, canceling 789 administrative approval projects, of which 14 were related to capital items, mainly to relax capital controls and open up the market. In November 2002, the CSRC, the Ministry of Finance and the State Economic and Trade Commission jointly issued the *Issues Relevant to the Transfer of State-owned Shares and Legal Person Shares in Listed Companies to Foreign Investors Circular*, adopting the method of public bidding to transfer state-owned shares and legal person shares of listed companies to foreign investors. Foreign investors may purchase and remit foreign exchange according to law after the liquidation of the listed company for the profits they receive from the listed company and the income they receive from the re-transfer of equity. In October 2001, the Ministry of Foreign Trade and Economic Cooperation and the CSRC jointly issued *Foreign Investment Issues Relating to Listed Companies Several Opinions* to allow qualified foreign-invested enterprises to apply for issuing A-shares or B-shares. Share-holding Corporations Ltd. with foreign investment with B-shares may apply for non-listed foreign capital shares to circulate in the B-share market, but foreign-invested companies were not allowed to transfer non-tradable shares of listed companies for the time being. In November 2002, the State Economic and Trade Commission, the Ministry of Finance, the State Administration for Industry and Commerce and the State Administration of Foreign Exchange jointly issued the *Provisional Regulations on Restructuring State-owned Enterprises with Foreign Capital*, allowing state-owned equity holders of state-owned enterprises and corporations to transfer all or part of their equity to foreign investors, and domestic creditors of state-owned enterprises to transfer domestic claims to foreign investors. In March 2003, the Ministry of Foreign Trade and Economic Cooperation, the State Administration for Industry and Commerce, the State Administration of Foreign Exchange and the State Administration of Taxation jointly issued the *Interim Provisions on Mergers and Acquisitions of Domestic Enterprises by Foreign Investors*, allowing foreign investors to conduct mergers and acquisitions of equity and assets in China.

We improved the equalization management of the outflow and inflow of foreign exchange funds, relaxed foreign exchange restrictions on overseas investment, and supported domestic enterprises to "go global". In October 2002, a pilot reform of foreign exchange management for overseas investment was started, with the risk review and profit margin return requirements for overseas investment eliminated, the quota for purchasing foreign currency to invest abroad by enterprises relaxed, and discrimination against private enterprises for purchasing foreign currency to invest abroad reduced. In 2006, the area quota restriction on purchasing foreign currency for overseas investment was lifted, allowing enterprises to remit related upfront expenses first.

(3) *Administration of foreign exchange market*

China's inter-bank foreign exchange market was established in 1994, marking a new stage with three major features in the reform of China's exchange rate system at that time. First, the national market unification was realized through the internet; Second, in the market, the market transaction subjects flatted the positions of foreign exchange settlement and sale through market transactions, forming the market exchange rate, effectively ensuring the development of foreign exchange settlement and sale business for banks and enterprises; Third, the central bank participated in market transactions as a special trading subject in this market, conducive for the central bank to better play its role in macro-control in the foreign exchange field by shifting from direct management to indirect management.

Since China's entry into WTO, the construction of China's inter-bank foreign exchange market was accelerated, especially since 2004, the reform of the foreign exchange market has reflected the orientation of marketization with expanded market scale. In 2005, the renminbi exchange rate formation mechanism took an important step. On July 21, 2005, the People's Bank of China announced the reform of the renminbi exchange rate formation mechanism. Instead of pegging to a single US dollar, it chose several major currencies to form a currency basket, taking into account the changes in the multilateral exchange rate index of the renminbi with reference to the basket of currencies at the same time, and began to implement a managed floating exchange rate system based on market supply and demand and regulated with reference to the basket of currencies. The USD/CNY exchange rate was adjusted from US$1 for RMB8.2765 to US$1 for RMB8.11, and the appreciation of renminbi against US dollar was about 2.01%. The daily closing price of a basket of inter-bank currencies against renminbi was the next day's trading intermediate price, with a fluctuation of 0.3%. On May 18, 2007, the People's Bank of China issued the *Announcement on Expanding the Floating Range of Stock Prices of renminbi against US Dollars in the Interbank Spot Foreign Exchange Market*, announcing that the floating range of stock prices of renminbi against US dollars in the interbank spot foreign exchange market would be increased from 3‰ to 5‰ from May 21, 2007, that is, the daily stock prices of renminbi against US dollars in the interbank spot foreign exchange market could float within the range of 5‰ of the same day's reference rate of renminbi against US dollars announced by the China Foreign Exchange Trading System. The smooth implementation of the new renminbi exchange rate system fully proved that "the managed system of floating foreign currency exchange rates based on market supply and demand, regulated with reference to a basket of currencies" met the requirements of initiative, controllability, and progressivity of China's exchange rate reform. This exchange rate reform not only meant the gradual establishment of a mechanism determined by market supply and demand that is in line with international standards, shaping a more international and standardized exchange rate formation mechanism, but also enriched China's foreign trade macro-control system, indicating that exchange rate policy would be increasingly applied in macroeconomic control in the future.

In terms of the subjects of the foreign exchange market, the number of trading subjects was increasing, and members of the inter-bank foreign exchange market were enlarged to include non-bank financial institutions and large non-financial enterprises. By the end of 2006, the total number of members in the inter-bank spot foreign exchange market had reached 262, including 150 foreign banks, 111 Chinese financial institutions, and one enterprise. Besides, 77 banks had been allowed to become a member of the inter-bank forward foreign exchange market, and 62 banks obtained membership in inter-bank renminbi foreign exchange swap transactions.

An important role of the inter-bank foreign exchange market was to serve the foreign exchange settlement and sale system. Since its realization in 1994, the designated foreign exchange banks have been subject to foreign exchange quota management on positions for turnover of foreign exchange settlement and sale, and the foreign exchange funds used by banks for the turnover of foreign exchange settlement and sale business must not exceed the approved range, otherwise they must enter the inter-bank foreign exchange market for flat compensation. With the deepening of financial reform, especially after the reform of the renminbi exchange rate mechanism, the demand for banks to manage foreign exchange funds flexibly and independently was increasing. In order to meet the developing needs of forwarding foreign exchange market and promote banks to improve the prevention mechanism of exchange rate risk, reform on the management of turnover positions in foreign exchange settlement and sale was also required. On September 23, 2005, the Administration of Foreign Exchange issued the *Notice on Adjusting the Management Measures for Banks' Foreign Exchange Settlement and Sale Positions*, extending the coverage of the past turnover positions of foreign exchange settlement and sale to foreign exchange positions held by designated foreign exchange banks as a result of transactions between renminbi and foreign currencies, implementing the comprehensive position management of foreign exchange settlement and sale. This position included foreign exchange positions formed by banks handling settlement and sale of foreign exchange business to customers, their own settlement and sale of foreign exchange business and participating in inter-bank foreign exchange market transactions in accordance with foreign exchange regulations. At this stage, the lower limit of the management range of the ceiling of the comprehensive position of foreign exchange settlement and sale was zero, while the upper limit was the limit approved by the Foreign Exchange Bureau. Therefore, the total limit of the banking system was significantly increased. This was conducive to enhancing the flexibility and initiative of banks in handling foreign exchange settlement and sale business and foreign exchange fund management, and helpful to achieve fair competition among banks by unifying the management policies and quota approval standards for Chinese and foreign banks. Since January 2006, market makers have been experimented with accrual-based position management, being allowed to incorporate long-term exposure into the comprehensive position management of settlement and sale of foreign exchange, that is, both the forward foreign exchange sales and purchase handled by banks to customers and the exposure formed by forwarding transactions between banks can be flattened at the spot foreign exchange market at the time of signing the contract. On June 2, 2006, the Administration of Foreign Exchange issued the *Notice on Adjusting the General Position Administration on Banking Exchange*, saying that from July 1, 2006, the overall position of banking exchange would be managed on an accrual basis instead of a cash basis, which would be implemented to all designated foreign exchange banks. Accrual position management has played a positive role in further developing the foreign exchange market, improving the trading mechanism of renminbi against foreign currency derivatives, and promoting banks to strengthen exchange rate risk prevention and enhance risk management. After 10 years of the development of forward settlement and surrender exchange market in China, especially the all-round development since the reform of renminbi exchange rate formation mechanism in 2005, the number of participating banks had expanded from originally the Bank of China to 71 at the end of July 2007, with the transaction volume increased from US$3.3 billion in 1998 to US$76.4 billion in January to July 2007. This has played an important role in broadening the management measures of exchange rate risk of domestic economic units, expanding the range of bank products and services, cultivating the domestic market of renminbi for foreign currency derivatives and perfecting the renminbi exchange rate formation mechanism.

In addition, the efficiency of China's foreign exchange market was further improved by opening foreign currency borrowing business, introducing market maker system, changing the standard delivery time, adopting the measures of futures / swaps agreement, unifying foreign and domestic banks' access standards for forward settlement and sale of foreign exchange business and the approval standards for settlement and sale of foreign exchange quotas, and changing the pricing of forward settlement and sale of foreign exchange from one price to multiple prices.

It is precisely because China has seized the opportunity of "joining the WTO" to actively promote its own domestic reform, better integrate itself into the international economic system and push forward the process of internationalization of China's economy that China can usher in a new round of high-speed growth in the first eight years of the new century. We have proved by our actions that the Chinese people can not only dance well with "wolves" but also benefit everyone, achieve win-win.

3.3.3 Achievements of China's economic internationalization at the beginning of the 21st century

At the turn of the century, when Chinese people were still hesitating about the pros and cons of "joining the WTO", maybe it was hard for them to imagine that in just a few years, great changes would be brought to China. China's entry into the WTO would probably have no less influence than the South Talks. China has successfully boarded the economic globalization express by joining the WTO as a driver rather than a passenger, pushed forward the reform and opening up in the domestic economic field, connected with the international community and gained new development opportunities.

Through this round of economic internationalization, China's economic development is catching up, with an open economy developed by leaps and bounds, and the national economy entered one of the best periods of development.

3.3.3.1 Rapid development in the field of trade

Since the reform and opening up, foreign trade has become the fastest growing area in China's economy by expanding the opening up and deepening the reform of the foreign trade system, with self-evident status and role in the national economy. China's entry into WTO has made unprecedented development in the field of trade.

After joining WTO, China's foreign trade development ushered in the best period in history. In the last 20 years of the 20th century, China's foreign trade developed at an extremely rapid speed, and China's accession to the WTO once again promoted the great development of foreign trade, made the scale of foreign trade rise sharply. By comparing data, we can find that from 1978 to 2000, China's total import and export volume expanded from US$20.64 billion to US$474.3 billion, achieving an increase of about 23 times and an average annual growth rate of 15.3%. Among them, the export volume rose from US$9.75 billion to US$249.2 billion, with an increase of 25.5 times and an average annual growth of 15.8%, while the import volume rose from US$10.9 billion to US$225.1 billion, with an increase of about 21 times and an average annual growth of 14.8%. Since China joined the WTO in 2001, China's import and export increased 4.58 times from 2000 to 2007 from the previous high level, with an average annual growth rate of 24.3%, with export increased 4.9 times, achieving an average annual growth rate of 25.4%, and import increased 4.25 times, achieving an average annual growth rate of 23%. As can also be seen from Figure 3-6, import and export have witnessed rapid growth after China's entry into the WTO. Although the speed declined and tended to stabilize after 2004, the growth rate of foreign trade after 2000, whether import or export, was higher than that before China's entry into the WTO.

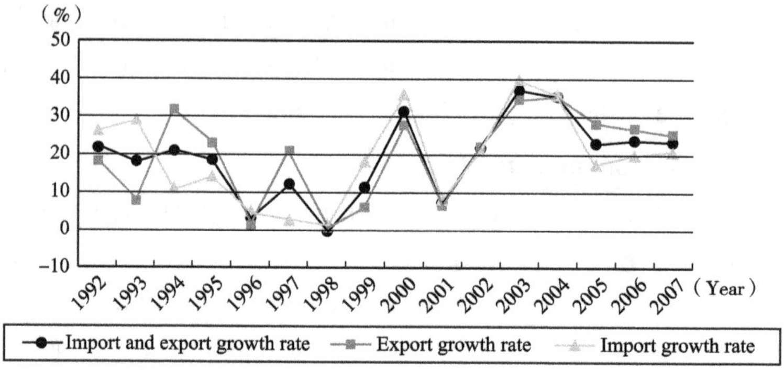

Figure 3–6 Changes in China's import and export growth rate from 1992 to 2007

Source: Data Center of Mofcom, http://data.mofcom.gov.cn/index.html.

Figure 3–7 shows China's fast-growing trade scale after China's entry into the WTO from another side. According to the proportion of world trade volume, it rose from 4.3% in 1992 to 15.5% in 2007, exceptionally rapid after 2001. In 2007, China's position in world trade rose to the third place, making China a real trading power. Moreover, the export of foreign trade played an amazing role in boosting China's economic growth. Throughout the 1990s, the proportion of China's foreign trade exports to GDP was hovering at 20%. While after China's accession to the WTO, the proportion of foreign trade exports continued to rise as shown in Figure 3–8 and remained 37% despite a slight decline in 2007, primarily established the position of foreign trade in the "troika" of China's economic growth.

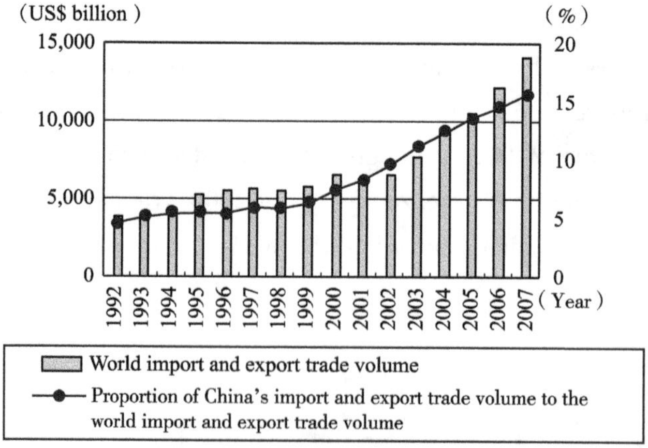

Figure 3–7 Proportion of China's import and export trade volume to the world import and export trade volume from 1992 to 2007

Source: National Statistics Bureau.

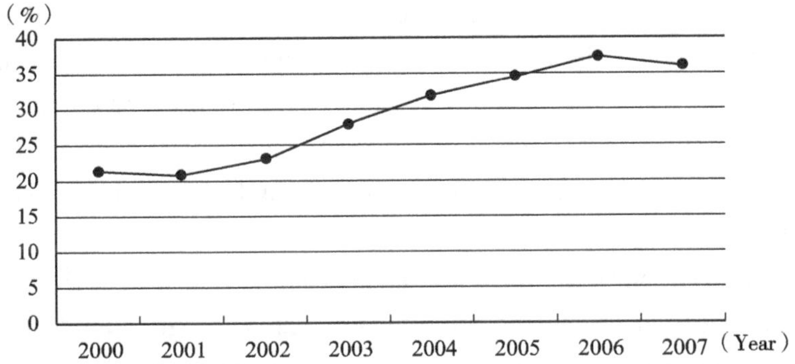

Figure 3-8 China's export trade as a proportion of GDP from 2000 to 2007

Source: World Bank Database, http://data.worldbank.org.cn/.

The increasing trade volume also enhanced the degree of dependence upon foreign trade.[1] From 1980 to 2000, China's dependence on foreign trade increased from 12.5% to 39.6%, with an increase of 27.1 percentage points and an average annual increase of about 1.7 percentage points. The dependence on exports increased from 6.1% to 20.8%, with a rise of 14.7 percentage points and an average annual increase of more than 0.7 percentage points. Dependence on imports increased from 6.4% to 18.8%, with an increase of 12.4 percentage points. The importance of foreign trade in the national economy has increased rapidly since China's entry into the WTO, with an increase of 9.2 and 7.9 percentage points in 2003 and 2004 respectively, which then stabilized. In 2007, China's dependence on foreign trade reached 62.2%. The increase in dependence on foreign trade reflects not only the deepening of China's participation in economic globalization but also the increased dependence of the national economy on the international market.

With the rapid development of the total trade volume, China's foreign trade structure also underwent great changes, which led to three industrial restructurings in China.

Agriculture was the focus of WTO negotiations. After China's entry into WTO, the import value of China's agricultural products, their proportion of world agricultural products imports, and their ranking in the world are all on the rise. In 2006, China's agricultural product imports rose from the previous 5th to 6th place in the world, and in 2007, China's agricultural product imports reached US$71.92 billion. The rapid growth of agricultural products imports resulted in a deficit in agricultural products

[1] The degree of dependence upon foreign trade is the total import and export/GDP.

trade. Since 2004, our agricultural products have been in an ongoing deficit. Large imports of soybeans, edible vegetable oils and cotton produced the world's largest import volume. However, as can be seen from Figure 3–9, China's grain production did not decline but instead, showed a momentum of accelerating growth. China's agricultural exports to the outside world also increased, but the import momentum was stronger. By importing land- and water-intensive agrarian products, such as grain, cotton, oil, and sugar, and exporting labor-intensive products, such as fruits, vegetables, flowers, aquatic products, and animal products, China's agricultural structure was adjusted to the rational use of resources and the pressure on domestic agricultural resources was reduced.

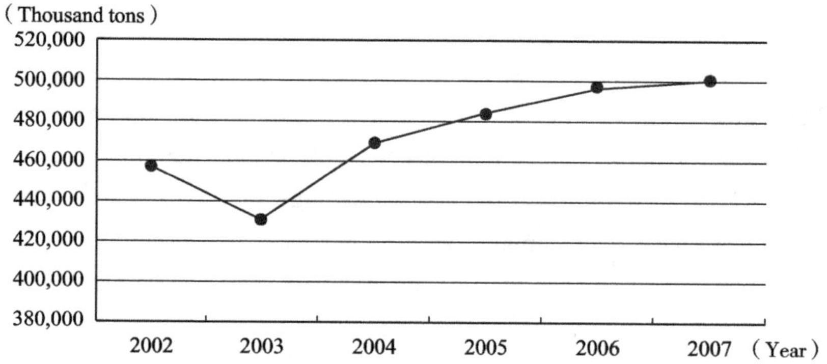

Figure 3–9 Production status of agricultural products in China from 2002 to 2007

Source: *China Statistical Yearbook.*

In the manufacturing sector, China gradually completed the upgrading of its export structure in the 1990s. In 2000, the ratio of industrial manufactures to primary products in China reached 90:10, far exceeding the level of 60:40 in developing countries and even the average level of 80:20 in OECD countries. Compared with the major countries and regions in the world, the proportion of manufactured goods exported from China's mainland was only slightly lower than those of Japan, South Korea, Israel, the Philippines, and Taiwan of China, by 6, 3, 6, 5, and 7 percentage points respectively, 5, 3, 7, 6, 24, and 59 percentage points higher than developed countries such as the US, Germany, France, the UK, Canada, and Australia, as well as 9, 29 and 66 percentage points higher than big countries such as India, Brazil, and Russia, respectively. By 2007, the proportion of manufactured goods exported by China had increased by 6.6 percentage points over 2000, much higher than the world average.

The improvement of trade structure was also reflected in the optimization of export commodity structure. After the 10th Five-year Plan period, China's foreign trade sector actively implemented the strategy of promoting trade and brand by science and technology, which promoted the optimization of export commodities. The rapid increase in the proportion of high-tech products exports was achieved, as is shown in Table 3–6, the trade volume of high-tech products in China increased nearly ten times from 2000 to 2007, from US$37.04 billion in 2000 to US$347.83 billion. Export growth is faster than import growth, with a surplus beginning in 2004 and continuing to expand. In 2007 there was a surplus of US$60.8 billion. In 2007, China's exports of high-tech products accounted for 28.6% of total exports, which was the same as that of the United States, 13 and 8 percentage points higher than those of Germany and Japan, two manufacturing powers, respectively.

Table 3–6 Import and export of high–tech products in China from 2000 to 2007

Unit: US$ billion

Item	2000	2001	2002	2003	2004	2005	2006	2007
Export volume	37.04	46.45	67.86	110.32	165.36	218.25	281.45	347.83
Import volume	52.51	64.11	82.84	119.3	161.34	197. 71	247.30	286.99
Total export and import volume	89.55	110.56	150.69	229.62	326.71	415.97	528.75	634.82
Balance	-15.46	-17.66	-14.98	-8.98	4.02	20.54	34.15	60.84

Source: Data Center of Mofcom, http://data.mofcom.gov.cn/index.html.

From Table 3–7, we can also see the foreign trade situation of China's mechanical and electrical products is very similar to that of high-tech products. From 2000 to 2007, the trade volume of China's high-tech products increased nearly sevenfold, and the growth of exports was also significantly faster than that of imports. Starting from 2002, the surplus continues to expand, realizing a surplus of US$202.19 billion in 2007.

Table 3–7 Import and export of mechanical and electrical products in China from 2000 to 2007

Unit: US$ billion

Item	2000	2001	2002	2003	2004	2005	2006	2007
Export volume	105.31	118.79	157.08	227.46	323.40	426.81	549.42	701.77
Import volume	102.87	120.52	155.60	224.99	301.88	350.38	427.73	498.98
Total export and import volume	208.18	239.31	312.68	452.45	625.28	777.19	977.17	1,200.15
Balance	2.44	−1.73	1.48	2.47	21.6	76.43	121.69	202.19

Source: Data Center of Mofcom, http://data.mofcom.gov.cn/index.html.

In 2007, China's exports of high-tech products and mechanical and electrical products accounted for 28.6% and 57.6% of the total export trade respectively, accounting for more than 80% of the total export altogether, and these two types of products have become the main products of China's foreign trade. The rapid growth of the export of these two kinds of products enabled China to transform its export commodity structure successfully, and at the same time, it promoted the upgrading of China's domestic industrial structure.

In terms of trade in services, before 2000, although China's trade in services continued to increase in the proportion of import and export trade and the growth rate of trade in services was slightly higher than the growth rate of trade in goods in the same period, there was still a wide gap between it and the world average. The proportion of world service export in international trade exports has remained above 20% since the 1970s, while China's service trade exports accounted for only 11.1% of import and export in 2001. After joining WTO, China opened up its service industry market. Although the proportion of China's service industry in GDP did not change much during this period (from 40.5% in 2001 to 38.6% in 2007), the service industry developed vigorously and the scale of service trade expanded rapidly, rising from US$72.61 billion in 2001 to US$252.32 billion in 2007, with a total amount exceeding US$200 billion for the first time, up four times from 2000, with an average annual growth rate of 21%, exceeding that of the previous 20 years (see Table 3–8). The proportion of service trade exports in world exports kept increasing. In 2007, service trade exports ranked 7th in the world and imports ranked 5th in the world. Of course, there were also problems behind the booming trade in services. One was that the deficit in trade in services had widened further since the 1990s, indicating that the level of domestic service industry still needed to be improved. The other was that although the service industry was growing at a fast speed, the total volume of trade in services was smaller than that of trade in goods, and was still smaller than that of developed countries such as the United States, not matching with China's status as a trading power.

Table 3–8 Development of China's service trade from 2001 to 2007

Year	Total import and export volume (US$ billion)	Export volume (US$ billion)	Import volume (US$ billion)	Trade balance (US$ billion)	Service industry accounts for GDP (%)
2001	72.61	33.34	39.27	-5.93	40.5
2002	86.27	39.74	46.53	-6.79	41.5
2003	102.04	46.73	55.31	-8.58	41.2
2004	134.56	62.43	72.13	-9.70	40.4
2005	158.19	74.40	83.79	-9.39	40.0
2006	192.83	92.00	100.83	-8.83	39.4
2007	252.32	122.21	130.11	-7.90	38.6

Source: *China Statistical Yearbook* of the past years.

3.3.3.2 "Bringing in" and "going global" are initially combined

Compared with the 1990s, after 2000, China not only further expanded the scale of foreign investment but also actively encouraged Chinese capital to go global. The 16th National Congress of the CPC proposed to adhere to the policy of "going global" and "bringing in" to comprehensively improve the level of opening to the outside world. China's entry into the WTO also provided a broad overseas market for Chinese enterprises. During this period, China made good achievements in both "bringing in" and "going global."

(1) *"Bringing in"*

Since China's entry into the WTO, the scale of our use of foreign capital has continued to expand. Foreign-funded enterprises were fully integrated into China, playing an important role in boosting China's economy. Especially after opening up the service industry market, a large number of foreign investors were attracted to invest in China, and China has become one of the world's most important investment places.

First, the amount of foreign capital utilized has increased year by year. As can be seen from Figure 3–10, China's actual use of foreign capital has maintained a steady growth since China's accession to the WTO. At the same time, the number of newly-established foreign-invested enterprises had increased sharply due to the opening up of the service industry, which did not slow down until 2006. The average size of foreign-funded enterprises was further improved. By the end of 2007, more than 480 of the World Top 500 MNCs(multinational companies) had invested or set up institutions in China, more than 980 research and development centers had been set up by MNCs in various forms, and more than 40 million people had been directly employed by foreign-invested enterprises in China. The influx of multinational companies enabled China to enter the global division of labor system rapidly and promoted the rapid growth of China's foreign trade by taking advantage of the market size, labor force, and other resource advantages. From 2002 to 2007, the import and export volume of foreign direct investment enterprises increased from US$330.22 billion to US$1,254.93 billion, accounting for more than 50% of China's foreign trade all along. It can be said that China's foreign trade could not have achieved such brilliant achievements without foreign-funded enterprises.

However, judging from the export commodity structure of foreign-invested enterprises, most of China's high-tech products were completed by foreign-invested enterprises. In 2006, exports of high-tech products of foreign-invested enterprises accounted for 88.06% of that of the country, and exports of mechanical and electrical products of foreign-invested enterprises accounted for 74.05% of that of the country. It is thus clear that though China's exports of high-tech products in trade grew rapidly, most of which were driven by foreign-invested enterprises, especially wholly-foreign-funded enterprises, indicating that the level of China to undertake the transfer of world industry was still low.

However, domestic enterprises also developed in this process. Foreign-invested enterprises had a substantial spillover effect. By absorbing their production factors such as technology, management experience, brands, and market channels, domestic enterprises were promoted, especially the service industry in China, which benefited greatly and achieved rapid development.

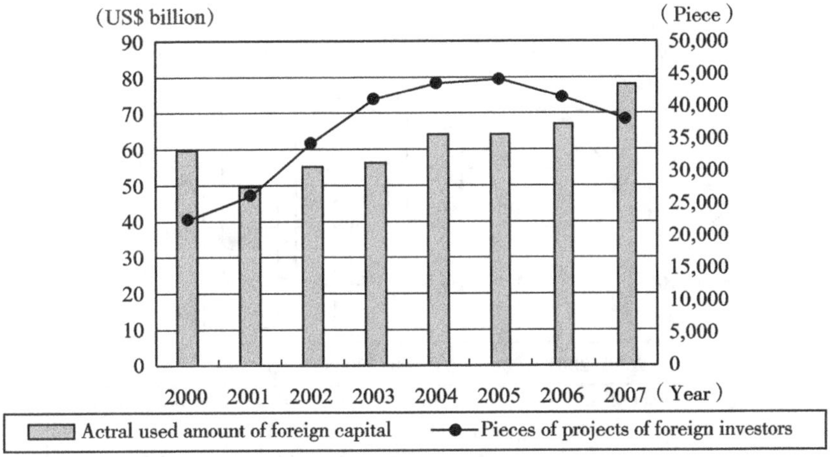

Figure 3–10 Actual used foreign capital in China from 2000 to 2007

Source: *China Statistical Yearbook*, http://www.stats.gov.cn/tjsj/ndsj/.

Second, foreign investment impacted China's industrial distribution. The industrial distribution of foreign investment in China after 2000 was similar to that in the 1990s, with a still relatively large proportion of foreign investment in the manufacturing industry. It is not difficult to find from Figure 3–11 that manufacturing still accounted for the bulk of the actual use of foreign capital, but its ability to absorb foreign capital was declining. In 2007, there were 19,193 newly-established foreign-invested enterprises in the manufacturing industry, and the actual amount of foreign investment used was US$40.9 billion, down 23% and 5% respectively from the same period in 2006. At the same time, there were 16,165 foreign-invested enterprises in the field of trade in services (excluding finance) in 2007, up 7% year on year. The actual amount of foreign investment used was US$36.8 billion, up 46% from the same period of last year, accounting for 41% of the total amount of foreign investment absorbed in the country, of which the use of foreign investment in the communications service industry increased 5.6 times. As can be seen from the flow of foreign capital, although China's service industry was still in the growth stage after China's entry into the WTO, it has already sprouted a strong vitality, and it can also be seen that China's domestic industrial structure has been quietly adjusted three times under the impetus of the new round of economic internationalization.

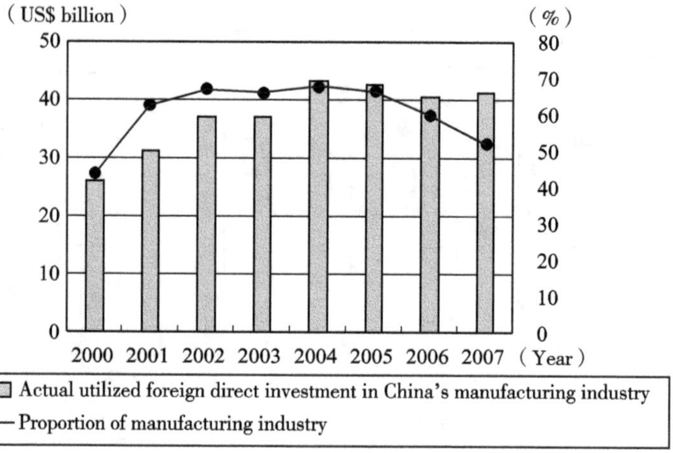

Figure 3–11 Actual utilization of foreign capital in China's manufacturing industry from 2000 to 2007

Source: *China Statistical Yearbook.*

Third, the taxation of foreign-funded enterprises steadily increased. In 2006, the national tax on foreign-invested enterprises in 2006 (excluding tariff and land tax) amounted to RMB797.694 billion, an increase of 24.81% over the previous year, accounting for 21.19% of the total tax revenue of RMB3,763.704 billion. Among them, foreign-invested enterprises paid RMB155.262 billion of enterprise income tax, an increase of 33.77% year on year, accounting for 21.93% of the national total of RMB708.09 billion of enterprise income tax. The personal income tax of foreign-invested enterprises was RMB50.998 billion, up 19.73% year on year, accounting for 20.79% of the national total personal income tax of RMB245.267 billion. The value-added tax of foreign-invested enterprises was RMB478.048 billion, up 21.24% year on year, accounting for 26.92% of the total value-added tax of RMB1,775.593 billion. The consumption tax of foreign-invested enterprises was RMB33.785 billion, up 37.79% year on year, accounting for 16.96% of the national consumption tax of RMB199.168 billion. Business tax on foreign-invested enterprises was RMB62.353 billion, up 27.27% year on year, accounting for 12.16% of the national business tax of RMB512.975 billion.[1]

(2) "*Going global*"

Foreign investment achieved remarkable results. Since China's entry into the

[1]Pei Changhong ed., *Research on Reform and Opening Up and Circulation Reform for 30 years of China*, Beijing: Economy & Management Publishing House, 2008, pp.212-213.

WTO, China's outward foreign direct investment has achieved sustained rapid development by speeding up the implementation of the "going global" strategy to actively promote economic internationalization. Great changes took place in both the annual scale of investment and the ranking of the world. China has changed from a potential big country to a real vast country of foreign direct investment, which is heading towards a powerful country of foreign direct investment.

First, the scale of foreign investment developed rapidly. China's foreign direct investment traffic increased from US$6.90 billion in 2001 to US$26.51 billion in 2007, an increase of about four times. The reserves of foreign direct investment increased about fourfold from US$27.2 billion in 2001 to US$117.91 billion in 2007 (see Table 3–9). With a rare quick speed of foreign investment development, China's ranking in the world for foreign direct investment has dramatically raised.

Table 3–9 China's foreign direct investment

Year	China's FDI traffic (US$ billion)	China FDI traffic growth rate (%)	World ranking
2001	6.90	590.0	19
2002	2.70	-60.9	26
2003	2.85	5.6	22
2004	5.50	93.0	21
2005	12.26	122.9	18
2006	21.16	72.6	13
2007	26.51	25.3	18

Note: China's foreign direct investment traffic was US$1 billion in 2000 and soared to US$6.9 billion in 2001, thus increasing by 590%. Data from 2001 to 2005 are China's non-financial FDI data, and data from 2006 to 2007 are industry-wide FDI data.[1]

Source: Pei Changhong ed., *Research on Reform and Opening Up and Circulation Reform for 30 years of China*, Beijing: Economy and Management Publishing House, 2008, p.59.

Second, the way of foreign investment was becoming more and more diversified. Greenfield investment, leasing, cross-border mergers and acquisitions, strategic alliances and joint investment coexist, but the status of mergers and acquisitions is increasingly prominent. In 2001, the number of overseas mergers and acquisitions was US$452 million, accounting for only 6.6% of China's foreign direct investment in that year. While in 2005, it increased to US$6.5 billion, accounting for 53% of the foreign

[1] Pei Changhong ed., *Research on Reform and Opening Up and Circulation Reform for 30 years of China*, Beijing: Economy & Management Publishing House,2008, pp.212-213.

direct investment flows in that year, more than half. Although the proportion decreased in 2006 and 2007, the amount of investment did not fall. From 2003 to 2007, foreign investment realized through cross-border mergers and acquisitions exceeded US$21 billion, accounting for about 37% of total foreign direct investment in the same period.

Third, the gap between the introduced foreign capital and outward foreign investment was narrowed. Since the implementation of the "going out" strategy, China's situation of stronger utilization of foreign capital and weaker foreign investment has been improved significantly. The ratio of foreign investment in the utilization of foreign capital was only 0.3%: 1 in 1994, which increased to 1.5%: 1 in 2000. Since then, foreign investment has expanded rapidly to 27.3%: 1 in 2007.

Fourth, the economic and social benefits were remarkable. Through foreign investment and cooperation, China coordinated the structural adjustment of its domestic industries and realized the origin diversification. About 1,000 overseas processing trade enterprises approved and filed by the Ministry of Commerce located in nearly 100 countries and regions. At present, the overseas Chinese enterprises (non-financial) have a total assets of about US$300 billion, employing 630 thousand people (including 268 thousand foreigners), paying about US$3 billion in taxes overseas each year, and the import and export volume of domestic investors through overseas enterprises is about US$100 billion. Through foreign investment and cooperation,China has accumulated more than 100 million tons of equity oil.[1]

3.3.2.3 Breakthroughs have been made in economic diplomacy[2]

The end of the 20th century was the era of economic globalization, while the beginning of the 21st century was the era when economic regionalization began to prevail. On the one hand, this was because the birth of the EU and euro allowed countries to see the benefits of regional organizations. On the other hand, because the WTO Doha Round had not been settled for a long time, blocking the process of economic globalization, many countries attempted to carry out regional economic cooperation under the WTO framework. Since the 1990s, China has actively participated in regional economic cooperation, which has been further developed in the new century. Hu Jintao pointed out at the 10th meeting of diplomatic envoys abroad in August 2004 that the creativity, initiative, and aggressiveness of diplomatic

---

[1] Wang Zixian ed., *30 Years' Foreign Economy and Trade of China Since Reform and Opening Up*, Beijing: Economy & Management Publishing House, 2008, p.70.

[2] Wang Zixian ed., *30 Years' Foreign Economy and Trade of China Since Reform and Opening Up*, Beijing: Economy & Management Publishing House, 2008, pp.176-177.

work should be enhanced to safeguard and expand China's national interests, economic diplomacy should be strengthened and the implementation of the opening-up strategy of "bringing in" and "going out" should be promoted; we should strengthen the ability to protect our overseas interests, improve relevant laws and regulations, as well as early warning and rapid response mechanisms to serve our citizens and institutions abroad.[1] China should not only use WTO rules to safeguard its own interests but also participate in the formulation of international economic rules to actively create a stable external environment for its own development.

Great progress was made in China's participating in regional economic cooperation. After its entry into the WTO, China accelerated the building of a surrounding free trade platform to gradually set up a global free trade network. The free trade zone strategy is an integral part of a country's opening-up policy and an important measure to expand the breadth and depth of opening up, improve the level of open economy and participate deeply in the process of economic globalization. In 2003, the Mainland, Hong Kong SAR, and Macao SAR signed the *Closer Economic Partnership Arrangement* and its *Supplementary Agreement.* On November 4, 2002, then Premier Zhu Rongji signed the *Framework Agreement on Comprehensive Economic Cooperation*, the *Agreement on Trade in Goods*, the *Agreement on Dispute Settlement Mechanism* and the *Agreement on Trade in Services* with the 10 ASEAN countries to continue promoting investment negotiations. On November 18, 2005, China and Chile signed the *Free Trade Agreement (Goods). The China-Pakistan Free Trade Agreement* was signed with Pakistan on November 24, 2006. In 2008, China's free trade zone negotiations made another breakthrough, that is, China successfully signed agreements with New Zealand and Singapore. At the same time, progress was made in the free trade zone negotiations with Australia, Peru, Iceland, and other countries. As of 2008, China had been building 12 free trade zones with 29 countries and regions in the world, including China-ASEAN free trade zone established in cooperation with neighboring developing countries, China-New Zealand free trade zone established in cooperation with developed countries, and China-Chile free trade zone spanning traditional geographical areas. The free trade zone strategy effectively promoted China's economic and trade relations with neighboring countries. For example, China-ASEAN free trade zone witnessed rapid growth in trade between China and ASEAN after its establishment, with an average annual growth of more than 20%

[1] "10th Diplomatic Conference held in Beijing", *People's Daily*, Aug.30, 2004.

since 2004, and by 2007, China and ASEAN had become each other's fourth largest trading partner.

China participated in and promoted the development of the international economic system under the WTO framework. As a big developing country, China should not only seek for its own interests and development in the formulation of international rules but also assume reasonable international obligations as far as possible. In September 2003, China attended the World Trade Organization Ministerial Meeting (Cancun) for the first time as a member. Lu Fuyuan, then commerce minister, apparently stood on the position of developing countries, claiming: "The rights of developed and developing members in the WTO are not symmetrical, the obligations are not balanced, and the benefits are not equal; Market access barriers of developed countries against developing countries are far from being eliminated;Instead of narrowing the gap between the north and the south, the gap has been widened ... As the vast majority of WTO members are developing countries, that developing members can truly benefit from the negotiations is the basic guarantee for the success of the Doha development agenda." China formed G21 with Brazil, India, Argentina, Pakistan, South Africa, and other developing countries to cope with the issue of agricultural products trade, demanding developed countries to open their markets, cancel subsidies and reduce trade protection for agricultural products. At this time, China spoke on behalf of the interests of developing countries. However, on some issues, such as market access for non-agricultural products, China's interests were not entirely consistent with those of most developing countries. Unlike in the past, China is not only a developing country but also a rising world power. This change of status requires us to adapt. Supachai Panitpakdi, the first director general of the World Trade Organization from a developing country, once pointed out: "China hopes to play an important role in the World Trade Organization. In the long run, China's most appropriate role may be one that is to build a bridge between developing and developed countries."[1]As a rising developing country, China, proceeding from its own interests and striving for the rights and interests of developing countries, really needs to act a "bridge" in the subsequent economic diplomacy and international multilateral negotiations.

---

[1] Shi Jianjun ed., *China's Entry into the World—Collected Papers by the University Of International Business And Economics on China's Entry into WTO for A Decade*, Beijing: the University Of International Business And Economics Press, 2011, p.59.

The impact of this round of economic internationalization on China's development is exceptionally far-reaching. It is by seizing this opportunity that China could achieve great development at the beginning of the 21st century, with its economy catching up with those of developed countries, and as its international economic influence was growing day by day, China became an economic power that surprised the world.

If China's rapid development was due to its practicing on the right road before the 20th century, then in the first eight years of the 20th century, after joining the WTO, the correctness and strength of China's road began to be demonstrated worldwide. The internationalization of China's economy not only brings us the dividend of globalization but also makes the people of the world enjoy the dividend of China.

We have proved to the world through practice that China is on a path of peaceful development and win-win cooperation. The 2008 financial crisis not only challenged the internationalization of China's economy but also made the world witness the strength of China's model once again.

3.4 Internationalization of China's economy in response to the financial crisis

In the first decade of the 20th century, two major events had a great impact on the internationalization of China's economy. One was to join the WTO; the other was the outbreak of the financial crisis in 2008. The difference is that the former has greatly promoted China's economic internationalization, while the latter has brought great challenges to it.

In 2008, the world economic situation was changing, and the financial crisis triggered by the US subprime mortgage crisis became more and more serious, which finally expanded to the whole world, spreading from the financial field to real economy, resulting in an international economic crisis that was rarely seen before with strong impact and wide sweep area. The inherent contradictions of capitalism burst forth with the form of economic crisis. Against the background of economic globalization, economic exchanges between countries were increasingly closer, through which any country's economic crisis may spread out, thus making the economic crisis stricken area wider and wider. Any country involved in international economic activities would not be spared, and eventually, a global economic crisis would be brought about.

With China's accession to the WTO, its opening up was dramatically accelerated, and the degree of economic internationalization increased day by day. By 2007, China had already become the world's third largest economy and second largest trading nation, whose economy was closely linked with the world economy. As the United States was China's third largest source of investment, second largest export market and the sixth largest source of imports, its domestic economy "earthquake" would naturally affect China with a severe impact on China's economic internationalization.

3.4.1 The financial crisis in 2008

The financial crisis in 2008 was the latest economic crisis to us and the most serious one since the Great Depression in the 1930s, whose consequences have profoundly impacted the current world economic structure. Some American scholars even call it "Great Depression 2.0", believing its severity can rival that of the Great Depression of 1929–1933, which had almost led to the collapse of the capitalist system and was also one of the main factors caused the Second World War.

A correct understanding of the seriousness of the financial crisis and its impact on China will enable us to understand the measures taken by China in coping with it, and where China's economic internationalization will be ahead in the post-crisis era.

(1) *Review of the financial crisis*

It is generally believed that the US subprime mortgage crisis in 2007 was the direct cause of the financial crisis, but most scholars at that time did not realize that its impact would be so great in the end. Coincidentally, 2007 coincides with the 10th anniversary of the Asian financial crisis. Some countries, particularly those in Asia, even held seminars, but none of them has imagined that a crisis much more severe than the 1997 Asian financial crisis was brewing.

Since the collapse of the United States NASDAQ bubble in 2001, the Federal Reserve has continuously cut interest rates in support of the US economy, resulting in lower interest rates in various countries and the rise of the housing market, especially in the US and UK. Low-interest rates led various financial institutions to borrow large amounts of debt, and the debt-equity ratio rose to a dangerously high level. Many US government agencies promoted the construction of housing for the poor, resulting in an increase of home ownership in the United States. A variety of financial innovation products emerged, including mortgage-backed securities, collateralized debt obligation, and credit default swaps. By November 2006, the precursor of the storm had already appeared—the ABX index, a composite index of the prices of subprime mortgage securities, had fallen by 1.5%.

In 2007, the United States real estate market bubble burst and year on year housing prices fell for the first time since 1991. The sudden collapse of subprime lending companies led to losses in many financial institutions and ran on money market funds, with tighter credit and higher interest rates. The unemployment rate was stable, hovering below 4.5% until the end of the year, but the oil price rose dramatically. By the middle of 2007, house prices had fallen by nearly 4% from their peak in 2006. From February to March, several subprime lending companies announced losses, including Accredited Home Lenders Holding Co., New Century Financial Corporation and Countrywide Financial Corporation. On March 5, HSBC announced that the default rate of some subprime loans purchased by the bank was higher than that contained in the pricing model of these products.On March 6, Federal Reserve Chairman Bernanke warned that the government-sponsored enterprises, Fannie Mae and Freddie Mac, were the source of systemic risks, and he suggested legislation to prevent potential crises. On June 7, Bear Stearns Cos. announced that its two funds stopped redemptions. On April 2, New Century Financial Corporation, the second largest subprime mortgage company in the US, filed for bankruptcy protection. On August 16, helped by a US$11 billion syndicated emergency loan, financial companies across the United States survived bankruptcy. On August 31, Ameriquest, the former leading company of the US subprime mortgage companies, went out of business. On November 1, the Federal Reserve injected US$41 billion into the banking system to facilitate banks to borrow money at low interest rates, which was the largest single injection by the Federal Reserve since 2001. On December 12, central banks including the Federal Reserve, the Bank of England, the European Central Bank, the Swiss National Bank and the Bank of Canada took measures to ease the pressure on the short-term financing market.

In early 2008, the economy began to show signs of depression. At that time, the financial market was chaotic, house prices fell, crude oil prices exceeded US$75 per barrel, and consumer spending was also slowing down. On February 11, American International Group Inc. (AIG) announced that its auditors had found significant deficiencies in the company's internal control over the valuation of credit default swap portfolios. On March 14, JP Morgan Chase announced that it would join hands with the Federal Reserve Bank of New York to provide Bear Stearns (BSC) with a 28-day secured financing and would acquire BSC with government support the next day. The disaster was temporarily avoided. There was a short-term stability in the market, but

BSC's problems also existed in other investment banks, and the systemic risks in the unregulated OTC derivatives market remained unresolved.

On July 11, the Independent National Mortgage Corporation, a US mortgage lender, entered bankruptcy custody. On July 13, the US Treasury Department launched a rescue plan for Fannie Mae and Freddie Mac. On September 7, Fannie Mae and Freddie Mac were taken over by the US government. On September 14, Bank of America Corp. bought Merrill Lynch & Co., and Lehman Brothers were on the verge of bankruptcy. On September 15, the US government decided not to rescue Lehman Brothers with a history of 158 years, which then filed for bankruptcy protection.

Harvey Miller, a lawyer in charge of Lehman's bankruptcy, said: "The collapse of Lehman has caused systematic disaster to the whole world. It has a negative impact on the fragile volatility of the financial system.The expectation of failure in the financial market has seriously undermined the confidence of the entire financial system".[1]This is the case. On the day Lehman filed for bankruptcy protection, the DJIA fell more than 500 points, or more than 4%, its biggest daily decline since September 11; US pension plans, government pension funds, and other portfolios lost US$700 billion; Lehman's bankruptcy also affected its 8000 subsidiaries with US$600 billion in assets and liabilities, more than 100,000 corporate creditors and more than 26,000 employees, and there were 660,000 claims (more than US$873 billion) against Lehman by September 2010. Lehman's bankruptcy was like a domino, causing investors to panic in the financial market, and Morgan Stanley, Bank of America, Citibank and Bank of America were all hit.

24 hours after Lehman's bankruptcy, the Federal Reserve provided US$85 billion in aid to AIG. However, this inconsistent behavior of the US government (the government did not save Lehman, but saved Bear Stearns and Fannie Mae and Freddie Mac before and then AIG) only increased the panic in the market. The impact of the crisis spread all over the world, so far the financial crisis caused by the subprime mortgage crisis had reached a catastrophic level.

(2) *The cause of the financial crisis*

It is generally believed that the formation of the US financial crisis is mainly due to improper use of monetary instruments by the Federal Reserve and lack of supervision, coupled with people's lack of understanding of financial derivatives and their uncertainties. Due to the improper use of monetary supply policy, the market had

---

[1] Miller, *Written Testimony for the FCIC*, Sep.2, 2010, Transcript, p.23.

been in a state of excess liquidity for a long time, so the excess liquidity blindly sought appreciation and accumulated huge risks. Due to the lack of supervision, the "three noes" (no fixed income source, no fixed assets, no good credit record) could also get large loans, so the root of the disaster was deeply buried. Due to inadequate supervision and lack of understanding of financial derivatives, subprime loans could also be turned into quality assets through financial derivatives, and no one knew how many and by whom these assets were held, so credit was lost. In this way, when the economic environment changed, the problem became a crisis.

However, this is only the superficial or direct reason. The fundamental reason should be that the energy accumulation caused by the deviation of a subjective value from objective value reached a level that could trigger a crisis. On the one hand, the United States needed to consume (and this rate of consumption was still increasing) a large amount of wealth to achieve its objective and subjective goals at home and abroad. Internationally, if the United States wanted to win the war on terror and to complete all the contents given by unilateralism, a large number of expenses were needed. At home, the United States also needed to meet the growing material and spiritual needs of the American people, such as living in larger houses and having better game software. On the other hand, the United States cannot increase the speed of wealth creation. In terms of labor, resources and technological development, the US could only create wealth at a low speed until it found a new economic growth point. The superposition of the two aspects undoubtedly resulted in a constant reduction of objective value. Therefore, in order to maintain the lining and face of a big country, the United States had to borrow from other countries and from the future by means of institutional innovation and dazzling financial means. As a result, the subjective value corresponding to the objective value of each unit grew larger and larger. When this deviation accumulated to a certain extent, the energy of the crisis released from the weakest link it could find, and finally, a crisis was formed.[1]

The devastating world-wide crisis has caused huge losses to the world economy, and its consequences still affect the world economy even to this day.

3.4.2 China's main measures to deal with the financial crisis

On September 15, 2008, Lehman Brothers of the United States declared

---

[1] Chen Jiangsheng, "An Analysis of World Economic Pattern after Financial Crisis", *Journal of The Party School of The Central Committee*, Feb. 2009.

bankruptcy, and the international financial crisis broke out in an all-round way, causing a severe impact on China's economy. In the fourth quarter of 2008, China's GDP dropped significantly to 6.8%, the number of new jobs in cities and towns dropped sharply, and the number of unemployed people increased. A large number of migrant workers returned home, and businesses were having difficulties. In 2009, despite some measures taken, the international financial crisis was still deepening and spreading, and the real economy of our country was still severely impacted by the crisis. In January 2009, China's PPI fell 3.3% year on year. The total value of foreign trade imports and exports fell by 29% year on year, and the decline in imports and exports set a record of the past decade. The difficulty of employment increased, with the employment situation of migrant workers especially grim, due to the economic downturn and layoffs in some enterprises. As of March 2009, of the 56 million migrant workers who returned to the city after the Spring Festival, only 45 million had found jobs, while the other 11 million were still unemployed.[1] In the first quarter of 2009, China's GDP growth dropped to 6.1%. At that time, the US *Time* magazine predicted, "China has already started its economic decline, which may be even worse than the US economy". On March 2, the magazine predicted that China's GDP growth rate would not exceed 4% in 2009. In the face of the increasingly severe situation, the Chinese government resolutely stepped in and responded quickly, adopting a series of macro-control policies and measures to effectively mitigate the impact of the crisis.

(1) *Adjust macro-control objectives in a timely manner*

China has a relatively perfect and efficient macroeconomic decision-making mechanism and can adjust it in time according to different situations, which provides an institutional guarantee for coping with the financial crisis.

As early as the beginning of 2008, Hu Jintao stressed on various occasions to "accurately grasp the slowing trend of global economic growth and its impact on China" and "improve China's international competitiveness and ability to resist risks".[2] In March 2008, when deploying the economic work of that year, the first Session of the 11th National People's Congress proposed that the spread of the sub-prime crisis, the continued depreciation of the US dollar and the high oil prices may have a negative impact on China's economic development. We must "pay close attention to the trend of the international economy and adopt flexible and timely

[1] "11 Million Migrant Workers Still out of Work",*People's Daily*, Apr.1, 2009.

[2] "Accomplishing All the Work for Transforming the Model of Economic Development and Constantly Obtain New Development Advantages and Create New Development Chapters", *People's Daily*, Apr.30, 2008.

countermeasures according to changes in the situation".[1] It can be seen that while the impact of the international financial crisis on China's real economy has not yet appeared, the CPC Central Committee and the State Council have repeatedly stressed the importance of having an awareness of hardship and making a plan to deal with the crisis, thus winning time and initiative for China to deal with the severe impact of the crisis. Despite the ideological preparations, no one thought that the financial crisis would come so quickly. At the Central Economic Work Conference held in December 2007, the Central Committee of the Communist Party of China also set the macro-control policy goal for 2008, namely, to prevent fast economic growth from overheating, and to prevent prices from changing from structural rise to evident inflation. That is the "double prevention" policy of "preventing overheating and inflation". Clearly, there was a flourishing scene at that time. However, by the middle of 2008, the adverse impact of the international financial crisis on China had appeared.

In the face of the increasingly obvious impact of the crisis, the Political Bureau of the Central Committee held a meeting on July 25, 2008, to determine the overall idea of doing a good job in the economic work in the second half of 2008. China's macroeconomic policy goal was changed from "double prevention" set in early 2008 to "one insurance and one control". This adjustment laid a policy foundation for effectively coping with the severe impact of the international financial crisis.

On October 7, 2008, shortly after the outbreak of the US financial crisis, General Secretary Hu Jintao chaired a meeting of the Standing Committee of the Political Bureau of the Communist Party of China Central Committee to analyze the situation of the international financial crisis and discuss countermeasures. The decision was made on the meeting to hold an economic briefing to inform the heads of provinces, autonomous regions, municipalities, central departments and major military units of the international financial crisis and related work, and a group was set up to deal with the global financial crisis. On October 17, 2008, the executive meeting of the State Council decided to adopt a flexible and prudent macroeconomic policy and introduce targeted finance, taxation, credit, foreign trade, and other policy measures as soon as possible. In late October, the fifth session of the Standing Committee of the 11th National People's Congress heard and deliberated the State Council's report on strengthening financial macro-control, and put forward some opinions and suggestions on strengthening macro-control and promoting structural adjustment, security

[1] "Premier Wen Jiabao's Meeting with the Press", *People's Daily*, Mar. 19, 2008.

financing and capital market stability, expanding domestic demand and enhancing economic vitality, stressing the need to unify ideas and actions into the spirit of the third Plenary Session of the 17th Central Committee of the Party and the central decision-making arrangements, to assess the situation and calmly deal with it. A series of intensive meetings and discussions provided reliable information for the Party and government to regulate the economy correctly.

With the deepening impact of the financial crisis, China's real estate, steel, automobile, and other important pillar industries began to be under hit, production and sales dropped sharply, and economic operation became more difficult. The Central Economic Work Conference held in December 2008 further analyzed the international and domestic situation comprehensively and put forward the overall requirements and key tasks of economic work in 2009. In his speech at the conference, general secretary Hu Jintao made a general judgment of "four changes and non-changes" on the latest trends and medium- and long-term trends of world economic development, pointing out that after the crisis, "the pattern of world economic growth will change, but the general trend of deepening economic globalization will not change; the government's responsibility to maintain the normal operation of the market will be strengthened, but the basic role of the market in the allocation of resources will not change; international currency diversification will be promoted, but the status of the US dollar as a major international currency has not changed fundamentally; the overall strength of the developing countries will rise, but the pattern of the developed countries leading in overall national strength and core competitiveness has not changed".[1] Practice shows that these judgments are correct. This overall judgment laid a strategic foundation for our country to form a clear idea of coping with the impact of the international financial crisis and planning for the long-term development of our economy and society. The Central Economic Work Conference proposed that the economic work in 2009 must take maintaining steady and relatively rapid economic development as its primary task and focus on maintaining growth, taking expanding domestic demand as the fundamental way to this end, taking accelerating the transformation of development mode and structural adjustment as the main direction of maintaining growth, taking deepening reforms in key areas and key links and improving the level of opening up as the dominant driving force for maintaining growth, and taking improving people's

[1] *Selection of Important Documents since the 17th Party Congress, Volume II*, Beijing: Central Party Literature Publishing House, 2011, p.448.

livelihood as the starting point and end point for maintaining growth. This shows that the main objective of China's macroeconomic policy begun to shift from "one insurance, one control" to "maintaining growth, expanding domestic demand and adjusting structure".[1] Also in this short year, the central economic policy underwent a "roller coaster style" change, reflecting the timely and efficient response of our policy.

(2) *A package economic plan of "4 Trillion" investment was issued*

On November 5, 2008, against the grim situation that China's economic growth declined rapidly from 9.9% of the first half of 2008 to 7.2% of the third quarter of 2008, then Premier Wen Jiabao presided over the executive meeting of the State Council and decided to deploy measures to further expand domestic demand and promote steady and rapid economic growth in order to counter the adverse impact of the international economic environment on China.

The meeting identified ten measures to further expand domestic demand and promote economic growth. First one was to accelerate the construction of affordable housing projects, increasing support for low-rent housing construction, accelerating efforts to improve conditions in shantytowns, implementing nomads' settlement projects, and expanding rural reconstruction pilot projects. The second was to speed up the construction of rural infrastructure, strengthening the efforts to promote projects on rural biogas and drinking water safety and construction of rural highway, improving rural power grid, speeding up the construction of major water conservancy projects such as the South-to-North Water Diversion Project and reinforcing decaying reservoirs, and strengthening the upgrading of water-saving systems in large irrigation areas, as well as increasing efforts to relieve poverty. The third was to speed up the construction of major infrastructures such as railways, highways, and airports, focusing on the construction of a number of passenger dedicated lines, coal transportation channel projects and western trunk railways, improving the highway network, arranging the construction of central and western trunk airports and regional airports, and speeding up the transformation of urban power grids. The fourth was to speed up the development health care, culture and education, strengthening the construction of primary medical and health service system, speeding up the transformation of middle school buildings in rural areas in the central and western regions, and promoting the construction of special education schools and comprehensive cultural stations in villages and towns in the central and western regions. The fifth was to strengthen the construction of ecological environment, to accelerate the

[1] "The Central Economic Work Conference Held in Beijing", *People's Daily*, Dec.11, 2008.

construction of urban sewage and garbage disposal facilities and the prevention and control of water pollution in key river basins, to strengthen the construction of key shelter-belts and natural forest resource protection projects, and to support the construction of key EMCs. The sixth was to speed up independent innovation and structural adjustment, supporting the construction of high-tech industrialization and industrial technology development, and supporting the development of the service industry. The seventh was to accelerate the reconstruction work in areas hit by the earthquake. The eighth was to improve the income of urban and rural residents. We would raise the minimum purchase price of grain next year, raise the standards for comprehensive direct subsidies for agricultural materials, subsidies for improved varieties and subsidies for agricultural machinery and tools, and increase farmers' income. We would improve the treatment level of social security recipients such as low-income groups, increase subsistence allowances for needy urban and rural residents, and continue to raise the basic pension level of enterprise retirees and the standard of living allowances for entitled groups. The ninth was to carry out VAT reform in all regions and all industries in the country, encouraging the technological transformation of enterprises and reducing the burden on enterprises. The tenth was to increase financial support for economic growth, lifting the restriction on the credit scale of commercial banks, reasonably expanding the credit scale, increasing credit support for key projects, agriculture, rural areas, and farmers, small and medium-sized enterprises and technological transformation, merger, and reorganization, and cultivating and consolidating consumer credit growth points in a targeted manner. According to preliminary calculations, from the 4th quarter of 2008 to the end of 2010, about RMB4 trillion would be invested to implement the above measures, including central investment and social investment, of which RMB1.18 trillion would be invested by the central government, and RMB2.82 trillion would be invested by local governments and others. This is the famous "4 trillion" investment plan, and China has also taken the lead in launching the "package" of the economic stimulus plan in the world, implementing a proactive fiscal policy and a moderately loose monetary policy.

The "4 trillion" plan was completed in a very short time, sending a strong signal of "sustaining growth". On November 8, the CPC Central Committee and the State Council officially approved the *National Development and Reform Commission's Ten Measures for Further Expanding Domestic Demand and Promoting Economic Growth*. On November 10, the State Council held a meeting of the heads of provincial, district and municipal people's governments and departments under the State Council to deploy for implementing those measures, stressing that "the general requirement is to act fast, be forceful, take targeted measures and stress implementation".[1] According to this, from the end of 2008 to the beginning of 2009, China raised export tax rebate rate three times, lowered the benchmark interest rate of deposit and loan of financial institutions five times, lowered the deposit reserve ratio four times, temporarily exempted personal income tax on deposit interest, lowered stamp duty on securities transactions, lowered taxes on housing transactions, and further increased credit support for small and medium-sized enterprises. These policies and measures have played an important role in alleviating outstanding contradictions in economic operation, enhancing confidence and maintaining steady and rapid economic development.

In 2009, the CPC Central Committee with Hu Jintao as general secretary, based on the overall goal of "maintaining growth, expanding domestic demand and adjusting structure", adhered to a positive fiscal policy and a moderately loose monetary policy, fully implemented and continuously improved the package plan to deal with the international financial crisis, massively increased government investment, continued to implement a two-year investment plan of RMB4 trillion, implemented structural tax cuts, expanded domestic demand, gave full play of the important "domestic demand", and improved China's high dependence on foreign trade for economic development. In 2008, China's dependence on foreign trade still reached 56%, but down to 45% by 2012.

(3) *Promote exchange rate system reform and renminbi internationalization*[2]

With the continuous improvement of China's economic internationalization, the requirements for exchange rate system reform and renminbi internationalization became higher and higher. Especially since the outbreak of the financial crisis, the internal impetus and external pressure for the reform of the renminbi exchange rate system and the internationalization of the renminbi were increasing, and the call for speeding up the reform of the exchange rate system and the internationalization of the renminbi became increasingly strong. In 2009, the Chinese government began to push forward the internationalization of renminbi, aiming to deepen reform at home for

---

[1] *Selection of Important Documents since the 17th Party Congress, Volume I*, Beijing:Central Party Literature Publishing House 2009, p.719.

[2] Chen Jiangsheng, "China's Exchange Rate Regime Reform and the renminbi Internationalization", *Think Tank*, 2011(12).

opening wider to the outside world and, in the worldwide, to establish a new international financial order to deal with the financial crisis and US dollar hegemony. In this process, the reform of the renminbi exchange rate system played a key role.

The reform of the renminbi exchange rate system and renminbi internationalization were closely related and mutually reinforced. On the one hand, the reform of the renminbi exchange rate system was a key factor affecting the process of renminbi internationalization. Because only when the exchange rate level was able to reflect the supply and demand situation in the foreign exchange market could the value of money be credible with high credibility and be truly accepted by the international community. Without the reform of renminbi exchange rate system, the sustainable development of renminbi internationalization could not be realized. On the other hand, renminbi internationalization was the fundamental way to solve the difficult problem of renminbi exchange rate system reform. Since the US dollar accounts for as much as 75% of China's foreign trade settlement, the establishment and implementation of renminbi exchange rate policy had to take the exchange rate against US dollar as the focus of consideration; thus the reform of exchange rate system was tied up. Only the renminbi internationalization could fundamentally solve the exchange rate problem, so the two needed to be coordinated and promoted as a whole.

The reform of the exchange rate system was always difficult, and the central government was thus careful in promoting it. After the financial crisis broke out, the renminbi returned to the system before the exchange reform in 2006. It was not until May 2010, when China announced that it had got rid of the impact of the financial crisis, that the central bank reaffirmed its reform position and promoted a managed floating exchange rate system for the renminbi. On April 16, 2012, the exchange rate of renminbi against US dollar expanded from 0.5% to 1%. However, the progress was still slow.

While the difficulties in reforming the exchange rate system made the Chinese government more aware of the importance of weakening the influence of US on China's monetary policy, the international economic pattern accelerated to adjust since the financial crisis. In 2010, China overtook Japan to become the world's second largest economy for the first time, with the world's first total import and export trade volume, accounting for more than 16% of the world's total trade. Renminbi issuance exceeded the pound and became one of the world's four major currencies alongside the dollar, euro, and Japanese yen. China's economic strength and international status also demanded the internationalization of renminbi.

The internationalization of renminbi began with border trade settlement. Since the 1990s, China has started to use renminbi for trade settlement with Russia, Mongolia, Vietnam and other neighboring countries. China signed a series of settlement clauses with these countries that included border trade in goods and services, providing institutional support for the extensive use of renminbi in border trade and tourism consumption. renminbi has also been widely used in trade settlement with these countries, enabling the renminbi to play the role of international currency in some surrounding areas.

Since the financial crisis in 2008, China has accelerated the pace of renminbi internationalization. The first is to develop overseas renminbi trade and investment settlement. On December 4, 2008, China and Russia held talks on speeding up their trade settlement in their own currencies. On the 25th, the State Council decided to conduct the trials of renminbi settlement of goods trade in Guangdong and Yangtze River Delta region, and Hong Kong and Macao, and in Guangxi and Yunnan and ASEAN region. In July 2009, six departments issued administration measures for the renminbi settlement pilots in cross-border trade, officially launching China's renminbi settlement pilots in cross-border trade. In June 2010, the pilot area for renminbi settlement of cross-border trade was expanded to include 20 provinces and cities in the coastal mainland, and the overseas settlement area was expanded to include all countries and regions. On January 13, 2011, the central bank issued the *Measures for the Administration of renminbi Settlement Pilot for Overseas Direct Investment* to clarify that banks and enterprises in the pilot areas of renminbi settlement for cross-border trade can conduct renminbi settlement for overseas direct investment. By the end of 2011, the BRICS countries had jointly signed agreements to promote settlement in local currencies among countries, and local currency trade settlement between China, Japan, and South Korea was on the agenda, after China had signed agreements on optional bilateral currency settlement with eight neighboring countries including Mongolia, Vietnam, and Myanmar. The second is to carry out the international swaps of renminbi. Bilateral currency swap agreements have been signed with the monetary authorities, including South Korea, Malaysia, Belarus, Indonesia, Argentina, Iceland, Singapore, New Zealand, and Hong Kong SAR(China), with a currency swap scale of RMB829.2

billion. The third is to build channels for the circulation and return of renminbi abroad. In August 2010, the central bank announced that foreign banks would be allowed to participate in bond trading in China's inter-bank market. Besides, measures are also being actively advanced to speed up the construction of renminbi offshore center, promote institutions to issue renminbi bonds in the Hong Kong market, and impose no restrictions on non-residents holding renminbi deposits in China. In 2011, renminbi deposits in Hong Kong SAR, exceeded RMB400 billion and were generally expected to reach RMB1 trillion by the end of the year. By the end of February 2011, 58 renminbi bonds had been issued in the Hong Kong market, with a total amount of RMB77.6 billion. The first renminbi -denominated share sale in Hong Kong SAR was a success, raising RMB10.48 billion. These measures have greatly promoted the internationalization of the renminbi. In 2009, the amount of renminbi cross-border trade settlement was only RMB3.6 billion, and in 2010 it rose rapidly to RMB502.8 billion, of which the amount of renminbi cross-border trade settlement between Hong Kong SAR and the mainland accounted for 73% of that in China.

On the whole, however, the renminbi is still in the initial stage of internationalization. Its further advancement requires not only the gradual acceptance by the international community, but also the follow-up of supporting facilities and systems such as the payment system of renminbi international settlement, the circulation system of renminbi outflow-offshore circulation-return, and the reform of exchange rate system. Factors such as capital account control, immature foreign exchange market, underdeveloped domestic financial market, low level of enterprise internationalization also restrict the process of renminbi internationalization. Therefore, there is still a long way to go for renminbi internationalization.

3.4.3 Achievements of China's economic internationalization in response to the financial crisis

Under the strong leadership of the CPC Central Committee and the State Council, with the joint efforts of the whole party and the people of all ethnic groups in the country, by the end of 2009, China had won a staged success in coping with the impact of the international financial crisis, and various economic indicators showed that China's economy was beginning to improve. Although at this stage, the internationalization of China's economy regressed for some time in response to the financial crisis. However, China's determination to open up to the outside world was not shaken by the financial crisis, and China's economic internationalization cannot be reversed. As General Secretary Hu Jintao pointed out at a forum for non-Party personage held by the CPC Central Committee on July 26, 2008, opportunities were unprecedented, challenges were also unprecedented, and opportunities outweighed challenges.[1] In resisting the financial crisis, China successfully "turned the crisis into an opportunity" and achieved remarkable results.

(1) *Economy continues to maintain high-speed and stable growth*

After the financial crisis, China's economy was the first in the world to recover. Affected by the financial crisis, the world GDP growth rate declined in 2008, and China was not an exception. It is the first time that China's growth rate has declined after China's accession to the WTO, but China still maintained a high growth rate of 9.7%, as shown in Figure 3–12. In 2009, the impact of the financial crisis broke out in an all-round way, and the world economy fell into negative growth. At this time, China's performance was brilliant, and its economic growth accelerated quarter on quarter, with 6.4%, 8.2%, 10.6% and 11.9% year-on-year growth in each quarter. The annual gross domestic product (GDP) was RMB34.9 trillion, an increase of 9.3% over the previous year, maintaining the consistent high growth rate, which was a beautiful scene in the world economy. Since then, due to the active cooperation of all countries in the world, the world economy began to recover sharply in 2010, in which the world economy grew by 4.4%, exceeding the average level of more than 20 years before the crisis. However, because of the deep unresolved impact of the financial crisis and the exposure of the European debt crisis, the world economic growth rate began to slow down since 2011. Affected by the overall economic situation in the world, China's economic growth rate also showed a downward trend, with 10.6% in 2010, 9.5% in 2011 and 7.8% in 2012. Compared with 2012 US GDP growth rate of 2.22%, Japan 1.74%, EU -0.4%, India 5.6%, it is clear that China's economy still maintained a high level of growth.

---

[1] "Given the Current Economic Situation and Economic Work, the CPC Central Committee Held A Symposium on Non-party Persons", *People's Daily*, Jul.26, 2008.

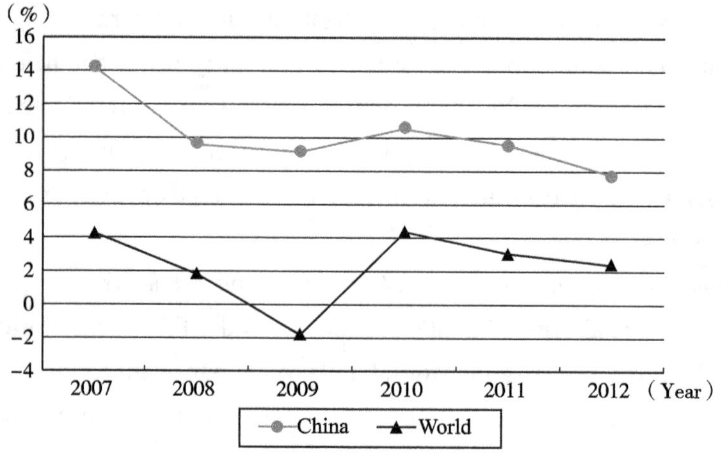

Figure 3–12 GDP growth rate of China and the world from 2007 to 2012

Source: World Bank Database, http://data.worldbank.org.cn/.

The relatively high economic growth ensured the steady growth of China's economic strength during this period. After its GDP reached US$4.6 trillion in 2008, China surpassed Germany to become the third in the world, and since its GDP reached US$6.1 trillion in 2010, surpassing Japan to become the second in the world, China has maintained this ranking. In 2012, China's GDP reached US$8.6 trillion, a fivefold increase from US$1.47 trillion in 2000 before China's entry into the WTO and a doubling from US$4.6 trillion in 2008 when the financial crisis broke out. China's GDP per capita reached US$6,337.9 in 2012, which nearly doubled that of 2008. Accounting for about 11.5% of world GDP, China's economy has become an extremely important pole in the world economy (see Table 3–10).

Table 3–10 China's GDP from 2007 to 2012

Item	2007	2008	2009	2010	2011	2012
GDP of China (US$ trillion)	3.5	4.6	5.1	6.1	7.5	8.6
World ranking	4	3	3	2	2	2
Per capita GDP (US$)	2,695.4	3,471.2	3,838.4	4,560.5	5,633.8	6,337.9
GNI per capita (RMB)	20,500	24,200	26,100	30,700	36,000	39,800

Source: World Bank Database, China National Statistics Bureau.

While the economy maintained high-speed growth, people's living standards also improved significantly. As can be seen from Table 3–11, the per capita disposable income of urban residents reached RMB24,564.7 million in 2012, doubling that of RMB12,785.8 million in 2007, an average annual real increase of 8.7%. The net income of rural households increased from RMB4,140.4 in 2007 to RMB7,916.6 in 2012, an average annual real increase of 10.2%. Engel's coefficients of urban and rural residents were both relatively stable. Looking horizontally, China was the fastest growing country in the world in terms of per capita income. The number of poor people in rural areas was dramatically reduced. In 2010, the number of poor people in China was about 165.67 million. By 2012, the number had dropped to 98.99 million, with an average annual decrease of 33.34 million.[1] The urban and rural markets were booming with the total retail sales of consumer goods in the whole society increased from RMB9,357.16 billion in 2007 to RMB21,443.27 billion in 2012, and the consumption level of residents increased from RMB7,572 to RMB14,699. Consumption has played a perfect role in boosting GDP growth.

From these data, it can be seen that despite the impact of the financial crisis, China's economy has continued to grow rapidly and steadily since 2008 with reasonable countermeasures. Compared with the situations of other countries in the world, China can be described as "nice scenery on this side only". China's development still enjoys great benefits from economic internationalization.

Table 3–11 Income of urban and rural residents in China from 2007 to 2012

Item	2007	2008	2009	2010	2011	2012
Per capita disposable income (RMB)	12,785.8	15,780.8	17,174.7	19,109.4	21,809.8	24,564.7
Engel's coefficient in town (%)	36.3	37.9	36.5	35.7	35.3	36.2
Per capita net income of rural residents (RMB)	4,140.4	4,760.6	5,153.2	5,919.0	6,977.3	7,916.6
Engel's coefficient in rural areas (%)	43.1	43.7	41.0	41.1	40.4	39.3

Source: China National Statistics Bureau.

[1] Poverty standards according to *China's Rural Poverty Monitoring Report 2015*.

(2) *The foreign economy is developing in twists and turns*

The most direct impact of the financial crisis on China's economy lies in the field of foreign trade.

As can be seen from Table 3–12, the amount of China's foreign trade, whether import or export, has been rising since 2000, only declined in 2009, growing in all the other years. In fact, due to the impact of the financial crisis, global trade fell by 13% in 2009, and China's foreign trade experienced the biggest negative growth of 13.9% for the first time in more than 30 years since the reform and opening up. We can see this change more intuitively from Figure 3–13. However, despite the rapid recovery in 2010 in response to policies, the growth rate began to decline year by year, reflecting that the overall depression of the world economy still affected China despite the encouraging trend of China's economy.

Table 3–12 Annual growth rate of China's import and export from 2000 to 2012 Unit: %

Year	Annual growth rate of import and export	Annual growth rate of export	Annual growth rate of import
2000	31.52	27.84	35.85
2001	7.45	6.78	8.20
2002	21.80	22.36	21.19
2003	37.09	34.59	39.84
2004	35.67	35.39	35.97
2005	23.16	28.42	17.59
2006	23.81	27.17	19.93
2007	23.62	25.91	20.80
2008	17.79	17.26	18.46
2009	-13.88	-16.01	-11.18
2010	34.72	31.30	38.80
2011	22.46	20.32	24.87
2012	6.19	7.92	4.30

Note: Annual growth rate= $\frac{X_t - X_{t-1}}{X_{t-1}} \times 100\%$, calculated according to the annual import and export figures given by the National Statistics Bureau.

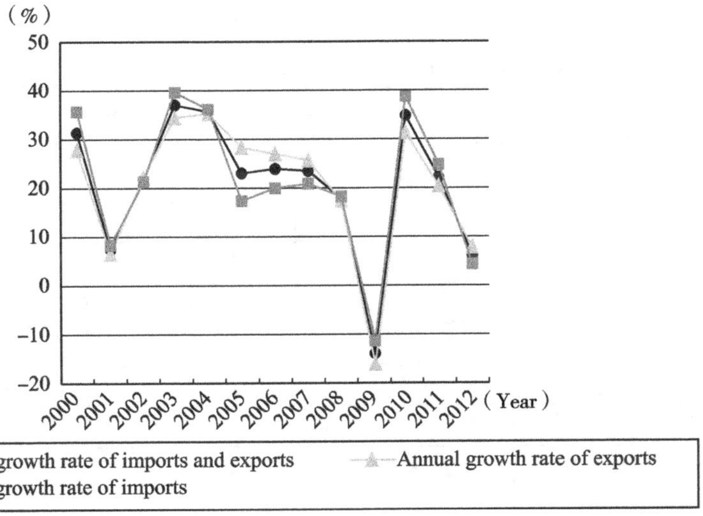

Figure 3-13 Changes in China's import and export growth rate from 2000 to 2012

Source: National Statistics Bureau.

As can be seen from Table 3-13 from the perspective of the contribution and pull of exports to GDP, the average annual contribution of net exports to GDP growth from 2002 to 2008 was 1.3 percentage points calculated at constant price, accounting for 12.4%, playing an important role in maintaining China's steady and rapid economic development. However, due to the continuous deterioration and spread of the financial crisis, the contribution of net exports to China's GDP became negative since 2009. Concurrent investment and consumption kept the same pull on GDP, while compared with the GDP growth rate in China, the pull has been in a decline since 2009. It is thus evident that the decline in import and export scale has undoubtedly affected the steady and rapid growth of China's economy.

Table 3-13 Contribution rate and pulling effect of three demands on GDP

Year	Final consumption expenditure		Gross capital formation		Net exports of goods and services	
	Contribution rate (%)	Pull (percentage point)	Contribution rate (%)	Pull (percentage point)	Contribution rate (%)	Pull (percentage point)
2000	65.1	5.5	22.4	1.9	12.5	1
2001	50.2	4.2	49.9	4.1	-0.1	-
2002	43.9	4.0	48.5	4.4	7.6	0.7
2003	35.8	3.6	63.2	6.3	1.0	0.1
2004	39.5	4.0	54.5	5.5	6.0	0.6
2005	38.7	4.4	38.5	4.3	22.8	2.6

(continued)

Year	Final consumption expenditure		Gross capital formation		Net exports of goods and services	
	Contribution rate (%)	Pull (percentage point)	Contribution rate (%)	Pull (percentage point)	Contribution rate (%)	Pull (percentage point)
2006	40.4	5.1	43.6	5.5	16.0	2.1
2007	39.6	5.6	42.5	6.0	17.9	2.6
2008	44.1	4.2	46.9	4.5	9.0	0.9
2009	49.8	4.6	87.6	8.1	-37.4	-3.5
2010	43.1	4.5	52.9	5.5	4.0	0.4
2011	56.5	5.3	47.7	4.4	-4.2	-0.4
2012	55.1	4.2	47	3.6	-2.1	-0.1

Source: *China's Statistical Yearbook of Foreign Trade (2014).*

Despite the harsh world trade environment, China's foreign trade in this period still achieved success. Although the growth rate of import and export showed a downward trend, the average level was still far higher than the world average. Regarding total volume, China's import and export has remained stable in the second place in the world since 2009. In 2012, China's total import and export accounted for more than 10% of the world's total for the first time. In fact, by 2013, China had surpassed the United States to become the world's first trading country. On the import side, when the effective global demand was insufficient after the financial crisis, China assumed an important role in exporting the aggregate demand to the world. In 2009, when the world aggregate demand fell by 0.6%, China's domestic demand increased by 13%, replacing Germany as the world's second largest importer, contributing 1.6 percentage points to global economic growth, and in 2012, China's import accounted for 9.8% of the global share. Regarding exports, we have made a great breakthrough. After overtaking Japan to become the third in the world in 2004 and overtaking Germany to become the second in the world in 2007, we succeeded in overtaking the United States to become the world's largest exporter in 2009 and have successfully maintained this ranking. In 2012, China's exports accounted for 11.1% of the world's exports. China has become one of the world's most important production bases and consumer markets (see Table 3-14).

Table 3–14 Proportion and ranking of China's import and export in the world from 2001 to 2012

Year	China's import and export to the world (%)	Import and export volume ranking	China's export to the world (%)	Export volume ranking	China's import to the world (%)	Import volume ranking
2001	4.0	6	4.3	6	3.8	6
2002	4.7	6	5.0	4	4.4	6
2003	5.6	4	5.8	4	5.3	3
2004	6.2	3	6.5	3	5.9	3
2005	6.7	3	7.3	3	6.1	3
2006	7.2	3	8.0	3	6.4	3
2007	7.7	3	8.8	2	6.7	3
2008	7.9	3	8.9	2	6.9	3
2009	8.8	2	9.6	1	7.9	2
2010	9.7	2	10.4	1	9.1	2
2011	9.9	2	10.4	1	9.5	2
2012	10.4	2	11.1	1	9.8	1

Source: Data from *China Statistical Yearbook (2015)* and *International Statistical Yearbook (2015)*.

At the same time, China's trade surplus in goods was significantly reduced during this period, with the import and export surplus as a share of GDP declined from 7.6% in 2007 to 6.6% in 2008 and to 4.0% in 2009 and kept declining at a rate of 3% in the next three years. China's international balance of payments was effectively improved through policy instruments, which played a positive role in promoting global trade balance.

At the same time as the great breakthrough made in the total amount, China's foreign trade continued to develop by the achievements of the previous stage. The structure of export products was still dominated by capital-intensive industrial products, of which electro-mechanical products and high-tech products accounted for 87% of total exports in 2012.[1]

Regarding trade in services, we can see from Figure 3–14 that China's trade in services has grown rapidly since China's entry into the WTO. Although it has been running a deficit for a long time, the amount is not significant. After the financial crisis, the growth of trade in services accelerated. In 2010, China's trade in services exports and imports ranked fourth and third in the world. However, it should also be noted that

[1] Data from the General Administration of Customs.

the deficit in China's trade in services has also increased since 2010.

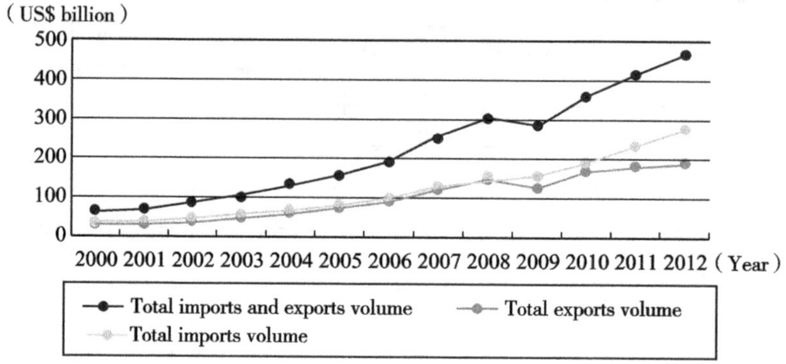

Figure 3–14 Total imports and exports of China's trade in services

Source: *China Statistical Yearbook (2015).*

Regarding investment, after the financial crisis, China's "going out" strategy has taken a new step, and a growing number of enterprises have started to move onto the international stage. Although the total amount of foreign capital utilized by China decreased in 2009 and 2012, the amount of foreign capital utilized still showed an upward trend overall with an average annual growth rate of about 5%,not as high as before. In 2012, China attracted US$113.294 billion of foreign investment, accounting for 8.2% of the world's total, ranking second in the world.

At the same time, China's foreign investment rose sharply. In 2007, China's foreign investment was only US$26.506 billion, about US$51.833 billion less than the actual amount of foreign investment utilized. In 2012, China's foreign investment reached US$87.804 billion, an increase of 3.3 times with an average annual growth rate of 35%, US$23.49 billion less than the actual amount of foreign investment utilized. Although the difference in absolute did not shrink much, which was mainly due to the large scale of China's use of foreign capital, the relative gap between the two has been dramatically narrowed (this is obvious in Figure 3–15). The increase in outward investment shows that more and more Chinese enterprises are expanding in various ways, such as cross-border mergers and acquisitions, overseas listing, etc., constantly expanding the investment field and improving cooperation. According to UNCTAD's *World Investment Report 2013*, global foreign direct investment in 2012 was US$1.39 trillion, down 17% from the previous year. Investment from China was rising, despite the adverse situation when global investment activity was weak, up

17.6% year on year, accounting for 6.3% of the world's total, ranking third in the world, only after the United States and Japan. China has become an important source of investment.

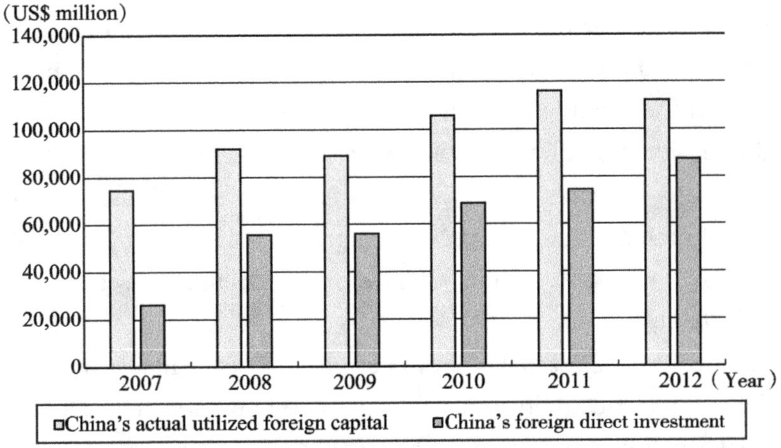

Figure 3–15 China's actual utilization of foreign capital and foreign direct investment from 2007 to 2012

Source: National Statistics Bureau.

(3) *The ability to participate in international economic cooperation enhanced significantly*

Historical experience tells us that the solution to the international economic crisis is cooperation rather than trade protection. One of the reasons why the 2008 financial crisis can be controlled in a short period without causing damage to the world economy as the long-lasting Great Depression is that countries have conducted more active cooperation and communication with each other after the crisis. As mentioned earlier, in 2009, China's foreign exchange reserves were the world's first, so were its foreign trade exports and economic growth rate, and China's GDP in 2010 ranked the world's second. With its strong economic strength and by playing a proactive role as a major power, the Chinese government did not take measures such as trade protection or currency devaluation that would hurt other countries, but took the lead in carrying out the economic stimulus package and expanding domestic demand, and actively engaged in international cooperation to help other countries get rid of the impact of the financial crisis, making China an important engine for global economic recovery. China's great role in stabilizing the world economy has also further enhanced China's international influence.

On the one hand, China actively participated in the construction of the international economic system. Economic crises are often accompanied by trade protectionism. Although the trend of globalization was inexorable, regional cooperation could be actively carried out under the original framework. As the financial crisis had a great impact on EU and the United States, which happen to be China's main partners in foreign trade whose insufficient demand greatly impacted China's exports, China actively adjusted its trade direction. On January 1, 2010, China-ASEAN Free Trade Area was officially launched, the first free trade area established by China to the outside world, forming a huge market covering 11 countries with a population of 1.9 billion and a GDP of US$6 trillion. China's export decline caused by the financial crisis was effectively solved.

On the other hand, China's discursive power increased. China actively participated in international economic affairs to play a major role in the world. From 2009 to 2010, then President Hu Jintao and Premier Wen Jiabao alone went abroad more than ten times, participated in 16 multilateral meetings and visited more than 20 countries, playing a constructive role in dealing with other global and regional hot issues. With China's unremitting efforts in 2009, the western developed countries agreed to increase the voting share of developing countries such as China in the IMF and the World Bank and to replace the G8 with the G20 as the primary platform for global economic governance. For the first time, developing countries such as China could achieve cooperation and co-governance with developed countries in the field of international finance and economy.

It is precisely because of the correct leadership of the Communist Party of China that China successfully survived this financial crisis and achieved its own great development. After the crisis, China's economic internationalization did not regress, but instead, progressed, achieved the best results in history. Facts have proved that the road to economic internationalization was not an easy one, so we must always remain calm when we enter the sea of "world economy", nor a wrong one, thus the twists and turns count for nothing. More than 40 years of historical experience have taught us that this is the right road to China's great rejuvenation. As long as we adhere to the correct leadership of the Party, we can surely overcome difficulties and move towards victory.

Chapter 4
Comprehensively Carrying Forward China's Economic Internationalization

Since the 18th National Party Congress, the CPC Central Committee with Xi Jinping at its core, by leading the people of all ethnic groups in the country, closely focusing on the Two Centenary Goals and the Chinese Dream of the rejuvenation of the Chinese nation, directing and planning, overcoming difficulties, satisfying basic needs and strengthening foundations, has created a new situation for the development of the Party and the state. In the aspect of opening to the outside world, the CPC Central Committee strongly advocates the concept of opening up for development, strives to build a new open-economy system, spares no effort for new achievements in opening up, puts forward the Belt and Road Initiative and promotes the construction of a community of human life, etc. China's economic internationalization has entered a stage of comprehensive advancement.

4.1 The background of China's overall economic internationalization: the historical trend of win-win cooperation

Today's world is undergoing profound and complex changes, but peace and development are still the main themes of our times, with the still stronger trend of peaceful development and win-win cooperation. General Secretary Xi Jinping pointed out: "If we want to keep up with the pace of the times, we cannot have our body step into the 21st century, but our head left in the past, in the old era of colonial expansion, of cold war thinking or of zero-sum game conventions."[1] Faced with a multi-polar world, the in-depth development of economic globalization and the continuous advancement of

[1] "Xi Jinping: Establishing An Asian Security Concept And Creating A New Situation of Security Cooperation", *People's Daily*, May 22, 2014.

cultural diversity and social informatization, today's humankind is better equipped than ever to move towards the goal of peace and development, and win-win cooperation is the realistic way to achieve this goal.

4.1.1 Win-win cooperation is the right choice to promote world peace and development

The development of the world results from the joint efforts of all countries. All countries and people should enjoy dignity, development, and security together. The only way for the world to continue to develop is win-win cooperation, both historically and practically.

History tells us that cooperation is conducive to economic development and only cooperation leads to win-win results. As shown in Figure 4–1, the period from the 1950s to present is the best period of economic development in human's history, and it is also in this period that the proportion of world trade in world GDP has increased at the highest speed since 1870 (this trend has been getting more evident since the 1980s). The indicators of world trade describe not only the transnational movement of goods and labor services itself but also the state of world exchanges and cooperation. From the changes in Figure 4–1, we see an increase in cooperation, and this increase correspondingly brings about an increase in economic growth and peace forces, from which all major economies in the world has benefited. History also tells us that this is the case with the economy as well as other sectors. Only through cooperation can there be a peaceful environment for cultural exchange. Only through communication and its result—innovation—can promote the world to develop. If communication is interrupted, it is likely that conflicts will burst out, or even the worse, peace will be torn apart, only producing a double loss.

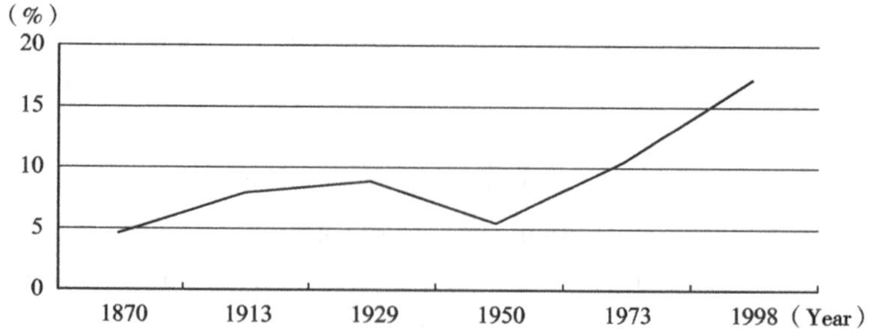

Figure 4–1 World merchandise exports as a percentage of GDP at 1990 prices

Source: [British] Angus Maddison, *The World Economy: A Millennial Perspective*, Beijing: Beijing University Press, 2003, p.360.

Looking at the present, humankind still faces many problems and challenges. The world pattern is in a historical process of accelerating evolution. On the one hand, the sunshine of peace, development, and progress is still strong enough to penetrate the haze of war, poverty, and backwardness. Economic globalization and social informatization are still greatly liberating and developing productive social forces, creating unprecedented opportunities for development. However, on the other hand, terrorism, financial turmoil, environmental crisis, and other issues are turning increasingly prominent, bringing us unprecedented challenges. Since the outbreak of the international financial crisis in 2008, the world economy has suffered serious setbacks: as for the economic growth, the average annual rate of 4.2% from 1998 to 2007[1] dropped to about 3% at present[2]; the growth rate of trade volume[3] decreased from an average annual of 6.7% in 1998–2007 to 2.8% in 2015[4]. Foreign direct investment even underwent negative growth, falling from US$1.87 trillion in 2007 to US$1.23 trillion in 2014[5]. With the world economy running at a trough, trade protectionism has risen again, and geopolitical relations have become more complicated. Besides, the aging population, declining capital accumulation and slowing down of productivity growth have altogether made the prospects for world economy even bleaker.

In the face of global challenges, only cooperation can achieve global development, a development no worse than that in the past 70 years. The current traffic, communication, and other conditions have pushed human life into the era of the global village. The degree of mutual contact, interdependence, cooperation and mutual promotion among countries has never been higher, and the international community is gradually becoming a community of common fate, which means that any economic shock is global, and the occurrence and influence of any terrorism and its activities are the interaction results of various factors in the global system. How to solve these global

---

[1] The average data for the year 1998–2007 is chosen based largely on the IMF's statistical habits with no special meaning, and this 10-year data is appropriate, basically reflecting the situation before the financial crisis.

[2] 2008–2005 years respectively for 3.0%, –0.1%, 5.4%, 4.2%, 3.5%, 3.3%, 3.4%, 3.1%. Data from IMF: *World Economic Outlook*, Apr. 2016.

[3] Trade volume as the main criterion, excluding the impact of exchange rate fluctuations.

[4] Data from IMF: *World Economic Outlook*, Apr. 2016.

[5] Data from UNCTAD, http://unctadstat.unctad.org/wds/TableViewer/tableView.aspx?Report Id = 96740. Although the World Investment Report 2016 shows a strong recovery of global FDI, the total inflow of FDI jumped by 38%, Reached US$1.76 trillion, the highest level since the 2008 global financial crisis, that does not mean the current economic upturn, as there are two major reasons for the growth of FDI in 2015: large-scale intra-firm restructuring and geopolitical factors.

challenges without cooperation? Almost impossible. So, if one wants harmony, peace, and development, in a community of destiny, the only way is to cooperate. Of course, cooperation is based on equality. Only through equal cooperation can we effectively create a community of destiny of all mankind, establish a partnership of equal treatment and mutual understanding, create a security pattern of justice, co-construction and sharing, seek for open and creative, inclusive and mutually beneficial prospects, promote all-embracing cultural exchanges that are harmonious but different, and build an ecological system that respects nature and pursues green development. Only then can we successfully adhere to multilateralism, create a global partnership, and blaze a new trail of "dialogue without confrontation, partnership without alliance" between countries. Only in this way can the people of all countries fairly enjoy the benefits brought about by world economic growth, promote exchanges and dialogues among different cultures and development models, complement each other from competition and comparison, and develop together in exchanges and mutual learning. By resolving the contradictions brought about by industrial civilization, aimed at harmonious coexistence between man and nature, we can realize the sustainable development of the world and all-round development of mankind to create a future in which each person does his best for win-win cooperation, observes rules and laws, practices fairness and justice, tolerance and mutual learning to seek joint development.[1]

4.1.2 Win-win cooperation is the inevitable way for China to achieve further development

Adhering to the principle of win-win cooperation and taking the road of peaceful development is a strategic choice made by China according to the trend of the times and the fundamental interests of the country, and it is also an inevitable move for China to achieve further and better development. General Secretary Xi Jinping pointed out that the Party's 18th congress had set the Two Centenary Goals and the goal of realizing the Chinese Dream of national rejuvenation. To achieve our goal, we must have a peaceful international environment. Without peace, neither China nor the world can develop smoothly. Without development, there can be no lasting peace in China and the world. Only by adhering to the road of peaceful development and maintaining world peace together with other countries can China achieve its goals and make

---

[1] *Reader on General Secretary Xi Jinping's Major Speeches*, Beijing: Xuexi Press & People's Publishing House, 2016, p.266.

greater contributions to the world.

China's pursuit of peaceful development is not an expedient choice, let alone diplomatic rhetoric, but a conclusion drawn from an objective judgment of history, present reality and future, which is an organic unity of self-confidence in thought and self-consciousness in practice. China's self-confidence and self-consciousness in taking the road of peaceful development come from the deep roots of Chinese civilization, from the understanding of the conditions for realizing China's development goals, and from the grasp of the world's development trend.

From the perspective of real economic and social development, China's current economic development needs to be more open and inclusive, and China needs to further deepen its opening to the outside world. China's domestic economic development is also seen as a mixture of hope and fear, leaving no ground for optimism. On the one hand, China's economic strength and development are constantly rising. Not only does the economic growth rate rank the top among major powers[1], but it is also the right time for economic transformation and upgrading[2].On the other hand, China also faces serious problems such as the slowing of economic growth[3], unbalanced, uncoordinated and unsustainable development[4].

Under the complicated international and domestic economic situation, China has made great theoretical and practical innovations in opening to the outside world and domestic economy. In the aspect of opening to the outside world, we put forward the concept of opening up for development, launched the Belt and Road Initiative, and accelerated the construction of a new open economic system. In the domestic economy, the development concept of innovation, coordination, green and sharing was put forward, and the strategies of innovation-driven development, Beijing-Tianjin-Hebei coordinated development and the Yangtze River economic belt development were put forward, to vigorously and comprehensively deepen the reform, promote the flow of

---

[1] In 2015, but the economic growth of China, the United States, Japan, the European Union, Brazil, and India was also 6.9%, 2.4%, 0.5%, 2.0%, -3.8% and 7.3%, respectively. Data from IMF: *World Economic Outlook*, Apr. 2016.

[2] An outstanding performance is the 2012 third industry value added more than secondary industry, and in 2015 the third industry value added accounted for 50.5% of GDP, for the first time more than half. Data from National Bureau of Statistics, http://data.stats.gov.cn/easyquery.htm?cn =C01.

[3] Since 2012, China's economic growth rate is gradually declining, from 2012 to 2015 economic growth was 7.7%, 7.7%, 7.3%, and 6.9%, respectively. Data from IMF: *World Economic Outlook*, Apr. 2016.

[4] Refer to *Recommendations of the CPC Central Committee on formulating the 13th Five-Year Plan for National Economic and Social Development on 3 Nov. 2015.* http://news.cnr.cn/native/gd/20151103/t20151103_520381646.shtml.

elements and enhance the vitality of the domestic economy.[1] China chooses these initiatives and strategies based on its own national conditions, social systems, and cultural traditions, which conforms to the trend of the times, to China's fundamental interests, to the interests of neighboring countries and to the interests of all countries in the world.

4.1.3 Win-win cooperation is the Party Central Committee's clear choice since the 18th CPC national congress

Since the 18th National Congress of the Communist Party of China, the Party Central Committee with Xi Jinping at its core, faced with new problems and situations, starting from China's national conditions and coordinating both international and domestic overall situations, has clearly advocated the concept of win-win cooperation to actively and effectively promote opening up, which has theoretically enriched the opening up theory of socialism with Chinese characteristics and pushed forward the process of deepening reform and opening up in an all-round way in practice.

After the 18th National Congress of the CPC, Xi Jinping suggested "opening up across the board and never cease to reform or open up"[2] during his visit to Guangdong, and issued a clear call to continue deepening reform and opening up. Xi Jinping stressed, "We will follow a more proactive opening-up strategy, improve the open economy which is mutually beneficial, diversified, balanced, secure and efficient, encourage coastal, inland and border areas to draw on each other's strengths in opening up, develop open areas that take the lead in global economic cooperation and competition, and establish pilot open areas that drive regional development. We will continue to attach equal importance to export and import, and promote balance in foreign trade. We will attract foreign investment and encourage companies to 'go global' at the same time, and enhance international investment cooperation. We will promote investment- and trade-related institutional reforms, and improve relevant legislation to create a legal environment in which foreign companies in China can operate in a fair manner. We will make overall planning for bilateral, multilateral, regional and sub-regional opening up and cooperation, accelerate the implementation of the FTA strategy, and promote communication and exchanges with our neighboring

---

1 Refer to *National Economic and Social Development of the People's Republic of China 13th Five-Year Planning Outline* on 17 Mar. 2016. http://www.xinhuanet.com/politics/2016lh/2016-03/17/c_1118366322.htm.

2 "Xi Jinping: Remarks during Guangdong Expedition", *People's Daily*, Dec.12, 2012.

countries."[1]

The goal of Xi Jinping's important remarks of opening to the outside world is to improve an open economic system that is mutually beneficial, diversified, balanced, secure and efficient. With the further development of economic globalization, all countries in the world are connected more closely. Establishing the sense of community of destiny and mutual benefit is the ideological basis for China to further expand its opening up and strengthen its economic cooperation. Xi Jinping pointed out that the community of destiny has the linkage effect in which "benefit to one means benefit to all, whereas harm to one means harm to all", and advocated countries to seek for all-win cooperation in the competition so that each country can develop in tandem with the growth of other countries and bring about positive externality to each other. In order to amplify the positive effect of the destiny community, all countries in the world should supply each other's needs with their complementary advantages, because they are closely connected with mixed interests. They should take into account the reasonable concerns of other countries when pursuing their own interests, promoting the common development of all countries in the pursuit of their own development so as to constantly expand the common interest. As for multiple equilibria, on the one hand, we should strengthen the cooperation of various forms, and utilize the function of organizations in the economic opening to promote bilateral and multilateral development. On the other hand, for it also includes balanced development of trade, we should continue to attach equal importance to stabilizing exports and expanding imports, strengthen the coordination of trade and industrial policies, speed up the opening up of service industries to promote balanced development of foreign trade and to better integrate into global value chains. We must adhere to the road of national security with Chinese characteristics based on economic security. Through various forms of cooperation in practice, new achievements in economic benefits have been gained continuously.

With regard to the ways and means of opening to the outside world, first of all, we should upgrade the overall partnership of cooperation. By strengthening cooperation with various regions and countries, deepening cooperation fields, and innovating cooperation methods, we have established different types of partnerships with different countries to form an all-round development cooperation situation of multi-level, multi-field, involving cooperation partners, friendly cooperation partners, strategic

---

[1] Xi Jinping, *The Governance of China*, Beijing: Foreign Languages Press, 2018, p.383.

cooperation partners and all-round strategic cooperation partners, and thereby have led to multilateral opening-up economic pattern of different forms with interwoven bilateral relations. Second, we should promote scientific and technological innovation. Xi Jinping pointed out that China's opening to the outside world was changing from factor- and investment-driven to innovation-driven. "Innovation is crucial for a nation's progress and an inexhaustible power source for a country's prosperity. It is also the most distinctive endowment of the Chinese nation."[1] Third, we should develop a balanced trade. Growth must be real, effective, quality and sustainable. Finally, we will promote the implementation of the Belt and Road Initiative and the construction of free trade zones. Considering the overall situation in the long run, the CPC Central Committee with General Secretary Xi Jinping at its core has proposed accelerating the advancing of the Belt and Road Initiative and the construction of free trade zones and setting up experimental free trade zones, thus to promote the construction of a new pattern of opening to the outside world. Among them, the Belt and Road Initiative connects East Asia, Southeast Asia, South Asia, the Middle East, and Africa, regions of the greatest potential for global economic growth of Asia-Europe continent, which will strongly promote the coordinated development of China and the countries along the line. The historical mission of the experimental FTZ is to accelerate the domestic economic restructuring through opening up to form a system that can be replicated and popularized throughout the country and to link the construction of the domestic FTZ with the negotiation of the international FTZ to lay a solid foundation for a high-standard FTZ network facing the world. Pushing forward the Belt and Road Initiative and speeding up the construction of free trade zones are significant not only for promoting sustainable and healthy economic and social development but also for enhancing China's discursive power and promoting world economic recovery. The opening-up theory, having reflected both the epochal character and succession since the 18th National Congress of the Communist Party of China, which is in line with China's national conditions, will better guide China's opening to the outside world in practice.

---

[1] "Xi Jinping: Speech during Meeting with the Representatives of Chang'E No. 3 Mission Participants", *People's Daily*, Jan.7, 2014.

4.2 Policies and measures for the comprehensive promotion of China's economic internationalization: comprehensively deepening reform and opening up

Since the 18th National Congress, China's economic development has entered a new normal, and the domestic and international situation has undergone profound changes. In order to cope with the new situation, the Central Committee of the Communist Party of China with Xi Jinping at its core has put forward a series of new visions, new ideas, and new strategies. As far as opening up is concerned, in the light of reality, the CPC Central Committee has a long-term perspective. Based on the Five Major Principles of Development, with the overall deepening of reform as the driving force and achieving sustainable and healthy economic development as the goal, a series of reforms have been carried out.

4.2.1 Improving the strategic plan for opening up[1]

Since the 18th National Congress of the Communist Party of China, the Party Central Committee has put forward new requirements for improving the strategic layout of opening up and has made great efforts to improve the layout of the opening up, foreign trade and investment. We have vigorously promoted the comprehensive deepening of reforms, the building of an open economy, and the new development in opening up.

(1) *Improving regional opening up*

We should improve the regional layout of opening up, mainly including strengthening the development of ports of entry and infrastructure in both inland and border regions and creating cross-border multimodal transport corridors; we will develop outward-oriented industrial clusters and create centers of opening up with specialized areas of focus. We will support coastal areas in fully participating in global economic cooperation and competition, and cultivate advanced manufacturing bases and economic zones with global influence; we will improve the development of both border and cross-border economic cooperation zones.

First, we will build pilot free trade zones. We will deepen the reform and the

[1] "The CPC Central Committee Recommendations for the 13th Five-Year Plan for Economic and Social Development", Xinhua News Agency, Nov.3, 2015.

opening up of China (Shanghai) Pilot Free Trade Zone, expand the opening up in the service industry and advanced manufacturing, and form a policy support system to promote investment and innovation. Some of the opening measures will be radiated to the Pudong New Area of Shanghai, and the experience of trial reform will be summarized in time to be replicated and promoted throughout the country. The existing new districts and parks will support the promotion of the full implementation of the overall plan of the experimental free trade zones in Guangdong, Tianjin, and Fujian. With the pilot content of the Shanghai Pilot Free Trade Zone as the main body and local characteristics combined, we will enrich the new pilot content, and promote the implementation of a new round of high-level opening up.

Second, we should develop overseas-oriented industrial clusters. Relying on inland central cities and city cluster and taking development zones and industrial agglomerations as platforms, we will seize the opportunity of global industrial re-layout and actively explore new paths for industrial transfer. We will innovate the processing trade mode and steadily promote the transfer of integrated equipment production, parts, raw materials matching, R&D and settlement to the inland areas in qualified enterprises based on the key points of the processing trade gradient transfer, thus forming industrial clusters and supporting the establishment of advanced manufacturing centers in inland central cities. We will encourage regional cooperation to jointly build industrial parks and promote coordinated development of inland trade, investment, and technological innovation. We will support the increase of international passenger and cargo routes in inland cities, develop combined river-ocean shipping, and multimodal transport such as rail, water, and land transport to form a foreign economic corridor that traverses eastern, central and western China and links together southern and northern China.

Third, we will create a new highland for coastal opening up. We will give full play to the role of portals of China's opening up of the Yangtze River Delta, the Pearl River Delta, and the Bohai Rim region, and build a number of international metropolises and city clusters serving the whole country and opening to the world to establish a coastal economic belt with stronger international influence. We will also promote the Integration of Beijing, Tianjin, and Hebei. We will support the development of high-end industries in coastal areas, strengthen scientific research and development, accelerate the transformation from global processing and assembly bases to R&D and advanced manufacturing bases, and promote early and pilot implementation of the opening in the service industry. Based on the Yangtze River golden watercourse, we will promote the development of the Yangtze River Economic belt, create a new supporting belt for

China's economy, and build a new corridor for the two-way opening of the land and sea.

Fourth, cultivating new pivot points along the border. We will build border pilot zones for development and opening up and border economic cooperation zones into important platforms for cooperation between China and neighboring countries, and accelerate the pace of opening up along the border. Key border ports, border cities, and border economic cooperation zones are allowed to implement special methods and policies in terms of personnel exchanges, processing logistics, and tourism. The establishment, adjustment, and expansion of border economic cooperation zones will be carried out by relevant regulations in an orderly manner. We will build an energy resources import and processing base and carry out industrial cooperation for the surrounding markets. We will encourage border areas to strengthen pragmatic cooperation with local governments of neighboring countries.

(2) *Improving the structure of foreign trade*

The main contents are as follows: We will enhance the level of foreign trade, innovate the development model of foreign trade, and strengthen the construction of marketing and after-sales service networks; we will improve the competitiveness of traditional products, consolidate the export market share, promote the transformation of foreign trade to higher prices for better quality as well as optimization of imports, and expand the export-oriented industries such as equipment manufacturing; we will develop trade in services and raise its strategic position.

First, we should innovate the development model of foreign trade and improving the level of trade facilitation. We will strengthen the cooperative mechanisms for achieving compatibility in customs clearance procedures, and realize the information exchange, mutual recognition of regulations, and mutual assistance in law enforcement among port management departments. We will accelerate the construction of the "single window" for international trade, and comprehensively implement new customs clearance modes such as "joint inspection and one release" in port management departments. Based on the electronic port platform, the operating systems of the relevant departments of port management will be promoted to interconnect horizontally, and an information-sharing mechanism will be established. We will innovate the port check and inspection mechanism and carry out the pilot project of comprehensive law enforcement of port management departments. We will accelerate the integration and upgrading of special customs control areas and the reform of the integration of regional customs clearance procedures and promote the paperless operation of customs clearance. We will carry out exchanges, cooperation and mutual recognition with major trading partners in inspection and quarantine, certification and accreditation, technical standards, etc. We will strengthen the construction of overall capacity in port inspection and quarantine, and improve the risk warning and rapid response system for product quality and safety. We will integrate and standardize the business services and charges in import and export.

Second, cultivating new advantages in foreign trade competition and optimizing the market layout and trade structure. We will stabilize the export of traditional competitive products, further promote the strategy of winning by quality, improve the quality, grade and proportion of innovation of export products, and expand the export of large-scale complete sets of equipment and technology. We will strengthen the construction of foreign trade credit system and standardize the import and export order. We will encourage enterprises to carry out innovation in science and technology as well as a business model and accelerate the cultivation of new advantages in foreign trade competition with technology, brand, quality and service as the core. We will encourage the development of new trade methods such as cross-border e-commerce and market procurement trade. We will actively solve the technical and policy problems of e-commerce development at home and abroad, and strengthen international coordination in standards, payment, logistics, customs clearance, inspection and quarantine, and taxation and at the same time participate in the formulation of relevant rules, innovate cross-border e-commerce cooperation methods, integrate into foreign retail systems, and resolve relevant trade barriers. We will optimize the structure of imported goods, encourage the import of advanced technologies, key equipment, and parts, stabilize the import of resource products, and rationally increase the import of general consumer goods. We will cultivate trading platforms for international commodities. We will increase the proportion of general trade and service trade, promote the transformation and upgrading of processing trade, enhance the industrial level, improve the quality and added value of processing trade, extend the processing trade industrial chain, and increase the value-added rate of processing trade.

Third, developing trade in services. We will enhance the strategic position of service trade, focus on expanding the scale of service trade and promote the facilitation and liberalization of service trade. We will encourage the development of trade in producer services. Based on new technologies such as big data, cloud computing, Internet of Things, and mobile Internet, we will promote the transformation of the service industry and foster new forms of business in the service sector. We will innovate the service trade financial system and establish port management and customs clearance cooperation model that is compatible with service trade. We will increase the added value of services in the goods trade and promote the coordinated development of manufacturing and service industries, goods trade and services trade. We will encourage the consolidation of system, standards, norms and a mechanism for oversight and management in the domestic service market to facilitate the cross-border movement of professionals and professional services. We will develop a service industry standardization system that is in line with international standards, and strengthen international cooperation in personnel training, mutual qualification recognition, and standards formulation related to service trade. We will promote the upgrading of service outsourcing, improve service cross-border supply capabilities, and build a demonstration city of service outsourcing.

(3) *Improving the investment layout*

To improve the investment layout, the main measures include promoting the "bringing in" of overseas funds and technologies as well as the "going global" of domestic equipment, technologies, standards, and services. Meanwhile, we will build a financial service platform for international industrial capacity and equipment manufacturing cooperation.

First, we should promote the "bringing in" of overseas funds and technologies. We will open more sectors to foreign investment, relax restrictions on market access, work proactively and effectively to bring in foreign capital and advanced technology, promote the orderly opening up of the finance, education, cultural, medical sectors, and other service areas, and to remove foreign investment access restrictions in child and old-age care, architectural design, accounting and auditing, commerce and logistics, electronic commerce, and other such service sectors, and further open up manufacturing sectors. On the premise of state security, the restrictions on foreign investment will be gradually reduced in infrastructure sectors such as transportation and telecommunications as well as other sectors such as the mining industry.

Second, we will promote greater use of Chinese equipment, technology, standards, and services in the international market. We will support enterprises to expand outbound investment, promote the "going global" of equipment, technologies, and standards, deeply integrate into global production, value, and logistics chains, establish overseas production centers and cultivate a batch of transnational corporations. We will permit enterprises and individuals to exert their advantages to carry out investment and cooperation abroad, to undertake engineering projects and labor cooperation projects in various countries and regions at their own risk, to "go global" and carry out greenfield investment, M&A investment, securities investment, and joint investment in innovative ways. We will encourage competitive enterprises to conduct overseas infrastructure investment and energy and resources cooperation in various ways. We will promote the "going global" of high-speed railway, nuclear power, aviation, machinery, electric power, telecommunications, metallurgy, building materials, light industry, textile and other advantageous industries, improve the internationalization level of modern service industries such as Internet information service and promote the "going global" of e-commerce as well as China's major technical standard.

4.2.2 Building a new open-economy system[1]

The system is long-term and fundamental. In the process of comprehensively deepening openness, institutional reform is at a critical position. We will construct a new system of opening up and work to create a business environment that is more internationalized, convenient and that is based on the rule of law, and to improve our institutions and mechanisms to make them more conducive to mutually beneficial cooperation and more compatible with international trade and investment rules. The main measures focus on four aspects: The first is to innovate the foreign investment management system; the second is to establish a new system to promote the strategy of "going global"; the third is to expand the new space for international economic cooperation; the fourth is to build an open and secure financial system.

(1) *Innovating foreign investment management system*

The main measures to innovate the foreign investment management system are as follows: We will improve the investment environment, unify laws and regulations for domestic and foreign capital, and create a standardized institutional environment and stable market environment; we will reform the management mode of approval process of foreign investment and industrial guidance, and work to transform the mode into pre-establishment national treatment plus a negative list. We will improve the foreign investment regulatory system and enhance the scientificity, normalization, and transparency of foreign investment regulation; we will promote the development of institutional mechanisms and the transformation and upgrading of development zones.

First, we should unify laws and regulations for domestic and foreign capital. We will revise *Law of the People's Republic of China on Chinese-Foreign Equity Joint*

[1] "Several Opinions of the CPC Central Committee and the State Council on Foster A New Open-Economy System", *People's Daily*, Sep.18, 2015.

Ventures, *Law on Sino-foreign Cooperative Joint Ventures* and *Law on Foreign Capital Enterprises*. Besides, we will introduce basic laws on foreign capital to involve the standardization and guidance of foreign investors and investment. The general contents of the organization form and business activities of foreign capital enterprises can be regulated by laws and regulations uniformly applicable to all kinds of market entities, in accordance with the principle of consistency between domestic and foreign capitals which unified laws and regulations shall apply to. We will keep the policy on foreign investment stable, transparent and predictable to create a standardized institutional environment and a stable market environment.

Second, we will promote the management model of "pre-establishment national treatment plus a negative list". We will improve the system of market access for foreign investment and explore the management model of pre-establishment national treatment plus a negative list for foreign investment. Based on risk assessment, we will relax restrictions on market access for foreign capital in service sectors in an orderly and focused manner, and promote the orderly opening up of the finance, education, cultural, medical sectors, and other service areas, and to remove foreign investment access restrictions in child and old-age care, architectural design, accounting and auditing, commerce and logistics, electronic commerce, and other such service sectors, and further open up manufacturing sectors. On the premise of state security, the restrictions on foreign investment will be gradually reduced in infrastructure sectors such as transportation and telecommunications as well as other sectors such as the mining industry.

Third, we will improve the foreign investment regulatory system. In accordance with the requirements of expanding opening up as well as strengthening supervision and synchronization, we will exercise stronger oversight both during and after the handling of matters, establish the report system for foreign investment and the public platform for foreign investment information and take full advantage of the system for releasing enterprise credit information to form an overall regulatory system for foreign investment in which all government departments share information and coordinate oversight and general public are involved so as to enhance the scientificity, normalization, and transparency of foreign investment regulation in case of being overly lax.

Fourth, we will promote the transformation, upgrading and innovative development of development zones. We will reinforce the planning and guiding, innovation and development of various development zones such as state-level economic and technological development zones, national high and new technology industrial development zones, special customs regulation zones, and provincial-level development zones. We will give play to the leading and driving role of development zones, vigorously develop advanced manufacturing and service sector of technology, advance the upgrading of the industries inside the region and establish collaborative innovation platforms to promote comprehensively in industrial structure, value-added of products, quality, brand, technical level, and innovation capability. We will encourage the green, low-carbon and circular development in development zones and continue to deepen international cooperation in energy conservation and environmental protection. We will constantly improve investment environment, further standardize administration and management system, improve the system of decision-making, implementation, supervision and assessment, avoid homogeneous competition, and strive to build development zones into an important carrier driving regional economic development and implement regional development strategies, construct a new open-economy system, and cultivate pacesetters in absorbing foreign investment as well as demonstration zones driven by scientific and technological innovation and green intensive development.

(2) *Establishing a new system to promote the strategy of "going global"*

We will establish a new system to promote the strategy of "going global", the main measures include implementing the national strategy of "going global" and enhancing overall plan and guidance; we will ensure the main status of enterprises and individuals in foreign investment, work to improve the quality and efficiency of foreign investment, and promote the convenience of overseas investment; we will explore new approaches to investment cooperation with other countries, promote infrastructure connectivity and the "going global" of competitive industries, carry out cooperation in advanced technology, strengthen the international operation capability of Chinese enterprises and avoid cut throat competition; we will maintain rights in overseas investment and perfect service systems for "going global"; we will promote the integration and cooperation between foreign capital and foreign investment.

First, we will establish and implement a national strategy of "going global" in the new era. According to the overall plan for national economic and social development and the overall strategy of opening-up, we will perfect medium and long-term development plans for overseas investment, strengthen the coordination and guidance for "going global", and provide policy support as well as investment facilitation. We will encourage enterprises to formulate medium and long-term internationalization development strategy, give consideration to both current and long-term interests and operate in accordance with the law abroad. We will urge enterprises to fulfill their social responsibilities and establish a good image.

Second, we should promote the convenience of overseas investment. We should enact laws and regulations on overseas investment. We will implement the principle of independent decision making as well as independent accounting and responsibility for profits and losses by enterprises in investment, relax restrictions on overseas investment, simplify overseas investment management, and implement the record-keeping system in overseas investment projects. We will promote the establishment of the accredited domestic individual investors system and strengthen the construction of overseas investment cooperation information platform.

Third, we will explore new approaches to investment cooperation with other countries. We will permit enterprises and individuals to exert their advantages to carry out investment and cooperation abroad, to undertake engineering projects and labor cooperation projects in various countries and regions at their own risk, to "going global" and carry out greenfield investment, M&A investment, securities investment, and joint investment in innovative ways. We will encourage competitive enterprises to conduct overseas infrastructure investment and energy and resources cooperation in various ways. We will promote the "going global" of high-speed railway, nuclear power, aviation, machinery, electric power, telecommunications, metallurgy, building materials, light industry, textile and other advantageous industries, improve the internationalization level of modern service industries such as Internet information service and promote the "going global" of e-commerce. We will also promote overseas agricultural investment cooperation positively and soundly as well as help Chinese manufacturing brands gain international recognition. We will explore new models for overseas economic and trade cooperation zones, and support independent construction and management of domestic investment entities.

Fourth, perfecting service systems for "going global". We will accelerate negotiating investment and trade agreements with relevant countries and regions, improve consular protection system, provide more services such as the safeguard of rights and interests, investment stimulation and risk warning to facilitate foreign investment. We will also work to guarantee the safety of persons and property overseas by giving play to the functions of intermediary institutions and establishing a batch of international intermediary institutions for design and consultation, capital assessment, credit rating, as well as legal service.

Fifth, we should integrate "bringing in" and "going global". We will enhance the integration and cooperation between foreign capital and foreign investment, promote industrial investment cooperation with countries and regions for mutual benefit, and give full play to China's advantages and favorable conditions to promote the common development of other countries and regions. We will encourage enterprises to carry out international cooperation in many aspects such as scientific and technological innovation, project integration, and human resource development. We will support local governments and enterprises in attracting investment, technology, and talents from overseas as well as proactively exploring the international market. Through various investment cooperation mechanisms, we will share the successful experience of "bringing in" and promote a good investment environment for the countries concerned.

(3) *Opening up new space for enhancing international economic cooperation*

First, we should adhere to the rules of the world trade system. We will maintain the multilateral trade system's status as the main channel of international trade in global trade and investment liberalization and facilitation, stick to the principle of balance, inclusiveness and mutual benefits, and oppose trade and investment protectionism. We will actively implement the "Bali Package" and promote the formulation of Post-Bali Work Program. At the same time, we will also support WTO in strengthening the oversight mechanism for trade policies, improving the dispute settlement mechanism, and further enhancing the compliance of trade policies.

Second, we will establish a network of high-standard free trade areas. We will accelerate the implementation of the free trade zone strategy, adhere to the targeted policies and intensive cultivation, gradually establish a global network of high-standard free trade areas based on surrounding areas and radiating the Belt and Road Initiative, actively expand the opening up of service industry, promote the negotiation of new issues such as environmental protection, investment protection, government procurement and e-commerce, as well as advance international cooperation in innovation. We will actively implement the outcomes in our negotiations of China-ROK Free Trade Zone and China-Australia Free Trade Area, build an upgraded version of the China-ASEAN Free Trade Area, advance the process of negotiations and construction on free trade agreements with relevant countries, steadily promote the construction of Central European Free Trade Area and Free Trade Area of the Asia-Pacific, and start negotiations on free trade agreements with other trading partners in due course.

Third, we will participate in global economic governance. We will promote the system reform of the global economic governance system, support United Nations and

Group of Twenty (G20) in playing the role as the main platform for global economic governance, and advance the functions of BRICS cooperation mechanism to increase the representation and say of emerging market and developing countries in the field of global economic governance. We will fully participate in the reform of the international economic system and rulemaking, actively propose new ideas, new initiatives and new action plans on global issues, and enhance China's voice in making international economic and trade rules and standards.

Fourth, we will establish a new mechanism for international economic and trade negotiations. We will promptly establish a negotiation mechanism that is legal, orderly, scientific, efficient, coordinated, and effective. We will coordinate resources and leverages in negotiations, make negotiation plans scientifically, and optimize the negotiation process. We will strengthen the implementation, supervision and performance assessment of negotiation plans, and improve the intensity and effectiveness of foreign negotiations. We will give full play to the positive role of the relevant coordination mechanism and improve the system of authorization and approval of international economic and trade negotiations.

(4) *Building an open and secure financial system*

The construction of an open and secure financial system is mainly aimed at expanding two-way opening up in the financial sector; we will extend the cross-border use of the renminbi, take systematic steps to realize renminbi capital items convertibility, to promote the process of renminbi being included in the SDR basket and being a convertible and freely usable currency; we will transform foreign exchange management and way of using from a positive list to a negative list, relax restrictions on foreign exchange and requirements on corporate as well as individual foreign exchange management, and also relax the restrictions on the overseas operation of multinational corporations' capitals. We will strengthen monitoring over the balance of payments and keep equilibrium in the balance of payments basically balanced. We will promote two-way opening up of capital markets, improve and gradually eliminate restrictions on domestic and foreign investment quotas.

First, we will expand the opening up in the financial sector. Based on the continuous evaluation, perfecting prudential supervision and effective risk-controlling, we will relax the ratio of stocks in the securities and promote the opening up of the banking industry in an orderly manner to form a fair, well-organized and benign financial environment. We will enhance the international operation level of financial institutions, encourage financial institutions to prudently conduct cross-border mergers and acquisitions, perfect the network of overseas branches, improve financial services level, and strengthen the international cooperation in the field of payment and market infrastructure. We will establish and perfect an international financial cooperation mechanism that supports the development of science and technology innovation.

Second, we will extend the cross-border use of the renminbi, take systematic steps to realize renminbi capital items convertibility, to promote the process of renminbi being included in the SDR basket and being a convertible and freely usable currency. We will deepen financial cooperation, and make more efforts in building a currency stability system, investment, and financing system and credit information system in Asia. We will promote local currency swap cooperation, further expand the scale of renminbi settlement of the current account, and support multinational enterprise groups in carrying out the concentrated operation of renminbi funds. Renminbi is used as the main currency of invoice in foreign economic management, accounting, and statistics. We will accelerate the construction of the renminbi cross-border payment system and further improve the renminbi global clearing system and further expand the renminbi output channels as well as encourage the use of renminbi to make loans and investments abroad. The construction of a regional renminbi bond market will further facilitate foreign institutions to invest in the domestic bond market, support overseas institutions in issuing renminbi debt financing instruments in China and steadily push domestic financial institutions and enterprises to issue renminbi bonds overseas. It will also support the innovation of renminbi-denominated financial products in the offshore market, accelerate the construction of the offshore renminbi market, and expand the offshore circulation of the renminbi.

Third, we should perfect the exchange rate regime and foreign exchange management system. We will work to expand the floating ranges of renminbi exchange rates and allow it to float more freely. We will deepen the reform of the foreign exchange management system, further facilitate the use of foreign exchange by market entities, and promote the reform of foreign exchange capital surrender management of foreign-invested enterprises in accordance with the principle of negative list. We will innovate the use of foreign exchange reserves to broaden the channels of diversified use.

Fourth, we will establish a financial support system of "going global". We will construct a financial support system for overseas investment that combines policy-based finance and commercial finance, and promote the joint "going global" of financial capitals and industrial capitals. We will perfect the overseas investment and financing mechanism, explore the establishment of a domestic trading financing platform for overseas stock equity assets, and provide enterprises with a financing method of "offshore guarantees for onshore loans". We will develop various forms of overseas investment funds, promote the establishment and operation of the Silk Road Fund as well as the Asian Infrastructure Investment Bank and BRICS New Development Bank, and establish Shanghai Cooperation Organization (SCO) financing institution. We will make good use of the international cooperation mechanism for investment and financing, select the key points, and actively promote the cooperation with countries along the Belt and Road.

Fifth, we should promote the two-way opening up of the capital market in an orderly way. We will work steadily to make the renminbi convertible under capital accounts to facilitate cross-border investment and financing of domestic and foreign entities. We will expand the opening up of the futures market and permit the eligible foreign institution to engage in futures trading of specific types. We will explore that financial institutions or enterprises such as banks, securities companies with true trading and investment in China are allowed to participate in overseas financial derivatives. Under the premise of controllable risks, the financial derivatives markets can be gradually opened up.

4.2.3 Accelerating the construction of the Belt and Road [1]

The Belt and Road Initiative is a major initiative of the Party Central Committee in the new era. It not only provides a broad space for China's economic development but also brings a powerful impetus to the recovery and development of the world economy. In the process of promoting the construction of the Belt and Road, China has always upheld amity, sincerity, mutual benefit, and inclusiveness as well as the principle of joint discussion, common development, and shared growth. With enterprises as the main entities, we implement market-oriented operation as we look to undertake practical and mutually-beneficial cooperation in multiple sectors with countries and regions involved in the Belt and Road Initiative, with the aim of developing a new picture of all-around opening up in which China is opened to the world through eastward and westward links and across land and sea.

(1) *Perfecting the Belt and Road cooperation mechanism*

We will improve the bilateral and multilateral cooperation mechanisms of the Belt and Road Initiative focusing on policy communication, infrastructure connectivity,

[1] "The 13th National Five-Year Plans", Xinhuanet, Mar.18, 2016.

trade facilitation, capital flow, and people-to-people exchanges.

First, we should strengthen bilateral cooperation, and promote the comprehensive development of bilateral relations through multilevel and multichannel communication and consultation. We should encourage the signing of cooperation MOUs or plans, and develop a number of bilateral cooperation pilot projects. We should establish and improve bilateral joint working mechanisms, and draw up implementation plans and roadmaps for advancing the Belt and Road Initiative. Besides, we should give full play to the existing bilateral mechanisms such as joint committee, mixed committee, coordinating committee, steering committee, and management committee to coordinate and promote the implementation of cooperation projects.

Second, we should enhance the role of multilateral cooperation mechanisms, make full use of existing mechanisms such as the Shanghai Cooperation Organization (SCO), ASEAN Plus China (10+1), Asia-Pacific Economic Cooperation (APEC), Asia-Europe Meeting (ASEM), Asia Cooperation Dialogue (ACD), Conference on Interaction and Confidence-Building Measures in Asia (CICA), China-Arab States Cooperation Forum (CASCF), China-Gulf Cooperation Council Strategic Dialogue, Greater Mekong Subregion (GMS) Economic Cooperation, and Central Asia Regional Economic Cooperation (CAREC) to strengthen communication with relevant countries, and attract more countries and regions to participate in the Belt and Road Initiative.

Third, we should continue to encourage the constructive role of the international forums and exhibitions at regional and subregional levels hosted by countries along the Belt and Road, as well as such platforms as Boao Forum for Asia, China-ASEAN Expo, China-Eurasia Expo, Euro-Asia Economic Forum, China International Fair for Investment and Trade, China-South Asia Expo, China-Arab States Expo, Western China International Fair, China-Russia Expo, and Qianhai Cooperation Forum. We should support the local authorities and general public of countries along the Belt and Road to explore the historical and cultural heritage of the Belt and Road, jointly hold investment, trade and cultural exchange activities, and ensure the success of the Silk Road (Dunhuang) International Culture Expo, Silk Road International Film Festival and Silk Road International Book Fair. We propose to set up an international summit forum on the Belt and Road.

(2) *Promoting the economic cooperation with countries along the routes*

First, we should promote connectivity of infrastructure and facilities. We should accelerate the formulation of international channels, build a comprehensive transportation network that connects inside and outside China and that is safe and fluent, and perfect the platform and mechanism for transportation cooperation. We should consolidate and expand cooperation in power transmission and optical cable communication. Besides, we should deepen the cooperation in energy resources development and channels construction.

Second, we will strengthen cooperation with international organizations including international financial organizations and institutions, work actively to participate in the development of the Asian Infrastructure Investment Bank and the New Development Bank, put the Silk Road Fund to effective use, and attract international capital for the creation of a financial cooperation platform that is open, pluralistic, and mutually beneficial.

Third, we should deepen economic and trade cooperation with countries along the routes. We will expand market opening to each other, deepen all-round cooperation in customs, inspection and quarantine, standards, certification, and transit transportation, foster and expand industries with distinctive advantages, and promote cooperation in large-scale complete sets of equipment, technologies, and standards between China and countries along the road. We will enhance the import of non-resource products to promote trade balance and promote the establishment of warehouse and logistics bases as well as allocating center in countries along the routes, and perfect regional marketing network. We will strengthen industrial investment cooperation with countries along the routes, and build a number of trade and economic cooperation zones to drive employment and improve people's livelihood in those countries. We will encourage the development of e-commerce in those countries and advocate multilateral cooperation in E-commerce.

Fourth, we will solidly promote the construction of China-Pakistan Economic Corridor and Bangladesh-China-India-Myanmar Economic Corridor. The China-Pakistan Economic Corridor and the Bangladesh-China-India-Myanmar Economic Corridor are closely related to the Belt and Road Initiative, and therefore require in-depth research and greater cooperation. We should actively explore the four-party cooperation model under the framework of the Bangladesh-China-India-Burma Economic Corridor, formulate a pragmatic cooperation plan for the economic corridor, and launch a batch of early harvest projects that are easy to operate and effective. We should work together to develop a long-term plan for the construction of the China-Pakistan Economic Corridor and guide Chinese enterprises in participating in construction activities in an orderly manner.

(3) *Strengthening cultural exchanges*

We will work to ensure the success of the International Summit for the Belt and

Road Initiative and give expression to the role of the Silk Road (Dunhuang) International Culture Expo. We will conduct extensive international cooperation in the areas of education, science, technology, culture, sports, tourism, environmental protection, health care, and traditional Chinese medicine. We will create mechanisms for official and nongovernmental cultural exchanges that involve the participation of multiple parties; hold events such as culture years, art festivals, film festivals, and expos with other countries; encourage diverse kinds of folk culture exchanges; and give full expression to the positive role of folk cultures such as Mazu culture. We will coordinate China's efforts with other countries to develop unique tourism products and increase the convenience of tourism. We will strengthen international exchanges and cooperation on health care and epidemic prevention and enhance our capacity to handle public health emergencies with other countries jointly. We will promote the establishment of think tank associations.

4.2.4 Accelerating implementation of the free trade zone strategy[1]

Accelerating the implementation of the free trade zone strategy is an important part of China's new round of opening up. The 18th National Congress set forth the requirement of accelerating the implementation of the free trade zone strategy. The Third and Fifth Plenum of the 18th CPC Central Committee further required accelerating the implementation of the free trade zone strategy based on surrounding areas to form a global network of high-standard free trade areas. Accelerating the implementation of the free trade zone strategy is an objective requirement for China to adapt to the new trend of economic globalization, and is an inevitable choice for comprehensively deepening reforms and building a new open economic system.

(1) *Further optimizing the construction of the free trade zones*

The optimization of the construction of the free trade zones will be carried out mainly through the three levels: surrounding areas, the Belt and Road and the world.

First, we will accelerate the construction of the surrounding free trade zone. We will strive to establish free trade zones with all neighboring countries and regions, continuously deepen economic and trade relations, and build a large market for win-win cooperation.

Second, we will actively promote the free trade zone along the Belt and Road.

---

1 "Several Opinions of the State Council on Accelerating the Implementation of the Free Trade Area Strategy", Chinese Government Network, Jan.17, 2015.

Integrating the construction of the surrounding free trade zones and the promotion of international cooperation in production capacity, we will actively establish free trade zones with countries along the Belt and Road to form a Belt and Road big market and make the Belt and Road a trade route that is unblocked and open.

Third, we will gradually form a global free trade zones network. We will strive to establish free trade zones with most emerging economies, large developing countries, and major regional economic blocs as well as some developed countries, and build large BRICS markets, large emerging markets, and large developing countries' markets.

(2) *Accelerating the construction of high-level free trade zones*

First, we should improve the openness of trade in goods. We will stick to placing equal importance on import and export, improve free trade zones and two-way market access with free trade partners to rationally design rules of origin in order to advance the development of trade with free trade partners and promote the construction of global and regional value chain that is more effective. On the premise of ensuring economic security, industrial safety and the dynamic development of the industry, we will steadily expand market access for goods trade. At the same time, we will continue to work with free trade partners to reduce tariffs and non-tariff barriers and open up the trade of goods to each other to achieve mutual benefit and win-win results.

Second, we should open service industries wider to the outside world. Implementing open strategies through ways such as free trade zones, we will fully give play to the function of the service industry and service trade in promoting the adjustment of China's economic structure, the transformation of the pattern in economic development, and expansion of employment. We will promote the orderly opening up of services such as finance, education, culture, and medical care. We will liberalize restrictions on foreign investment in service industries such as child care, building design, accounting and auditing, business logistics, and e-commerce.

Third, we should relax market access restrictions on investment. We will vigorously promote the opening up of the investment market and the reform of the foreign investment management system to further optimize the foreign investment environment. We will accelerate the negotiation of investment areas in the free trade zones, and carry out negotiations in an orderly manner with the model of "pre-establishment national treatment plus a negative list". On the premise of safeguarding China's interests as an investment host country and regulatory rights, we will create better market access and investment protection conditions for Chinese investors to "go global" and substantially improve the two-way investment access with free trade partners. We will actively and steadily promote various pilot projects for the convertibility of the renminbi capital projects to facilitate cross-border investment and financing of domestic and foreign entities. We will also strengthen currency cooperation with free trade partners to promote trade and investment facilitation.

Fourth, we should advance negotiations of rules. Integrating with the requirement of comprehensively deepening reforms and governing the country by law, we will actively participate in the free trade zones negotiations on issues that are in line with the need of construction of China's socialist market system and the stable development of the economy as well as society. With reference to international rules and its development trends, combined with China's development level and governance capabilities, we will accelerate negotiations on new issues such as intellectual property protection, environmental protection, e-commerce, competition policy, and government procurement. In terms of intellectual property protection, through the construction of free trade zones, we will create a more equitable intellectual property protection environment for Chinese enterprises to "go global" and promote the improvement of intellectual property protection systems to strengthen the protection and enforcement of intellectual property rights, enhance the awareness of intellectual property protection of enterprises and the public, and enhance the adaptability and response capabilities of Chinese enterprises in the field of intellectual property protection. In terms of environmental protection, we will further strengthen environmental protection legislation and law enforcement through the construction of free trade zones, and draw on international experience to explore the feasibility of establishing environmental impact assessment mechanisms to promote the harmonious development of trade, investment, and the environment. In the area of E-commerce, through the construction of free trade zones, we will encourage cooperation in E-commerce between our country and free trade partners, and create a mutually beneficial environment for E-commerce rules. In terms of competition policy, we will make the market a decisive role in the resources allocation, further promote the improvement of the legal environment of China's competition policy through the construction of free trade zones and establish a legal and international business environment. Regarding government procurement, we will conduct open negotiations on government procurement markets within the framework of free trade zones with free trade partners when conditions are right, and promote the reciprocal and equal opening up of government procurement markets.

Fifth, improving the level of trade facilitation. We will strengthen the management of origins, promote the construction of the electronic network, strengthen the electronic data exchange with free trade partners of origins, and actively explore the implementation of the origin independent declaration system for the authorized exporters in a broader range. We will reform management systems such as customs supervision, inspection, and quarantine, strengthen cooperation in areas such as inspections, and gradually realize the "single window" acceptance of international trade. We will simplify customs clearance procedures and links, accelerate the release of low-risk goods, strengthen coordination and cooperation with customs of free trade partners, and promote the mutual recognition of "certified operators" to improve the level of customs clearance. We will also enhance the efficiency of inspection and quarantine, and implement dynamic adjustment of the catalog of laws and regulations. We will accelerate the implementation of paper-free inspection and quarantine declarations, improve the e-certification network verification of inspection and quarantine, and strengthen the exchange of electronic certificates with free trade partners. We still need to enhance the transparency of inspection and quarantine standards and procedures.

Sixth, promoting regulatory cooperation. We will strengthen information exchange with free trade partners on their respective regulatory systems, and accelerate mutual recognition of technical barriers to trade, sanitary and phytosanitary measures, regulatory standards and qualifications for specific industry sectors to promote moderate integration of regulatory systems, procedures, methods and standards and reduce trade costs and at the same time increase trade efficiency.

(3) *Improving the social security system*

First, continuing to deepen the construction of experimental free trade zones. The experimental free trade zones such Shanghai is a test field in which China actively adapt to the new trends of economic development and new changes in international economic and trade rules to promoted reforms and development. We should put the common difficulties and focus issues in the negotiation of the free trade zones in the free trade pilot zone such as Shanghai, and accumulate experience in prevention and control of risks, to explore the best opening up model, and provide a practical basis for external negotiations by conducting stress tests in some areas.

Second, we should improve laws and regulations on foreign investment. We will promote the revision of the *Law on Sino-foreign Equity Joint Ventures* , the *Law on Sino-foreign Cooperative Joint Ventures* and the *Law on Foreign Capital Enterprises*, study and formulate new basic laws on foreign capital, reform the foreign investment management system, implement the management model of "pre-establishment national treatment plus a negative list", and improve the national security review system for foreign investment and keep the foreign investment policy stable, transparent and predictable.

Third, we should improve the basic system of ongoing and ex-post regulation. In accordance with the requirements of comprehensively governing the country according to law, with the transformation of government functions as the core, we will strengthen on-going and ex-post supervision while strengthening the decentralization of power, and promote the establishment of a social credit system, information sharing and comprehensive law enforcement system, corporate annual report disclosure and abnormal business activities register system, social forces engaging in market supervision system, foreign investment information report system, foreign investment information disclosure platform system, overseas reimbursement guarantee mechanism, etc. and strengthen the process supervision and follow-up management after the "widening" of market entities.

Fourth, we will continue to do a good job in trade remedy. While expanding the opening up of the industry, we should effectively use legal rights of the WTO and Free Trade Agreement to conduct trade remedy investigations in accordance with the law, and enhance diplomatic involvement as well as maintain the legitimate rights and interests of domestic industrial enterprises. We will strengthen the comprehensive trade friction response mechanism coordinated by the central, local, industry association, chambers of commerce and enterprises, and guide enterprises to do a good job in trade friction warning, consultation, dialogue, consultation, litigation, etc.

Fifth, we will study and establish a trade adjustment assistance mechanism. Based on reducing policy distortions and standardizing industrial support policies, we will learn from the relevant countries' practical experience to study and establish a trade adjustment assistance mechanism that conforms to WTO rules and China's national conditions. We will provide assistance for industries, enterprises, and individuals affected by tariff reductions to enhance their competitiveness, and promote industrial restructuring.

4.2.5 Promoting the all-round development of trade internationalization

As China continues to integrate into the world economy, foreign trade, especially exports, has become more and more important to China. The healthy development of foreign trade has effectively promoted the development of China's labor productivity and economic level. Since the 18th National Party Congress, the CPC Central

Committee has firmly grasped the key area of foreign trade and vigorously promoted the healthy development of processing trade and service trade.

4.2.5.1 Accelerating the cultivation of new advantages in foreign trade competition[1]

Facing the new situation and new requirements of world trade development, the CPC Central Committee has set out from the overall situation of domestic and international affairs and proposed to work hard to consolidate the traditional advantages of foreign trade and accelerate the cultivation of new competitive advantages, making export an important role in the economic development.

(1) *Promoting the structural adjustment of the international market*

First, we should promote the structural adjustment of the international market. We should promote the transformation of the import and export market structure from the traditional market to the diversified market and deeply develop traditional markets such as the United States, Europe, and Japan. We should increase the development of emerging markets such as Latin America and Africa, and comprehensively consider factors such as economic scale, development speed, natural resource, and risk level, and select several emerging markets to focus on so as to gradually increase the proportion of emerging markets in China's foreign trade. We should expand the import of advanced technologies and equipment; promote the export of industries and products with good quality, high grade, and comparative advantages.

Second, we should promote balanced development among domestic regions. In accordance with the state's overall deployment of key industries and industrial transfers, a new dimension that is conducive to giving play to regional comparative advantages and that has a rational division of labor is created. We will encourage the eastern region to focus on developing high-end industries, high value-added links, and headquarters economy, to improve the quality and efficiency of trade and play an exemplary and leading role. We will support the central and western regions in combining local realities to actively undertake industrial transfer in the eastern region, with equal emphasis on scale and quality. We should accelerate the pace of opening up along the border, develop cross-border economic cooperation zones in an orderly manner, and expand economic and trade exchanges with neighboring countries.

Third, we should promote the coordinated development of all types of foreign trade

[1] "Several Opinions of the State Council on Accelerating the Cultivation of New Advantages in Foreign Trade", Chinese Government Network, May 12, 2015.

entities. We should encourage leading enterprises in industries to extend the industrial chain and improve the level of international operations. We should encourage well-established enterprises to work with each other, promote cross-regional mergers and reorganization as well as foreign investment cooperation. We should accelerate the formation of a large number of large-scale enterprises capable of international operations which allocate factor resources internationally and lay out market networks. We should encourage the development of small and medium-sized enterprises, and support enterprises which are innovative, entrepreneurial and labor-intensive and support enterprises to take the road of increasing their capacity to turn out products that are new, distinctive, specialized and sophisticated as well as cooperating with large enterprises to promote overall development in all related fields in a coordinated way. We should also support the development of export-oriented private enterprises with innovative capabilities.

Fourth, we should promote the restructuring of foreign commodities. We should strengthen the classification and guidance of exports in key industries. We should continue to consolidate and enhance the global dominance of labor-intensive products such as textiles, clothing, bags, shoes, hats, toys, furniture, and plastic products as well as improve the in-depth processing capacity and characteristic development level of agricultural products. We should strengthen the overall competitive advantages of equipment manufacturing and large-scale equipment exports in power, rail transit, communication equipment, ships, engineering machinery, aerospace, and other equipment and at the same time focus on expanding the export of investment products. We should further improve the international competitiveness of strategic emerging industries such as energy conservation, environmental protection, next-generation information technology, and new energy sources. The import of advanced technologies, equipment, and important parts and components will be increased to promote the adjustment and upgrading of industrial structure, and we should stabilize the import of energy resources products and improve the strategic reserve system. We should reasonably increase the import of general consumer goods and guide the return of overseas consumption. We will promote trade balance and continue to implement zero-tariff treatment for some imported products of the least developed countries.

Fifth, we should promote the optimization of trade forms. We should strengthen general trade, expand the general trade scale, increase the added value of export products in general trade as well as the export of branded products, and exert a brand value-added effect to improve profitability. We will innovate the processing trade mode, accelerate the transformation and upgrading of processing trade in coastal areas to extend to the high-end industrial chain such as brand, R&D, allocation and settlement center, steadily promote the transfer of whole-machines, parts and components, raw materials, R&D and settlement to inland and border areas in competitive enterprises in order to form industrial clusters and build a new development pattern. We should also accelerate the innovation, development, transformation, and upgrading of frontier trade.

(2) *Accelerating the international competitiveness of foreign trade*

We should accelerate the international competitiveness of foreign trade mainly from three aspects: improving product quality, cultivating new trade forms and platform construction.

First, we should improve the quality of export products. We should actively adopt advanced international quality standards, establish an internationally recognized product testing and certification system, and encourage enterprises to organize production and quality assessment by international standards. We should promote the construction of quality and safety demonstration zones of exports. We should also work to accelerate the mutual recognition of the testing system and certification of key export markets. We should strengthen the construction of traceability systems in important products, improve safety risk early warning and rapid response mechanisms in product quality, establish and improve a public platform for quality inspection of exports and support export enterprises to carry out quality management system certification. We will strengthen the quality improvement of agricultural exports, promote negotiations on foreign technical quality, and stabilize the quality and safety of food and agricultural exports. We will carry out an intense crackdown on violations of intellectual property rights and the manufacture and sale of counterfeit or substandard goods.

Second, we will accelerate the cultivation of new trade forms. We will vigorously promote the development of cross-border e-commerce, actively carry out pilot projects for comprehensive reform of cross-border e-commerce, and promptly study and formulate guiding opinions for promoting the development of cross-border e-commerce. We will cultivate a number of cross-border e-commerce platforms and enterprises, and vigorously support enterprises to explore the international market with cross-border e-commerce. We should encourage cross-border e-commerce companies to integrate into overseas retail systems through standardized "overseas warehouses" and other models. We will promote the development of market procurement trade, foster a number of commodity markets with domestic and foreign trade combined, promote the implementation of market procurement trade in the integrated commodity markets of domestic and foreign trade, and expand commodity exports. We will cultivate a number of enterprises that provide comprehensive foreign trade services and strengthen their comprehensive service capabilities such as customs clearance, logistics, tax rebates, finance, and insurance.

Third, we should accelerate the construction of a foreign trade platform. We will accelerate foreign trade transformation and upgrading of bases construction, and cultivate a number of comprehensive, professional and entrepreneurial bases. We will accelerate the construction of trade promotion platform and cultivate a number of state-level exhibition platforms with a high international reputation and great influence. We will create internationally renowned professional exhibitions in key industries and cultivate a number of import promotion platforms to play their role in promoting imports. We will work to cultivate internationally influential securities, commodities, and financial derivatives markets, and enhance the ability to participate in the international market competition. We will accelerate the construction of international marketing networks and encourage enterprises to build exhibition centers, distribution centers, wholesale markets, retail outlets, etc. overseas.

(3) *Striving to build a new pattern of international cooperation for mutual benefits and win-win results*

First, we should accelerate the effective interaction between foreign trade and foreign investment. We will deepen the reform of the foreign investment management system and implement a record-based management model to improve the level of foreign investment facilitation. We will work to accelerate the signing of high-level investment agreements and promote the formulation of investment rules. We will vigorously promote the "going global" of Chinese equipment, promote international cooperation in production capacity, and enhance the level of cooperation. We will make efforts to accelerate competitive and qualified enterprises in industries such as household appliances and machinery equipment to accelerate overseas industrial cooperation, to actively and steadily carry out mergers and acquisitions such as overseas technology and marketing networks. We will deepen international cooperation in the development and processing of energy resources, steadily promote overseas agricultural investment cooperation, and promote the import and export of related products. We should explore new approaches to investment cooperation with other countries, support the development of Greenfield investment, joint investment, etc., and drive the export of China's products, technologies, standards as well as services.

Second, we should further improve the quality and level of using foreign direct investment. We should stabilize the scale and speed of foreign investment and improve the quality of foreign investment. We will innovatively utilize the foreign investment management system and explore the management model of "pre-establishment national treatment plus a negative list". We will combine the transfer of international manufacturing industry with the transformation and upgrading of domestic industries, and actively lead foreign investment to fields like emerging industries, high-tech, energy conservation, and environmental protection. We will encourage multinational corporations to set up regional headquarters, procurement centers, and financial management centers in China to promote the combination of attracting investment and attracting talent, and further exert foreign capitals' function as a carrier to introduce advanced technology, management experience, and high-quality talents.

Third, we will accelerate the implementation of the free trade zone strategy. We will continue to maintain the leading position of the multilateral trading system in the development of global trade, accelerate the implementation of the free trade zone strategy with an open attitude, and promote the role of the free trade zone in promoting trade and investment. We will sign and implement Free Trade Agreement between China and South Korea and Free Trade Agreement between China and Australia as soon as possible, actively promote the negotiation of China-ASEAN Free Trade Zone upgrading, advance the negotiation and construction of RCEP among China, Japan and South Korea, Cooperation Committee between China and Gulf Countries, China-Israel Free Trade Area and China-Sri Lanka Free Trade Area, steadily promote the construction of Asia-Pacific Free Trade Area and launch the negotiation of Free Trade Agreement with other trade partners in due course. We will vigorously promote the economic integration of the Mainland, Hong Kong, and Macao, and continue to promote the institutionalization of cross-strait economic and trade cooperation. We should strengthen the top-level design, actively build free trade zones with countries and regions along the Belt and Road, and accelerate the formation of a high-standard global network of free trade zones based on the surrounding areas and radiating the Belt and Road.

4.2.5.2 Promoting the innovation of processing trade[1]

Processing trade is an important part of China's foreign trade and open economy and plays an important role in promoting industrial upgrading and stabilizing

[1] "Several Opinions of the State Council on Promoting the Innovation and Development of Processing Trade", Chinese Government Network, Jan.18, 2016.

employment. To meet the requirements of the new situation, we should encourage the innovation and development of processing trade, and improve the quality and efficiency of development. Since the 18th National Party Congress, the state has continued to exert its strength in processing trade and actively promote the innovation and development of processing trade.

(1) *We should extend the industrial chain and enhance the position of processing trade in the global value chain*

First, we should strengthen labor division and cooperation in the industrial chain. We should encourage enterprises to actively integrate into the global industrial labor division and collaboration, and make better use of the resources of both international and domestic markets in a more open manner, and strive to enhance the status of processing trade in the global value chain.

Second, we will promote industrial integration and upgrading. We should stabilize the expectations of foreign investment and support foreign capital enterprises in taking root in China. We should attract more investment, focus on attracting advanced manufacturing and emerging industries, further expand the opening up of service industries, encourage foreign capital enterprises to set up procurement center in China and develop Headquarters Economy. We should support coastal areas in developing competitive industries such as electronic information, and encourage enterprises to take root, transform and upgrade. We will promote the gradient transfer of labor-intensive industries to the inland areas along the border and realize the development of integrated clusters. We should encourage enterprises to go global together and extend industrial chain offshore in an orderly way through developing foreign investment cooperation and exerting the platform function of overseas economic and trade cooperation zones.

Third, we should enhance innovation abilities of enterprises. We will promote the transformation of development in processing trade enterprises from simple OEM to ODM and OBM. We should encourage greater investment in R&D and technological transformation, strengthen collaboration with universities and research institutions, and improve automatic and intelligent production. We should support enterprises in creating and acquiring brands, expanding marketing channels, and transforming from the passive order receiving to active marketing. We should comply with the new opportunities brought about by the development of the internet and realize the rising of the value chain.

(2) *We will give play to the leading role of coastal areas, promote transformation and upgrading as well as improve quality and efficiency*

First, we should stabilize traditional competitive industries. We should continue to develop traditional labor-intensive processing trade industries such as textile, garments, shoes, furniture, plastic products, and toys to consolidate traditional advantages. We will support enterprises in promoting technology R&D, equipment upgrading, raising the technological content and added value of products to strengthen the core competence of enterprises.

Second, we will vigorously develop advanced manufacturing and emerging industries. We should encourage the development of sophisticated manufacturing processing trade that with strong radiation and overflowing capabilities such as electronic information, mobile communications, automobiles, and parts, integrated circuits, medical service equipment, and aerospace. We will promote the development of emerging industrial clusters such as biomedicine, new energy, new materials, energy conservation, and environmental protection. We should support processing trade enterprises in entering key parts and integrated manufacturing sectors, to master core technologies and improve overall manufacturing level.

Third, we will support the development of service for production. We should promote the transformation of manufacturing from production to both production and the provision of services. We should promote the deep integration of processing trade and service trade, and encourage processing trade enterprises to undertake service outsourcing services such as R&D and design, inspection and maintenance, logistics and distribution, financial settlement, and distribution and warehousing. We should carry out high-tech and high-value-added inspection, maintenance and remanufacturing service in eligible areas both domestic and overseas.

Fourth, we should continue to give play to the role of demonstration zones in coastal areas. We will give play to the advantages of complete processing, industrial agglomeration, convenient logistics and efficient supervision in the processing trade industry in the coastal regions to promote industrial transformation and upgrading. We will accelerate the transformation and upgrading of the processing trade in the Pearl River Delta and the pilot cities for transformation and upgrading of processing trade in Dongguan and Suzhou, as well as the construction of demonstration enterprises, and foster a batch of new transformation and upgrading demonstration enterprises for processing trade. We should support a group of capable processing trade enterprises to cultivate regional and industry-owned brands, build domestic and overseas marketing networks, and expand the producer-service industry. We will support coastal areas in cultivating advanced manufacturing bases and economic zones with global influence.

(3) *We should support inland areas along the border in undertaking industrial gradient transfer to promote coordinated development among regions*

First, we will promote the development of processing trade industry clusters. We will support inland areas along the border in accelerating the transfer of labor-intensive industries and processing and assembly capacity in accordance with crucial national industry layout. We should encourage inland areas along the border to develop processing trade based on local environment capacity and carrying capacity. We will steadily promote the transfer of whole-machines, parts, and components, raw materials, R&D and settlement to inland and border areas in domestic and overseas enterprises in order to form industrial clusters.

Second, we should establish a cooperation mechanism for the industrial transfer of processing trade. We should promote the establishment of a coordination mechanism for the industrial transfer of processing trade, focusing on solving such problems as information asymmetry, imperfect supporting services, and insufficient talents to promote the launch of projects. We should encourage coastal areas and inland areas to jointly build industrial cooperation parks, and carry out industrial connection as well as talent exchange and training in accordance with the principles of mutual complementarity, joint investment, joint development, and benefit sharing.

Third, we will support the development of key areas for gradient transfer. We will increase support for the key areas of processing trade gradient transfer, focus on strengthening the construction of public service platforms, employee skill training, investment promotion, and employment promotion in these areas. Special funds for transfer can be set up to promote related work in eligible areas. We should cultivate and build a batch of key regions and demonstration sites of processing trade gradient transfer.

Fourth, we will formulate a differentiated policy to support gradient transfer. On the premise of strictly prohibiting the transfer of polluting industries and backward production capacity, combined with the layout of national key industries, we will study and formulate policies and measures to support the gradient transfer of processing trade in inland areas.

(4) *We should guide enterprises to carry out international cooperation in production capacity in an orderly manner and coordinate two resources in the international and domestic markets*

First, we will plan the layout of overseas cooperation in processing trade. We will do a good job in the layout of key countries and key industries for overseas cooperation, and guide the overseas cooperation of building materials, chemicals, nonferrous metals, light industry, textiles, and food industries. We will transform the "going global" approach of processing trade enterprises and support enterprises to rely on overseas economic and trade cooperation zones, industrial parks, special economic zones, and other cooperative parks to achieve chain-shifting and cluster-based development. We will support enterprises to expand outbound investment, promote the "going global" of equipment, technologies, and standards, deeply integrated into global production, value, and logistics chains, establish overseas production centers and cultivate a batch of transnational corporations.

Second, we should perfect the mechanism for the cooperation of processing trade industries. We should strengthen the existing bilateral and multilateral cooperation mechanisms, promote the cooperation with key countries of "going global" in investment protection, finance, taxation, customs, quality inspection, and personnel exchanges to provide support for enterprises. We should establish a foreign cooperation platform, organize exchanges between domestic processing trade enterprises and those in key countries, and carry out industrial collaborations.

Third, we should deepen industrial cooperation with countries along the Belt and Road. We should support traditional competitive industries in establishing production bases in countries with abundant labor and energy resources to develop entrepot trade and processing trade. We should support the active gradient transfer of processing trade in key developing and pilot zones, border cities, border economic cooperation zones and cross-border economic cooperation zones.

Fourth, we will enhance cooperation level in China-Africa industrialization. By the principles of gradual progress, key breakthroughs, and pilot demonstrations, we will actively promote the China-Africa Industrialization Partnership Action Plan with labor-intensive industries as carriers. We should choose countries with relatively mature conditions such as Ethiopia, Egypt, Nigeria, Angola, and South Africa to carry out processing trade capacity cooperation.

(5) *Reforming and innovating management system to enhance momentum for development*

First, we should deepen the reform of the administrative examination and approval for processing trade. We should summarize the experience of Guangdong Province's pilot work in canceling processing trade approval and domestic sales approval to comprehensively promote the reform process of administrative approval in processing trade. We should implement a dynamic management mechanism for prohibitive and restricted catalogs in processing trade. We will improve the access management of key sensitive commodities in processing trade enterprises.

Second, we will establish a new mechanism for processing trade industries. We should strengthen ongoing and ex-post regulation, improve verification regime for enterprise management condition and production capacity in processing trade, urge enterprises to undertake social responsibilities such as production safety, energy saving, and low carbon and environmental protection. We should promote the network of departments such as business, customs, quality inspection, taxation, foreign exchange, and processing trade enterprises to achieve inter-departmental coordination. On the premise of effectively preventing risks and ensuring taxation, we will improve the existing deposit account system of banks in due course. We should establish a scientific and rational evaluation system for transformation and upgrading of processing trade.

Third, we should optimize the supervision method. We should accelerate the reform of integrated regional customs clearance, paper-free customs clearance to further improve the level of customs clearance. We should enhance the supervision method and gradually implement enterprise-based supervision. We will explore the implementation of self-verified unit consumption for enterprises with good credit, transparent information and that are up to requirements of customs. We should standardize the outbound processing regulatory process.

Fourth, we will promote the convenience of domestic sales. We should explore the elimination of approval for domestic sales to further simplify the procedures of taxation and verification. We should promote the implementation of centralized taxation for domestic sales. We will make expo of processing trade products play a role as a platform, advance the cooperation between processing trade enterprises and large-scale domestic logistics enterprises, and promote online and offline integration. We should support enterprises to expand sales channels through various methods such as e-commerce.

Fifth, we will accelerate the integration of special customs control areas. We should give full play to the role of the special customs supervision area to connect the two resources in the international and domestic markets, actively promote its radiation to drive the surrounding economic development, and vigorously develop advanced manufacturing, producer-service industry, and science and technology services to advance industrial upgrading in the area. In the special customs supervision area of the experimental free trade zones, we will actively promote the pilot preferential tariff policy for domestic sales, and timely study and expand the pilot. We should encourage diversified businesses such as bonded processing, bonded logistics, and bonded services for the development of special customs regulation zones.

(6) *Improving our policies and measures and creating a better development environment*

First, we will increase financial support. We should give full play to the guidance of existing financial funds, encourage the introduction of advanced technology and equipment, support product innovation, R&D and design, brand cultivation and standard setting to promote transformation and upgrading of processing trade as well as gradient transfer. We should strengthen the guidance of social funds, and improve various public services through government and social capital cooperation models as well as industrial funds.

Second, we should improve the level of financial services. We should encourage financial institutions to innovate financial products and services in line with the principle of business sustainability and risk control, provide credit support for inland and border areas to undertake industrial transfer, and provide diversified financing services for the transformation and upgrading of processing trade enterprises. We should innovate overseas insurance business varieties, expand the scale and coverage of export credit insurance, and improve the efficiency of underwriting and claims. We should work to guide financial guarantee institutions to promote services for small and medium-sized processing trade enterprises. We will encourage financial institutions to provide financing support for processing trade enterprises to operate overseas through onshore guarantees for offshore loans and so on.

Third, we will improve the social security system. We should reduce insurance premiums and the burden on processing trade enterprises appropriately according to the state's regulations. We should accelerate the realization of the national network of social insurance, enhance the management services of the convenience of social insurance, and facilitate the transfer of social insurance relationship of mobile workers. We should do a good job in social insurance for mobile workers in key development areas of processing trade.

Fourth, we should optimize the legal environment. We will improve the system of laws and regulations of processing trade in line with China's national conditions and international practices. We will strengthen the classification management of processing trade enterprises, establish coordination mechanisms for business, environmental protection, customs, industry and commerce, quality inspection and other departments, and promote the construction of credit evaluation system for processing trade enterprises associated with the system for releasing enterprise credit info. We should establish a mechanism in which enterprises get convenience for law-abiding and penalty for lack of credibility. We should strengthen the regulation, supervision, and guidance of the protection and application of intellectual property rights such as trademarks and business secrets of OEM enterprises. We should intensify the training of relevant laws and regulations on intellectual property rights and raise awareness of enterprises on intellectual property rights protection.

Fifth, we should create a fair external environment. We should actively participate in bilateral and multilateral negotiations, promote the formulation of multilateral, regional and bilateral international economic and trade rules, and strengthen the bilateral cooperation mechanism such as the Economic and Trade Joint Commission to effectively resolve trade frictions and disputes. We should give full play to the promotion role of free trade agreements. We will establish a stable and institutionalized cooperation platform to further improve the conditions two-way cargo, service, and investment market access with major trading partners, and promote trade and investment liberalization and facilitation. We will vigorously promote the economic integration of the Mainland, Hong Kong SAR, and Macao SAR, and continue to promote the institutionalization of cross-strait economic and trade cooperation.

Sixth, we should create a public opinion environment conducive to the development of manufacturing. We should stabilize processing trade policies to provide a predictable long-term development environment. We should encourage and protect innovation, respect and promote entrepreneurship, support manufacturing enterprises to operate in a specialized and refined way, and strive to become century enterprises. We should encourage enterprises to focus on R&D and technology applications and improve management. We will strengthen the promotion of demonstration enterprises' experience in transformation and upgrading of processing trade.

4.2.5.3 Promoting the healthy development of service trade[1]

Since the 18th National Party Congress, China's service trade has developed rapidly, but overall its international competitiveness is relatively inadequate and is still a weak spot in foreign trade. We will vigorously develop service trade which is an important focus for expanding opening up and development space. It is conducive to stabilizing and increasing employment, adjusting economic structure, improving development quality and efficiency, and cultivating new growth points. To adapt to the new normal of the economy and accelerate the development of service trade, the CPC Central Committee has put forward the requirements for promoting the healthy development of service trade.

(1) *The main tasks of promoting the healthy development of service trade*

First, we will expand the scale of service trade. We should consolidate the scale advantages of exports in labor-intensive service such as tourism and construction; we should focus on the development of capital-and-technology-intensive service areas such as transportation, communications, finance, insurance, computer and information services, consulting, R&D and design, energy conservation and environmental protection, and environmental services. We should meet not only domestic demand by expanding imports but also foster industrial competitiveness and new advantages in foreign trade competition by encouraging exports; we should actively promote the export of cultural services that support the core values of Chinese culture, such as cultural arts, radio, film, and television, journalism and publishing as well as education, and vigorously promote the export of new cultural services such as cultural creativity, digital publishing, and animation games. We should also work to strengthen international exchanges and cooperation in special service fields such as traditional Chinese medicine, sports, catering to enhance the soft power and influence of Chinese culture.

Second, we will optimize service trade structure. We will optimize the structure of the service trade industry, actively open up new areas of service trade, and steadily increase the proportion of high value-added services such as capital-intensive services and featured services in service import and export. We should optimize the international market layout, continue to consolidate the traditional market, and increase the import potential of capital-and-technology-intensive services while exploiting the potential of

---

[1] "Several Opinions of the State Council on Accelerating the Development of Service Trade", Chinese Government Network, Feb.14, 2015.

services export; we should vigorously develop the national markets along the Belt and Road, increase the market share of emerging countries, actively develop service trade such as transportation and construction, and cultivate international boutique tourism routes and products with the characteristics of the Silk Road. We will promote the development of special service trade that carries Chinese culture and increases the proportion of capital-and-technology-intensive service trade. We should optimize the regional layout of the country, consolidate the scale and innovation advantages of the eastern coastal areas, accelerate the development of capital-and-technology-intensive service trade, and give play to the resource advantages of the central and western regions. We should cultivate characteristic industries and encourage dislocation competition and coordinated development.

Third, we will plan to build a service trade function area. We should give full play to the role of the modern service industry and service trade agglomeration, and carry out pilot projects for service trade innovation development in qualified regions. We will plan to build a number of special service export bases based on the existing development zones and experimental free trade zones. We will expand the service export function of special customs regulation zones and bonded supervision places, and expand functions such as international entrepottrade, international logistics, transfer service, research and development, international settlement, distribution, and warehousing.

Fourth, we will innovate the model of service trade development. We should actively explore new service trade development models under the background of informatization, and promote service trade model innovations based on new technologies such as big data, Internet of Things, mobile Internet, and cloud computing to create a new network platform for service trade, and promote the integration and development of manufacturing and service industries. We should take outsourcing service as an important means to improve China's service level and international influence, expand the scale of the outsourcing service industry, increase the proportion of high-tech and high value-added outsourcing businesses, expand the service outsourcing business area to improve the capability of cross-border service delivery. We should promote the coordinated development of offshore and onshore service outsourcing, and gradually expand the scale of the onshore market while actively undertaking international service outsourcing.

Fifth, we will cultivate the market entities of service trade. We should create a number of large-scale multinational service enterprises with outstanding main business and intense competitiveness, and cultivate a number of service brands with strong international influence; we should support the development of distinctive and innovative small and medium-sized enterprises and guide them to integrate into the global supply chain. We should encourage service enterprises of designated scale to take the international development path, actively exploit overseas markets, and strive to achieve import and export performance in service enterprises of designated scale. We should support service trade enterprises to strengthen independent innovation and encourage technology introduction, digestion, absorption and innovation in service sectors.

Sixth, we will further expand the opening up of the service industry. We will apply the management of "pre-establishment national treatment" plus a negative list to foreign investment to improve the quality and level of foreign capital utilization. We will promote the opening up of the service industry and advance the orderly opening up of the service sectors such as finance, education, culture, and medical care to achieve a high-level opening up gradually; We should liberalize restrictions on foreign investment in service industries such as child care, building design, accounting and auditing, business logistics, and e-commerce. We should actively participate in multilateral, regional service trade negotiations and the formulation of global service trade rules. We should establish a global network of high-standard free trade areas based on the implementation of the free trade zone strategy, and actively promote the two-way reciprocal opening up of the service industry. We will also work to realize the liberalization of trade between the mainland and Hong Kong as well as Macao and at the same time promote mutually beneficial opening up in the service industry between the mainland and Taiwan.

Seventh, we should vigorously promote foreign investment in the service industry. We should support various enterprises in the service industry in carrying out investment cooperation abroad through new establishments, mergers and acquisitions, cooperation, etc., to accelerate the construction of overseas marketing networks, and increase the commercial presence overseas. We should support enterprises in the service industry to participate in investment, construction, and management of overseas economic and trade cooperation zones. We should encourage enterprises to build overseas bonded warehouses, actively build cross-border industrial chains, and drive domestic labor export as well as exports of goods, services, and technologies. We should support overseas registration of intellectual property rights, strengthen the overseas distribution of intellectual property rights, advance overseas rights protection, and safeguard rights and interests of enterprises. At the same time, supervision, planning, and guidance should be strengthened. We should give play to the guiding role of planning and regularly develop a service trade development plan. We should guide local governments to do well in planning, establish leading industries and development priorities, and support the development of industries with distinctive advantages. We will strengthen support and guidance for key areas and develop guidelines for the export of key services. We should establish exchange systems for key enterprises at different levels.

(2) *The main measures of promoting the healthy development of service trade*

First, we should improve finance and taxation policies. We should make full use of policies such as special funds for foreign trade and economic development, increase support for the development of service trade, further optimize the structure of financial arrangements, and highlight key points of policy support, improve and innovate supporting ways to guide more social funds to increase support for service trade development so as to broaden financing channels, and improve public services. We should promote service exports integrating the full implementation of the "replacing business tax with a value-added tax", zero-tax or tax-free tariffs on service exports.

Second, we will improve financial services. We should strengthen the construction of the financial service system, encourage financial institutions to innovate financial products and services on the premise of risk control, and carry out supply chain financing, overseas M&A financing, the pledge of accounts receivable, warehouse receipt pledge loans, financial leasing, etc. We should encourage policy-based financial institutions to increase support for service trade enterprises to explore international markets and conduct international mergers and acquisitions and support the construction of key trade projects within the existing business scope. We should encourage insurance institutions to innovate insurance products and insurance business, explore and research to introduce more and more convenient foreign exchange rate hedging insurance, and adopt flexible insurance policies on the premise of risk control as well as simplify the insurance procedures. We should guide service trade enterprises to actively use various policy tools such as finance and insurance to explore the international market and expand financing channels. We will work to promote the construction of financing guarantee system for small and micro enterprises, and actively promote their comprehensive information sharing. Besides, we should increase support for service trade enterprises in multiple levels of capital markets, and support qualified service trade enterprises to list on the exchange market, list in the national small and medium-sized enterprises share transfer system, issue corporate bonds as well as small and medium-sized enterprise placement bonds.

Third, we will improve the level of facilitation. We will establish and perfect a management model port customs clearance that is compatible with service trade. We will explore the innovation of the supervision mode of special items such as international exhibits, artworks, e-commerce express shipments, etc. required for service companies such as exhibitions, auctions, and express delivery and improve cross-border e-commerce customs clearance services. We should strengthen the construction of financial infrastructure, facilitate cross-border renminbi settlement, encourage domestic banking institutions and payment institutions to expand the scope of cross-border payment services, and support service trade enterprises to increase the efficiency of foreign exchange funds by using export revenues to store overseas. We should strengthen international negotiation and cooperation on personnel mobility, mutual recognition of qualifications, standardization, etc. and facilitate the "bringing in" and "going global" of professional talents and services. We will also work to provide facilitation for the permanent foreign high-end talents on permanent residence in China.

Fourth, we will create a promotion platform. We should support associations and promotion agencies in carrying out various forms of service trade promotion activities and propagandize "Chinese services" in the form of government procurement services to improve the service trade brand and corporate image. We should support enterprises to participate in key service trade exhibitions abroad. We will actively cultivate an exchange and cooperation platform for service trade, and form a service trade exhibition structure with China (Beijing) International Service Trade Fair as the leading role and various professional exhibition forums as the supporting role to encourage other investment and trade exhibitions to add service trade exhibition areas. We should actively sign service trade cooperation agreements with major service trade partners and countries along the Belt and Road to carry out pragmatic cooperation in a bilateral framework.

(3) *Security system promoting the healthy development of service trade*

First, we should perfect the legal system. We should accelerate the revision of basic regulation in relevant service industries, gradually establish and improve the legal and regulatory systems in all areas of service trade, and standardize the market access and business order of service trade. We will study and develop relevant regulations on services of import and export. We should encourage areas with suitable conditions to lay down local regulations on service trade. We will establish producer service standards more in line with international standards.

Second, we will establish a coordination mechanism. We should establish the State Council's service trade development coordination mechanism, strengthen macro guidance on service trade, coordinate the opening up of the service industry, coordinate the service export policies of various departments, and promote the facilitation and liberalization of service trade. All localities should take the development of service trade as an important part in stabilizing foreign trade growth and cultivating new advantages of foreign trade competition, and incorporating it into the government evaluation and evaluation index system to improve the assessment mechanism.

Third, we will improve statistical work. We will establish and improve the statistics monitoring, operation, and analysis system in international service trade, improve the service trade statistical indicator system, strengthen the exchange of data and information with international organizations and industry associations and regularly publish service trade statistics. We should innovate service trade statistics methods, strengthen guidance on local service trade statistics, and conduct direct data reporting for key enterprises.

Fourth, we should strengthen the cultivation of talents. We will vigorously cultivate service trade talents and accelerate the formation of mechanisms for joint training of talents by government departments, research institutes, universities, and enterprises. We should intensify the training, support, and introduction of core talents, key talents, high-skilled talents, and international talents. We should encourage the major of international economy and trade in higher education institutions to add courses related to service trade. We should encourage all market players to advance their talent training, conduct service trade management, and marketing service personnel training, and build a team of high-quality professionals.

Fifth, we should optimize the development environment. We should actively create a good atmosphere in which the whole society attaches importance to the development of service industry and service trade. We will clean up and standardize laws and regulations as well as departmental regulations related to service trade, unify laws and regulations for domestic and foreign capital, and foster a business environment in which all market players enter and trade in an equal manner according to law. We will promote industry associations and chambers of commerce to establish and improve self-regulation, self-discipline and professional ethics, regulate member behaviors, promote industry integrity and consciously maintain market order.

4.2.6 Promoting rapid development of capital internationalization

Capital internationalization is an important part of economic internationalization. Since the 18th National Party Congress, the CPC Central Committee has attached great importance to the promotion of capital internationalization. On the basis of emphasizing the further utilization of foreign capital, we will vigorously promote the "going global" of the Chinese capital.

4.2.6.1 Making better use of foreign capitals[1]

The use of foreign capital is an essential part of China's basic national policy and an open economic system and has played a positive role in the process of economic development and deepening reform. At present, global transnational investment and industrial transfer have shown a new trend. China's economy has deeply integrated into the world economy, and economic development has entered a new normal. The use of foreign capital is facing new situations and new tasks. Therefore, Xi Jinping repeatedly stressed that China will continue to adhere to the basic national policy of opening up to the outside world, and further actively use foreign capital to create an excellent business environment. We will continue to deepen the streamline administration and delegate government powers, enhance oversight where appropriate and improving government services and reduce institutional transaction costs to achieve mutual benefit and win-win results.

(1) *Further expanding opening up*

First, we should promote a new round of high-level opening up guided by the concept of open development. We will revise the *Catalog of Industries Open to Foreign Investment*, and make service industries, manufacturing, and mining more open to foreign investment. We should support foreign to play a role in the strategy of innovation-driven development, transformation and upgrading of manufacturing industry as well as the entrepreneurial development of overseas talents in China.

Second, the service industry will focus on relaxing foreign investment access restrictions for banking financial institutions, securities companies, securities investment fund management companies, futures companies, insurance institutions, and insurance intermediary institutions. We will liberalize the restrictions on foreign investment in accounting auditing, architectural design, rating services, etc., and promote the orderly opening of telecommunications, Internet, culture, education,

---

[1] "Several Opinions of the State Council on Measures of Expand Opening Up and Actively Utilizing Foreign Capitals", Chinese Government Network, Jan.17, 2017.

transportation, and other fields.

Third, the manufacturing sector has focused on eliminating foreign investment access restrictions in rail transit equipment manufacturing, motorcycle manufacturing, fuel ethanol production, oil processing, etc. The mining industry has relaxed restrictions on foreign investment in oil shale, oil sands, shale gas, and other non-conventional oil and gas resources as well as mineral resources. The foreign cooperation projects in the oil and natural gas fields were changed from the examination and approval system to the filing system.

Fourth, foreign-invested enterprises and domestic enterprises are equally applicable to measures in "Made in China 2025" strategic policy. We should encourage foreign investors to invest in high-end manufacturing, smart manufacturing, green manufacturing, and producer-service industry such as industrial design and creativity, engineering consulting, modern logistics, inspection, and testing, etc. to transform and upgrade traditional industries.

Fifth, we will support foreign investment in the construction of infrastructure, including energy, transportation, water conservancy, environmental protection, municipal public works, etc., by franchising according to the law. Relevant support policies are equally applicable to the construction and operation of foreign franchise projects.

Sixth, we should support domestic and foreign-funded enterprises as well as scientific and research institutions in carrying out research and development cooperation. We should support foreign-invested enterprises in building R&D centers, enterprise technology centers, and apply for post-doctoral research stations. We will permit foreign-invested enterprises to take part in national science and technology projects under the principle of reciprocity. Foreign-invested enterprises are equally eligible for preferential policies such as deductions for research and development expenses, high-tech enterprises, as well as research and development centers.

Seventh, we should support high-level overseas talents in starting a business in China. Foreign-level high-level talents holding foreigners' permanent residence shall be granted with equal treatment as Chinese citizens in establishing science and technology enterprises. Foreign high-level talents, as well as their spouses and children who apply for multiple visas or residence permits, shall be provided convenience in accordance with the law.

(2) *Further creating a level playing field*

First, we should promote the fair participation of domestic and foreign-funded enterprises in China's standardization work. We should further deepen the reform of standardization work and improve the transparency and openness of standard revision. We should promote information disclosure and strengthen information sharing and social supervision in the process of standard setting and revision.

Second, we will deepen the reform of government procurement; adhere to the principle of openness, transparency, and fair competition. We will treat products produced by foreign-invested enterprises equally according to the law and promote the fair participation of domestic and foreign-funded enterprises in government procurement bidding.

Third, we will strictly protect the intellectual property rights of foreign-invested enterprises in accordance with the law and regulation. We will improve the enforcement mechanism for intellectual property rights, strengthen the enforcement of intellectual property rights, rights assistance, and arbitration mediation. We will strengthen the construction of international cooperation mechanisms for intellectual property rights and promote relevant international organizations to establish intellectual property arbitration and mediation sub-centers in China.

Fourth, we will support foreign-invested enterprises in expanding financing channels. Foreign-invested enterprises can be listed on the Main Board, SME Board, and GEM Board and the New Third Board by the law. It also can issue enterprise bonds, corporate bonds, and convertible bonds as well as use non-financial corporate debt financing instruments for financing.

Fifth, we should deepen the reform of the registered capital system of foreign-invested enterprises. The minimum registered capital requirement of a foreign-invested company shall be abolished and the unified registered capital system of domestic and foreign-funded enterprises shall be implemented unless otherwise provided for in administrative laws and regulations.

(3) *Further attracting foreign investment*

First, we should support the central and western regions and northeast China in undertaking industrial transfer industries. We will revise *Catalogue of Priority Industries for Foreign Investment in the Central-Western Regions* to expand the scope of industries in which foreign investors are encouraged to invest in central and western regions and northeast China. We should implement preferential corporate income tax policies for eligible foreign-invested enterprises of encouraged industries in the west region. Foreign-invested enterprises that have moved to the central and western regions and northeast China shall enjoy preferential policies such as state funds and land for supporting industrial transfer and processing trade. For foreign-invested enterprises in the eastern region that transfer to the central and western regions and northeast China, Ministry of Human Resources and Social Security shall promptly handle the transfer of social insurance in different places according to the application.

Second, we will support the land use of foreign-invested projects. Foreign-invested enterprises and domestic enterprises are equally applicable to related land use policies. We will continue to preferentially supply land to encouraged foreign-invested industrial projects in case of intensive land use. The basic price of land transfer shall be at least 70% of the minimum national price for the corresponding industrial land transfer.

Third, we should promote the reform of centralized operation and management of domestic and foreign currency in foreign-invested multinational corporations. We will actively attract multinational companies to set up regional headquarters, procurement centers, settlement centers, and other functional institutions in China, allowing foreign multinational companies to carry out centralized operations of domestic and foreign currency funds to promote two-way flow of funds and improve the efficiency of capital use and the level of investment facilitation.

Fourth, we will perfect the foreign debt management system of foreign-invested enterprises. We should unify the management of foreign debts of domestic and foreign-funded enterprises, improve enterprises' foreign exchange management, and improve the overseas financing capabilities and convenience of foreign-invested enterprises.

Fifth, we should deepen the reform of the foreign investment management system. We will apply the management of "pre-establishment national treatment plus a negative list" to foreign investment to simplify and alter management procedure in foreign investment projects. We should advance the joint operation during approval procedures, shorten the time needed in customs registration, invoices application, etc. We will promote e-government construction, implement "applying at one window", limited time settlement, and queryable progress to improve the level of foreign investment management informatization. We should advance the construction of experimental free trade zones, promote and replicate the experience on a larger scale. All regions and departments must fully understand the importance of making good use of foreign capital under the new situation, attach great importance to it, take the initiative, strengthen responsibility, and cooperate closely. The National Development and Reform Commission and the Ministry of Commerce should strengthen supervision and inspection with relevant departments to ensure that all policies and measures are implemented. Integrating the implementation of various policies and measures, we will vigorously create a more open, convenient and transparent business environment, and actively attract foreign investment, advanced technology, and management experience. We should also stabilize the scale and speed of foreign investment, improve the level and quality of foreign capital utilization, and strive to promote a new round of high-level opening up to promote reform and development.

4.2.6.2 Promoting the "going global" of capitals[1]

Internationalization is not one-way, but two-way and comprehensive. With the continuous development of China's economy, China has accumulated a lot of funds and technology. How to promote the better use of these funds and technologies is the focus of current work as well as the key to the formation of a new impetus for economic development.

(1) *Establishing a new system to promote the "going global" strategy and the healthy development of foreign direct investment*

Since the 18th National Party Congress, China has taken the following measures in order to promote the healthy development of foreign direct investment:

First, establishing and implement a national strategy of "going global" in the new era. In accordance with the overall plan for national economic and social development and the overall strategy for opening up, we will improve the medium- and long-term development plans for overseas investment, strengthen the overall planning and guidance for "going global" and provide policy support and investment promotion. We should encourage enterprises to formulate medium- and long-term international development strategies, take into account current and long-term interests, and operate according to law abroad. We will urge enterprises to fulfill their social responsibilities and establish a good image.

Second, we will promote the convenience of overseas investment. Laws and regulations on overseas investment should be formulated. We will implement the principle of self-determination and independent accounting and responsibility for profits and losses on corporate investment, relax overseas investment restrictions, and simplify overseas investment management. Except for a few special regulations, overseas investment projects will be subject to a filing system. We will promote the establishment of an accredited domestic individual investors system. We should

---

[1] "The 13th National Five-Year Plan", Xinhuanet, Mar.18, 2016.

strengthen the construction of overseas investment cooperation information platform.

Third, we should explore new approaches to investment cooperation with other countries. We will permit enterprises and individuals to exert their advantages to carry out investment and cooperation abroad, to undertake engineering projects and labor cooperation projects in various countries and regions at their own risk, to "go global" and carry out greenfield investment, M&A investment, securities investment, and joint investment in innovative ways. We will encourage competitive enterprises to conduct overseas infrastructure investment and energy and resources cooperation in various ways. We will promote the "going global" of high-speed railway, nuclear power, aviation, machinery, electric power, telecommunications, metallurgy, building materials, light industry, textile and other advantageous industries, improve the internationalization level of modern service industries such as Internet information service and promote the "going global" of e-commerce. We will also promote overseas agricultural investment cooperation in a positive and sound manner as well as we will promote greater use of China's major technical standard, explore new models for overseas economic and trade cooperation zones, and support domestic investment entities in self-construction and self-management.

Fourth, we will improve the service systems for "going global". We will accelerate negotiating investment and trade agreements with relevant countries and regions, improve consular protection system, provide more services such as the safeguard of rights and interests, investment stimulation and risk warning to facilitate foreign investment. We will also work to guarantee the safety of persons and property overseas. By giving play to the functions of intermediary institutions, we should establish a batch of international intermediary institutions for design and consultation, capital assessment, credit rating, as well as legal service.

Fifth, we should integrate "bringing in" and "going global". We will enhance the integration and cooperation between foreign capital and foreign investment, promote industrial investment cooperation with countries and regions for mutual benefit. We should give full play to China's advantages and conditions to promote the common development of other countries and regions. We will encourage enterprises to carry out international cooperation in many aspects such as scientific and technological innovation, project integration, and human resource development. We will support local governments and enterprises in attracting investment, technology, and talents from overseas as well as proactively exploring the international market. Through various investment cooperation mechanisms, we will share the successful experience of "bringing in" and promote a good investment environment for the countries concerned.

(2) *Building an open and secure financial system to promote renminbi internationalization*

We should steadily carry out reforms to make interest rates and the renminbi exchange rate more market-based, expand cross-border use of the renminbi and gradually achieve the renminbi's convertibility under capital accounts.

First, we should expand the opening up in the financial sector. Based on the continuous evaluation, perfecting prudential supervision and effective risk-controlling, we will relax the ratio of stocks in the securities and promote the opening up of the banking industry in an orderly manner to form a fair, well-organized and benign financial environment. We will enhance the international operation level of financial institutions, encourage financial institutions to prudently conduct cross-border mergers and acquisitions, perfect the network of overseas branches, improve financial services level, and strengthen the international cooperation in the field of payment and market infrastructure. We will establish and perfect an international financial cooperation mechanism that supports the development of science and technology innovation.

Second, we should promote the two-way orderly opening of the capital market. We will work steadily to make the renminbi convertible under capital accounts and facilitate cross-border investment and financing of domestic and foreign entities. We will expand the opening up of the futures market and permit the eligible foreign institution to engage in futures trading of specific types. We will explore that financial institutions or enterprises such as banks, securities companies with true trading and investment in China are allowed to participate in overseas financial derivatives. On the premise of controllable risks, we will explore the gradual opening up the financial derivatives market.

Third, we will establish a financial support system of "going global". We will construct a financial support system for overseas investment that combines policy-based finance and commercial finance, and promote the joint "going global" of financial capitals and industrial capitals. We will perfect the overseas investment and financing mechanism, explore the establishment of a domestic trading financing platform for overseas stock equity assets, and provide enterprises with a financing method of "offshore guarantees for onshore loans". We will develop various forms of overseas investment funds, promote the establishment and operation of the Silk Road Fund as well as the Asian Infrastructure Investment Bank and BRICS New Development Bank, and establish Shanghai Cooperation Organization (SCO) financing institution. We will make good use of the international cooperation mechanism for investment and financing, select the key points, and actively promote the cooperation with countries along the Belt and Road.

Fourth, we should expand the cross-border use of renminbi. We should advance the construction of a currency stability system, investment and financing system and credit information system in Asia. We will promote local currency swap cooperation, further expand the scale of renminbi settlement of the current account, and support multinational enterprise groups in carrying out the concentrated operation of renminbi funds. The renminbi is used as the main currency of invoice in foreign economic management, accounting, and statistics. We will accelerate the construction of the renminbi cross-border payment system and further improve the renminbi global clearing system and further expand the renminbi output channels as well as encourage the use of renminbi to make loans and investments abroad. The construction of a regional renminbi bond market will further facilitate foreign institutions to invest in the domestic bond market and support overseas institutions to issue renminbi debt financing instruments in China. We will steadily push domestic financial institutions and enterprises to issue renminbi bonds overseas. We should support the innovation of renminbi-denominated financial products in the offshore market, accelerate the construction of the offshore renminbi market, and expand the offshore circulation of the renminbi.

Fifth, we should improve the exchange rate regime and foreign exchange management regime. We will work to expand the floating ranges of renminbi exchange rates and allow it to float more freely. We will deepen the reform of the foreign exchange management system, further facilitate the use of foreign exchange by market entities, and promote the reform of foreign exchange capital surrender management of foreign-invested enterprises in accordance with the principle of negative list. We will innovate the use of foreign exchange reserves to broaden the channels of diversified use.

4.3 The solid foundation of China's overall economic internationalization: the sustained and healthy development of domestic economy[1]

Since the 18th National Party Congress, the whole nation puts into practice the principles from General Secretary Xi Jinping's major addresses and his new vision, thinking, and strategies for China's governance, implement Five Major Principles of Development, solidly and comprehensively deepen reform, actively adapt to and guide the economic "new normal" to ensure the sustained and healthy development of China's economy as well as progress in overall national strength and international influence and lay a solid foundation for the comprehensive promotion of China's economic internationalization.

4.3.1 The healthy and stable operation of the economy

In the past five years, China's economy has been running smoothly and steadily. First, the economy maintains a medium-high rate of growth. From 2013 to 2016, GDP grew at an average annual rate of 7.2%, higher than the average global rate of 2.5% and the average rate of other developing economies of 4% for the same period. The economic growth is increasing year by year. The economic growth in 2013, 2014, 2015 and 2016 were RMB4,325.3 billion, RMB4,382.4 billion, RMB4,447.7 billion, and RMB4,609.7 billion respectively calculated at constant prices of 2015. China's comprehensive strength has been remarkably enhanced. In 2016, China's GDP reached RMB74 trillion, which was 1.32 times that of 2012 calculated at constant prices (see Table 4-1).

[1] Data in this section from "New Concepts Leads the New Normal, and New Practice Writes A New Chapter—Achievements of Social and Economic Development Since the 18th National Congress, Part Ⅰ, National Bureau of Statistics, Jun.16, 2017. International Status has been Significantly Elevated, and International Influence has been Significantly Enhanced—Achievements of Social and Economic Development Since the 18th National Congress, Part Ⅱ", National Bureau of Statistics, Jun.21, 2017.

Table 4–1 Economic growth rate of major countries in the world from 2013 to 2016

Unit: %

Country or region	2013	2014	2015	2016	2013–2016 average growth rate
China	7.8	7.3	6.9	6.7	7.2
World	2.5	2.7	2.6	2.3	2.5
Developed economies	1.1	1.9	2.1	1.6	1.7
Developing economies	4.7	4.3	3.5	3.4	4.0
The United States	1.7	2.4	2.6	1.6	2.1
Eurozone	2.0	0.3	1.2	1.6	1.3
Japan	-0.3	1.1	2.0	1.0	1.0
South Korea	2.9	3.3	2.6	—	2.9
Mexico	1.4	2.2	2.5	2.0	2.0
Brazil	3.0	0.1	-3.8	-3.4	-1.1
Russia	1.3	0.7	-3.7	-0.6	-0.6
India	6.6	7.2	7.6	7.0	7.1
South Africa	2.3	1.6	1.3	0.4	1.4

Source: Database of the World Bank.
http://data.worldbank.org.cn/.

Second, the situation of employment and price is stable. The proactive employment policy has continued to take effect, and the role of entrepreneurship in promoting employment has been prominent. The employment situation has remained stable, which has become a prominent highlight in economic operations. From 2013 to 2016, a total of 13 million more urban residents entered the workforce every year (see Figure 4–2). The surveyed urban unemployment rate in 31 major cities is stable at around 5%, and the average annual increase in migrant workers is 1.8%. The prices increase moderately. Consumer prices have risen at an average annual rate of 2% from 2013–2016. In all, with an average annual economic growth rate of 7.2%, an inflation rate of 2%, and a surveyed unemployment rate of around 5%, such a pattern of operation is commendable, and it is in line with the inherent laws of economic development and stands out in the world.

Again, per capita GDP has steadily increased. In 2016, China's per capita GDP was RMB53,980. With price factor deducted, it increased by 29% compared with 2012, and the average annual growth rate was 6.6%. From 2012 to 2016, China's per capita gross national income (GNI) increased from US$5,940 to over US$8,000, which is close to the average of the upper-middle income countries. According to the data released by the World Bank, among the 219 countries and regions, China's per capita GNI ranking rose from 112th in 2012 to 96th in 2015 and advanced by 16 places. The per capita national income of China and the world is shown in Table 4–2.

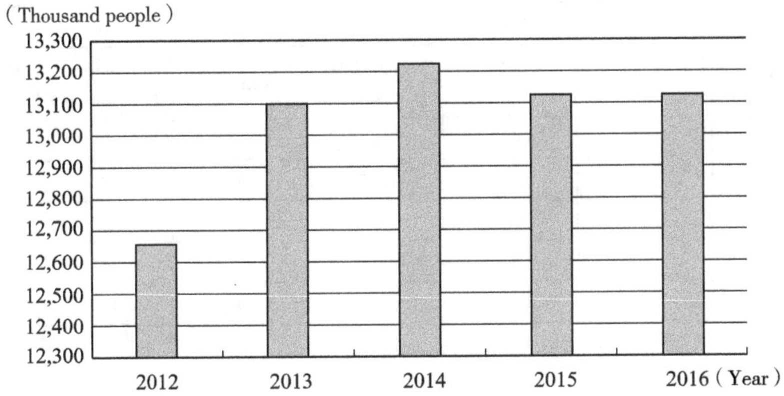

Figure 4–2 Number of the new employed from 2013 to 2016

Source: National Bureau of Statistics.
http://www.stats.gov.cn/.

Table 4–2 Per capita GNI of China and the world Unit: US$

Country or region	2012	2013	2014	2015
World	10,446	10,799	10,898	10,552
High-income countries	42,390	43,165	43,218	41,932
Middle-income countries	4,553	4,908	5,086	4,957
Upper-middle-income countries	7,503	8,163	8,498	8,260
Lower-middle-income countries	1,887	1,984	2,042	2,032
Low-income countries	563	598	628	619
China	5,940	6,800	7,520	7,900

Source: Database of the World Bank.
http://data.worldbank.org.cn/.

The healthy and stable development of the economy has significantly increased China's international influence. China is the source of power for the world's economic growth and the anchor of stability, making a major contribution to the painful recovery of the world economy. In 2016, China's GDP was equivalent to US$11.2 trillion, accounting for about 15% of the world's total economy; more than three percentage points higher than in 2012, ranking second in the world (see Table 4–3). From 2013 to 2016, China's average contribution rate to world economic growth reached more than 30%, more significant than that of the United States, Japan, and the Eurozone combined, ranking first in the world (see Table 4–4).

Table 4–3 GDP and world share of major countries or regions in the world

County or region	2012			2016		
	Ranking	GDP (US$ billion)	World share (%)	Ranking	GDP (US$ billion)	World share (%)
World		74,437.7			75,278	
The United States	1	16,155.3	21.7	1	18,569.1	24.7
China	2	8,570.3	11.5	2	11,218.3	14.9
Japan	3	6,203.2	8.3	3	4,938.6	6.6
Germany	4	3,545.9	4.8	4	3,466.6	4.6

Source: Database of the World Bank.
http://data.worldbank.org.cn/.

Table 4–4 The contribution rate of major countries or regions in the world to the growth of world economy

Unit: %

Country or region	2013	2014	2015	2016	Average annual contribution rate
China	32.5	29.7	30.0	34.7	31.6
The United States	15.2	19.6	21.9	15.4	18.2
Eurozone	-1.9	7.6	13.6	12.2	8.0
Japan	6.7	1.0	3.8	3.5	3.7

Source: Database of the World Bank.
http://data.worldbank.org.cn/.

4.3.2 Outstanding achievement in economic structure adjustment

Since 2012, China has vigorously optimized its industrial structure, continuously improved its demand structure, promoted supply-side structural reforms, actively promoted new urbanization, and encouraged regional coordinated development. China's economic restructuring has accelerated, transformation and upgrading have achieved remarkable results, and economic growth is moving forward to the medium- and high-end.

First, the industrial structure has been optimized and upgraded. The service industry has continued to develop rapidly, and its support for economic and social development is increasing with each passing day. From 2013 to 2016, the annual growth of the service sector's added value is 8.0%, 0.8 percentage points higher than that of GDP. In 2013, the added value (current price) of service industry (i.e., the tertiary industry) surpassed that of the secondary industry in terms of the GDP share for the first time, and service industry became the largest industry in the national economy. In 2016, it increased to 51.6%, an increase of 6.3 percentage points compared with that in 2012 (See Figure 4–3). The implementation of "Made in China 2025" was accelerated, and industrialization and informatization were deeply integrated. The equipment manufacturing and high-tech industry grew significantly faster than traditional industries. From 2013 to 2016, the annual growth rate of the added value of equipment manufacturing and high-tech industries were 9.4% and 11.3% respectively, 1.9 and 3.8 percentage points higher than that of industries above designated size. In 2016, the added value of equipment manufacturing and high-tech industries accounted for 32.9% and 12.4% of the added value of industrial enterprises above designated size, 4.7 and 3 percentage points more than 2012.

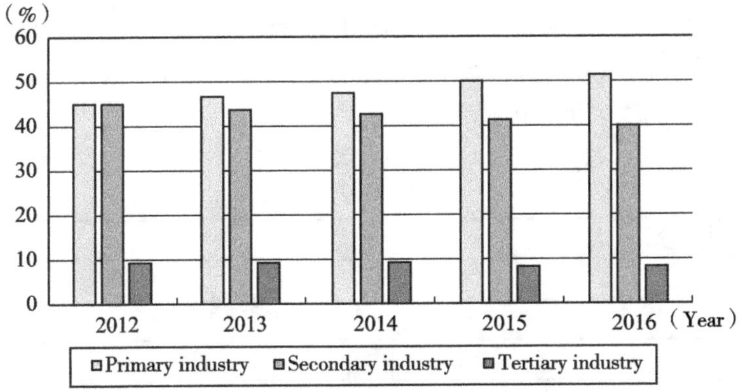

Figure 4–3 The growth portion to GDP of three industries

Source: National Bureau of Statistics.
http://www.stats.gov.cn/.

Second, consumption has become the main driving force of economic growth. Under the effect of expanding domestic demand policy measures, the consumption potential of residents has been released in an orderly manner, and the potential of consumption upgrading has continued to increase. Consumption has continued to play a basic role and has become the main driving force for economic growth. From 2013 to 2016, the average annual contribution rate of final consumption expenditure to economic growth was 55%, higher than the contribution rate of capital formation by 8.5

percentage points. The contribution rate for four years was 47%, 48.8%, 59.7%, and 64.6% respectively, showing a steady increase. Finally, the consumption rate steadily increases. In 2016, China's final consumption rate was 53.6%, 3.5 percentage points higher than that in 2012; the capital formation rate is 44.2%, three percentage points lower than that in 2012.

Third, the new urbanization is in solid progress. The level of urbanization has constantly been improving. At the end of 2016, permanent urban residents accounted for 57.35% of the total population, 4.78 percentage points higher than that at the end of 2012. From 2013 to 2016, the urban population has increased by more than 20 million people every year, which has driven huge investment and consumer demand. We have comprehensively promoted reform of the household registration system and the residence permit system, accelerated the process of urbanization of rural people who have moved to cities, promoted the equalization of the basic public services between rural people who have moved to cities and urban residents, and significantly improved the quality of new urbanization. At the end of 2016, the urbanization rate of China's registered population was 41.2%, 6.2 percentage points higher than that at the end of 2012. The difference from permanent resident urbanization rate is 16.1 percentage points, 1.4 percentage points lower (see Figure 4-4).

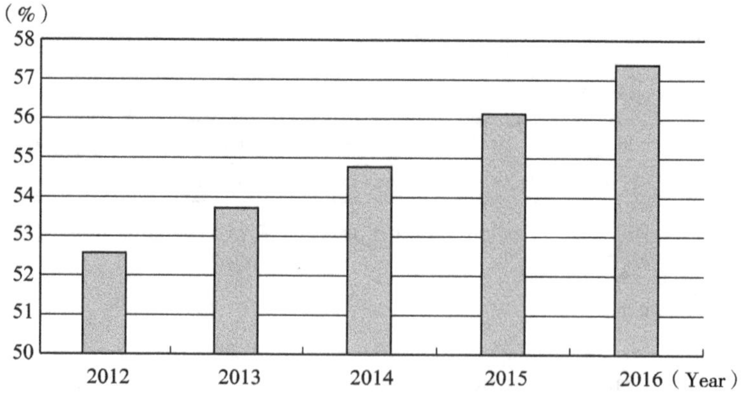

Figure 4-4 Permanent urban residence rate in 2012-2016

Source: National Bureau of Statistics.
http://www.stats.gov.cn/.

Fourth, optimizing and reshaping regional development pattern. The implementation of the "three major strategies" is progressing smoothly. The development of the Belt and Road is in active progress, and regional opening up is accelerated. The coordinated development of the Beijing-Tianjin-Hebei region is promoted in an orderly manner, and the Xiong'an New Area has been launched; the development of the Yangtze River Economic Belt has achieved a lot, and its environmental protection and economic radiation have been enhanced. Many national and regional central cities such as Chongqing, Guangzhou, Chengdu, Wuhan, and Zhengzhou have developed rapidly, and new growth poles and growth belts have gradually formed. We have coordinately promoted "four major sectors" as follows: development of the western region, revitalization of northeast China, the rise of the central region, and the support for the eastern region as it leads the country. We have continued to exert late-mover advantage in the west and central regions, and the growth rate of major development indicators is significantly faster than that of the whole country. From 2013 to 2016, the annual growth of GDP of the central and western regions was 8.6% and 9.1%, a respective increase of 1.4 and 1.9 percentage points over national growth. The transformation and upgrading of the eastern region as well as open innovation are at the forefront, new growth drivers and highlights in regional development continue to emerge, and eastern region's supporting and leading role in national development has become increasingly prominent.

4.3.3 Innovation-driven development achieving initial success

Since the 18th National Party Congress, the innovation-driven development strategy has won people's support. It has built up powerful new drivers and accelerated the development of new industries. We have continued to promote mass entrepreneurship and innovation. The innovation vitality and creative potential of the whole society have been stimulated, and new economic growth points have emerged. New and old drivers are in orderly transformation.

First of all, technological innovation continues to make breakthroughs. The state's support for scientific and technological innovation has increased, and R&D investment has increased rapidly. In 2016, research and development (R&D) expenditures were RMB1.55 trillion, an increase of 50.5% over 2012. The ratio to GDP is 2.08% with an increase of 0.17 percentage points (see Figure 4–5).A number of major scientific and technological achievements with a marked significance have emerged, and breakthroughs have been made in manned spaceflight, lunar exploration, quantum communication, radio telescope, manned deep-sea submersible, supercomputer, etc., leading to a steady increase in labor productivity. In 2016, the total labor productivity (calculated with price in 2015) reached RMB94,825 per person, a rise of 30.2% over 2012 with an annual growth of 6.8%.Major progress has been made in the construction of an innovative country. In 2016, China's innovation index ranked 25th in the world, 9 places higher than in 2012, and ranked first among middle-income countries.

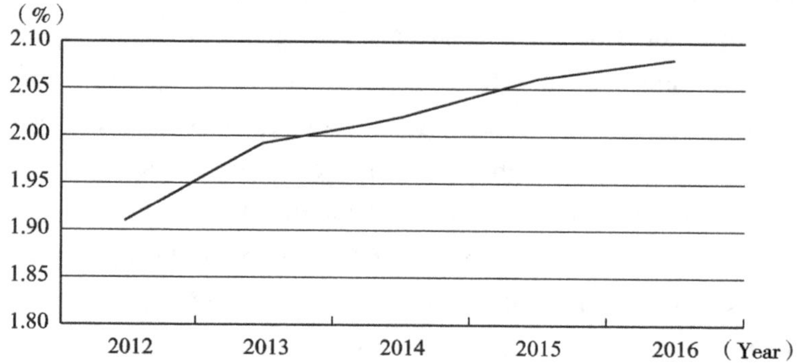

Figure 4–5 Proportion of China's R&D expenditures to GDP in 2012–2016

Source: National Bureau of Statistics.
http://www.stats.gov.cn/.

At the same time, mass entrepreneurship and innovation have become a common practice. With the continuous deepening of the reform of the commercial system and the reform of "streamlining administration and delegating power, strengthening supervision, and optimizing services", the multiplier effect of gathering public's wisdom is constantly emerging. The construction of 28 national entrepreneurship and innovation demonstration centers has been comprehensively promoted. From 2014 to 2016, there were more than 44 million new registered market entities in the whole country, including 13.62 million new registered enterprises, with an average annual growth rate of 30%. In 2016, an average of 15,000 new registered companies per day set off a new upsurge since the reform of the commercial system. The number of patent applications and grants has increased substantially, and innovations have continued to emerge. In 2016, 3.465 million domestic and foreign patent applications were accepted, and 1.754 million were granted, a respective growth of 68.9% and 39.8% over 2012. The number of effective invention patents exceeded 1.1 million, which is the third country with more than one million invention patents after the United States and Japan in the world; the technical contract turnover exceeded RMB1.1 trillion.

Finally, new industries, new models and new formats emerge in an endless stream. The "Internet +" plan has been promoted intensely. The rapid growth of online shopping has driven the rapid expansion of the express delivery business. From 2015 to 2016, the online retail sales of physical goods increased by an average of 28.6%, 18.1 percentage points faster over the total volume of retail sales of consumer goods. In 2016, the volume of express delivery was 31.28 billion, 4.5 times more than 2012 with an annual growth of 53.2%. New formats such as platform economy, economic sharing, and coordinated economy have been widely infiltrated, and new models such as online and offline integration, cross-border e-commerce, smart home, and intellectual exchanges are on the rise.

Reading material 4-1

Rapid Development of China's High–speed Rail[1]

In general, China's high-speed rail development can be roughly divided into two stages.

In the first stage, from 1990 to 2007, during the five times of national railway speed increase, the imported technologies from German, Japanese and French high-speed EMUs were digested and absorbed. Especially after 2004, with the principle of "introduction of advanced technology and joint design creating Chinese brand", a large number of high-speed rail technologies were introduced, of which direct technology transfer fees were as high as RMB2.3 billion.

In the second stage, from 2008 to the present, the high-speed rail industry entered the stage of independent innovation marked by the launching of the "Chinese High-speed Train Independent Innovation Joint Action Plan". At present, China has established the technology policy-guided, market-oriented, enterprise-centered innovation model integrating efforts of enterprises, universities, research institutes, and end-users; taking high-speed train design and manufacturing enterprises as the leader, a number of universities, research institutes and high-speed train parts and components enterprises, develop their respective advantages in scientific and technological resources and industrial resources, work together, break through the key technologies of high-speed trains, and have built a high-efficiency innovation mechanism for high-speed trains which has brought China's high-speed railway development technology innovation into a new stage.

It should be pointed out that the rapid development of China's high-speed rail technology in the stage of independent innovation has benefited not only from China's obvious institutional advantages and strong scientific research capabilities but also from the protection of high-speed rail technology, which has enabled a large number of digested, absorbed andre-innovated results in our control. In general, the development of domestic high-speed rail takes on the following characteristics:

---

[1] Sun Yongfu, "Experience and Enlightenment of China's High-speed Rail Technology Innovation", *Oil Forum*, 2015(5).

First, the domestic high-speed rail mileage has grown rapidly. China's high-speed railway network was built in 2004. The first high-speed railway line Beijing-Tianjin intercity railway was opened to traffic in August 2008. Since then, it has become the top priority of railway investment. In 2017, the rapid railway network with high-speed railway as the main skeleton was mainly built with a total scale of more than 40,000 kilometers, of which the high-speed railway covered 22,000 kilometers, which is doubled compared with 2012. The express passenger transport network formed by high-speed railway and other railways can cover cities with a population of more than 500,000. In the past five years, the length of China's high-speed rail has increased by 12,000 kilometers, exceeding the total mileage of high-speed railway in other countries in the world. In the lead, China's high-speed rail has become a new shining business card as well as a new engine for economic development.

Second, domestic high-speed rail technology and standards are developing rapidly. From 2004 to 2008, although China introduced a large number of high-speed rail technology, it always insisted on its own standards and continuous innovation. After more than ten years of development, China's high-speed rail technology and standards have achieved remarkable progress. In June 2017, the China Standard EMU, which was led by the China Railway Corporation and developed with completely independent intellectual property rights and that reached the world's advanced level, was named "Revival". "Revival" employs a large number of technical standards such as China's national standards, industry standards, and corporate standards of China Railway Corporation. At the same time, it adopts a number of international standards and advanced foreign standards and has good compatibility performance. Among 254 important standards, Chinese standards account for 84%. All vehicles in the future can be interconnected, and all core standard components on the train can be interchanged. The most important thing is that "Revival" has built a complete technical standard system with reasonable structure and advanced science. A dozen of aspects including the general basics, the car body, the walking device, the cab layout and equipment, the traction electricity, braking and air supply, network standards, application, and maintenance have reached the advanced international level.

Third, the momentum of "going global" in high-speed rail is strong. Compared with other countries, China's high-speed railway construction has low construction cost, short construction period, and excellent quality, so it is very competitive. The close cooperation among financial enterprises in China makes it easier to enter the high-speed rail international market. In May 2017, during the Belt and Road International Cooperation Summit, witnessed by the heads of China and Indonesia, China Development Bank officially signed a loan agreement with the Indonesia-China High Speed Rail Co., Ltd. on Indonesian Jakarta to Bandung High-Speed Railway Project in Beijing with the credit line being US$4.5 billion. This marks the first step of "going global" of China's high-speed rail coming into rapid implementation.

4.3.4 Promoting green development

Since the 18th National Party Congress, with the concept of green development, China has advanced environmental management, focused on improving the ecological environment, comprehensively saving and efficient use of resources to build an ecological safety barrier. The total discharge of major pollutants has been controlled. The construction of a resource-saving, environmentally friendly society has achieved great progress.

First of all, energy saving and emission reduction have achieved remarkable results. The efficiency of energy resource utilization has been generally improved, and the consumption of energy per unit of GDP has decreased significantly (see Figure 4–6). In 2016, energy consumption and water consumption per unit of GDP declined by 17.9% and 25.4% over 2012. The main pollutants have achieved a significant reduction in emissions. In 2015, the national chemical oxygen demand emissions decreased by 8.3%, ammonia nitrogen emissions by 9.3%, sulfur dioxide emissions by 12.2% and nitrogen oxide emissions decreased by 20.8%.

Second, environmental governance and protection continue to increase. The pace of afforestation continues to accelerate. In 2016, the whole country completed afforestation area of 6.79 million hectares, an increase of 21.3% over 2012. The forest coverage rate increased from 20.36% in the 7th National Forest Resources Inventory (2004–2008) to 21.63% in the 8th National Forest Resources Inventory (2009–2013) by 1.3 percentage points. The net increase in forest accumulation was 1.416 billion m^3.

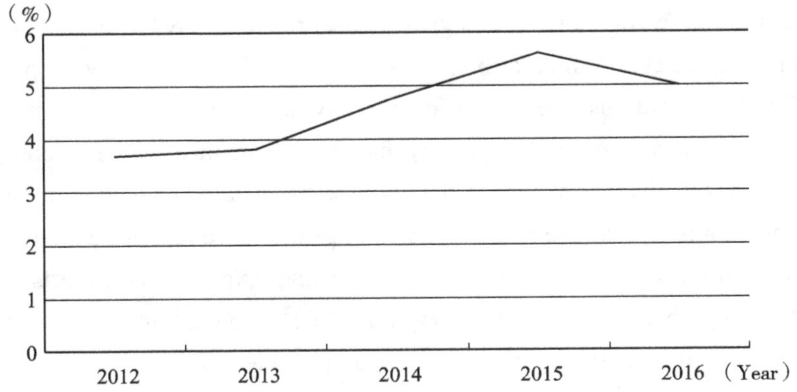

Figure 4–6 Decrease rate of energy consumption per unit of GDP

Source: National Bureau of Statistics.
http://www.stats.gov.cn/.

Soil erosion control is progressing steadily. In 2016, national newly-added soil erosion control area reached 54,000 square kilometers, an increase of 24.5% over 2012. Comprehensive management capacity of the urban environment has improved. At the end of 2016, the daily treatment capacity of urban sewage treatment plants was 148.23 million cubic meters, an increase of 26.3% over the end of 2012. Urban household refuse safely disposal rate was 95.0%, an increase of 10.2 percentage points; the green area rate of urban built-up areas was 36.4%, an increase of 0.7 percentage points.[1]

Finally, environmental quality has improved steadily. We resolutely fought to defend the blue sky and city's air condition tended to improve. In 2016, among the 338 cities monitored, the cities standard air quality reached 24.9%, an increase of 3.3 percentage points over the previous year; the annual average concentration of PM2.5 in cities at and above the prefectural level missing the target was 52 μg per cubic meter, a decrease of 8.8% over the previous year. The marine environment has improved. Among the coastal water quality monitoring points in the coastal waters, the monitoring points meeting the national quality standards of category one and two accounted for 73.4%, an increase of 4 percentage points over 2012; sea water at category four accounted for 16.3%, a decrease of 7.6% over 2012.[2]

4.4 Overall promotion of China's trade internationalization: transforming from a trader of quantity to a trader of quality

Since the 18th National Party Congress, the world economy has been in a period of deep adjustment after the international financial crisis, and the recovery process has been difficult and tortuous; the domestic economy has entered a new normal, and the pressure for transformation and upgrading has increased. In the face of complex and severe situations, China has always adhered to the basic national policy of opening up, implemented a more proactive opening up strategy, advance reform, development and innovation to promote domestic and external demand, exports and imports, "bringing in" and "going global" as well as the coordinated development among eastern, central and western regions, and opening up has been at a new level.

As far as the trade sector is concerned, China is on the road of becoming a trade of

1 Source: National Bureau of Statistics.

2 Source: National Bureau of Statistics.

quality based on the consolidation of trade of quantity. This transformation is reflected in the entire trade area: from the microscopic elements to the mesoscopic industrial chain to the macro institutional environment.

4.4.1 Comprehensive performance of China's foreign trade development since the 18th national party congress

Since the 18th National Party Congress, despite the continued sluggish development of world trade, China's foreign trade has achieved good results, and the total volume of foreign trade in goods and services ranks among the top in the world.

(1) *The trade in goods has developed steadily*

In general, China's total cargo volume has increased first and then decreased since 2012, but China has achieved excellent results considering the downturn in world trade and the statistical impact of exchange rate fluctuations. Especially since 2009, China has become the world's largest trader of goods and has maintained this status; since 2013, China has surpassed the United States to become the world's largest trader of goods and has maintained this status for three consecutive years. Total import and export value of China's goods trade (2013–2016) is shown as Table 4–5.

Table 4–5 Total import and export value of China's goods trade Unit: US$ trillion

Item	2013	2014	2015	2016
Total value of import and export	4.16	4.30	3.96	3.68
Total export value	2.21	2.34	2.27	2.10
Total export value	1.95	1.96	1.68	1.59

Source: Commercial Data Center.
http://data.mofcom.gov.cn/index.html.

Specifically, China's import and export of goods continues to increase in proportion to the world. From 2013 to 2015, China's total import and export of goods ranked first in the world. In 2016, China's total volume of import and export in goods reached US$3,685.6 billion, ranking second in the world, accounting for from 10.4% in 2012 to 11.5% of the world's total. From 2012 to 2016, China's total import volume ranked second in the world after the United States. Under the background of the downward pressure on the international economy, China has made outstanding contributions to the recovery of the world economy (see Table 4–6).

Table 4–6 Comparison of the total volume of import and exportamong Top 10 countries (Regions) in 2012, 2015, 2016

Ranking	2012			2015			2016		
	Country or region	Total volume of import and export (US$ billion)	World share (%)	Country or region	Total volume of import and export (US$ billion)	World share (%)	Country or region	Total volume of import and export (US$ billion)	World share (%)
	World	37,201.0		World	33,232.0		World	32,180.0	
1	The United States	3,882.2	10.4	China	3,953.0	11.9	The United States	3,706.0	11.5
2	China	3,867.1	10.4	The United States	3,817.9	11.5	China	3,685.6	11.5
3	Germany	2,556.0	6.9	Germany	2,378.2	7.2	Germany	2,394.5	7.4
4	Japan	1,684.4	4.5	Japan	1,272.8	3.8	Japan	1,251.9	3.9
5	France	1,243.1	3.3	The United Kingdom	1,086.5	3.3	France	1,074.3	3.3
6	Netherlands	1,242.3	3.3	Netherlands	1,082.9	3.3	Netherlands	1,073.1	3.3
7	The United Kingdom	1,168.0	3.1	France	1,079.2	3.2	Hong Kong, China	1,064.1	3.3
8	South Korea	1,067.5	2.9	Hong Kong, China	1,069.8	3.2	The United Kingdom	1,045.1	3.2
9	Hong Kong, China	1,046.4	2.8	South Korea	963.3	2.9	South Korea	901.6	2.8
10	Italy	989.9	2.7	Italy	868.5	2.6	Italy	866.0	2.7

Source: Database of the World Bank.
http://www.wto.org/english/res_e/statis_e/statis_e.htm.

In addition, according to customs statistics, in 2016, the total value of China's import and export of goods trade was RMB24.33 trillion, a decrease of 0.9% over 2015. Among them, the export totaled RMB13.84 trillion, a decrease of 2%; imports totaled RMB10.49 trillion, an increase of 0.6%; trade surplus was RMB3.35 trillion, a decrease of 9.1%.[1] First, the trade structure has been optimized. In 2016, China's general trade import totaled 13.39 trillion, an increase of 0.9% and it accounted for 55% of China's

[1] General Administration of Customs. http: //www.customs.gov.cn/publish/portal0/.

import and export trade, an increase of 1 percentage point over 2015. Second, the export to some countries along the Belt and Road increased. In 2016, China's exports to Pakistan, Russia, Poland, Bangladesh, and India increased by 11%, 14.1%, 11.8%, 9%, and 6.5% respectively. During the same period, China's exports to the EU increased by 1.2%, exports to the United States increased slightly by 0.1%, and exports to ASEAN fell by 2%. Exports to these three countries together accounted for 46.7% of China's total exports. Third, the proportion of exports of private enterprises continued to rank first. In 2016, the import and export of China's private enterprises totaled 9.28 trillion, increasing by 2.2% and accounted for 38.1% of China's total foreign trade value. Among them, export totaled RMB6.35 trillion, decreasing by 0.2% and accounted for 45.9% of total export volume, maintaining the top position in export share; the total import and export value increased by 8.1%. Fourth, mechanical and electrical products and traditional labor-intensive products took the big share. In 2016, China's mechanical and electrical products exports reached RMB7.98 trillion, a decrease of 1.9%, and accounted for 57.7% of China's total exports, among which medical equipment and equipment exports increased by 6.1%, and battery exports increased by 4%. In the same period, the export of traditional labor-intensive products totaled RMB2.88 trillion, a decrease of 1.7%, and it accounted for 20.8% of the total export. The export of textiles, toys and plastic products increased, and still maintained a good competitive advantage.[1]

(2) *Promoting the development of service trade*

Since the 18th National Party Congress, China's foreign trade in services has grown substantially, and it has entered a new stage every year. In 2012, China's total foreign trade in services ranked fourth in the world. In 2013, it rose to the third place. From 2014 to 2016, it ranked second in the world. In 2016, China's foreign trade in services totaled US$657.5 billion. According to the World Trade Organization, the proportion rose from 5.5% in 2012 to 6.9% in 2016 (see Table 4–7).

[1] General Administration of Customs. http: //www.customs.gov.cn/publish/portal0/.

Table 4-7 Comparison of total foreign service trade among Top10 countries in 2012, 2015, 2016

Ranking	2012			2015			2016		
	Country	Total service trade volume (US$ billion)	World share (%)	Country	Total service trade volume (US$ billion)	World share (%)	Country	Total service trade volume (US$ billion)	World share (%)
	World	8,773.2		World	9,432.0		World	9,501.8	
1	The United States	1,057.7	12.1	The United States	1,197.7	12.7	The United States	1,214.5	12.8
2	Germany	540.9	6.2	China	649.8	6.9	China	657.5	6.9
3	The United Kingdom	498.3	5.7	Germany	557.2	5.9	Germany	578.4	6.1
4	China	480.9	5.5	The United Kingdom	546.9	5.8	The United Kingdom	518.2	5.5
5	France	435.9	5.0	France	472.5	5.0	France	471.3	5.0
6	Japan	316.7	3.6	Netherlands	343.9	3.6	Japan	351.4	3.7
7	Netherlands	309.0	3.5	Japan	335.0	3.6	Netherlands	346.6	3.6
8	India	274.2	3.1	Singapore	302.6	3.2	Ireland	338.1	3.6
9	Singapore	257.8	2.9	Ireland	301.8	3.2	Singapore	304.7	3.2
10	Ireland	228.7	2.6	India	278.4	3.0	India	294.3	3.1

Source: Database of the World Bank.
http://www.wto.org/english/res_e/statis_e/statis_e.htm.

Specifically, the total import and export volume of China's service trade in 2016 was RMB5,348.4 billion, a year-on-year increase of 14.2%, among which service exports reached RMB1,819.4 billion, an increase of 2.3%; the service import was RMB3,529.1 billion, an increase of 21.5%. The development of service trade showed the following characteristics[1]:

First, the status of service trade has been continuously improving. In recent years, the proportion of China's trade in services to foreign trade (the sum of imports and exports of goods and services) has continued to rise, from 10.3% in 2011 to 15.3% in 2015. In 2016, the scale of China's service import and export continued to expand, and the proportion of service trade to total foreign trade further rose to 18%, an increase of 2.7 percentage points over 2015. The rapid development of service trade has enefited

[1] Data source: *Report on China's Foreign Trade Situation, Ministry of Commerce (Spring 2017)*, http: //zhs.mofcom.gov.cn/article/cbw/201705/20170502569655.shtml.

from China's growing service industry, the further expansion of the service industry, and the policy effects of the country's support for service trade innovation. From 2012 to 2015, China's service import and export trade volume increased by 16.1% annually, which was higher than the average annual growth rate of gross domestic product (GDP) by nearly eight percentage points and seven percentage points higher than its nominal growth rate. In 2016, China's service import and export trade volume increased by 14.2% annually, which is higher than the average annual growth rate of gross domestic product (GDP) by nearly 6.7% and higher than its nominal growth rate by 8%. Service trade has made important contributions to the steady development of China's foreign trade and economic growth.

Second, the traditional service trade deficit has continued to rise. In 2016, the import and export of the three traditional service industries (transport, travel, and construction services) totaled RMB3,922 billion, accounting for 73.3% of total service trade, an increase of 2.4 percentage points over 2015. The transportation service was affected by the downturn in international trade in goods. Import and export only increased slightly by 1%, with a total amount of RMB717.4 billion. The import and export of construction services were RMB141 billion, registering a 15.6% year-on-year decrease. Unlike the downturn in transportation and construction services, travel services maintained rapid growth, with a growth rate of 22.6% in import and export. It reached RMB2,513.6 billion, further accounting for 57.3% of service trade with imports and exports grew by 3.1% and 28% respectively. Due to the slowdown in export growth and continued fast growth in imports, the travel service deficit in 2016 further expanded, reaching RMB1,597.0 billion, a growth rate of 44%.

Third,the performance of emerging service trade is eye-catching. China's emerging service trade grew fast in 2016. The import and export of information services grew by as much as 74%, of which exports increased by 49.1% and imports increased by 96.2%. Advertising services grew 37.9%, of which imports increased by 46.7%, and imports increased by 20.2%. Imports and exports in insurance services, computer services, management consulting and public relation services, advertising, exhibitions, intellectual property, personal cultural entertainment, maintenance, and repair services all grew by more than 10%. The increase in the share of information services, advertising services, and insurance services indicates that the service trade industry structure has been further optimized.

Fourth, the regional distribution structure of service trade development tends to be optimized. The eastern coastal areas have a relatively high level of economic growth and an excellent service industry foundation. Besides, most of the service trade innovation development pilots are concentrated in these areas so system innovation and preferential policies there have achieved remarkable results, and these areas have always been the leading force in the development of China's service trade. In 2016, the top five provinces or cities in China's service import and export scale were Guangdong, Shanghai, Beijing, Jiangsu, and Zhejiang, with an amount of RMB978.7 billion, RMB965.1 billion, RMB932.8 billion, RMB414 billion, and RMB295 billion respectively, accounting for 67% of the total import and service exports. Compared with the eastern region, the scale of service import and export in China's central and western regions are still at a relatively low level, but its share in national service trade has increased. In 2016, the import and export of services in the central and western regions reached RMB905.3 billion, accounting for 17% of the national total, an increase of 2 percentage points over 2015. The gap in service trade development between the eastern and western regions has narrowed, and the regional distribution structure has tended to be optimized.

Fifth, the pilot reform of service trade innovation has achieved remarkable results. In 2016, 15 service trade innovation and development pilot areas attained a total of RMB2,678.5 billion in service imports and exports, accounting for 50.8% of national service imports and exports. In 11 provinces and cities along the Yangtze River Economic Belt, the total import and export of services reached RMB2,176.2 billion, accounting for 40.7% of the national total. Shanghai's service import and export accounted for 18% of the country and 44.3% of the Yangtze River Economic Belt provinces. The total import and export of services in the Beijing-Tianjin-Hebei region reached RMB1,154.3 billion, accounting for 21.6% of national imports and exports.The import and export of Beijing's service trade accounted for 17.4% of the national total and 80.8% of the total in the Beijing Tianjin Hebei region.

4.4.2 From the introduction of factors to the cultivation of factors: the microcosmic foundation of a trader in quality

The introduction of factors is a stage of development that developing countries must experience against the context of globalization. Developing countries increase the level of development of the entire economy through the introduction of factors, and in turn promote the cultivation of their own elements. China at present is already at a critical stage from the introduction of factors to factor cultivation.[1]

(1) *Capital from scarcity to abundance*

From the perspective of capital, the capital factors are no longer so scarce like in the past, and even in some areas, there is surplus. There are two examples. First, China's foreign direct investment increased rapidly from US$0.43 billion in 1982 to US$145.7 billion in 2015; second, China's foreign exchange reserves are enormous, even if this data has declined in the past one or two years, China is still the country with world's largest foreign exchange reserve (see Table 4–8).

Table 4–8 Top 10 Countries (Regions) in outward foreign direct investment from 2012 to 2015

Unit: US$ billion

Ranking	2012		2013		2014		2015	
	Country or region	Amount	Country or region	Amount	Country or region	Amount	Country or region	Amount
	World	1,308.8	World	1,310.6	World	1,318.5	World	1,474.2
1	The United States	318.2	The United States	307.9	The United States	316.5	The United States	300.0
2	Japan	122.5	Japan	135.7	Hong Kong, China	125.1	China	145.7
3	Luxembourg	89.8	China	107.8	China	123.1	Japan	128.7
4	China	87.8	British Virgin Islands	103.3	Japan	113.6	Netherlands	113.4
5	Hong Kong, China	84.1	Hong Kong, China	81.0	Germany	106.2	Ireland	101.6
6	Germany	62.2	Russia	70.7	British Virgin Islands	81.2	Germany	94.3
7	Canada	55.9	Netherlands	70.0	Russia	64.2	British Virgin Islands	76.2
8	British Virgin Islands	54.1	Canada	54.9	Netherlands	56.0	Switzerland	70.3
9	Switzerland	43.3	Germany	40.4	Canada	55.7	Canada	67.2
10	Belgium	33.8	Singapore	39.6	Ireland	43.1	Hong Kong, China	55.1

Source: Database of the World Bank.
http://www.wto.org/english/res_e/statis_e/statis_e.htm.

[1] Zhang Youwen et al., *Factors Benefits and the Path of Strengthening the Country by Trade*, Beijing: People's Publishing House, 2016, p.276.

(2) *Talent cultivation and introduction have been tangibly developed*

Since the 18th National Party Congress, the CPC Central Committee has attached great importance to talents. General Secretary Xi Jinping has repeatedly emphasized that talent is the foundation of innovation and a powerful driving force for economic development. China has made considerable achievements in the cultivation and introduction of talents. It not only has the largest number of colleges and universities in the world but also has continuously enhanced its ability to attract talents. In 2015, the "Talent 10,000 Initiative" completed the selection of the second batch of young talent and 354 new candidates were selected. The high-end talents have steadily improved the quality of the whole team. China has initially formed a large team of professional and technical personnel with reasonable structure, high quality and certain pioneering and innovative capabilities, which has effectively promoted the improvement of China's scientific research level. The number of Chinese college graduates from 1979 to 2015 is shown in Figure 4–7.

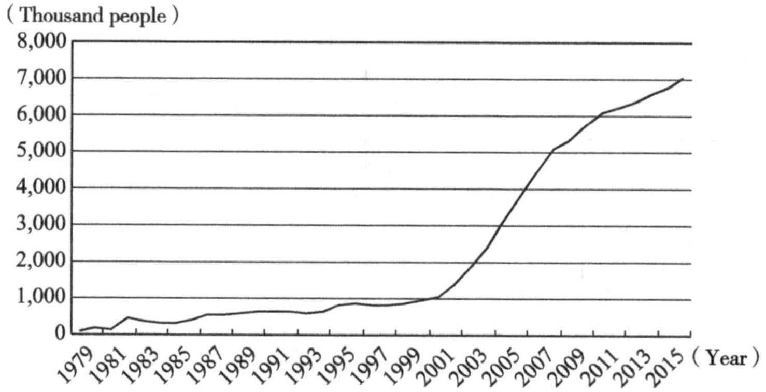

Figure 4–7 Number of college graduates in China from 1979 to 2015

Source: National Bureau of Statistics.
http://www.stats.gov.cn/.

(3) *Innovation and technology are developing rapidly*

With the development of China's economy and science and technology, especially the promotion of innovation-driven strategy, China has continuously made new progress in innovation and technology development. According to *the Global Innovation Index Report 2016* by WIPO, China's innovation index ranked 25th in the world, nine places higher than in 2012, and ranked first among middle-income countries. According to *Global Competitiveness Report 2015–2016* by World Economic Forum, in 2015, China's international competitiveness ranked 28th among 140 countries and regions, an increase of 1place over 2012 and among the best in developing countries.

We can take the United States as a reference in order to more clearly examine China's development in this regard.

Firstly, in terms of the investment in scientific innovation, the ratio of R&D to GDP in the United States was steadily 2.7% from 2008 to 2014, much higher than that in China. But it needs to be pointed out that this index in China was increasing rapidly with an average annual growth of 5.8% and it reached 80% of that in the United States (see Figure 4–8). It fully demonstrated that although the scientific innovation investment was not as many as that in the United States, yet it tended to catch up.

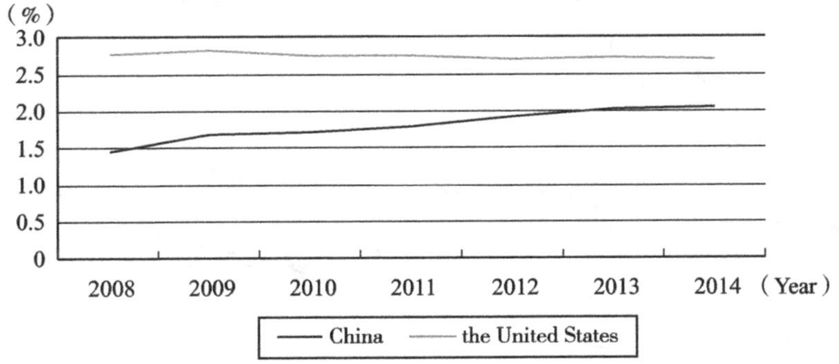

Figure 4–8 The proportion of R&D to GDP of China and the United States

Source: Database of the World Bank.
http://www.worldbank.org/.

Secondly, from the perspective of technological innovation output, two indicators are selected here, namely, the number of patent applications and the number of scientific papers published. From the perspective of the number of scientific articles published, as shown in Figure 4–9, this indicator in the United States is basically stable, while China has a significant growth in it: In 2008, the United States still had a tremendous advantage, almost twice which of China, and as in 2013, this advantage has been basically lost. Similarly, from the perspective of the number of patent applications, as shown in Figure 4–10, China's catch-up in recent years has become more evident and prominent. From the statistics of the World Bank, China has completely surpassed the United States in this indicator, which is almost twice as large as that of the United States. It should be pointed out that this indicator is only a reflection of quantity, and does not reflect the quality and transformation effect of patents. Therefore, this indicator only shows that China has caught up with the United States in terms of innovation output.

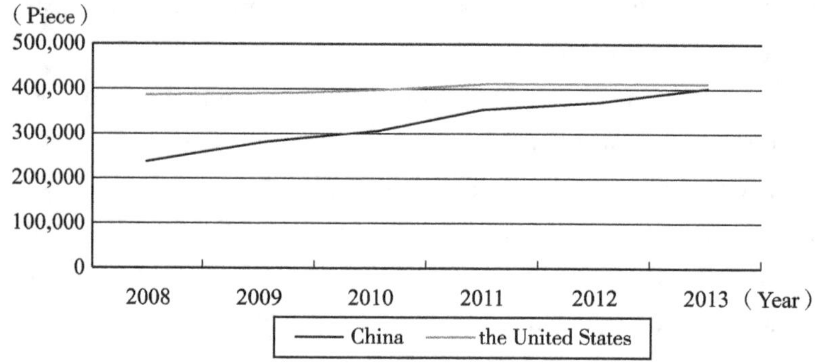

Figure 4–9 The number of scientific papers published in China and the United States

Source: Database of the World Bank.
http: //www.worldbank.org/.

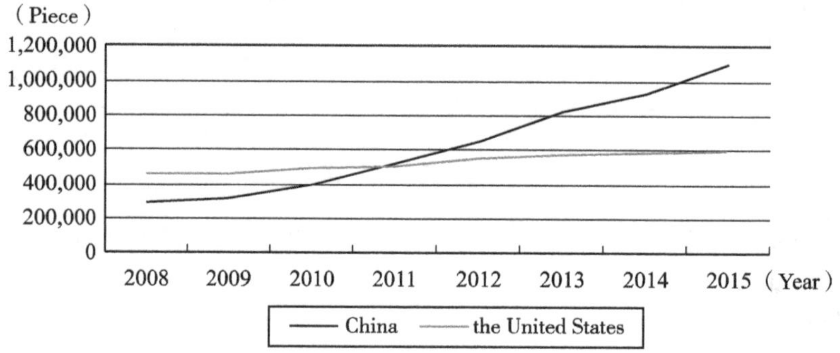

Figure 4–10 The number of patent applications in China and the United States

Source: Database of the World Bank.
http: //www.worldbank.org/.

Finally, examine the introduction of innovation. As an important channel for technology introduction, FDI plays a key role. It can be seen from this indicator that China's FDI level is lower than that of the United States as a whole, but due to the violent fluctuation of this indicator in the United States, the average gap between the two is not very large. Considering the gap in the degree of development between China and the United States (in terms of per capita GDP, China is only 1/7 of the United States), China is more likely to increase total factor productivity through FDI. Therefore, in terms of innovation, the gap between China and the United States is not very big.

These data are not isolated, but linked together, reflecting that China has made considerable achievements in the cultivation of economic factors, and these are the fundamental forces for China to achieve innovation-driven development and promote trade transformation and upgrading.

4.4.3 From the low end to the high end of the industrial chain: mesoscopic performance of a trader of quality[1]

From a mesoscopic perspective, the symbol of a trader of quality is the status of labor division, including its position in the division of the value chain and its position in the division of industrial chain. The continuous innovation of the industry, especially the current industrial revolution, has constantly been changing the status of countries in the international division of labor. After years of hard work, China's position in the global value chain has risen steadily. The effectiveness of foreign trade transformation and upgrading has begun to manifest itself, mainly in the following aspects.

First, the trend of export-led industries shifting from traditional competitive industries such as light industry, textile and home appliances to capital and technology intensive industries such as equipment manufacturing has gradually emerged. The new and old advantages of international competition are changing, with technology, brand, quality and service as the core competitiveness in the making. In 2014, China's exports electromechanical products and high-tech products accounted for 56.3% and 28.2%; the export of equipment manufacturing reached RMB2.1 trillion, accounting for 17% of the total exports.

Second, the transformation and upgrading of import and export enterprises have made new achievements. In 2016, the imports and exports of private enterprises achieved RMB9.3 trillion, an increase of 2.2%, accounting for 38.1% of the national foreign trade. Exports reached RMB6.4 trillion, a decrease of 0.2%, accounting for 46% of the total exports.Imports and exports of state-owned enterprises reached RMB3.8 trillion, a decrease of 5.6%. The imports and exports of foreign-funded enterprises were RMB11.1 trillion, a decrease of 2.1%. Many foreign trade enterprises have increased their investment in independent innovation, actively cultivated their own brands, developed products with independent intellectual property rights, built independent marketing channels, participated in the higher-level international division of labor and cultivated new outbound economic advantages with technology, standards, brand,

[1] Unmarked data in this section from "2015 Statistical Bulletin of China's Outward Foreign Direct Investment", China Statistical Press, 2016.

quality and service as the core. New economic advantages, new achievements in innovation and development, transformation and upgrading have been achieved and made positive contributions to the stabilization of foreign trade.

Third, goods trade and service trade are in coordinated development. In 2016, China's service trade maintained a good momentum of development. The annual import and export volume was RMB5.4 trillion, an increase of 14.2% over 2015. It broke the RMB5 trillion mark and ranked second to the United States in the world. Imports and exports of services accounted for 18% of China's total foreign trade, an increase of 2.6 percentage points over 2015.

Fourth, new trade forms such as cross-border e-commerce, market procurement trade, and foreign trade comprehensive services enterprises have flourished. In the past three years, the growth rate of cross-border e-commerce has exceeded 30%.[1] This also reflects the positive results of the construction of the cross-border e-commerce comprehensive pilot zone. The China (Hangzhou) Cross-border E-commerce Comprehensive Experimental Zone is the country's first cross-border e-commerce comprehensive pilot zone (hereinafter referred to as the comprehensive pilot zone). In January 2016, the State Council approved the establishment of a number of cross-border e-commerce integrated experimental zones in 12 cities including Tianjin, Shanghai, Chongqing, Hefei, Zhengzhou, Guangzhou, and Chengdu, through institutional innovation, management innovation, service innovation, and coordinated development. We can accumulate experience that can be replicated and promoted and provide new support for foreign trade development with a new model to promote the development of cross-border e-commerce in China. At present, the construction of 13 comprehensive pilot zones has achieved initial results. Among them, the Hangzhou Comprehensive Pilot Zone has explored the beneficial experience with the "six systems and two platforms" as the core. Twelve cities including Tianjin have successively issued "implementation plans" for pilot work and advance the pilot task in an orderly manner.

4.4.4 From environment adaptation to institutional construction: macro path of a trader of quality

Xi Jinping pointed out: "The fundamental purpose of our participation in global governance is to serve the Two Centenary Goals and realize the Chinese Dream of national rejuvenation. It is necessary to size the situation, strive to seize opportunities,

[1] "Splendid Achievements in China's Open Economy Development since 12th Five-Year Plan, especially since the 18th National Congress", *Guangming Daily*, Oct.20, 2015.

properly cope with challenges, coordinate domestic and international situations, promote the development of a global governance system in a more just and rational direction, and create more favorable conditions for China's development and world peace".[1] Since the 18th National Congress, China has actively participated in global economic governance and has continuously strengthened its say over international regimes. In terms of trade, China promoted the Belt and Road Initiative and the free trade zone strategy.

The Belt and Road Initiative has formed a new strategy for the development of China's foreign economic and trade relations, and together with the national financial strategy such as the Asian Infrastructure Investment Bank, constitutes the overall strategy for the development of China's foreign economic relations. Under such a grand strategy, the strategy of strengthening the country in the sense of trade has become an integral part of the overall reinvigoration. Specifically, the Belt and Road Initiative's institutional role to make China a trader of quality is mainly reflected in the following aspects: First, the Belt and Road Initiative is in line with the country's external financial strategy, effectively leveraging the national strategic advantage. AIIB, Silk Road Fund, BRICS, emergency reserve arrangements, etc. reflect the leading role of national strategic advantages in developing investment and trade relations. Second, the state's strategic investment and financing opens the way for private investment and trade relations, and the effectiveness of the country's development financing is guaranteed by the pragmatic development of the local economy. The long-term macro interaction is the essence of strategic integrity. Third, China's national strategy and financial cooperation with other countries will effectively make up for the shortcomings of the current international financial system on the requirements for the world's development, especially in infrastructure construction, which reflects the influence and dominance of a major country. This is what a strong country, as well as a responsible major country, does in a comprehensive sense.

The Belt and Road Initiative has been put forward for more than three years and has made a number of important early achievements. It has become an important way for all parties to strengthen international cooperation as well as an important international public product. In accordance with the unified arrangements of the CPC Central Committee and the State Council, the Ministry of Commerce strengthened

[1] Xi Jinping, "The Fundamental Purpose of Our Participation in Global Governance is to Realize the Chinese Dream", Chinese People's Political Consultative Conference Network, Oct.13, 2015, http: //www.rmzxb.com.cn/c/2015 - 10 - 13/596085.shtml.

coordination with relevant departments, deepened economic and trade cooperation with countries along the routes, and made positive progress.

First, we will promote communication and pragmatic cooperation with countries along the routes. We will make the best use of the existing mechanisms such as the bilateral economic and trade joint commissions and the mixed commission, as well as regional or sub-regional cooperation platforms, give play to role of foreign-invested economic institutions, strengthen exchanges and dialogues with countries along the routes, and actively promote policy communication and strategic alignment. We have successfully reached a consensus on the Belt and Road Initiative to link with the EU's "Junker Investment Plan", Cambodia's "Four Corners Strategy", and Laos' "transformation from a landlocked to a land-linked country" strategy, and promote the alignment of development strategies between Belt and Road Initiative with the Czech Republic, Poland, Uzbekistan, countries such as Brunei as well as other Eurasian Economic Union.

Second, we should promote trade with countries along the routes. We will actively improve trade and investment promotion policies and facilitation measures, expand mutual market opening, and use export credit and export credit insurance to support the export of large-scale complete sets of equipment. We will actively expand imports from countries along the line, develop cross-border e-commerce, and support the orderly development of China-Europe freight train. A series of trade investment promotion activities were held, and large-scale comprehensive exhibitions such as China-ASEAN Expo and China-Eurasia Expo were held, which achieved good results. In 2016, with the continued sluggish demand in the international market, China's trade cooperation with countries the Belt and Road Initiative has achieved gratifying results. In 2016, the trade volume between China and the countries along the routes was RMB6.3 trillion, an increase of 0.6%, among which exports amounted to RMB3.8 trillion, an increase of 0.7%; imports totaled RMB2.4 trillion, an increase of 0.5%.

Third, expand two-way investment with countries along the routes. The Ministry of Commerce, together with relevant departments, will introduce the promotion policies and facilitation measures for improving the "going global" of enterprises, optimizing the model of foreign investment management, strengthening service guarantees. We will take engineering contracting as the guide and supporting financial services as the support to drive the united "going global" of equipment products, technologies, standards as well as services and to promote international production capacity and equipment manufacturing cooperation. In 2016, China's investment in these countries reached US$14.5 billion, accounting for 8.5% of its total outbound investment. China's new signed overseas engineering contracts are worth US$126 billion, an increase of 36%. At the same time, China continues to optimize the foreign investment environment to attract more companies from countries along the routes to invest in China. In 2016, 2,905 new enterprises were established in China along the Belt and Road, an increase of 34.1% and the actual amount of foreign investment is US$7.1 billion.

Fourth, we will build a "going global"platform with industrial cluster-style. We will give full play to the role of the overseas trade and economic cooperation zones and cross-border economic cooperation zones, and promote the "going global" of manufacturing and supporting service enterprises to form industrial clusters in order to promote common development and reduce the risk of "going global". Chinese companies have set up 56 economic cooperation zones in over 20 countries, generating some US$1.1 billion of tax revenue and 180,000 jobs for them.[1]

Fifth, we will promote the implementation of a number of major projects. We should comprehensively use policy, development, and commercial funds to promote positive progress in the construction of major projects. The second phase of Pakistan Karakoram Highway, Karachi Motorway and the China-Laos railway have started construction, and the projects such as Turkey's east-west high-speed rail and the Budapest-Belgrade Railway are being promoted in an orderly manner.

The Belt and Road Initiative has reaped a series of early harvests and benefited the world. It fully demonstrates the great potential and broad prospects of this initiative. It also reflects China's active participation in global economic governance and its own say over international regimes and its constant contribution to the development of global economic governance in a more just direction.

4.5 Overall promotion of China's capital internationalization: "bringing in" and "going global" under the Belt and Road Initiative

Since the 18th National Party Congress of China, the Party Central Committee with General Secretary Xi Jinping as the core has scientifically applied dialectics in opening up to the outside world and proposed the Belt and Road Initiative to realize the

[1] "China's Foreign Trade Situation Report (Spring 2017)"Column II, Department of General Affairs of the Ministry of Commerce, May 4, 2017.

negation of the negation of opening up. In theory, the law of the negation of negation is to achieve a deeper understanding of objective things through continuous abandonment, which requires us to negate the existing things affirmatively; in practice, with the deepening of opening up, China has accumulated a large number of funds, technology, and information. Some of these factors have reached the point where it is necessary to seek higher efficiency. Therefore, we will promote the cooperation between "bringing in" and "going global" to improve the efficiency and performance of the information, technology, and capital, and accelerate the formation of a new engine for China's economic and social development.

4.5.1 Comprehensive performance of China's capital internationalization since the 18th national party congress

In general, since the Belt and Road Initiative was put forward and implemented, China's capital internationalization has been comprehensively promoted and has developed rapidly by optimizing "bringing in". It can be seen from the data of outward foreign direct investment and attracting foreign direct investment, this value in China has been growing steadily and rapidly since 2012, reflecting the rapid advancement of China's capital internationalization (see Figure 4–11).

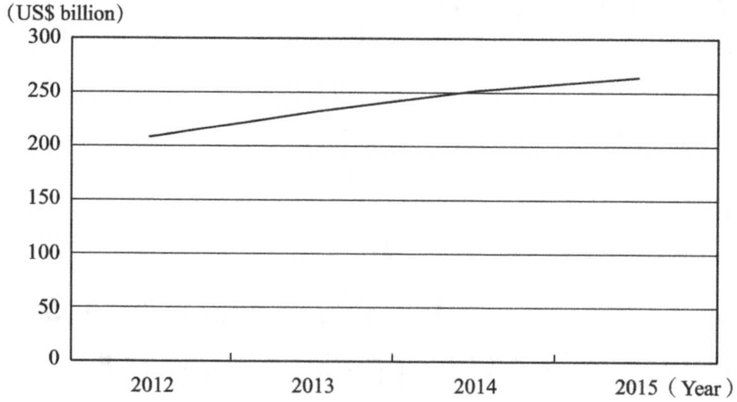

Figure 4–11 Total amount of Chinese FDI and OFDI

Source: UNCTAD.
http: //unctadstat.unctad.org/wds/TableViewer/tableView.aspx.

In fact, the high level of "bringing in" and the large-scale "going global" have become important features of China's open economy in the new era. From "attracting investment" to "selecting an investment", from commodity output to capital output—

under the new normal, Chinese economy further integrates itself into the world economy, and the two-way investment is becoming more balanced and coordinated. The internationalization of China's capital has shown a comprehensive advancement.

The quantity and quality of "bringing in" should both be promoted. Around the globe, China's use of foreign capital is undoubtedly a shining pearl, and the scale of foreign investment has continuously hit a new high. China's overseas investment utilization increased by 6.4% over the previous year. The foreign-invested industrial structure was further optimized, and the service industry utilized RMB477.05 billion of overseas investment, a year-on-year increase of 17.3%. "Going global" is in steady progress. Haier Group acquired the home appliance unit from General Electric for US$5.4 billion and Dalian Wanda Group acquired Legendary Entertainment of Hollywood for US$3.5 billion...In 2015, China's foreign direct investment flows ranked 3rd in the world and stocks ranked 8th in the world. China's foreign investment played an important role in driving world economic growth and promoting mutual benefits.[1]

Reading material 4-2

A-Shares Successfully Added to the MSCI Index[2]

In June 2017, A-shares were successfully added to the MSCI Index. Before this entry, A-shares had been "rejected" by MSCI three times. How did it make it the fourth time? MSCI answered: International investors have widely recognized the significant improvement in China's A-shares market access over the past few years. It is now an appropriate time for MSCI to take the first step in adding China's A-shares. At present, the A-shares market is already the world's second largest capital market as well as the world's largest emerging capital market, and the fastest growing capital market in the world. What is gratifying is that during the process of continuous growth and internationalization, China's capital market is becoming more confident in the exchange with the world. Although the initial inclusion is just a debut, it is also a critical step. This step not only brings important opportunities for reform and opening up of China's capital market but also makes the international capital market more exciting because of A-shares.

4.5.2 Improving the quality and efficiency of "bringing in"

Since the opening up, China has actively implemented the strategy of "bringing in", mainly introducing foreign capital and advanced technology in which China has made

---

1 Statistics Center of the Ministry of Commerce.

2 "Final Success at the Fourth Try!China A-shares Debuted on MSCI's Emerging Markets Benchmark", China Finance Information.

tremendous achievements. First, foreign direct investment continued to increase, from US$0.43 billion in 1982 to US$126.27 billion in 2015. From 2012 to 2016, China attracted foreign direct investment was in a steady increase, with an annual growth of 3.5%. In 2016, China attracted foreign direct investment of US$126 billion (utilized foreign capital), ranking the top three in the world for five consecutive years (see Table 4–9); second, the structure of foreign capital was further optimized. During the four years from 2011 to 2014, the proportion of foreign investment in the service industry was as high as 55.4% and even 61.1% in 2015.

Table 4–9 Comparison between Top 10 countries (regions) of foreign direct investment from 2012 to 2016

Unit: US$ billion

Ranking	2012		2013		2014		2015		2016	
	Country or region	Amount	Country or region	Amount	Country or region	Amount	Country or region	Amount	Country or region	Amount
	World	1,510.9	World	1,443.2	World	1,277.0	World	1,762.2	World	1,525.0
1	The United States	188.4	The United States	201.4	China	128.5	The United States	379.9	The United States	391.0
2	Luxembourg	143.0	China	123.9	Hong Kong, China	114.1	Hong Kong, China	174.9	The United Kingdom	253.8
3	China	121.1	British Virgin Islands	110.0	The United States	106.6	China	135.6	China	133.7
4	Brazil	76.1	Hong Kong, China	74.3	Brazil	73.1	Ireland	100.5	Hong Kong, China	108.1
5	British Virgin Islands	74.5	Canada	69.4	Singapore	68.5	Netherlands	72.6	Netherlands	92.0
6	Hong Kong, China	70.8	Singapore	64.7	Canada	58.5	Switzerland	68.8	Singapore	61.6
7	Australia	59.0	Australia	56.3	The United Kingdom	52.4	Singapore	65.3	British Virgin Islands	59.1
8	Singapore	57.2	Russia	53.4	Netherlands	52.2	Brazil	64.6	Brazil	58.7
9	The United Kingdom	55.4	Brazil	53.1	British Virgin Islands	50.0	British Virgin Islands	51.6	Australia	44.0
10	Ireland	45.3	The United Kingdom	51.7	Australia	39.6	Canada	48.6	Cayman Islands	45.0

Source: "China's International Standing Has Risen Noticeably, and International Influence Has Improved Greatly—Achievements of Economic and Social Development since the 18th National Party Congress (Part II)", website of National Bureau of Statistics, Jun. 21, 2017, http://www.stats.gov.cn/tjsi/siid/201706/t20170621_1505616.html.

Statistics of 2013 and 2016 from UNCTAD database: http://unctadstat.unctad.org/wds/ ReportFolders/reportFolders.aspx.

With the in-depth promotion of the Belt and Road Initiative, China's "bringing in" has entered a new phase. In 2016, the main features of China's "bringing in" are as follows:[1]

First, the scale of foreign investment in the country has remained generally stable. In 2016, there were 27,900 foreign-invested enterprises newly established nationwide, a year-on-year increase of 5%; China utilized RMB813.22 billion of overseas investment, a year-on-year increase of 4.1%.

Second, the overseas investment continues to gather in high-end industries. Service industry utilized RMB571.58 billion of overseas investment, a year-on-year increase of 8.3%, Accounting for 70.3% of the total foreign investment. Of this sum, incoming foreign investment information and consulting services, computer application services industry, integrated technology services industry, distribution services and retail industry increased by 59.8%, 112.8%, 66.4%, 42.9% and 83.1% respectively over the previous year. High-tech service industry utilized RMB95.56 billion of foreign investment, a year-on-year increase of 86.1%. In the manufacturing industry, the year-on-year increase in foreign investment utilization in medical manufacturing, medical equipment, and instrumentation manufacturing industry was 55.8% and 95% respectively. High-tech manufacturing industry utilized RMB59.81 billion, a year-on-year increase of 2.5%.

Third, the dividends of the institutional reform continued to emerge. The total inward foreign investment in the four pilot zones of Shanghai, Guangdong, Tianjin, and Fujian reached RMB87.96 billion, a year-on-year increase of 81.3%. They utilized 10.8% of the national foreign investment with five hundred thousands of land area. After the approval of foreign-invested enterprises was changed to record-keeping, the establishment and modification of 95.3% foreign-invested enterprises were record-based, which make foreign investment much more convenient. The comprehensive pilot reform of the service industry in Beijing has achieved remarkable results. The inward foreign investment in the service industry in Beijing accounted for 13% of the national total.

Fourth, the intake of foreign capital in the western region increased slightly, and in the eastern region, it maintained steady growth. The western region utilized RMB62.69 billion of foreign investment, a year-on-year increase of 1.6%.Of this sum, the inward

[1] "MOFCOM Department of Foreign Investment Administration Comments on China's Intake of Foreign Investment in January-September, website of Ministry of Commerce", Jan.13, 2017, http://www.mofcom.gov.c// article/ae/ag/201701//0170102 501364.shtml.

foreign investment of agriculture, forestry, animal husbandry and fishery, manufacturing, the production and supply industry of electricity, gas and water, information transmission, computer services and software industry, leasing and commercial services increased 457.7%, 11.3%, 30.6%, 115.6% and 24.9% respectively over the previous year. The proportion of foreign investment in agriculture, forestry, husbandry and fishery, manufacturing and service industries is 7.6%, 34.3% and 58%. The eastern region utilized RMB704.7 billion of foreign investment, a year-on-year increase of 7.6%.[1]

4.5.3 Fast development of "going global"[2]

In the face of the development and changes in opening up, the CPC Central Committee proposed to insist on the integration of "bringing in" and "going global" as early as 1997. Since the 18th National Party Congress, with the further development of opening upward, there has been further progress in "going global".

4.5.3.1 Outward Foreign direct investment has developed rapidly

From 2012 to 2015, China's outward foreign direct investment grew rapidly, with an average annual growth rate of 18.4%. In 2015, China's outward foreign direct investment entered a new phase. The annual investment amount reached US$145.7 billion, ranking second in the world for the first time (see Table 4–10), a record high.

Table 4–10 Comparison between Top 10 countries (regions) of outward foreign direct investment from 2012 to 2015 Unit: US$ billion

Ranking	2012		2013		2014		2015	
	Country or region	Amount	Country or region	Amount	Country or region	Amount	Country or region	Amount
	World	1,308.8	World	1,310.6	World	1,318.5	World	1,474.2
1	The United States	318.2	The United States	307.9	The United States	316.5	The United States	300.0
2	Japan	122.5	Japan	135.7	Hong Kong, China	125.1	China	145.7
3	Luxembourg	89.8	China	107.8	China	123.1	Japan	128.7

1 "MOFCOM Department of Foreign Investment Administration Comments on China's Intake of Foreign Investment in January-September, website of Ministry of Commerce", Jan.13, 2017, http: //www.mofcom.gov.c// article/ae/ag/201701//0170102 501364.shtml.

2 Unmarked data in this section from "2015 Statistics Bulletin of China's Outward Foreign Direct Investment", China Statistics Press, 2016.

(continued)

Ranking	2012		2013		2014		2015	
	Country or region	Amount	Country or region	Amount	Country or region	Amount	Country or region	Amount
4	China	87.8	British Virgin Islands	103.3	Japan	113.6	Netherlands	113.4
5	Hong Kong, China	84.1	Hong Kong, China	81.0	Germany	106.2	Ireland	101.6
6	Germany	62.2	Russia	70.7	British Virgin Islands	81.2	Germany	94.3
7	Canada	55.9	Netherlands	70.0	Russia	64.2	British Virgin Islands	76.2
8	British Virgin Islands	54.1	Canada	54.9	Netherlands	56.0	Switzerland	70.3
9	Switzerland	43.3	Germany	40.4	Canada	55.7	Canada	67.2
10	Belgium	33.8	Singapore	39.6	Ireland	43.1	Hong Kong, China	55.1

Source: UNCTAD.
http://unctadstat.unctad.org/wds/ReportFolders/reportFolders.aspx.

In 2016, China carried out non-financial direct investment in 7,961 overseas enterprises in 164 countries and regions, with an accumulated investment of RMB1.12992 trillion (equivalent to US$170.11 billion, a year-on-year increase of 44.1%). The foreign contracted project completed a turnover of RMB1.05892 trillion (equivalent to US$159.42 billion, a year-on-year increase of 3.5%). The value of new contracts reached RMB1.62079 trillion (equivalent to US$244.01 billion, a year-on-year increase of 16.2%). At the end of 2016, there were about 970,000 Chinese overseas laborers, a slight decrease of 5.6%. Specifically, in recent years, China's outward foreign direct investment has made progress in the following four aspects:

(1) *The regional distribution is more concentrated*

It can be seen from the stocks of China's outward foreign direct investment regions that China's outward foreign direct investment regions are increasingly concentrated. In 2015, China's outward foreign direct investment covered 80.7% of the globe, in 188 countries and regions. Among them, the total number of countries and regions with the top 20 outward foreign direct investment stocks reached US$988.059 billion, accounting for 89.8% of the total stock.

Judging from the flow of China's outward foreign direct investment in various regions, at present, China has formed a distribution of investment that is dominated by Asian regions and developing economies, and thus radiates globally. Asia is still China's largest investment destination. China's outward foreign direct investment flows to Asia, Latin America and North America have grown rapidly, while investment flows to Europe, Oceania and other regions have declined, especially for Europe, which has fallen by nearly 30%. Eighty percent of China's foreign direct investment stock is concentrated in developing economies. As of the end of 2015, China's direct investment stock in developing economies reached US$920.887 billion, accounting for 83.9% of the total. The direct investment volume in developed economies is US$153.652 billion, accounting for 14% of the total. The direct investment in economies in transition is US$23.321 billion, accounting for 2.1% of the total (see Table 4–11).

Table 4–11 Constitution of areas with China's outward foreign direct investment flow and stock in 2015

Continent	Flow			Stock	
	Sum (US$ billion)	Year-on-year growth rate (%)	World share (%)	Sum (US$ billion)	World share (%)
Asia	108.37	27.5	74.4	768.9	70
Europe	7.12	−34.3	4.9	83.68	7.6
Latin America	12.61	19.6	8.6	126.32	11.5
North America	10.72	16.4	7.4	52.18	4.8
Oceania	3.87	−10.7	2.7	32.09	2.9
Africa	2.98	−7.0	2.0	34.69	3.2

Source: *2015 Statistics Bulletin of China's Outward Foreign Direct Investment*, China Statistics Press, 2016.

It is worth mentioning that the countries and regions where China's outward foreign direct investment flows are highly concentrated, and cooperation with countries along the Belt and Road has become a highlight. In 2015, Chinese enterprises' investment in the Belt and Road countries increased rapidly, with a volume of US$18.93 billion, accounting for 13% of the annual total.[1]

(2) *The industry structure was further improved*

The industrial structure of China's outward foreign investment has been further improved, and a basic pattern has been formed in which the tertiary industry is the leading factor, the investment in the secondary industry is accelerating, and the

1 *2015 Statistics Bulletin of China's Outward Foreign Direct Investment*, China Statistics Press, 2016.

investment potential of the first industry is gradually released[1]. The tertiary industry maintains a dominant position in China's outward foreign direct investment (see Table 4–12). The investment of the tertiary industry in 2015 was US$105.984 billion, 9.3 times that of 2006 (US$11.381 billion), accounting for 72.8% of the total outward foreign direct investment in 2015.The stock of investment increased to US$822.69 billion, 13.2 times that of 2006 (US$62.37 billion), accounting for 74.9% of the total outward foreign direct investment. The secondary industry has also accelerated the pace of foreign investment. The outward foreign direct investment flow of China's secondary industry grew from US$9.598 billion in 2006 to US$37.1 billion in 2015, an increase of 2.9 folds.Also, China began to strengthen the strategic layout of the primary industry's foreign investment: The outward foreign direct investment of China's primary industry increased from US$0.185 billion in 2006 to US$2.57 billion in 2015, the proportion from 0.87% to 1.8%.[2]

Table 4–12 Constitution of industries with China's outward foreign direct investment flow and stock in 2015

Industry	Flow			Stock	
	Sum (US$ billion)	Year-on-year growth rate (%)	World share (%)	Sum (US$ billion)	World share (%)
Leasing and business services	36.26	-1.6	24.9	409.57	37.3
Financial industry	24.25	52.3	16.6	159.66	14.5
Manufacturing industry	19.99	108.5	13.7	78.53	7.2
Wholesale and retail industry	19.22	5.1	13.2	121.94	11.1
Mining industry	11.25	-32.0	7.7	142.38	13
Real estate industry	7.79	17.9	5.3	33.49	3.1
Information transmission, software and IT service industry	6.82	115.2	4.7	20.93	1.9
Building industry	3.74	10.0	2.6	27.12	2.5
Scientific research and technology service industry	3.35	100.5	2.3	14.43	1.3
Transporting, warehousing and postal services	2.73	-34.7	1.9	39.91	3.6
Agriculture, forestry, animal husbandry and fishery	2.57	26.4	1.8	11.48	1.0

[1] Wang Xiaohong, "Strategic Thoughts on Promoting China's Foreign Direct Investment in the New Era", *Globalization*, 2017(1).
[2] *2015 Statistics Bulletin of China's Outward Foreign Direct Investment*, China Statistics Press, 2016.

(continued)

Industry	Flow			Stock	
	Sum (US$ billion)	Year-on-year growth rate (%)	World share (%)	Sum (US$ billion)	World share (%)
Electricity, heat, gas and water production and supply	2.13	21.0	1.5	15.66	1.4
Culture, sports and entertainment	1.75	236.6	1.2	3.25	0.3
Resident services, repairs and other services	1.60	−3.2	1.1	14.28	1.3
Water, environmental and public facilities management	1.37	148.1	0.9	2.54	0.2
Accommodation and catering industry	0.72	195.5	0.5	2.23	0.2
Other	0.13	—	0.1	0.46	0.1

Source: *2015 Statistics Bulletin of China's Outward Foreign Direct Investment*, China Statistics Press, 2016.

(3) *Investment entities are constantly developing*[1]

From the perspective of dividing investment entities into state-owned enterprises and non-state-owned enterprises, state-owned enterprises are still playing a major role in outward foreign investment. Although the share of non-financial outward foreign direct investment stocks of state-owned enterprises in the total stock of US$938.2 billion fell from 81% in 2006 to 50.4% in 2015, due to the advantages of resources, funds, policies, etc., state-owned enterprises still play a leading role in outward foreign direct investment, especially in resources and energy industries. The outward foreign direct investment strength and internationalization level of non-state-owned enterprises increased significantly. The entities of China's outward foreign direct investment changed from a single state-owned enterprise to a multi-ownership economic entity. Non-state-owned enterprises had higher enthusiasm and success rate in outward foreign direct investment than state-owned enterprises. The share of non-state-owned enterprises in non-financial outward foreign direct investment stocks rose from 19% in 2006 to 49.6% in 2015, an increase of 3.2 percentage points over the previous year, basically equivalent to state-owned enterprises.

From the perspective of dividing investment entities into state-owned enterprises and non-state-owned enterprises, state-owned enterprises are still playing a major role in outward foreign direct investment. Regarding investment volume, non-financial direct investment flows of local enterprises were US$93.6 billion, a year-on-year

[1] *2015 Statistics Bulletin of China's Outward Foreign Direct Investment*, China Statistics Press, 2016.

increase of 71%, accounting for 77% of the total non-financial outward direct investment nationwide, with a stock of US$344.48 billion, which accounts for 36.7% of the total stock. In terms of the subordination of non-financial enterprises abroad, state-owned enterprises and units account for only 13.1% of the total, while local enterprises account for 86.9%.

The classification of domestic investors in 2015 is shown in Table 4–13.

Table 4–13 Classification of domestic investors by registration type

Business registration type	Quantity	World share (%)
Limited liability company	13,612	67.4
Private enterprise	1,879	9.3
Company limited by shares	1,559	7.7
State-owned enterprise	1,165	5.8
Foreign-invested enterprise	562	2.8
Joint stock company	458	2.3
Hong Kong, Macao and Taiwan-funded enterprise	385	1.9
Individual business	186	0.9
collectively-owned enterprise	88	0.4
Other	312	1.5
Total	20,207	100.0

Source:*2015 Statistics Bulletin of China's Outward Foreign Direct Investment*, China Statistics Press, 2016.

(4) *The investment method is more extensive*

Cross-border mergers and acquisitions, new enterprises, sole proprietorships, and joint ventures are the main ways for Chinese enterprises to invest abroad. In recent years, the status and role of cross-border mergers and acquisitions have become prominent, and it has become an essential way for China to obtain global high-end factors and resources and has played a positive role in promoting the transformation and upgrading structural adjustment and global value chain deployment of related industries in China.

M&A targets are mainly concentrated in developed countries and offshore financial centers. After the international financial crisis, the lower prices of high-quality assets in developed countries and the mergers and acquisitions of multinational corporations provided a historic opportunity for corporate mergers and acquisitions in China. At present, the main features of cross-border M&A projects of China's enterprises are full coverage, large amounts, large projects, etc. In 2015, China's enterprises carried out 579 cases in 62 countries and regions around the world, and the actual transaction amount totaled US$54.44 billion. Of this sum, outward foreign direct investment reached US$37.28 billion, accounting for 68.5% of the total mergers and acquisitions, 25.6% of the national outward foreign direct investment for the whole year. The most typical case is that ChemChina purchased 60% of the stocks of Pirelli with US$5.29 billion. China's outward foreign direct investment and M&A are shown in Table 4–14.

Table 4–14 China's outward foreign direct and M&A

Year	Sum①(US$ billion)	Year-on-year growth rate (%)	World share② (%)
2004	3.00	—	54.5
2005	6.50	116.7	53.0
2006	8.25	26.9	39.0
2007	6.30	−23.6	23.8
2008	30.20	379.4	54.0
2009	19.20	−36.4	34.0
2010	29.70	54.7	43.2
2011	27.20	−8.4	36.4
2012	43.40	—	31.4
2013	52.90	21.9	31.3
2014	56.90	7.6	26.4
2015	54.44	−4.3	25.6

Note: ①The amount of M&A from 2012 to 2015 includes the offshore financing component.
②The proportion of M&A from 2012 to 2015 is the proportion of direct investment in the current year's flow.
Source: *2015 Statistics Bulletin of China's Outward Foreign Direct Investment*, China Statistics Press, 2016.

4.5.3.2 New progress has been made in the renminbi internationalization

First, the renminbi was successfully included in the IMF's SDR basket. The inclusion of the renminbi in the IMF's SDR basket is an important milestone for the renminbi to integrate into the global system, and it shows that the international society affirms the achievements of the renminbi internationalization reform.

Second, the international business of the renminbi continued to expand, and the level of opening up of commercial banks was significantly improved. By June 2015, the renminbi payment ranked 6th in the world, accounting for 1.9%. At the same time, with Hong Kong SAR, China as the mainstay, the development pattern of parallel multi-point renminbi offshore market has taken shape, and financial assets such as renminbi-denominated credit, bonds and funds are increasingly enriched. By the end of March 2016, the balance of renminbi offshore market deposits was approximately RMB1.36 trillion.

Third, international cooperation between central banks. As of the end of June 2016, the currency with 36 countries and regions reached RMB3.3 trillion. In addition to the US dollar, the renminbi achieved direct transactions with a dozen currencies such as the Australian Dollar, Great Britain Pound, and South Korean Won. At the same time, in the regional market, or on the bank counter, direct transactions between the renminbi against neighboring countries such as Thailand, Laos, and Kazakhstan were realized.

Fourth, the renminbi internationalization infrastructure is well-established. In October 2016, the cross-border renminbi internationalization clearing system was put into operation, realizing a breakthrough in the liquidation and operation path. At present, 20 countries and regions have established the renminbi clearing arrangements.[1]

Reading material 4-3

Renminbi joins SDR[2]

On November 30, 2015, the International Monetary Fund (IMF) Chairman Christine Lagarde announced that the renminbi would be included in the IMF Special Drawing Rights (SDR) basket, and the resolution would take effect on October 1, 2016. The latest weight of the SDR basket is 41.73 percent for the U.S. dollar, 30.93% for the Euro, 10.92% for the Chinese yuan, 8.33% for the Japanese yen, and 8.09% for the Pound sterling.

For China, the renminbi's inclusion in the SDR basket enables central banks to increase their willingness to hold the renminbi and provide a strong guarantee for the renminbi's early realization of operational standards for "freely usable currency". The renminbi became the currency of SDR basket under certain conditions, and it enabled China to obtain important financial institutionalization rights, enhance the internationalization level of the renminbi, and enhance China's say over international economic affairs.

In the short term, as the first emerging market country currency to be included in the SDR basket, the importance of the renminbi is officially recognized by the IMF, which helps to promote the application and internationalization of the renminbi in the international financial arena, and is a milestone in promoting the internationalization of the renminbi. In the long run, the renminbi's inclusion in SDR would help to force the internationalization of the renminbi. The renminbi becomes an international reserve currency in line with our long-term interests. The renminbi's inclusion in SDR basket would help China's implementation of the strategy of "promoting reform through opening up" and force domestic reforms with external forces. Besides, it can also promote the diversification of the international reserve currency. To break

---

[1] Zhou Yan and Chen Yulu, "Preparations of the renminbi's Inclusion in the SDR Central Bank's Five Major Measures to Promote the renminbi Internationalization", *Financial Times*, Jul.25, 2016.

[2] "IMF Announced Chinese Renminbi (RMB) to Be Included in SDR Basket as Fifth Currency", Phoenix Net Finance, Dec.1, 2015.

US's global hegemony position must first break the dollar hegemony and establish a diversified national monetary system. The renminbi's inclusion in the SDR basket would make the renminbi a more globally recognized reserve currency, which would further challenge the hegemony of the dollar and facilitate the development of a multi-polar world.

4.6 Overall promotion of China's human resources internationalization: from one-way flow to two-way flow coordinated development

The expansion of international trade and international exchanges will bring about the international flow of production factors, and will inevitably bring about the global flow of people. The opening up of the labor market is not only an inevitable outcome of in-depth economic exchanges between countries but also an important indicator of economic internationalization. However, for a long time, our opening up has paid more attention to the "going global" and "bringing in" of capital while laying little emphasis on the flow of human resources on the macro level, lacking management on the micro level. With the acceleration of China's economic globalization, deepened internationalization of production and capitals, the internationalization of human resources in China has inevitably developed rapidly, and has become an important part of the internationalization of China's economy under the new situation. The development of the internationalization of human resources, first, increases the flow of human resources, which is conducive to raising the level of openness, and only when the amount of mobility reaches a certain level can we better regulate and consider the qualitative improvement; second, under the new opening up situation, China's economic development needs more high-level talents and needs to make more use of world resources. Human mobility is the basis of these two. Since the 18th National Party Congress, the Party Central Committee with General Secretary Xi Jinping as the core has attached great importance to the cultivation and development of people, and has further established a pleasant atmosphere of respecting talents in the whole society, constantly improving the institutional construction of China's human resources internationalization, and promoting the internationalization process of China's human resources.

4.6.1 New ideas and new systems laid a solid foundation of the system for the internationalization of human resources

"Of all things in the world, people are the most precious".[1] Mao Zedong's words profoundly clarify the importance of human beings. China has always attached great importance to the role of talents, especially in terms of talent cultivation, but how to make good use of the world's human resources has been still in the process of exploration. The United States has established itself as an immigrant country. The reason why it can become the world's largest country and dominate the world in the fields of economy, science and technology, and culture is inseparable from its emphasis on and utilization of the world's human resources and is inseparable from a relatively complete mechanism for extracting human resources from all over the world. Today China's economic openness is at a new height. We must not only focus on the development of trade internationalization and capital internationalization, but also promote the internationalization of China's human resources. This requires us first to improve the institutional basis of human resources.

Apparently, the country has paid more and more attention to this issue. The report of the 18th National Congress proposed the establishment of an "internationally competitive personnel system". General Secretary Xi Jinping has made important remarks on the work of talents and put forward a series of views on the talents of internationalization. For example, we should implement a more open talent policy, introduce talents from all regions, not seek all talents but make full use of talents in all shapes and forms.

"We need to open up the road to the sages and recruit talents from all over the world more than at any time in history...While vigorously cultivating innovative domestic talents, we should be more proactive in introducing foreign talents, especially high-level talents"[2],etc. The Fifth Plenary Session of the Eighteenth CPC Central Committee adopted the 13th Five-year Plan proposal and proposed to "deeply implement the strategy of prioritizing talent development" during the 13th Five-year Plan period.

Since 2015, China's immigration management system framework has begun to be built. The *Several Opinions of the CPC Central Committee and the State Council on Deepening the Reform of Institutional Mechanisms and Accelerating the Implementation of Innovation-Driven Development Strategies* issued in March 2015 pointed out that it is

[1] Mao Zedong, *The Bankruptcy of the Idealist Conception of History* (Sep. 16, 1949), People's Network.

[2] Xi Jinping, "China Must Be A Major Country That Learns Forever", People's Daily, May 24, 2014.

necessary to explore the establishment of a skilled immigration system to attract overseas high-level talents. On June 9, 2015, the Ministry of Public Security expanded the scope of work units for foreigners who apply for permanent residence in China. In February 2016, the General Office of the CPC Central Committee and the General Office of the State Council issued the *Opinions on Strengthening the Management of Permanent Residency Services for Foreigners* (hereinafter referred to as the *Opinions*) to comprehensively reform and innovate the management system for permanent residency of foreigners. The "Opinions" systematically reformed the existing problems of the permanent residency system for foreigners. The conditions for foreigners to apply for permanent residence in China are more flexible and pragmatic, the acceptance and approval procedures are more standardized and optimized, and the permanent residence qualifications will be fully implemented. The level of permanent residence-related services will also be substantially improved. This is an important reform document issued since the establishment of the permanent residence system for foreigners in 2004. It also marks that the permanent residency system for foreign talents will be more pragmatic and international.

The perfection of the permanent residence system and its consistency with the international community is one of the most important indicators for measuring the competitiveness of a country's talent system. In the United States, Canada, Australia, and European developed countries, the ability to obtain permanent residency has become an important criterion for selecting immigrant talents and has become a "welfare" issued by the state to immigrants. The perfection of the permanent residence system for foreigners in China is an embodiment of China's self-confidence and ability to recruit talents from all over the world and is also an important basis for enhancing the international competitiveness of China's talent system.

Concerning the export of labor services, along with the promotion of the Belt and Road and the promotion of related constructions, the number of people exporting foreign labor services is growing rapidly, and the various cross-border labor disputes that have followed are beginning to increase. It is urgent to establish some institutional foundations to protect the interests of Chinese overseas workers and enhance the exchange of personnel between countries. On June 12, 2012, the Ministry of Commerce issued the *Regulations on the Administration of Foreign Labor Cooperation* for the first time, and for the first time, foreign laborers were protected with legal regulations. On July 18, 2014, the Ministry of Commerce and the Ministry of Finance issued the *Measures for the Administration of Risks for Handling Foreign Labor Cooperation*

Risks (Trial), requiring all enterprises involved in foreign labor cooperation to pay a reserve fund to protect the legitimate interests of the dispatched laborers better. In 2015 and 2016, for two consecutive years, the Ministry of Commerce issued a notice requesting to strengthen the management of foreign labor cooperation. At the same time, it also actively requested all provinces, autonomous regions and municipalities to guide and supervise the service platform and dispatched enterprises to do a good job in the information management of people working abroad in foreign investment and cooperation. After that, integrating the development of foreign contracted projects and labor service business in the past two years, the Ministry of Commerce revised the *Statistical System for Outsourcing Engineering* and the *Statistical System for Foreign Labor Cooperation Business* in 2017. In June 2017, the Ministry of Commerce also issued a notice on the special action to regulate the order of the dispatched labor market. From this series of close actions, it is not difficult to find that the CPC Central Committee and the State Council still attached great importance to foreign labor services, and gradually began to formulate and improve relevant regulations to better protect the legitimate interests of Chinese multinational labor and laid the foundation for more overseas labor services.

In addition, we have not relaxed the promotion of civil exchanges. In March 2015, the Chinese government published the *Vision and Actions on Jointly Building Silk Road Economic Belt and 21st-Century Maritime Silk Road* white paper, which stated that "civil exchanges" were the social foundation of the Belt and Road Initiative. We should carry forward the spirit of friendly cooperation of the Silk Road by promoting extensive cultural and academic exchanges, personnel exchanges and cooperation, media cooperation, youth, and women exchanges and volunteer services, so as to win public support for deepening bilateral and multilateral cooperation. We should send more students to each other's countries and promote cooperation in jointly running schools. China provides 10,000 government scholarships to the countries along the Belt and Road every year. We should hold culture years, arts festivals, film festivals, TV weeks and book fairs in each other's countries; cooperate on the production and translation of fine films, radio, and TV programs and jointly apply for and protect World Cultural Heritage sites. We should also increase personnel exchange and cooperation between countries along the Belt and Road.

4.6.2 "Going global" of China's human resources

Different from China's capital flows in the modern times in which "bringing in" is the priority, China's human resources internationalization should first "go global". The pace of Chinese "going global" can be traced back to ancient times. Today, Chinese in many countries in Southeast Asia are proof that the Chinese have "gone global". In modern times, Chinese people's "going blobal" can be divided into two categories: First, people went overseas as a laborer to survive; second, people studied abroad to learn advanced scientific and cultural knowledge. With the development of China's economy, especially since the 18th National Party Congress, this situation has undergone qualitative changes: Overseas study began to show a personalized trend, and the living conditions and basic guarantees of expatriate workers are constantly improving. The "going global" of China's human resources began to be consciously and unconsciously linked to the overall situation of China's economic internationalization and the great rejuvenation of the Chinese nation.

(1) *New developments in talent exchange overseas*

At the beginning of reform and opening up, the state began to send international students, 3,000 people each year. In 1985, China canceled the "self-funded study abroad qualification review" and the door to study abroad was fully opened. More and more Chinese people chose to apply for study abroad through the TOEFL test. The "outbound fever" also warmed up rapidly throughout the country. During the 20 years after that, the state's support for studying abroad has also been increasing. The overseas study work was carried out with the words "supporting study abroad, encouraging those who complete their studies to return home and coming and going freely" as a guideline. Many overseas study funds and projects were established, and the number of government-funded students was increasing day by day. At the same time, due to the improvement of people's income, the number of self-sponsored overseas study students increased sharply. According to the data released by the Ministry of Education on March 1, 2013, the number of students studying abroad in China reached 399.6 thousand in 2012. Among them, there were 13.5 thousand government-funded students, 11.6 thousand unit-funded students, and 374.5 thousand self-funded students. China has become the country with the most students studying abroad in the world. In comparison, from 1872 to 1978, the total number of Chinese students studying abroad was 130,000. In the 22 years from 1978 to 2000, the number was about 340,000. In 2012 alone, the number of Chinese students studying abroad was equivalent to the sum of the number of people in the past 100 years before 1978.

Since the 18th National Party Congress, there has been a new development in overseas study. The CPC Central Committee centered on Comrade Xi Jinping, attaches great importance to studying abroad. Xi Jinping made important instructions at the National Overseas Study Work Conference held on December 13, 2014: Under the new situation, the work of studying abroad should adapt to the general trend of the country's development and the overall situation of the Party and the state, coordinate studying abroad and studying in China, comprehensively use both domestic and international resources to cultivate more outstanding talents and strive to create a new chapter for studying abroad so as to continuously make new and more significant contributions to the realization of Chinese Dream of the Two Centenary Goals and the great rejuvenation of the Chinese nation. It is hoped that the majority of overseas students will keep up with the trend of the times, have a global perspective, be determined, study hard, master new knowledge, enhance their skills, and contribute their wisdom and strength to the motherland and the people. In 2015, when he visited the United States, he also announced that China supported the exchange of 50,000 international students from each other in the next three years to study in the other country. The changes in Chinese students studying abroad these years can be seen in Figure 4–12. After becoming the country with the most students studying abroad in the world in 2012, the number was still growing rapidly. In 2016, the number of Chinese overseas students exceeded 25% of the total number of international students in the world, and status of the country with the largest number of international students in the world has been maintained for a long time. At the same time, the purposes of studying abroad changed a lot.

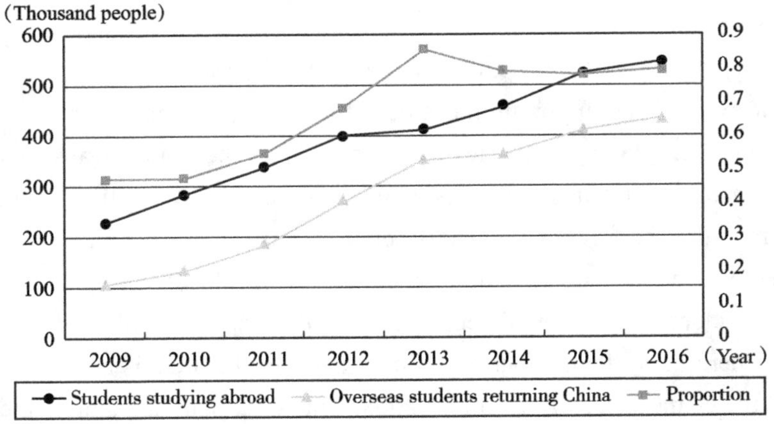

Figure 4–12 Number of Chinses students studying abroad

Source:Ministry of Education website.http://ww.moe.gov.cn/.

In 2011, the number of overseas students returning to China was less than 50%, but there was a rapid change later. By 2016, nearly 80% of students studying abroad chose to return home. These returnees brought advanced foreign visions and made great achievements in innovation in new fields such as the Internet, robots, new energy, and big data. They also helped solve the problem of Chinese companies' dissatisfaction after going abroad.

While the number of students studying abroad was growing, new forms of overseas exchanges emerged. In the past, Chinese scholars visited the country more with the aim of the study, while those with international influence often worked in foreign institutions. However, today, as the status of Chinese and Chinese scholars in the world is constantly improving, the voices of Chinese scholars on the world stage are becoming more and louder. More and more countries have begun to invite Chinese scholars to give lectures to them, with their expenditures covered. Because of the Belt and Road, the value of Chinese scholars has begun to exist, which has rarely been seen in the past. We need to make good offerings for foreign scholars to come to China and even pay a large number of appearance fees to some famous Western scholars.[1] This new form is essential because the "going global" of talents is not only to study foreign advanced science and technology culture but also to spread Chinese culture, tell Chinese stories and enhance the world's understanding of China. Many foreigners look at China through our overseas scholars and exchangers. Now, not only are you listening to others, but also others are listening to you, of course, the impact is much greater. This, in turn, can increase China's influence in the world and make better use of the world's resources.

(2) *The protection of expatriate laborers is strengthened*

Labor export is an important measure for a country's human resources to "going global". Many developing countries even use this as the main means of creating a foreign exchange. Since modern times, Chinese society has been filled with the view that "the moon of the foreign country is better than the domestic one". Therefore, not only the elites liked to study abroad, but the ordinary people also hoped to work abroad. With the development of China's economy and the improvement of its international status, the increase in the number of Chinese overseas laborers is as surprising as the growth of the Chinese economy. Before 2008, China's expatriate laborers increased by more than 10% annually[2]. After the financial crisis, this growth rate began to slow down,

[1] Wang Wen, "The Belt and Road Initiative Is a Real benefit for China", Global Network, Jun.4, 2017.

[2] Data are from the Ministry of Commerce with related statistics dating from 2014.

falling by 1.2% in 2009 and only 4% in 2010. Since the 18th National Party Congress, because of the new normal of China's society and changes in the world economic situation, especially the implementation of the Belt and Road Initiative, the situation of overseas laborers has changed in three aspects:

First, the number of people changes. From Table 4–15, it is not difficult to see that although the growth rate of overseas laborers was on average more than 10% in 2011 and 2012, it soon began to decline again. In 2015 and 2016, there was even negative growth.

Table 4–15 China's expatriate laborers dispatched in foreign labor cooperation

Item	2011	2012	2013	2014	2015	2016	2017 (January-April)
The number of dispatched laborers (thousand people)	452	512	527	562	530	494	147
Year-on-year growth (thousand people)	41	60	15	35	−32	−36	6
Year-on-year growth rate (%)	9.97	13.20	2.90	6.60	−5.70	−6.79	4.20

Source: The data center of the Ministry of Commerce.The number of dispatched laborers from January to April in 2016 was 141,000.

This change in numbers is due primarily to the downturn in the overall world economy, but it should not be excessively pessimistic. Data from January to April in 2017 indicate that this data was starting to pick up. As long as China's Belt and Road Initiative and related construction can be implemented, in the foreseeable future, the number of overseas labor will inevitably increase rapidly.

Second, the direction of personnel flow remains unchanged. At present, overseas labor service mainly flows to Asian and African countries. As shown in Table 4–16, the number of labor dispatched by China in Asia and Africa in recent years has continued to increase on the original large base, while the number of people dispatched to Europe has decreased significantly. This is because China's laborers in Europe are mostly engaged in low-end industries. When the economy is not prosperous, they often become the primary targets for layoffs, and with the proposal of the Belt and Road Initiative and its great appeal to countries along the routes, many Chinese engineering projects are being sent to these countries, which will inevitably lead to the flow of laborers. Moreover, Chinese laborers are technical personnel for many developing countries in Asia and Africa, which can greatly promote technological advancement and development in these countries. In the future, with the promotion of the Belt and Road construction, this trend of personnel mobility will remain unchanged for some time.

Table 4–16 Destinations distribution of China's dispatched laborers Unit: %

Continent	2011	2012	2013	2014	2015
Asia	81	77	78	76	78
Africa	8	8	9	10	9
Europe	9	6	4	4	4

Source: Calculated by the National Bureau of Statistics. The numbers in North America, Latin America, and Oceania were not calculated because the number of dispatchers was too small and they are not along the Belt and Road. From the data point of view, Latin America has become a new growth point since 2012.

Third, the basic welfare benefits of overseas laborers have been improved. As mentioned above, in the past few years, China's institutional guarantees for foreign laborers have been continuously improved, and various relevant administrative regulations have been continuously introduced. For example, the *Regulations on the Administration of Foreign Labor Cooperation* in 2012 has detailed and targeted norms, but at present, it is only a form of administrative regulations, the legal level is low, and the state still needs to enact relevant laws to protect it in the future. Besides, China has proved to the world that we can protect overseas residents. Whether it was the evacuation of Libya in 2011 or the evacuation of overseas Chinese in Yemen, Nepal and New Zealand in 2015, China showed the world the strong organizational capabilities of China and the firm determination to protect overseas nationals. In the construction of the China-Pakistan Economic Corridor of the Belt and Road, Pakistan specially established a force to protect Chinese workers at the request of the Chinese government. With the further improvement of China's strength, the basic guarantees of China's overseas laborers will be further improved in the future, and will also help promote the output of Chinese laborers.

As China's supply-side structural reforms are further deepened, the labor structure is further changed, and the country's strength is further enhanced, the number of laborers dispatched abroad will further increase in the future, and the industries and jobs covered will further increase, and per capita income will increase, and the security guarantees provided by the state will be more comprehensive.

4.6.3 "Bringing in" of China's human resources

"Gathering and recruiting the talents worldwide for our own sake" is an attitude that every open country should have. Concerning human resources, "bringing in" is more difficult than "going global", which requires further recognition of China's development. Since the 18th National Party Congress, thanks to the sustained and healthy development of the Chinese economy and its continuous integration into the world economy, China is becoming more and more attractive to international talents, and more and more international talents are pouring into China. This also means that China's human resources internationalization is shifting from "bringing in" to a new phase of development integrating "bringing in" and "going global".

The "bringing in" of human resources in China is mainly aimed at overseas high-level talents. On the one hand, we do not lack the general labor force. On the other hand, it is an indisputable fact that the current foreign technology level is still ahead of China. There is an urgent need for high-level talent in our economic transformation and development.

First, the state has introduced a series of policies to attract overseas students and Chinese to return home. In September 2013, Xi Jinping emphasized in the ninth collective study of the Political Bureau of the Central Committee that it is necessary to deepen education reform, promote quality education, innovate educational methods, improve the quality of personnel training, and strive to form an educational environment conducive to the growth of innovative talents. It is necessary to actively introduce overseas talents, formulate more active international talent introduction programs, and attract more overseas innovative talents to work in China. The Central Committee of the Chinese Communist Party, at its third plenary held in November 2013, adopted the *Decision by the CPC Central Committee on Certain Issues Concerning the Integrated Deepening of the Reform* (hereinafter referred to as the *Decision*). It pointed out that we should accelerate the formation of an internationally competitive talent system, improve the talent evaluation mechanism, enhance the openness of the talent policy, and widely attract overseas talents to return to China or to start businesses in China. From 2012, China plans to use 10 years to select and cultivate 4,000 national-level candidates, focus on selecting and training high-level young and middle-aged talents who are at the forefront of the world's science and technology, and that can lead and support the country's major science and technology and achieve leapfrogging development in key areas. Among them, 10,000 leading talents are included in the basic disciplines and research fields. In the face of the new situation and new tasks, in 2013, China's relevant departments issued a series of supporting policies, and the talent introduction policy was more open, pragmatic and standardized. In 2013, the Ministry of Human Resources and Social Security funded 494 overseas students to return to China to carry out scientific and technological activities and start businesses, and supported 30 projects for Returned Overseas Students to Serve the Country. 305 entrepreneurial parks for all types of students studying at all levels have been established nationwide and 22,000 enterprises have entered these parks as well as 63,000 overseas talents have started businesses there. It can also be seen in the previous Table 4–12 that after the 18th National Party Congress, returning home to work has become a mainstream choice for Chinese overseas students at present.

Second, we actively introduced foreign talents. In August 2013,the Organization Department of the Central Committee, the Ministry of Human Resources and Social Security, the Ministry of Public Security, the Ministry of Foreign Affairs, and the State Administration of Foreign Experts Affairs issued the *Notice on the Relevant Matters Concerning the Procedures for Visa and Residence Procedures for Foreign High-Level Talents*, which required all departments, localities and units to organize and record the overseas high-level talent introduction plan, and clarify the visa and residence procedures foreign high-level talents. On September 1, the *Regulations on the Administration of Entry and Exit of Foreigners* was officially implemented, clarifying that foreign high-level talents and foreigners who meet the conditions and requirements for the introduction of urgently needed specialists can apply for a talent visa and enjoy appropriate entry and exit conveniences as required.[1] The United Nations estimated that in 2013, the number of foreigners residing in China was 848.5 thousand, with an annual increase of 3.9% over the past 10 years, higher than 3% in 2000. The *HSBC Expat Explorer 2014* released in October 2014 showed that China ranked third in the "most attractive countries or regions for expatriates to live in", ahead of some developed countries such as the United States, Japan, France, and the United Kingdom, etc.[2]Besides, the number of international students coming to China is increasing year by year, and the source of international students covers a wide range, among which the countries along the Belt and Road have become an important source. The data for international students in China are shown in Table 4–17.

1 Yang Jianhui, Sun Dawei and Zhang Jin, "Chinese Talents Development Report (2014)" (main highlights and inspirations of Chinese talent development since 2013), 2014, p. 27.

2 Wang Huiyao, "The Chinese Government Wants to Set up an Immigration Bureau in order to Recruit International Talents?" Phoenix International Think Tank, Sep.28, 2016.

Table 4–17 Statistics of foreign students in China

Continent	2015			2016		
	Total number (person)	Proportion (%)	Year-on-year change(%)	Total number (person)	Proportion (%)	Year-on-year change(%)
Asia	240,154	60.40	6.50	264,976	59.84	10.34
Europe	66,746	16.79	-1.08	71,319	16.11	6.85
Africa	49,792	12.52	19.47	61,594	13.91	23.70
America	34,934	8.79	-3.34	38,077	8.06	9.00
Oceania	6,009	1.50	-4.19	6,807	1.54	13.28

Source: Ministry of Education.http://www.moe.gov.cn/.

It can be expected that with the further implementation of the concept of open development, as China's economic strength is further strengthened, China will become more open and inclusive, and China's human resources internationalization will undoubtedly continue to develop. The free flow of the "human resources" element will inevitably inject new vitality into the Chinese economy and promote the internationalization of China's economy to a higher level.

Conclusion
Retrospect and Prospect of China's Economic Internationalization

The process of China's economic internationalization is part of China's economic and social development and part of the Chinese Path. The internationalization of China's economy was erratic in the turmoil and turning of the old China. It had neither an equal status of international exchange nor a stable domestic development environment; only in the long-term stability of the new China has it been nourished and strengthened, not only to achieve independence, but also to achieve stable development. Today, we are closer, more confident, and more capable than ever before of making the goal of a reality. Similarly, the promotion of China's economic internationalization is more active and conscious than at any time in history, and the future of China's economic internationalization is brighter and greater.

1. Retrospect: the success of the Chinese path promoted the internationalization of China's economy

Looking back on the history of the past two hundred years, China's economy and society have changed from a relatively closed and backward natural economy to a fairly open and vibrant socialist market economy. This includes the great struggle of the Chinese nation and is the success of the path to great rejuvenation—the socialist path with Chinese characteristics led by the Communist Party of China. Along this road, we can see tremendous changes in Chinese society. China has completely ended the situation of backward poverty and achieved prosperity and success of our country. What we can see is the great improvement of China's economic internationalization. China's opening up has ended the passive and one-sided situation and formed an active and comprehensive layout; we have also seen the real improvement of the living standards of Chinese people, the great improvement of material life and the gradual enrichment of spiritual life.

First of all, the success of the Chinese Path has enabled the Chinese people to truly stand firm forever among the nations of the world. Only Chinese who stand up are more likely to interact with other ethnic groups on an equal footing and actively and consciously promote opening up. The internationalization of China's economy has evolved from the forced opening of the old China to the independent opening up at the beginning of reform and opening up, to the current situation of leading the open trend in the world and promoting the world's development towards a more inclusive and open direction. It can be said that to what extent the Chinese Path have succeeded, and to what extent China's economic internationalization has developed.

Secondly, the success of the Chinese Path has realized the great rise of the Chinese economy. It is the continuous growth of the domestic economy that enables the Chinese economy to be independent in the process of internationalization and to improve the living standards of its people as well as to be sustainable. China's nominal GDP increased from US$148 billion in 1978 to US$11.2 trillion in 2016. The per capita nominal GDP rose from US$155 in 1978 to US$7,900 in 2015, an increase of 76 times and 51 times respectively. China has maintained its position as the world's largest trader in goods for three consecutive years from 2012 to 2015, and China has also become a major country of foreign investment. Behind these data is a tangible fact that the people have enjoyed a better life, the comprehensive national strength of our country has been greatly enhanced, and our country's status in the international community has been significantly improved.

2. Prospect: the Chinese path will surely expand the new realm of economic internationalization

Looking forward to the second of the Two Centenary Goals, we believe that since mankind has developed into the 21st century, as long as the forces of peace and justice including China in the world make unremitting efforts, peace and development will always be the theme of the entire century. Under this theme, China's economic internationalization will continue to develop in the next 30 years, not only as part of the great rejuvenation of the Chinese nation but also as a driving force of the other parts in the great rejuvenation of the Chinese nation. Whether it is the production and exchange of material products or spiritual products, whether it is the flow of capital or the flow of human resources, whether it is the exchange of technology or culture, with the great rejuvenation of the Chinese nation, China and the world will have more and more similarities. By then, we will see:

First, the world's total output and commodity exchange patterns will change unprecedentedly, and China will become the most important participant in globalization. According to the annual growth rate of 6% of China's economy before 2030, 5% from 2030 to 2040, and 4% from 2040 to 2049, China's GDP in 2049 will quadruple the GDP in 2020, more than US$40,000 per capita (calculated at 2010 constant prices). And if the world can maintain an annual increase of 3.6%, China's GDP will account for about a quarter of the world's total, ranking first in the world. The Per capita GNP will reach the level of moderately developed countries, and the people will live a more affluent life. This also means that China will have to import tangible and intangible products whose value are several times that of 2020 from the rest of the world, and export products in the corresponding volume. The rest of the world will also reciprocate from China the magnitude of value several times more than the value of products and currencies obtained from China in 2020.

Second, China's economic internationalization has reached a higher level. Especially under the Belt and Road Initiative, the scope, field, and scale of China's opening up will be further enhanced. In terms of scope, on the one hand, China will continue to develop and optimize the opening up to developed economies, and further get it expanded and improved; on the other hand, it will vigorously develop and promote openness to developing countries, and exchange opportunities with developing countries to find more opportunities for mutual benefits. China will strengthen economic exchanges with all countries and regions in the world and form a broader new pattern of opening up. In terms of the fields, China's opening up to the outside world will not only pay attention to trade and investment, but also pay more attention to exchanges and cooperation in the fields of finance, humanities, science and technology, infrastructure construction, etc., and realize large-scale exchange of elements of technology, information and human resources with other countries. In terms of level, China will work with the world peace-lover to further and deeply promote the construction of a community with a shared future. It is necessary to continue to strengthen cooperation with other parts of the world in all sectors of the world economy, and to build a rational system of world economic rules with the rest of the world, and to maintain this system of rules with the rest of the world; we will not only learn from the wisdom and achievements of the development of world civilization outside of China, but also promote China's wisdom and creation to the world, effectively promote the development of China's innovative economy, and inject new impetus into the growth of the world economy.

We are looking forward to the continuous development of China's economic internationalization. We look forward to it that this development will continue to promote China's influence in the world economic and political governance system, and a more just system of world economic governance, and a more open and inclusive development of the world economy.

Wish China's economic internationalization a better future.

Bibliography

[1] "A.M. Ledovskikh, "Secret Talks between Mikoyan and Mao Zedong (January- February, 1949)", Part II, *Literature of Chinese Communist Party*, 1996(3).

[2] Accomplishing All the Work for Transforming the Model of Economic Development and Constantly Obtain New Development Advantages and Create New Development Chapters", *People's Daily*, Apr.9, 2008.

[3] Adrian · Buckley, translated by Wang Nianyong, *Financial Crisis: Causes, Context and Consequences*, Dalian: Dongbei University of Finance and Economics Press, 2013.

[4] Angus Maddison, *The World Economy: A Millennial Perspective*, Beijing: Beijing University Press, 2003.

[5] Bai Hejin ed., *Economic Summary of the People's Republic of China (1978–2001)*, Beijing: China Planning Press, 2002.

[6] Basic Construction Comprehensive Bureau of State Development Planning Commission, "Construction Condition of 156 Projects during the First Five-Year Plan (150 implemented)", Jun. 8, 1983.

[7] *Biography of Li Xiannian* Writing Group, *The Chronicle Biography of Li Xiannian, Volume V*, Beijing: Central Party Literature Publishing House, 2011.

[8] Cao Pu, "Gu Mu and Reform and Opening up during 1978–1988", *Hundred Year Tide*, 2001(11).

[9] Cao Pu, *Contemporary Chinese Reform and Opening Up, Part II*, Beijing: People's Publishing House, 2016.

[10] Cao Pu, *Several Major Problems in the Research of the History of Reform and Opening Up*, Fuzhou: Fujian People's Publishing House, 2014.

[11] "Central Economic Work Conference Held in Beijing", *People's Daily*, Dec.11, 2008.

[12] Chen Jiangsheng, "An Analysis of World Economic Pattern after Financial Crisis", *Journal of the Party School of the Central Committee*, Feb. 2009.

[13] Chen Jiangsheng, "China's Exchange Rate Regime Reform and the renminbi Internationalization", *Think Tank*, 2011(12).

[14] Chen Jinhua, *State Memory*, Beijing: Central Party History Publishing House, 2005.

[15] Chen Xiaohong ed., *Basic Knowledge of WTO*, Haikou: Hainan Publishing House, 2002.

[16] "China Cannot Fully Implement Market Economy", *Guangming Daily*, Oct.28, 1989.

[17] *China's Economic Development by Liu Shaoqi*, Beijing: Central Party Literature Publishing House, 1993.

[18] Chinese Academy of Social Sciences & the State Archives Administration of the People's Republic of China, *Selected Files Data of People's Republic of China's Economy during 1953–1957(of basic construction investment and building industry)*, Beijing: China City Economy and Society Press, 1989.

[19] City History Office of Shenzhen Municipality, *Interview with Li Hao on Shenzhen Special Economic Zone*, Shenzhen: Haitian Publishing House, 2010.

[20] *Collected Works by Deng Xiaoping on Military Affairs, Volume III*, Beijing: Military Science Publishing House & Central Party Literature Publishing House, 2004.

[21] *Compiled Documents of Successive Third Plenary Sessions since the Reform of Opening Up*, Beijing: People's Publishing House, 2013.

[22] Cultural and Historical Records Committee of CPPCC National Committee of Guangdong Province, *Origins of Special Economic Zones*, Guangzhou: Guangdong People's Publishing House, 2002.

[23] Dong Fureng ed., *Economic History of People's Republic of China,Volume II*, Beijing: Economic Science Press, 1999.

[24] Dong Zhikai, et al., *Mao Zedong's Economic Thinking during Yan'an Period*, Xi'an: Shaanxi People's Education Press, 1993.

[25] Fan Ying, "An Analysis of China's Openness since the Entry into WTO", *Intertrade*, 2012(10).

[26] Fang Weizhong ed., *Major Economic Events of the People's Republic of China (1949–1980)*, Beijing: China Social Sciences Press, 1984.

[27] Feng Wenli, *From the Asian Financial Crisis to International Financial*

Crisis, Beijing: Metallurgical Industry Press, 2009.

[28] Gao Debu and Wang Jue, *An Economic History of the World*, Beijing: China Renmin University Press, 2001.

[29] Gu Mu, *Reminiscences of Gu Mu*, Beijing: Central Party Literature Publishing House, 2014.

[30] Gu Wenfu and Ding Wen, "Opening up Will Not Lead to Capitalism with Socialism Taking the Priority", *People's Daily*, Jan.20, 1985.

[31] Guo Xianglin and Zhang Liying, *Research on Chinese Modern Market*, Shanghai: Shanghai University of Finance and Economics Press, 1999.

[32] Han Qiaowen ed., *100 Questions of WTO: Reflections of Industry Associations after China's Entry into WTO*, Shanghai: Shanghai People's Publishing House, 2002.

[33] Hu Naiwu and Yuan Zhenyu, "Create an Operation Mechanism Coordinating Planned Economy and Market", *People's Daily*, Nov.27, 1989.

[34] Huang Zhongping, et al., *Records of 30 years' Reform and Opening Up*, Beijing: People's Publishing House, 2009.

[35] Huangfu Ping, "Reform and Opening up Need New Ideas", *Jiefang Daily*, Mar.2, 1991.

[36] Huangfu Ping, "Strengthening the Awareness of Reform and Opening Up", *Jiefang Daily*, Mar.2, 1991.

[37] Jiang Xuemo, "China's Reform Cannot Take the Path of Private Market", *People's Daily*, May 29, 1991.

[38] Jiang Yuanming, *The Past—Pictures in 1966*, Tianjin: Baihua Literature and Art Publishing House, 1999.

[39] Jiang Zemin, "Accelerating Reform and Opening Up and Modernization Construction and Seize a Larger Success in Socialism with Chinese Characteristics—Report at the 14th National Congress of the Communist Party of China", *People's Daily*, Oct.21, 1992.

[40] Jiang Zemin, "Speech at the 70th Anniversary of Communist Party of China", *People's Daily*, Jul.2, 1991.

[41] Jin Zhesong and Li Jun, *Foreign Trade Growth and Economic Development of China—Retrospect and Prospect of the 30 Years' Reform and Opening Up*, Beijing: China Renmin University Press, 2008.

[42] Lao Haiyan, "Research on the Currency and Regulation Policies of All Countries Tackling Financial Crisis", *Southwest Finance*, 2010(4).

[43] Li Gongchang and Yang Guang ed., *Focus: Ten Major Questions Facing China in the 21st Century*, Urumqi: Xinjiang People's Press, 2000.

[44] Li Lanqing, *Breaking Out—Days of Early Opening Up*, Beijing: Central Party Literature Publishing House, 2008.

[45] Li Shujin, *Research on Thinking of Chinese Modern Foreign Trade*, Shanghai: Fudan University Press, 1996.

[46] Li Zhenghua, "An Important Meeting for Preparing Reform and Opening Up", *Reference Data of State History*, Vol. 214.

[47] Liang Lingguang, *Reminiscences of Liang Lingguang*, Beijing: Central Party History Publishing House, 1996.

[48] Liu Tianfu, *Reminiscences of Liu Tianfu*, Beijing: Central Party History Publishing House, 1995.

[49] Liu Zhenying and Sun Benyao, "Deepen Reform and Enhance Open Economy to Usher the Convening of the 14th National Party Congress", *People's Daily*, Jan.20, 1985.

[50] Lu Dan, "The Connotation and Relevant Concepts on Economic Internationalization", *Economic Research Guide*, 2009(5).

[51] Lu Qi ed., *A Summary of WTO(2nd Edition)*, Shanghai: Fudan University Press, 2008.

[52] Lu Xinde, "The Connotation and Features of Economic Internationalization", *Journal of Shandong University of Finance and Economics*, 2000(2).

[53] Luo Hongxi, "Research on China's Foreign Trade Diplomacy during the Republican Period", Doctoral Dissertation, Changsha: Hunan Normal University, 2014.

[54] Luo Musheng, *Draft of the development History of Chinese Special Economic Zones*, Guangdong: Guangdong People's Publishing House, 1999.

[55] Ouyang Song and GaoYongzhong ed., *Oral History of Reform and Opening Up*, Beijing: China Renmin University Press, 2013.

[56] Party Literature Research Center of the CPC Central Committee, *Memories of Deng Xiaoping*, Beijing: Central Party Literature Publishing House, 1998.

[57] Party Literature Research Center of the CPC Central Committee, *The Chronicle Biography of Zhou Enlai 1949–1976, Volume II*, Beijing: Central Party Literature Press, 1997.

[58] Party Literature Research Center of the CPC Central Committee, *The Chronicle Biography of Deng Xiaoping 1975–1997*, Beijing: Central Party Literature

Publishing House, 2004.

[59] Pei Changhong ed., *Research on Reform and Opening Up and Circulation Reform for 30 years of China*, Beijing: Economy & Management Publishing House, 2008.

[60] Peng Min ed., *Basic Construction of Contemporary China, Volume I*, Beijing: China Social Sciences Press, 1989.

[61] "Premier Wen Jiabao's Meeting with the Press", *People's Daily*, Mar.19, 2008.

[62] "Premier Zhu Rongji's Meeting with the Press at the Second Session of the 9th National Party Congress", *People's Daily*, Mar.16, 1999.

[63] *Reader on General Secretary Xi Jinping's Major Speeches*, Beijing: Xuexi Press & People's Publishing House, 2016.

[64] "Report on the Implementation of Plan for National Economic and Social Development 2008 and Draft for National Economic and Social Development 2009",*People's Daily*, Mar.16, 2009.

[65] Research Institute of Ministry of Commerce, *China's 30 years of Foreign Trade*, Beijing: China Commerce and Trade Press, 2008.

[66] *Selected Works of Chen Yun*, Beijing: People's Publishing House, 1995.

[67] *Selected Works of Deng Xiaoping*, Beijing: People's Publishing House, 2011.

[68] *Selected Works of Jiang Zemin*, Beijing: People's Publishing House, 2006.

[69] *Selected Works of Mao Zedong on Diplomacy*, Beijing: Central Party Literature Publishing House & World Affairs Press, 1993.

[70] *Selected Works of Mao Zedong since the Foundation of PRC*, Beijing: Central Party Literature Publishing House, 1987.

[71] *Selected Works of Mao Zedong*, Beijing: People's Publishing House, 1991.

[72] *Selected Works of Zhou Enlai on Diplomacy*, Beijing: Central Party Literature Publishing House, 1990.

[73] *Selected Works of Zhou Enlai on Economy*, Beijing: Central Party Literature Publishing House, 1993.

[74] *Selected Works of Zhou Enlai*, Beijing: People's Publishing House, 1984.

[75] *Selections of Party Literature of the CPC Central Committee*, *Volume XVIII*, Beijing: Party School of the Central Committee of CPC Press, 1992.

[76] Shen Jiawu, et al., *Selected Economic Data during Zhang Qian's Tenure as Secretary of Agriculture and Commerce*, Nanjing: Nanjing University Press,1987.

[77] Shen Zhihua, *Soviet Experts in China (1948–1960)*, Beijing: China Radio International Press, 2003.

[78] Shi Jianjun ed., *China's Entry into the World—Collected Papers by University Of International Business And Economics on China's Entry into WTO for A Decade*, Beijing: University of International Business and Economics Press, 2011.

[79] Song Jihe, "Similarities and Differences of Thinking on Chinese Economy's Independent Development between Mao Zedong and Deng Xiaoping", *Journal of the Party School of CPC Jinan Municipal Committee*, 1999(4).

[80] "Speech by Comrade Wang Quanguo at Central Working Conference with Central South Group", *Documents of the Third Enlarged Meeting of the Fourth Standing Provincial Party Committee in Guangdong*, Apr.10, 1974.

[81] "Speech by Comrade Xi Zhongxun at Central Working Conference with Central South Group", *Documents of the Third Enlarged Meeting of the Fourth Standing Provincial Party Committee in Guangdong*, Apr.8, 1974.

[82] Su Ling, "Strategic Decisions and Basic Experience of Foreign Trade during the Early Foundation of New China", *Research Collections of New China's 60 Years, Volume IV*, Beijing: Central Party Literature Publishing House, 2009.

[83] Sun Yat-sen, *A Plan for Industrial Development*, Beijing: Foreign Language Teaching and Research Press, 2011.

[84] *The Chronicle Biography of Chen Yun, Volume II*, Beijing: Central Party Literature Publishing House, 2000.

[85] "The CPC Central Committee Convenes A Symposium for Non-Party Members to Seek Views on Such Issues As the Current Economic Situation and Economic Work", *People's Daily*, Jul.26, 2008.

[86] The National Development and Reform Commission of the People's Republic of China, "Issues in Economic Guidance after the Crushing the 'Gang of Four'", Nov.15, 1980.

[87] The State Committee Office for Economic System Reform, *Compilation of Economic System Reform Documents (1978–1983)*, Beijing: China Financial & Economic Publishing House, 1984.

[88] "The State Council of the CPC Central Committee Convenes a Conference with Comrades from Central Departments As Well As Provinces and Municipalities in Beijing", *People's Daily*, Jun.14, 2008.

[89] "Vice Premier Deng's Meeting with the Press in Tokyo", *People's Daily*,

Oct.26, 1978.

[90] Wang Huanpei, *Research on Current Chinese Private Economy*, Changsha: Hunan Science and Technology Press, 2006.

[91] Wang Jingyu, "The Development and Stagnation of Modern Chinese Capitalism", *Historical Research*, 1985(5).

[92] Wang Jingyu, *Chinese Modern Economic History (1895–1927)*, Beijing: People's Publishing House, 2012.

[93] Wang Jingyu, *Data of Chinese Modern Industrial History, Volume II*, Beijing: Zhonghua Book Company, 1962.

[94] Wang Xinqing, "Jiang Zeming Emphasized at the Graduation Ceremony of a Senior Course for Ministerial Officials and Provincial Heads at the CPC Central Committee's Party School: Hold High the Banner of Deng Xiaoping Theory of Socialism with Chinese Characteristics and Grasp the Opportunity to Promote Our Career in the 21st Century", *People's Daily*, May 30, 1997.

[95] Wang Ying, "The Development History of China National Capitalism", *Journal of Fujian Institute of Socialism*, 2005(1).

[96] Wang Zhangbao, "50 Years' Technology Introduction in Chinese Mechanical Industry", *Journal of Dialectics of Nature*, 2000(1).

[97] Wang Zixian ed., *30 Years' Foreign Economy and Trade Of China Since Reform and Opening Up*, Beijing: Economy & Management Publishing House, 2008.

[98] Wu Chengming, *Imperialism's Investment in Old China*, Beijing: People's Publishing House, 1956.

[99] *Wu Jinglian, Planned Economy or Market Economy*, Beijing: China Economic Publishing House, 1993.

[100] Wu Jinglian, *Tutorial on Economic Reform in Contemporary China*, Shanghai: Shanghai Far East Publishers, 2015.

[101] Wu Nansheng, "The Foundation of Special Economic Zones", *Guangdong Party Committee History*, 1998(6).

[102] Wu Shuchun, "Reform and Opening Up Must Maintain Socialist Orientation", *People's Daily*, Nov.17, 1989.

[103] Xi Jieren ed., *Encyclopedic Dictionary on Scientific Outlook of Development*, Shanghai: Shanghai Lexicographic Publishing House, 2007.

[104] Xi Jinping, *The Governance of China*, Beijing: Foreign Languages Press, 2014.

[105] *Xi Zhongxun Administrating Guangdong Province* editorial committee, *Xi Zhongxun Administrating Guangdong Province*, Beijing: Central Party History Publishing House, 2007.

[106] Xi Zhongxun, "Summary Speech at the Second Enlarged Meeting of the Fourth Standing Provincial Party Committee", Jan.25, 1979.

[107] Xiao Guoliang and Sui Fuming, *Economic History of People's Republic of China 1949–2010*, Beijing: Peking University Press, 2011.

[108] Xie Zhenmin, *Legislative History of Republic of China*, Beijing: China University of Political Science and Law Press, 1999.

[109] Xinhua News Agency, "Jiang Zemin Chairs the Plenary Meeting of Political Bureau of the Central Committee of CPC Discussing Several Major Issues of China's Reform and Development", *People's Daily*, Mar.12, 1992.

[110] Yan Zhongping, *Selections of Data on Chinese Modern Economic History*, Beijing: China Social Sciences Press, 2012.

[111] Yao Xianhao, *Data of China's Modern Foreign Trade History*, Beijing: Zhonghua Book Company, 1957.

[112] Zhang Gui, et al ed., *China's Entry into WTO: Blessing or Curse*? Tianjin: Nankai University Press, 1992.

[113] Zhang Hanqing, "Xi Zhongxun in the Reform and Opening Up of Guangdong Province", *Reform Career of Xi Zhongxun*, Beijing: Central Party History Publishing House, 2002.

[114] Zhang Jian and Ma Xiaoning, "Jiang Zemin Points out Planning and Economy Are Both Economy Regulation Measures, not the Symbol Differentiating Socialism from Capitalism while meeting Karimov", *People's Daily*, Mar.14, 1992.

[115] Zhang Shoupeng, "Changes in Chinese Modern Economic Thinking", *Qinghai Social Sciences*, 1987(3).

[116] Zhang Shujun and GaoXinmin, *People's Republic of China in 1978*, Shijiazhuang: Hebei People's Publishing Houe, 2001.

[117] Zhang Ying and Zhang Aiping ed., *Modem Market Economy Foundation*, Harbin: Northeast Forestry University Press, 2006.

[118] Zhang Youwen, et al., *Factors Benefits and the Path of Strengthening the Country by Trade*, Beijing: People's Publishing House, 2016.

[119] Zhao Dexin, *Chinese Modern Economic History (1842–1949)*, Zhengzhou: Henan People's Publishing House, 2003.

[120] Zhao Dongrong, *Policy Research on Chinese Economic Internationalization*, Nanjing: Nanjing University Press, 2000.

[121] Zhong Jian, *Report of Chinese Economic Special Zones Development (2010)*, Beijing: China Social Sciences Academic Press, 2010.

[122] Zhou Hanmin, *China's Entry into WTO*, Shanghai: Wenhui Publishing House, 2011.

This book is the result of a co-publication agreement between Economic Science Press (China) and Paths International Ltd (UK).

Title: The Internationalization of China's Economy
Author: Chen Jiangsheng
Translated by Duan Feng, Zhang Yan, Liao Dongqiong
Proofread by Li Weibin
ISBN: 978-1-84464-587-9
Ebook ISBN: 978-1-84464-588-6

Paths International Ltd
Published in the United Kingdom
www.pathsinternational.com

www.ingramcontent.com/pod-product-compliance
Lightning Source LLC
LaVergne TN
LVHW081209240426
836338LV00004B/50